T0375247

GLOBAL
DERIVATIVE
DEBACLES
From Theory to Malpractice

GLOBAL DERIVATIVE DEBACLES

From Theory to Malpractice

Laurent L Jacque

Tufts University, USA & HEC School of Management, France

 **World Scientific**

NEW JERSEY · LONDON · SINGAPORE · BEIJING · SHANGHAI · HONG KONG · TAIPEI · CHENNAI

Published by

World Scientific Publishing Co. Pte. Ltd.

5 Toh Tuck Link, Singapore 596224

USA office: 27 Warren Street, Suite 401-402, Hackensack, NJ 07601

UK office: 57 Shelton Street, Covent Garden, London WC2H 9HE

Library of Congress Cataloging-in-Publication Data
Jacque, Laurent L.
    Global derivative debacles : from theory to malpractice / by Laurent L. Jacque.
        p. cm.
    Includes bibliographical references and index.
    ISBN-13: 978-981-283-770-7
    ISBN-10: 981-283-770-1
    1. Derivative securities. 2. Finance. I. Title.
    HG6024.A3J335 2010
    332.64'57--dc22
                                        2010000773

British Library Cataloguing-in-Publication Data
A catalogue record for this book is available from the British Library.

In-house Editor: Juliet Lee Ley Chin

Typeset by Stallion Press
Email: enquiries@stallionpress.com

Printed in Singapore by B & Jo Enterprise Pte Ltd

A la mémoire de ma mère.

PREFACE

At a time when the global financial system is engulfed into the mother of all financial crises, it is indeed tempting and opportune to charge derivatives for creating mayhem. Are derivatives indeed "*the financial weapons of mass destruction*" as vilified by Warren Buffet? This book is not another treatise on financial derivatives. The purpose of this project instead is to unlock the secrets of mystifying derivatives by telling the stories of institutions, which played in the derivative market and lost big. For some of them, it was honest but flawed financial engineering which brought them havoc. For others, it was unbridled speculation perpetrated by rogue traders, whose unchecked fraud brought their house down.

Each story is unique reflecting in part the idiosyncratic circumstances of derivative use and/or misuse but, as the reader will discover, a number of key themes keep reappearing under various guises: flawed financial engineering, poor auditing, ill-designed risk management and control systems, weak governance, old-fashioned fraud . . . Each chapter addresses one major derivative debacle by first narrating the story before deconstructing the financial architecture behind the debacle. In the process, the reader will become acquainted with institutions encompassing universal banks, hedge funds, industrial firms, trading companies and municipalities, and their lead character or villain. Like many I find myself mesmerized by the ingenuity of these infamous derivatives and the saga of powerful institutions in the hands of which they misfired: This book is their story.

ACKNOWLEDGMENTS

Over the years, research projects, consulting assignments and discussions with many savvy executives and academics have helped me challenge received wisdom in the area of financial engineering, risk management, and derivatives: for their insight this book is a better one. Most notably I wish to thank Daniel Ades (Kawa Fund), Y.D. Ahn (Daewoo), Bruce Benson (Barings), Alex Bongrain (Bongrain, S.A.), Eric Bryis (Cyberlibris), Gaylen Byker (Calvin College), Brian Casabianca (International Finance Corporation), Asavin Chintakananda (Stock Exchange of Thailand), Georg Ehrensperger (Garantia), Myron Glucksman (Citicorp), Anthony Gribe (Natexis Finance), Charamporn Jotishkatira (Siam Commercial Bank), Margaret Loebl (ADM), Oliver Kratz (Deutsche Bank), Rodney McLauchlan (Bankers Trust), Avinash Persaud (State Street), Gabriel Hawawini (INSEAD), Jacques Olivier (HEC), Christoph Schmid (Bio-Diesel), John Schwarz (Citicorp), Manoj Shahi, Pat Schena, Roger Sung (GIC, Singapore), Roland Portait (ESSEC), Charles Tapiero (Polytechnic University), Adrian Tschoegl (Wharton) and Seck Wai Kwong (Singapore Exchange Limited).

I am indebted to several individuals who selflessly read and edited several versions of the manuscript and wish to express my appreciation to Darius Haworon, Ellen MacDonald, Manoj Shahi, Scott Strand, and Rajeev Sawant. Timely help for graphics and word processing is gratefully acknowledged from Jordan Fabiansky, Martin Klupilek, and Lupita Ervin. Last but not least, I wish to thank my editor-in-chief — Olivier Jacque — who painstakingly reviewed the entire manuscript and asked all the hard questions.

Yet, with so much help from so many, I am still searching for the ultimate derivative which would hedge me from all remaining errors: but there is no escape — they are all mine.

LLJ
Winchester and Paris
June 2009

ABOUT THE AUTHOR

Laurent L. Jacque is the Walter B. Wriston Professor of International Finance & Banking at the *Fletcher School of Law and Diplomacy* (Tufts University) and Director of its International Business Studies Program. From 2004 to 2007, he was Fletcher's Academic Dean and as such responsible for the design and the establishment of the new Master of International Business degree and the Center for Emerging Market Enterprises. Since 1990, he has also held a joint appointment at the *HEC School of Management* (France) as a Professor of Economics, Finance, and International Business. From 1976 to 1987, he was on the faculty of the Wharton School where he held a joint appointment in the Management and Finance departments.

He is the author of two books, *Management and Control of Foreign Exchange Risk* (Kluwer Academic Publishers, 1996), *Management of Foreign Exchange Risk: Theory and Praxis* (Lexington Books, 1978) as well as more than 25 articles on International Risk Management Multinational Control Systems, Capital Markets, which have appeared in the *Journal of International Business Studies, Journal of Operations Research Society, Columbia Journal of World Business, Journal of Applied Corporate Finance, Insurance Mathematics and Economics, Management Science*, etc.... He served as an advisor and consultant to the Foreign Exchange Rate Forecasting Service of Wharton Econometrics, Forecasting Associates and as a member of Water Technologies Inc.'s board of directors.

A recipient of four teaching awards at The Wharton and Carlson Schools, Jacque received the James L. Paddock award for teaching excellence at The Fletcher School in 1996. He has taught in many Management Development Programs and is a consultant to a number of firms in the area of corporate finance and risk management including Manufacturers Hanover Trust, Merck, Sharp & Dohme, Philadelphia National Bank, General Motors, Bunge and Born (Brazil), Rhone-Poulenc (France), Siam Commercial Bank (Thailand), Daewoo (South Korea), General Electric, Dupont de Nemours, Norwest Bank, Bangkok Bank (Thailand), INSEAD, Pechiney, Petrobras, and the IFC (World Bank group).

Laurent Jacque is a graduate of HEC (Paris) and received his MA, MBA, and PhD from the Wharton School (University of Pennsylvania).

CONTENTS

LIST OF FIGURES

Chapter 6

Chapter 8

Chapter 9

Chapter 10

LIST OF TABLES

LIST OF BOXES

DERIVATIVES AND THE WEALTH OF NATIONS

Derivatives are financial weapons of mass destruction.

Warren Buffet

At a time when the world economy is engulfed into the mother of all financial crises, it is indeed tempting and opportune to find derivatives guilty as charged for creating financial chaos. This book is not an indictment of financial derivatives to be feared as "*financial weapons of mass destruction*" nor is it a call for multilateral disarmament or signing a nonproliferation treaty! Derivatives may be feared but they cannot be avoided nor ignored (abstinence is not an option) as they permeate many of the key goods and services which are at the core of modern life: for example, the price of energy is largely influenced by oil and natural gas derivatives and the cost of securitized consumer finance (variable rate home mortgages and automobile loans) embodies interest rate derivatives and credit default swaps.

Instead this book recounts the financial debacles which — triggered by the misuse of derivatives — devastated both financial and nonfinancial firms. By presenting a factual analysis of how the malpractice of derivatives played havoc with derivative end-user and dealer institutions, a case is made for vigilance not only to market and counter-party risk, but also operational risk in their use for risk management and proprietary trading. Clear and recurring lessons across the different stories should be of immediate interest to financial managers, bankers, traders, auditors, and regulators who are directly or indirectly exposed to financial derivatives. The second purpose of this book is more modest: by telling real-life "horror" stories it purports to debunk the mystifying pseudocomplexity of derivatives and to take the uninitiated reader on a "*grand tour*" of financial engineering and derivatives. Indeed the reader is introduced step by step to real-life companies and the vicissitudes that they experienced in misusing the arcane derivatives.

WHAT ARE DERIVATIVES?

Derivatives are financial contracts, whose value is "derived" from the future price of an underlying asset such as currencies, commodities, interest rates, and stock price indices. Even though each chapter will introduce one specific derivative in much detail, it is helpful at this early stage to provide definitions for the four major families of derivatives, whose architecture is identical across different classes of underlying assets:

- *Forwards* are legally-binding contracts calling for the future delivery of an asset in an amount, at a price and at a date agreed upon today. For example, a 90-day forward purchase of 25 million pound sterling (£) at the forward rate of $1.47 = £1 signed on April 13, 2009 happens in two steps: today, April 13, 2009 a contract is signed spelling out the nature of the transaction (forward purchase of the pound sterling), the amount (£25 million), the price ($1.47), the time of delivery (90 days hence or July 17, 2009) but nothing happens physically beyond the exchange of legal promises. Ninety days later, the contract is executed by delivering £25 × 1.47 = $36.75 million and taking delivery of £25 million. The contract is carried out at the forward rate regardless of the spot price (that is the price prevailing on delivery day) of the pound sterling. Forwards are tailor-made contracts also known as over-the-counter and — as such — expose the signatories to counter-party risk — that is the risk that the other party may default on its delivery obligations. Forwards are available on commodities such as copper or oil and other assets. Forwards will be the "*financial weapon of mass destruction*" in the first three chapters involving respectively a major Japanese oil company Showa Shell, Citibank, and Bank Negara — the Central Bank of Malaysia.
- *Futures* are close cousins of forward contracts with some material differences. Futures are standardized contracts, whose amount and delivery date are set by an organized exchange: for example, sterling futures can only be delivered in March, June, September, and December (third Wednesday of calendar month) and are available in multiples of £62,500). The lack of flexibility in designing a tailor-made contract (as in the case of forwards) is compensated by the liquidity of the contract, which can be closed at any time before expiry. Because futures are entered with well-capitalized exchanges such as the Chicago Board of Trade or the New York Mercantile Exchange, there is no counterparty risk to be concerned with as the

exchange will require any contract holder to post a margin — a form of collateral — which ensures that the contract holder is able to fulfill the terms of the contract at all times regardless of the spot price. Futures will be the *"financial weapon of mass destruction"* in Chapters 5, 6, and 7 featuring respectively the hedge fund Amaranth Advisors LLC, the German metal-processing and engineering firm Metallgesellschaft and the Japanese trading company Sumitomo.

- *Options* are securities which give you the right to buy (call option) or sell (put option) an asset (currency, commodity, stocks, bonds) for an extended period (American option) or at a particular future point in time (European option) at an agreed price today (strike price) for an upfront cash-flow cost (premium). In one of the largest options ever contracted, U.K. company Enterprise Oil Ltd. paid more than $26 million for a 90-day currency option to protect against exchange rate fluctuations on $1.03 billion of the $1.45 billion that it had agreed to pay for the oil exploration and production assets of U.S.-based transportation company Texas Eastern Inc. The option — a dollar call option — gave Enterprise the right to buy dollars at a dollar/sterling rate of $1.70. The dollar/sterling exchange rate was $1.73 when Enterprise Oil bought the option on March 1: "We are bearish on sterling," says group treasurer Justin Welby. *"And we did a very careful calculation between the price of the option premium (which is cheaper the further out-of-the-money) and how much we could afford the dollar to strengthen. We decided that this was the best mix between the amount of protection we could forgo and the amount of up-front cash we were prepared to pay out for the option.*[1]*"* Ninety days later, the pound stood at $1.7505, which made the call option just about redundant at the modest cost of $26 million for Enterprise Oil Ltd. Options are available not only on currencies, but also on stock price indices, interest rates, and commodities. They are the *"financial weapon of mass destruction"* in Chapters 8, 9, 10, and 11 featuring respectively Allied Lyons, Barings Bank, Allied Irish Banks, and Société Générale.
- Swaps are contracts between two parties agreeing to exchange (swap) cash-flows over a determined period. The most common swaps are interest rate swaps — where one party pays a fixed interest rate based on a notional amount and the counter-party pays a floating rate keyed to the same notional amount. Cross-currency and commodity swaps are also common. Mexicana de Cobre — a Mexican copper-mining company — decided to hedge against volatile copper prices on the London Metal Exchange[2] to secure medium-term financing at significantly more favorable terms than it was currently paying. It entered into a copper price swap with Metallgesellschaft (one of the leading metal-processing firms) whereby for a period of 3

---

[1] "Enterprise Oil $25 million call option", *Corporate Finance* (April 1989).

[2] Jacque, L. L. and G. Hawawini. Myths and realities of the global market for capital: Lessons for financial managers, *Journal of Applied Corporate Finance* (Fall 1993).

years it committed to deliver monthly 4,000 metric tons of copper at a guaranteed price of $2,000 per metric ton regardless of the spot price on the world market. In effect the swap was tantamount to a portfolio of 36 forward contracts with maturities ranging from 1 to 36 months at a forward rate of $2,000 per metric ton. Most swaps are over-the-counter rather than exchange-traded. They are the *"financial weapons of mass destruction"* in Chapters 12, 13, 14, 15 and 16 featuring respectively Procter & Gamble, Gibson Greeting Cards, Orange County, Long-Term Capital Management and last but not least AIG.

A BRIEF HISTORY OF DERIVATIVES

From immemorial times, traders have been faced with three problems: how to finance the physical transportation of merchandise from point A to point B — perhaps several hundreds or thousands of miles apart and weeks or months away — how to insure the cargo (risk of being lost at sea or to pirates) and last, how to protect against price fluctuations in the value of the cargo across space (from point A to point B) and over time (between shipping and delivery time). In many ways, the history of derivatives contracts parallels the increasingly innovative remedies that traders devised in coping with their predicament.

Ancient Times. Trade carried over great distance is probably as old as mankind and has long been a source of economic power for the nations which embraced it. Indeed international trade seems to have been at the vanguard of human progress and civilization: Phoenicians, Greeks, and Romans were all great traders, whose activities were facilitated by marketplaces and money changers which set fixed places and fixed times for exchanging goods. Some historians even claim that some form of contracting with future delivery appeared as early as several centuries BC. At about the same time in Babylonia — the cradle of civilization — commerce was primarily effected by means of caravans. Traders bought goods to be delivered in some distant location and sought financing. A risk-sharing agreement was designed whereby merchants-financiers provided a loan to traders, whose repayment was contingent upon safe delivery of the goods. The trader borrowed at a higher cost than ordinary loans would cost to account for the purchase of an "option to default" on the loan contingent upon loss of cargo. As lenders were offering similar options to many traders and thereby pooling their risks they were able to keep its cost affordable.[3]

Middle Ages. Other forms of early derivatives contracts can be traced to medieval European commerce. After the long decline in commerce following the demise of the

---

[3] Jorion, P. *Big Bets Gone Bad* (Academic Press, 1995), p. 138.

Roman Empire, Medieval Europe experienced an economic revival in the twelfth century around two major trading hubs: in Northern Italy, the city-states of Venice and Genoa controlled the trade of silk, spices, and rare metals with the Orient; in Northern Europe, the Flanders (Holland and Belgium) had long been known for their fine cloth, lumber, salt fish, and metalware. It was only natural that trade would flourish between these two complementary economic regions and somehow, as early as the 1100s, Reims and Troyes in Champagne (Eastern France) held trade fairs, which facilitated their mercantile activity: there, traders would find money changers, storage facilities, and most importantly protection provided by the Counts of Champagne. Soon rules of commercial engagement started to emerge as disputes between traders hailing from as far-away as Scandinavia or Russia had to be settled: a code of commercial law — known as "law merchant" — enforceable by the "courts of the fair" was progressively developed. Although most transactions were completed on a spot basis *"an innovation of the medieval fairs was the use of a document called the* "lettre de faire" *as a forward contract which specified the delivery of goods at a later date."*[4]

In 1298, a Genoese merchant by the name of Benedetto Zaccharia was selling 30 tons of alum[5] for delivery from Aigues Mortes (Provence) to Bruges (Flanders).[6] Maritime voyage around Spain and the Atlantic coast of France was then hazardous and fraught with dangers: the cargo could be lost at sea or to pirates. Zaccharia found two compatriot financiers Enrico Zuppa and Baliano Grilli, who would assume the risk. Here is how it worked: Zaccharia sold "spot"[7] the alum to Zuppa and Grilli and entered into a *forward* repurchase contract contingent upon physical delivery. The repurchase price was significantly higher than the spot price in Aigues Mortes. It reflected the cost of physical carry from Aigues Mortes to Bruges (several months at sea), insurance against loss of cargo and the *option to default* granted to Zaccharia in the case of nondelivery. The merchant Zaccharia had secured financing and insurance in the form of a *forward* contingent contract.

Renaissance. If medieval fairs had gone a long way in establishing the standards for specifying the grading and inspection process of commodities being traded as well as date and location for delivery of goods, it fell short of the modern concept of futures traded on centralized exchanges. The first organized futures exchange was the Dojima rice market in Osaka (Japan), which flourished from the early 1700s to World War II. It grew out of the need of feudal landlords whose income was primarily

---

[4] Teweles, R. J. and F. J. Jones, edited by Ben Warwick, *The Futures Game: Who Wins, Who Loses and Why* (McGraw Hill, 1999, 3rd edn.), p. 8.

[5] White mineral salt.

[6] Favier, J. *Les Grandes Découvertes* (Le Livre de Poche, 1991), cited in Bryis and de Varenne (2000).

[7] Spot sale is for immediate delivery and cash payment.

based on unsteady rice crops to cope with a growing money economy. By shipping surplus rice to Osaka and Edo, landlords were able to raise cash by selling warehouse receipts of their rice inventory in exchange for other goods on sale in other cities. Merchants who purchased these warehouse receipts soon found themselves lending to cash-short landlords against future rice crops. In 1730, an edict by Yoshimune — also known as the "rice Shogun" — established futures trading in rice at the Dojima market apparently in an effort to stem the secular decline in rice prices. It certainly allowed rice farmers to hedge against price fluctuations between harvests. Interestingly all the hallmarks of modern standardized futures contract were found in the Dojima rice futures market[8]: each contract was set at 100 *koku*[9] and contract durations were set according to trimester trading calendars consisting of a spring semester (January 8– April 28), summer term (May 7–October 9), and a winter term (October 17–December 24). All trades were entered in the "book" transaction system, where the names of the contracting parties, amount of rice exchanged, futures price, and terms of delivery were recorded. Transactions were cash-settled (delivery of physical rice was not necessary) at the close of the trading term. Money changers soon functioned as clearinghouses de facto eliminating the counterparty risk by forcing margin requirements on individual rice traders, which were marked-to-market every 10 days.[10]

Industrial Revolution. Forward contracts progressively evolved from the need to hedge price risk associated with international trade: consider the case of a mining firm in California shipping copper to London and wanting to lock in the value of its merchandise by selling "forward" (known then as on "*a to arrive basis*") its cargo — possibly at a lower price that it would expect to receive several months later. A copper processing firm in London may want to lock in the value of its core raw material input so that, in turn, it could bid on construction projects at firm prices. Neither firm would know of each other being domiciled far apart. A middle man would act as a match-maker: merchant banks (or their ancestors) having representation in the two distinct physical locations would be able to arrange the trade: They would receive a handsome fee for bringing the two parties together and acting as a guarantor of the good execution of the transaction.

In the early 1800s, grain commerce in the United States was vulnerable to large swings in prices: upon harvesting farmers would flood the market with their crop and grain prices would collapse. Within a few months shortages would develop and prices would rebound. Instead of shipping their crop all at once and face up to inadequate

---

[8] West, M. D. Private ordering at the world's first future exchange, *Michigan Law Review* (August 2000).
[9] Koku is a unit of measurement used in medieval Japan and which corresponds to the amount of rice consumed by a Japanese in one year. It is equal to 180 Litres.
[10] Op. Cit. p. 2588.

storage facilities, farmers (sellers) and millers (buyers) increasingly turned to forward contracting as a way to cope with price volatility while staggering over time grain delivery: Chicago was rapidly emerging as a hub for grain storing, trading, and subsequent distribution eastwards along rail lines or through the great lakes. In 1848, organized futures trading made its debut with the Chicago Board of Trade: forward contracts were morphed into futures through standardization of contracts which allowed easier (uniform grading of commodities) and safer trading (margin requirement eliminates counter-party risk). Physical commodities both hard (minerals) and soft (agricultural) became the object of futures trading.

Information Age. More than a century later, the burst of innovation in financial derivatives (as opposed to commodity-linked derivatives) was generally associated with the break-down in 1971 of the Bretton-Woods system of fixed exchange rates. Volatile exchange rates ushered the world financial system in a new era of deregulation and financial innovation with the introduction of currency futures, options, swaps, swaptions, etc… as illustrated in Figure 1. As early as 1972, currency futures started to trade at the newly established International Monetary Market (a subsidiary of the Chicago Mercantile Exchange). Soon the deregulation of interest rates in the United

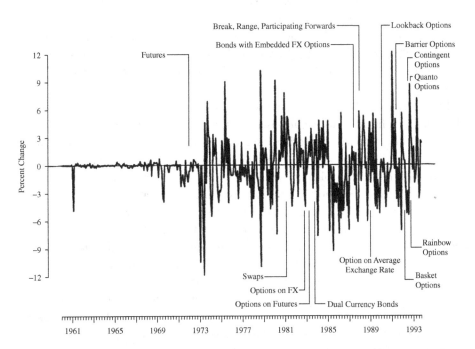

Figure 1 Percent change in yen/USD exchange rate. *Source*: Smithson, C. W. and C. W. Smith, Jr., with D. Sykes Wilford. *Managing Financial Risk* (Irwin, 1995), p. 22.

States set in motion the introduction of interest rate derivatives, which eventually would dwarf currency and commodity derivatives. In 1977, the Chicago Board of trade introduced what was soon to become the most successful contract of all times — US Treasury bond futures. When the world became a riskier place firms and financial institutions naturally sought safe harbor by hedging with financial derivatives.

DERIVATIVES AND THE WEALTH OF NATIONS

Indeed derivatives are sophisticated instruments whose spiraling success over the years has largely been driven by increased price volatility in commodities, currencies, stock prices, and interest rates. They fundamentally facilitate efficient risk transfer from firms, which are ill-equipped to bear risk and which would rather not be exposed to risk to firms which have excess risk-bearing capacity and are willing to take on exposure to risk. The first group is known as *hedgers*, who participate in derivatives trading for reducing or eliminating a pre-existing price risk: for example, airline companies are active participants in kerosene derivatives to limit their exposure to fluctuations in jet fuel prices. The second group is loosely known as *speculators*, who trade derivatives in the pursuit of profit and therefore willingly accept an increase in their exposure to risk: proprietary trading desks of investment banks or hedge funds are archetypical speculators. Thanks to derivatives risk transfer has become far more precise and efficient as its cost plunged because of breakthrough in computer technology and financial theory.

Thus derivatives allow for economic agents — households, financial institutions, and nonfinancial firms — to avail themselves of the benefits of division of labor and comparative advantage at risk-bearing: but are derivatives indeed value creating and contributing to the wealth of nations? Shouldn't the major derivatives-linked disasters (the subject of this book) which are striking with predictable frequency some of the best managed firms in the world be construed as evidence of wealth destruction rather than wealth creation? After all, the cumulative losses of recorded derivatives, debacles are well in excess of $25 billion and if one includes AIG the total is approaching $200 billion. The answer is neither: derivatives are zero-sum games and what one side of a derivative contract loses the other side gains. Unlike physical destruction brought about by Mother Nature such as Hurricane Katrina or the Kobe earthquake, derivative debacles are at worst wealth transfer rather than wealth destruction. Unfortunately, for the shareholders of any of the derivative-stricken firms portrayed in this book who suffered dramatic and at times total losses on their investment, the impeccable economic rationalization that their wealth had been transferred (rather than lost) to lucky bankers, traders, or hedge funds holding the other side of the derivative contract brings them little solace! Shouldn't regulation be tightened to save managers from the abyss of derivative debacles?

As the allegoric cover of this book purports to illustrate the "tight rope walker" or "funambulist" (trader, treasurer, or risk manager) can walk the straight path from one peak to the next (wealth creation) thereby avoiding the costly and time-consuming path down the mountain before climbing up again provided that he handles with aplomb the balancing pole (derivatives): otherwise he will lose his balance and fall in the abyss (death on landing or wealth destruction)!

ORGANIZATION OF THE BOOK

This book is not another treatise on financial derivative products. The purpose of this project instead is to unlock the secrets of derivatives by telling the stories of institutions, which played in the derivative market and lost big. For some of these unfortunate organizations, it was honest but flawed financial engineering which brought them havoc. For others it was unbridled speculation perpetrated by rogue traders, whose unchecked fraud brought their house down.

Each story is unique — reflecting in part the idiosyncratic circumstances of the firm's misuse of derivatives and allows the reader to familiarize himself with one derivative product at a time. Each chapter addresses one major derivative debacle by first narrating the story before deconstructing the financial architecture behind the flawed scheme. Each chapter is self-contained to facilitate the reading and comprehension: as a result, a number of key concepts are revisited under various guises throughout the book. Each chapter concludes with the lessons learnt or the "moral of the story": unsurprisingly organizational learning is found lacking as mistakes made by one firm keep being repeated by others.

In the process, the reader will discover various institutions ranging from multinational corporations to universal banks, central banks, trading companies, hedge funds, and municipalities while becoming acquainted with the lead character of the saga. Rather than following a chronological order, the book is organized along the families of derivative products: forwards, futures, options, and swaps (see Table 1 for short summaries of each debacle). Fortunately, the reader will discover that the basic architecture of each product is the same whether it is "derived" from currencies, commodities, interest rate products, or stock market indices.

The book is written for a general college-educated audience and does not presuppose any training in finance: as the reader explores each debacle key technical concepts are introduced and illustrated in the form of boxes set apart from the text. Simple numerical and graphical illustrations are built into the story to facilitate the

Table 1   Contents of the Book

Chapter 1	**Introduction: derivatives and the wealth of nations**

Part I FORWARDS

Chapter 2	**Shell Showa (1993).** Currency traders rolled over dollar forwards hoping to recover initial losses. Concealed losses eventually amount to $1.07 billion.
Chapter 3	**Citibank (1964).** Currency trader speculates that the pound sterling will not devalue. Speculative scheme is aborted early at a loss of $8 million.
Chapter 4	**Bank Negara (1994).** Speculates in the foreign exchange market through forwards and incurs losses of $3.16 billion.

Part II FUTURES

Chapter 5	**Amaranth (2006).** A hedge fund corners the natural gas futures market. After initial billions of speculative profits, Amaranth finally collapses for failing to meet margin calls losing $5 billion for its investors.
Chapter 6	**Metallgesellschaft (1993).** Sells long-dated oil forwards hedged by "stacking and rolling" oil futures. Unable to meet margin calls, Metallgesellschaft has to be rescued by a consortium of banks after losing $1.6 billion.
Chapter 7	**Sumitomo (1995).** Its chief copper trader corners the copper market first realizing large profits until regulators forced the firm to resume normal trading: $2.6 billion lost.

Part III OPTIONS

Chapter 8	**Allied Lyons (1991).** Its treasury speculates on lower volatility of the dollar-pound exchange rate during the Gulf war by selling currency options.
Chapter 9	**Allied Irish Bank (2002).** Currency trader conceals a streak of speculative losses on yen forwards by writing deep-in-the-money currency options. Losses totaled $694 millions.
Chapter 10	**Barings (1995).** Nick Leeson conceals a streak of speculative losses on Nikkei 225 futures leading to losses of $1.4 billion and the collapse of the venerable House of Barings.
Chapter 11	**Société Générale (2008).** Jerome Kerviel undertakes wild proprietary trading on stock index futures first generating $1.5 billion of gains before losing $7.4 billion for SoGen.

Part IV SWAPS

Chapter 12	**Procter & Gamble (1994).** Purchases leveraged interest swaps hoping to lower its cost of capital failing to understand that it effectively sold interest rate put options for financing the reduction of its cost of capital.
Chapter 13	**Gibson Greeting Cards (1995).** Purchases leveraged interest swaps to reduce its cost of capital. Lost $27 million partially recovered after suing Bankers Trust which sold the swaps.

(Continued)

Table 1 (*Continued*)

Chapter 14	**Orange County (1995).** Municipal finance pool uses excessive leverage and interest rate derivatives to turbo-charge its earnings. Forced into bankruptcy after $1.5 billion of losses.
Chapter 15	**Long-Term Capital Management (1998).** Exploits quasi-arbitrage convergence trades in US treasuries using extreme leverage until the Asian financial crisis turns illiquidity into insolvency.
Chapter 16	**AIG (2008).** Sells credit default swaps without proper reserving for actual defaults. Losses in excess of $150 billion forced the US government to the largest bail-out ever to stave off systemic financial collapse.
Chapter 17	**From Theory to Malpractice: Lessons Learnt**

intuition behind each story and to smooth the reader's discovery journey into the uncharted territories of derivatives. Safe travel and happy discovery!

Bibliography

Briys, E. and F. de Varenne. *The Fisherman and the Rhinoceros: How International Finance Shapes Everyday Life* (John Wiley & Sons Inc., 2000).

Chew, L. *Managing Derivative Risks: The Use and Abuse of Leverage* (John Wiley & Sons, 1996).

Edwards, F. R. and C. W. Ma. *Futures and Options* (McGraw Hill, 1992).

Jorion, P. *Value at Risk: The New Benchmark for Managing Financial Risk* (McGraw Hill, 3rd edn., 2007).

Marthinsen, J. *Risk Takers: Uses and Abuses of Financial Derivatives* (Pearson Addison-Wesley, 2005).

Miller, M. H. *Merton Miller on Derivatives* (John Wiley & Sons, 1997).

Teweles, R. J. and F. J. Jones, edited by Ben Warwick. *The Futures Game: Who Wins, Who Loses and Why* (McGraw Hill, 1999 3rd edn).

Part I
FORWARDS

SHOWA SHELL SEKIYU K.K.

First rule of holes: when you are in one, stop digging.

Anonymous

Showa Shell Sekiyu K.K. is the 50%-owned Japanese subsidiary of the oil giant Royal Dutch Shell. In early 1993, it announced a staggering foreign exchange loss amounting to ¥125 billion or $1.07 billion (five times the company's pretax profit). In fact, when Showa Shell's President, Takashi Henmi, first informed the Anglo–Dutch parent's executives, they assumed that the decimal point was erroneously transmitted and they kept requesting a correction expecting losses in million rather than billion of dollars.[10]

"SHELL-SHOCKED BY SHELL GAMES": THE SHOWA SHELL DEBACLE

It appears that the losses could be traced back to 1989 when Showa Shell treasury had hedged through 90-day forward contracts the company oil bill against the risk of an appreciating dollar. Somehow, what had started as a legitimate hedge in the normal course of business morphed mysteriously into a currency exposure of $6.4 billion — a position which was clearly in breach of the company's internal control procedures. To conceal its losses, the treasury department rolled over — at the expiration of the forward contracts — its currency position to avoid settling the cash losses. As the yen kept rising the foreign exchange losses were soon starting to balloon out of control.

---

[10] Y. Shibata, Japan's currency scandal could spread, *Global Finance*, **7**(3), 111.

Lax internal controls and dysfunctional auditing of foreign exchange trading operations kept the problem hidden from Showa Shell's senior management. It was not until late 1992 that a banker casually informed a Showa Shell treasury executive about the size of the position. The loss disclosure on February 20, 1993 amounted to 82% of Showa Shell's shareholder equity and precipitated a free fall in the stock price from ¥1500 to less than ¥800. The next day the treasurer was sacked and the company's Chairman and President announced their resignation.

How can a Japanese oil company whose main activities center around the refining and retail distribution of petroleum products for the Japanese market suffer huge foreign exchange losses amounting to five times its annual profit? Was it an ill-devised hedging strategy that went awry or was it reckless speculations by rogue currency traders? This chapter recounts how "shell games" eventually "shell-shocked" the senior management of both Shell Showa Sekiyu K.K. and its Anglo–Dutch parent Royal Dutch Shell. Of special interest is understanding how unsupervised currency traders could hide large scale forward speculation from their bosses' not so watchful eyes under the pretense of hedging oil imports.

HEDGING CURRENCY RISK AT OIL COMPANIES

To better understand why Showa Shell would want to hedge its oil imports bill against the risk of dollar appreciation, it is helpful to first profile the economics of its activities. Unlike giant multinationals such as Exxon or Royal Dutch Shell which are vertically integrated from oil exploration and extraction all the way to distribution, Japanese oil companies are primarily engaged in down-stream activities — namely, domestic refining and distribution operations through company-owned service stations. Such activities are almost exclusively focused on the Japanese market — with international dealings limited to importing petroleum products. As such, Showa Shell would import crude oil to refine into gasoline products for distribution to the retail market. Because the price of crude oil is set in dollars, Showa Shell was exposed to the twin risks of oil price and $/¥ exchange rate:

(1) Fluctuations (or lack thereof) in the dollar price of oil depend upon whether Showa Shell procured oil from the spot market[11] or through long-term fixed price contracts from its Anglo–Dutch parent (see Box A for an introduction to the oil market and Figure 1 for oil prices at the time of this debacle).

---

[11] The spot oil market refers to transactions which call for immediate delivery of physical oil as opposed to forward and futures markets which specialize in time-deferred delivery contracts.

Box A. The Oil Market. *Until the early 70s, the oil market was relatively stable with prices tightly controlled by the Organization of Oil Exporting Countries (OPEC).*[12] *In fact, there was not much of an oil market as crude oil was directly sold through long-term agreements between oil-rich countries and major globally integrated oil companies such as Exxon, British Petroleum, and Royal Dutch Shell ... also known as the Seven Sisters. The dramatic oil price increase triggered by the first oil embargo of 1973 encouraged energy conservation and the development of non-OPEC oil reserves most notably in the North Sea and the former Soviet Union. Soon, as demand contracted and oil supply expanded, a surplus of crude oil started to undermine the official OPEC-determined price. By the late 70s, OPEC was starting to lose its monopolistic grip on oil prices as national quotas were increasingly difficult to enforce and Saudi Arabia relented on its role of swing producer and price stabilizer. Oil companies naturally started to rely increasingly on the spot market for an ever larger percentage of their total supplies. By the mid-80s, more than two-thirds of global oil procurement was sourced from the spot market; the remaining one-third of total oil transactions was now locked into contracts of much shorter duration. This led in turn to greater price volatility for crude and refined petroleum products, which soon fostered the establishment of futures markets in petroleum products.*

---

(2) Fluctuations in the yen price of the dollar (see Figure 2 for exchange rates fluctuations) or so called exchange rate.

Figure 3 maps out the cash flow configuration characteristic of a domestic oil refiner and distributor such as Showa Shell. On the revenue side, Showa Shell would derive yen-denominated cash inflows from the sale of refined gasoline products to Japanese automobilists, transportation and airline companies as well as utilities. Showa Shell could depend on very stable market conditions in terms of price controlled by the Japanese government and quantity sold (relatively stable with a 12.5% share of the Japanese market). On the cost side, Showa Shell had to reckon with two somewhat correlated sources of risks which could — over relatively short period — result in major jumps (or declines) in the cost of procuring crude oil. Thus, any surprise spike in operating costs due to jumps in the price of oil or the yen price of the dollar would squeeze operating income since Showa Shell would not be able to translate or pass-through immediately its higher costs into higher price (because of governmental price

---

[12] OPEC was first established as the world oil cartel in 1960 and currently includes 12 members: Iran, Iraq, Kuwait, Qatar, the United Arab Emirates, Saudi Arabia, Libya, Algeria, Ecuador, Venezuela, Nigeria, and Angola. Collectively, it controls about two-thirds of known oil reserves and accounts for approximately one-third of world oil production. By setting national semiannual oil quotas for its members which reflects global demand for oil and likely production by non-OPEC oil exporters, it seeks to influence world oil prices.

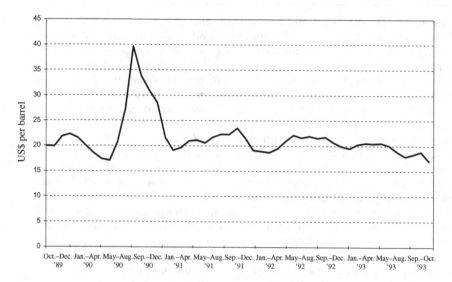

Figure 1   Monthly spot oil prices (1989–1993).

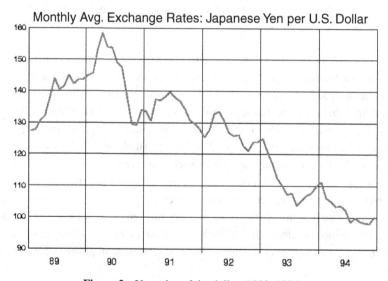

Figure 2   Yen price of the dollar (1989–1994).

controls). Hence, the rationale for hedging the dollar transaction exposure and possibly
the oil price exposure; this latter oil price exposure would depend upon how much of
Showa Shell's total oil was procured from Royal Dutch Shell through long-term fixed
price contracts.

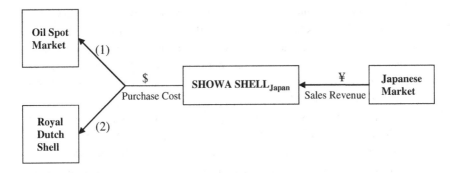

(1) Showa Shell purchases oil from the world spot oil market and faces oil price risk and exchange rate risk.

(2) Showa Shell purchases oil from parent company through long-term purchase contract at a fixed oil price. It faces exchange rate risk.

Figure 3   Showa Shell's economic exposure.

THE MECHANICS OF HEDGING DOLLAR EXCHANGE RATE RISK AND OIL PRICE RISK

Showa Shell would routinely import an average of 15 million barrels a month (its refining capacity stood at about 500,000 barrels a day) and would typically hedge its currency exposure by entering into 90-day forward contracts. This would lock in the yen cost of dollar-denominated petroleum imports (see Box B for a definition of

Box B. What Are Forward Contracts?   *A forward exchange contract is a commitment to buy or sell a certain quantity of foreign currency on a certain date in the future (maturity of the contract) at a price (forward exchange rate) agreed upon today when the contact is signed. For example, on September 30, 1989 Showa Shell could buy 90-day dollar forward at ¥145 in the amount of $300 million. On December 31, 1989, Showa Shell would deliver $300 million × ¥145 = ¥43.5 billion and receive $300 million regardless of the spot value on delivery day; if the dollar is worth ¥140, Showa Shell would lose from the forward contract having paid ¥5 more per dollar than it had to, thereby incurring a cash-flow loss of $300 million (140−145) = −¥1.5 billion ($10,714,285 at the exchange rate of ¥140 = $1.00). It is important to understand that a forward contract, when signed, is an exchange of irrevocable and legally binding promises (with no cash changing hands and no margin posted) obligating the two parties to go through with the actual transaction at maturity and delivering the respective currencies (or cash settlement) regardless of the prevailing spot exchange rate on that day.*

forward contracts) thereby hoping to protect itself against any appreciation in the value of the US dollar (same thing as the depreciation of the Japanese yen).

Alternatively, Showa Shell could borrow yens from a Japanese bank, immediately convert the loan proceeds into an interest-bearing dollar account which would grow into the exact amount of $300 million. This is known as a "money market hedge" or a "synthetic forward contract" (see Box C).

Last but not least, Showa Shell could have purchased a dollar call option at the money: if the dollar appreciated beyond ¥145 (the strike price), Showa Shell would exercise the option to purchase dollars at ¥145; conversely, should the dollar depreciate below ¥145, Showa Shell would simply abandon the option and purchase dollars at the more favorable spot rate. For the flexibility of having the best of both worlds, Showa Shell would have to pay a cash premium upfront, which could amount to as much as 3% of the face value of the contract — for example $0.03 \times \$300$ million $= \$9$ million. The reader is referred to Box C for the numerical illustration of hedging mechanics.

The currency traders at Showa Shell chose the forward hedging path for a simple reason: the money market hedge and the call option would have left an easily traceable mark on financial statements. More specifically, the money market hedge would have

---

Box C. How to Hedge a $300 Million Monthly Oil Bill? *To protect itself against a dollar appreciation (higher ¥ price of one dollar), Showa Shell can lock in the yen cost of oil purchases through:*

(1) *Forward Hedge: Showa Shell would purchase $300 million forward at the forward rate of $F(90) = 145$ for a yen cost of $\$300$ million $\times 145 = $ ¥43.5 billion.*

(2) *Money Market Hedge (synthetic forward contract): Showa Shell would deposit in a dollar-denominated interest-bearing account the present value of $\$300$ million discounted at the quarterly US interest rate $i_{US} = 0.06/4$ or $\$300$ million$/(1 + 0.06/4) = \$295$ million; this repayment would necessitate a yen loan given the spot rate of $S(0) = 147$ of $[\$300 \text{ million}/(1+0.06/4)]147 = $ ¥43,448 billion and a final cost in yen 90 days later at a given interest rate in Japan of $i_{Jap} = 0.03/4$ of $[\$300 \text{ million}/(1 + 0.06/4)]147(1 + 0.03/4) = $ ¥43,774 billion.*

(3) *A Dollar Call Option: Showa Shell would purchase a dollar call option at the money (strike price of ¥145 = \$1 which equals the forward rate) and pay an upfront premium of $\$9$ million $= 0.03 \times \$300$ million.*

The reader will note that in the first two cases Showa Shell will neutralize its dollar liability exposure (due to its commitment to purchasing for $300 million of oil) by creating a dollar-denominated asset exposure either through the medium of the forward contract or a combination of money market positions (borrow yen now and invest in a dollar time deposit). The forward hedge is slightly cheaper than the money market hedge.

shown up as both an additional yen liability and dollar short-term asset time deposit on Showa Shell's balance sheet while the currency option would have resulted in a cash-flow cost on its income statement.

As noted above, Showa Shell was also exposed to oil price risk, which can be as catastrophic as exchange risk; it could be eliminated through a forward oil contract which operates on the same principles as a forward exchange contract. Assuming that the spot price for West Texas Intermediate crude oil was $21 per barrel on September 30, 1989, Showa Shell could hedge its monthly purchase of 15 million barrels by buying crude oil forwards for the corresponding delivery date. On September 30, 1989 oil forwards stood at $20 per barrel, which allowed Showa Shell to lock in its December delivery purchase at $300 million. It seemed, however, that oil price risk was of no concern to Showa Shell presumably because oil supplies were protected by long-term purchase contracts or met through Royal Dutch Shell worldwide production.

WAS SHOWA SHELL HEDGING OR SPECULATING?

At a price of $20 per barrel, Showa Shell would purchase [15 million barrels of oil] × $20 = $300 millions at the forward rate of ¥145 per dollar and would therefore be hedging a transaction exposure in the amount of $300 million per month. This, in turn, would translate into a maximum of $900 million of outstanding forward dollar purchase contracts over the entire 90 days hedging/payment cycle. In other words, at any given point in time, Showa Shell — on account of hedging its oil imports bill — should have an outstanding dollar exposure of no more than a $900 million. Given the position limits of $200 million per month, Showa Shell should have kept its overall dollar forward position to 3 × $200 million = $600 million. They were far from the reported $6.4 billion outstanding balance indicating that $5.5 billion of the total outstanding balance was pure speculation and could not be explained by normal hedging. The only rational explanation for this huge discrepancy between a defensible hedge and a delirious speculative gamble is that Showa Shell currency traders were simply doubling up on their dollar position hoping to recoup their losses faster when the dollar would finally rebound. "Cut your losses and ride your gain" was not part of the gospel of our currency traders, who seemed consumed by the *loss realization aversion* syndrome whereby traders consistently hold on to losing trades longer than winning trades. Indeed, there is a well-documented human tendency to irrationally hold on to large speculative positions to avoid small realizable losses.[13]

---

[13] Locke, P. R. and S. C. Mann, *Do Professional Traders Exhibit Loss Realization Aversion?* (Georges Washington University: working paper, 2000).

CONCEALING CURRENCY LOSSES

Under normal practices, forward exchange contracts are cash settled at maturity. When, on September 30, 1989, Showa Shell first purchased 90-day forward dollar at the exchange rate of ¥145, it committed to taking delivery of $300 million and delivering ¥43.5 billion. On December 30, the $300 million at the spot rate of ¥140 was now worth only ¥42 billion for a cash flow loss of ¥1.5 billion or approximately $10 million. In an opportunity cost sense, Showa Shell would have been better off not hedging and riding the appreciation of the yen. Because of the currency loss on cash-settling, the forward contract would have been reported as a separate entry on the income statement; it would have attracted attention from senior management, the company's board of directors, bankers, and investors. However, a quirk in Japanese accounting rules and the cooperation of Japanese banks (which were Showa Shell counterparties on the forward contracts) allowed for the foreign exchange losses to be rolled over at the initial forward rate of ¥145. The actual cash-flow losses did not materialize — instead they became paper losses buried in a footnote since forward contracts are reported as off-balance sheet items. In effect, Japanese banks did not insist on a cash settlement from their valued customers agreeing instead to let the foreign exchange losses ride until the currency traders' unlucky streak turned lucky. That never happened. As stubborn Showa Shell currency traders entered into new forward dollar contracts — still convinced that the dollar would rise rather than decline — they compounded their foreign exchange losses month after month. The losses themselves were never settled — instead they accumulated into a burgeoning liability which must have made Showa Shell's friendly bankers more than concerned. In fact, Showa Shell's bankers had to face up to very significant counter-party risk. Could Showa Shell write a mammoth check for ¥125 billion ($1.07 billion) to their bankers when the day of reckoning would finally come? At five times Showa Shell's 1992 estimated profit, default on the forward contract was a real possibility .... Of course, the indigent Japanese "child" could always turn to its rich Anglo–Dutch "parent" as few — if any — oil multinationals would ever allow one of their foreign affiliates to descend into infamous bankruptcy![14]

THE STORY UNFOLDS

It was not until late 1992 when one of Showa Shell's bankers made a casual reference to the outsize forward contracts to one of the firm's senior executives that the concealed speculative gambit was unveiled. By then, our currency traders had already confided

---

[14] This is known as "letter of comfort" whereby a multinational — foreign based — parent would feel morally obligated to come to the rescue of a struggling foreign affiliate.

in two treasury senior managers, who took another nine months to inform President Hemni. Losing face and owning up to such considerable losses are never easy and certainly not in the land of the valiant samurai. Interestingly, the currency traders came from the Shell side of Showa Shell Sekiyu K.K., which had been created when it merged with Showa in 1985; the managers they confided in were also Shell alumni as was the President of the company. Rivalry between the two corporate cultures probably exacerbated the complex process of bringing the plot to an early resolution. As it turned out, Showa Shell was not an isolated case: Several other energy and transportation companies were similarly facing up to considerable forex losses on forward contracts, which had been rolled over a period and never cash-settled. Most notably, on April 9th, 1994 Kashima Oil disclosed $1.5 billion in forex losses on a script which shared much with Showa Shell's debacle.[15] It was not long before Japan's Ministry of Finance banned the roll-over of "out-of the-money" forward contracts; delinquent firms such as Showa Shell and Kashima Oil were advised to unwind forward contracts in short order which they did between 1993 and 1995. In both cases sizeable real-estate holdings had to be liquidated and common equity issued to settle the huge cash-flow losses.

FORECASTING EXCHANGE RATES: TREACHEROUS AT BEST

Behind a "risk-paranoid"[16] hedging strategy, stands a foreign exchange forecast. For initially hedging their dollar transaction exposure, Showa Shell currency traders must have had strong sentiments about the future value of the yen against the dollar. Clearly, their concern was a continuous weakening of the Japanese currency. As Figure 2 shows, except for a brief period when the dollar rose against the yen in 1989, the yen strengthened steadily over the period 1989–1994. Perhaps more revealing — Japan throughout this period ran a consistently high current account surplus on its Balance of Payments while the Bank of Japan's international reserves showed steady increases indicating that it was intervening heavily in the forex market to slow down the yen appreciation. Both trends pointed to strong fundamentals, which are generally associated with an appreciating yen. Similarly, over that period the forward rate for 1, 3, 6, and 12 months shows the yen at a premium against the US currency. This was, of course, explained by the relatively low Japanese interest compared to US interest rate — a relationship which drives the value of forward contracts through the theory of Interest Rate Parity (see Box D).

---

[15] *The Economist*, "Determined Loser" (April 16, 1994).

[16] Risk-paranoia refers to a policy of hedging all risks all the time — as opposed to risk aversion, which is characterized by selective hedging (that is, hedging some of the time less than 100% of exposure).

Box D. Valuing Forward Exchange Rates and the Interest Rate Parity Theory.
*Forward exchange rates are primarily determined by interest rates according to
the theory of Interest Rate Parity. Consider the example of Fuji Finance Company's treasurer, who has to invest ¥100 billion for the next 360 days. According
to Fuji Finance's charter, the funds should be kept in very low-risk securities —
say US one year treasury note yielding 6% and/or Japanese treasury notes of
similar maturity yielding 3%; the higher yield in dollar is enticing (¥3 billions of
additional interest income would be earned) but assumes that the spot exchange
rate between dollar and yen will remain steady at ¥145. Otherwise, the interest rate differential may be partly or fully wiped out by a dollar devaluation of
up to 3%.*

*Thus our treasurer would compare the yield on a domestic investment (no credit
risk and no currency risk), which would return ¥100,000,000,000 (1 + 0.03) =
¥103,000,000,000 with the higher yield on a dollar-denominated investment.
Specifically to take advantage of the higher US yield, our treasurer will*

(1) *purchase spot dollar in the amount of ¥100,000,000,000/145 =
$689,655,170,*
(2) *invest at the rate of 6% to receive in 360 days $689,655,170 (1 + 0.06) =
$731,034,480, and*
(3) *secure the yen value of the dollar investment by selling forward both dollar
principal and interest income at the forward exchange rate F = 140 and be
guaranteed to receive in 360 days $731,034,480 × 140 = ¥102,344,827,228.*

*In effect, the comparison between the two investment options will determine where
the funds will be invested: In this case, there is a small advantage to investing in
yen. More generally, if the return on covered investment in dollar is somewhat
higher short-term funds will migrate from Tokyo to New York, thereby exercising
upward pressure on Japanese interest rate and the spot yen price of one dollar
while putting downward pressure on the US interest rate and the forward rate
until both investment options are equal: this state of equilibrium is also known as
Interest Rate Parity.[17] More formally, the theorem of Interest Rate Parity establishes a very simple relationship between domestic (i), foreign (i^*) interest rates,
the spot (S) and forward (F) rates:*

$$(1 + i) = (1/S)(1 + i^*)F \quad or \quad F = S(1 + i)/(1 + i^*).$$

*The reader should understand that even though tight limits may be imposed on the
spot exchange rate the interest rate differential $i - i^*$ will determine the forward
rate which in equilibrium would settle at*

$$F = 145[(1 + 0.03)/(1 + 0.06)] = 141.$$

---

[17] The reader will note that Interest Rate Parity does not mean equality of nominal interest
rates but equality of nominal interest rates adjusted for the cost of a forward cover against the
exchange risk.

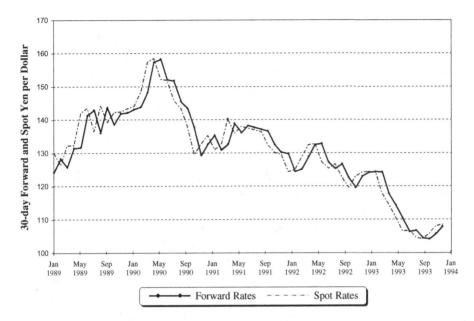

Figure 4 Forward rates as unbiased predictors of future spot exchange rates. Monthly Data 30 day Forward vs. Spot Yen per Dollar.

Forward rates are generally considered *unbiased predictors* (in a statistical sense) of future spot exchange rates. Of course, this does not mean that forward rate predicts where future spot rates are precisely going to be in 30, 60, 90, or 180 days. What it does tell us is that the mean or expected value of the random variable representing the future spot price is the forward rate prevailing today. Over time, the actual future spot price will fall higher or lower than the forward rate had anticipated but the algebraic sum of the forecasting errors — defined as the difference between the forward rate prevailing at time 0 for delivery at time t denoted as $F(0, t)$ and the future spot rate $S(t)$ prevailing at time t or $F(0, t) - S(t)$ tends toward zero. Here again the evidence pointed to an appreciation, not a depreciation of the yen (see Figure 4).

THE MORAL OF THE STORY

Lesson 1: Failure to Control. Most trading rooms within large industrial or financial institutions have reporting guidelines in place with tight position limits. Showa Shell claimed to have had position limits of $200 million, which were easily circumvented by scheming traders. Position limits are actually not enough and should be superseded by far more revealing *trading loss limits*, which can be enforced by a *"marking-to-market"* of each outstanding forward contract. Because forward contracts are not traded continuously — unlike currency futures — *"marking them to market"* would require their valuation at the close of every business day. This can be readily done through the Interest Rate Parity theorem (see Box D). Each trade, when executed, should be recorded via a trade ticket with the "back-office" accompanied by its rationale. Presumably, an industrial corporation such as Showa Shell only traded currencies paired with real transactions — that is transactions having to do with imports/exports of goods or services. Speculation of any kind should be outlawed. Unfortunately, at Showa Shell, overly lax controls allowed currency traders to roll over $6.4 billion of forward contracts, which had nothing to do with the course of normal business for a Japanese oil refiner and distributor.

Lesson 2: Failure to Report. These were sizeable transactions, which should have been continuously scrutinized by senior management (possibly at the board level) outside the treasury department. What to report, when to report, and to whom to report are often key questions ill addressed by large organizations. A breakdown of aggregate positions by tenor/maturity is necessary to avoid creative yet noxious speculative schemes (see Citibank's case in Chapter 3). Reporting should be daily and reach not only Treasury's senior management, but also the very governance of the firm. At Nippon Oil, Japan's largest oil refiner, the Treasury's deputy manager of foreign exchange is required to report to the company's Board of Directors at their monthly meeting on their foreign exchange positions and associated hedging policy.[18]

Lesson 3: Failure to Audit. Given the complexity and multitude of transactions flowing through a trading room, systematic audits are a vital complement to reporting. Auditing should be internal and external to the firm and based on principles of independence between the auditor and "auditee." Trade tickets are the informational foundation on which auditors will be able to uncover illicit transaction when they reconcile trades recorded by the "front" and "back" offices. But any transaction engages a counter-party: establishing channels of communications with such independent parties — typically the trading rooms at banks — is a critical adjunct to this process. In fact in several instances of major derivative malpractices — including the case of Showa Shell — the plot was uncovered through counter-parties which had commented on abnormal trades.

Lesson 4: Failure to Communicate. The procurement department in charge of oil purchase was not communicating with the treasury department nor were they in contact with the currency traders who were, presumably, hedging the yen cost of the company's oil bill. Close coordination between these different departments is clearly crucial to an

---

[18] Cf. Shibata, op. cit. p. 111.

effective hedging policy. For a domestic Japanese company whose international price risk exposure is limited to the dollar and oil it seems surprising — to say the least — that hedging exchange rate risk would be conducted independently from oil price risk management. Oil procurement managers and treasury executives should make their decisions conjointly rather than independently or sequentially.

Questions for Further Discussion

1. Should equal emphasis be placed on hedging oil price risk and exchange rate risk? On what criteria would you rely to decide which one to emphasize?
2. Show how Showa Shell could hedge its oil price exposure: 90-month oil forwards are at $21 and the annual cost of storing/insuring a barrel of oil is $0.45 and interest rate in the United States and Japan are, respectively 5% and 2% per annum?
3. Why were the two currency traders persisting in hedging their dollar exposures in spite of economic data pointing to an appreciating — not a depreciating — yen?

CITIBANK'S FOREX LOSSES[19]

A speculator is a man who observes the future and acts before it occurs.

Bernard Baruch

On June 19, 1965, in the heyday of the Bretton-Woods system of fixed exchange rates, the First National City Bank — the second largest American commercial bank with 177 offices in 58 countries — announced a loss of $8 million. The loss was attributed to unauthorized forward speculation on the pound sterling by a Belgian trader in the bank's Brussels branch. The amount of the underlying transactions was rumored to be close to $800 million. For First National City Bank — also known as Citibank — the year 1965 had commenced with a two-for-one stock split and ended with record operating profit of $94 million in spite of the one time loss of $8 million.

How could a single employee fool one of the largest and most sophisticated commercial banks? How could such a large speculative bet go undetected by the firm's Accounting and Control department and lose so much money for the bank when — for all practical purposes — currency prices were quasi-fixed? In this chapter, we reconstruct the speculative scheme elaborated by the bank's Belgian trader: in the process the reader is introduced to the "mother" of all financial derivative products — the old fashioned forward contract, its valuation, and how it can be used for speculating.

---

[19] This incident was widely reported in the financial press. See also Rodriguez, R. M. and E. M. Carter's *International Financial Management* (Prentice Hall: Englewood Cliff, New Jersey, 1979).

CURRENCY TRADING IN THE TRANQUIL DAYS
OF BRETTON WOODS

First, some background discussion of the foreign exchange (forex) trading room setting within which our Belgian trader played Russian roulette with the pound sterling before we review the process of exchange rate determination at the time of Citibank's forex losses.

Unlike the New York Stock Exchange or the Chicago Board of Trade which are physically organized exchanges for trading stocks, bonds, or commodities, the foreign exchange market is made up of a network of trading rooms found mostly in commercial banks and brokerage firms — hence its name as an *Interbank Market*. In the 60s, foreign exchange trading rooms were linked by telephones (and later telexes) which allowed for very fast communication (but not quasi-instantaneous as today with computer terminals and the Internet) in this *over-the-counter market*. Each currency trader would have

> *"before him a special telephone that links the trading room by direct wire to the foreign exchange brokers, the cable companies, the most important commercial customers.... The connections are so arranged that several of the bank's traders can 'listen in' on the same call."*[20]

Citibank was then trading in 50 currencies although the bulk of its activities was in dollar-sterling ($/£) and to a lesser extent in dollar-deutsche mark ($/DM) and dollar-yen ($/¥) in as many as 500 daily transactions worth as much as $50 million. Indeed, forex trading was playing a very critical role in Citibank's fast-paced international expansion. As Citibank was opening new foreign branches in Europe and Asia

> *"Forex trading was Citibank's passport to new countries and eventually a mainstay of Citibank's trading. Traders were under the gun to support the bottom line while the branch tried to develop other business."*[21]

Although forex trading is often shrouded in secrecy, there is a widespread consensus that forex trading profits come primarily from trades carried by the bank on behalf of corporate customers, e.g., IBM repatriates £50 million of dividends from its British subsidiary and purchases the amount on the spot market through the London branch of Citibank; it does not come from directional trades — an euphemism for outright speculation through the spot or forward currency market based on forecasting of exchange rates.

---

[20] Holmes, A. R. and F. H. Schott. *The New York Foreign Exchange Market* (Federal Reserve Bank of New York: New York, 1965).

[21] Zweig, P. L. *Walter Wriston, Citibank, and the Rise and Fall of American Financial Supremacy* (Crown Publishers: New York, 1995), p. 172.

Box A. The Bretton Woods System of Fixed Exchange Rates. *From 1944 to 1971, all industrialized countries maintained their exchange rates within a 3/4 of 1% margin on either side of their currency par value against the US dollar. The US dollar in turn was the only currency convertible in gold at a fixed price of $35 per ounce. Each currency — by defining a parity against the US dollar — would de facto define itself in terms of gold, which is actually the strict definition of a par value. For example if FF5 = $1 the French Franc (FF) par value against gold is (1 ounce of gold) × (1/5)=0.20 ounce of gold. Today gold is worth around $1,000 per ounce and is no longer linked to the US dollar; its price — like that of any other precious metal — is set by market forces. Most Central Banks continue to hold gold reserves, which can be used along with other convertible currencies to stabilize the price of their currency in the foreign exchange market.*

In 1965, the pound sterling (£) was pegged (tied) to the US dollar by its par value at the price of $2.80 = £1.00 and indeed this arrangement known as the Bretton-Woods agreement had been in place since 1944 (see Box A); par values were decided conjointly by the International Monetary Fund and the interested country's Central Bank. Par values were deemed public commitments made by respective Central Banks and were not altered lightly. A number of devaluations/revaluations in the range of 10–25% — most notably by France — from time to time realigned single currencies' par values in their relationship against the US dollar which then anchored the world monetary system.

Even though it was squarely associated with fixed exchange rates, Bretton-Woods did allow for a modicum of foreign exchange rate flexibility around each currency's par value. Referring to the dollar-sterling exchange rate relationship, this is how it worked: the Bank of England would set a floor for the price of its currency at −0.75% of the par value — that is $2.80 (1 − 0.0075) = $2.78 — and whenever the spot price determined by the interplay between supply and demand forces would fall below 2.78, the Bank of England would immediately step in the market and buy as many pounds as necessary to bring it back above the floor rate; this is also known as *Central Bank intervention* and it can be carried out as long as the Central Bank has sufficient foreign exchange reserves available. Conversely, the Bank of England would set a ceiling at 0.75% above the par value — or $2.80 (1 + 0.0075) = $2.82 at which it would sell sterling to bring its price back below the ceiling of $2.82 should market forces push the spot price above it. Both floor and ceiling exchange rates were publicly defined as was the par-value of the currency: in effect, the Central Bank would act as a guarantor of exchange rate stability. For all practical purposes, spot (currency purchase or sale for immediate delivery) forex transactions would be carried out between $2.78 and $2.82 — the Bank of England would make sure of it; in a way the Bank of England provided to all participants in the foreign exchange market an insurance against price

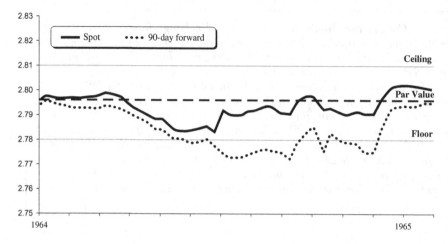

Figure 1 $/£ exchange rate fluctuations (1964–1965).

risk which was free of charge (Figure 1 illustrates the tunnel within which the spot exchange rate fluctuated over the period 1964–1965).

Of course, from time to time, par values were devalued/revalued as a result of balance of payments crises, bouts of inflation, speculative attacks, natural disasters, or political upheavals. In the fall of 1964, Britain under the leadership of its newly elected Labor government found itself under strong pressure to devalue the pound sterling (due to deepening balance of payments deficits) but staved off the crisis with heavy intervention by the Bank of England in the forex market and by hiking short-term interest rates to entice short-term capital inflows. It is precisely in this context that our Belgian trader had elaborated his speculative scheme betting that the pound sterling would not devalue — that is — its price would remain at or above $2.78 for the foreseeable future of 9–12 months.

GAMBLING ON CURRENCIES WITH FORWARD CONTRACTS

Speculating in the forex market can be carried out either through outright spot trans-actions or more complex forward contracts:

(1) Spot speculation consists of buying a currency — say the dollar — perceived to be cheap (undervalued) in terms of another currency say — pound sterling, holding it until its appreciates and selling it at a higher price in a month, two months or later. With the anticipation of a sterling devaluation (dollar appreciation), spot speculators would buy spot dollars (sell pound sterling), wait out the devaluation before buying back pound sterling at a much cheaper rate: for example, assume that the pound sterling is expected to devalue from $2.80 to $2.40 = £1.00; one pound sterling would buy $2.80

> **Box B. What Are Forward Contracts?** *A forward exchange contract is a commitment to buy or sell a certain quantity of foreign currency on a certain date in the future (maturity of the contract) at a price (forward exchange rate) agreed upon today when the contract is signed. For example on September 30, 1964, one could buy 30 day sterling at $2.7650 in the amount of £10 million. On October 30, 1964 (30 days later), you would deliver $27.65 million and receive £10 million regardless of the spot value on delivery day; if the pound is worth $2.80, you obviously benefit from the forward contract having paid 3.5 cents less ($2.80– $2.7650) per pound and generating a profit $350,000. Clearly, it is important to understand that a forward contract when signed is an exchange of irrevocable and legally binding promises (with no cash changing hands) obligating the two parties to going through with the actual transaction at maturity and delivering the respective currencies (or cash settlement) regardless of what the prevailing spot exchange rate may be on that day.*

before the devaluation and $2.80 which then buy back $2.80/2.40 = £1.1667 after the devaluation for a cash profit of £1.1667 − £1.00 = £0.1667 if one disregards the time value of money. Funds would be tied up for the entire duration of the (unknown) speculative period and financial cost would have to be incurred if the funds had to be borrowed: this indeterminate interest burden tied to the "cost of carry" would rule out speculation through the spot market for our Belgian trader since it would have immediate cash-flow implications and therefore attract attention from the branch control department.

(2) Alternatively one can speculate with a forward contract (see Box B), which by its very nature does not tie up cash and is therefore a good deal more discreet. To take a numerical example, consider the following situation prevailing on September 30, 1964: pound sterling can be purchased forward at $2.72 for delivery in 9 months on March 31, 1965 while we expect the spot rate for pound sterling to remain at or above its floor of $2.78. If our Belgian trader bought forward £100 million at $2.72 and proved to be right in his expectation of the spot price remaining at or above $2.78 on March 31, 1965, he would deliver $272 million receive £100 million now worth $278 million (or more) for a profit of $6 million — a nice return on an investment of — yes — $0.00…. Now of course — if he bets wrong and the pound sterling had devalued to say $2.40, our Belgian trader would still be obligated to deliver $272 million, receive £100 million worth now only $240 million for a staggering loss of $32 million.

HOW DO BANKS KEEP A LID ON THEIR FOREIGN EXCHANGE TRADING OPERATIONS?

Before sketching the actual speculative gamble elaborated by our Belgian trader, we need to profile the basic rules of engagement that every currency trader would have

Table 1   Matrix of currency positions by maturity.

Tenors:	30 days	60 days	90 days	180 days	360 days
£	−10 million			+10 million	
DM		−5 million	−5 million		+10 million

to follow. Currency traders are required to observe trading limits applying to single transaction; for example, the bank may mandate that no single forex trade be in excess of $10 million and that the aggregate limit of a trader's net position be no more than $25 million during the day to be reduced to very close to zero by the end of the business day to avoid overnight unwelcome surprises. Otherwise our bank CEO would lose sleep at night with too many creative gamblers like our Belgian trader manning the forex desk in far-flung foreign branches. Indeed banks, for the most part, earn a living by buying and selling foreign currencies at slightly different rates — also known as the bid/ask spread — mostly on a spot basis and to a lesser extent on a forward basis for corporate customers (and more recently on options, swaps, and other derivative products that the reader will discover throughout this book); this is indeed a relatively safe way to make a living as it does not entail outright speculative positions on currencies as the one we have just described. In fact, most banks have set in place control systems aimed at keeping traders honest by implementing the *square position* requirement: this is nothing more than requiring that each trader keep his trades in balance and that for each currency the amount sold forward would equal the amount purchased forward. For example, our Belgian trader could sell one month short £10 million at $2.77 = £1 and buy 6 month long £10 million at $2.75 = £1. Should sterling devalue to $2.40 after 15 days, the trader would generate a gain on the forward sale contract maturing on day 30 in the amount of £10,000,000 (2.77–2.40) = $370,000 but incur a loss on the six month forward contract to the tune of £10,000,000 (2.40–2.75) = $350,000. In this example, the bank's net exposure was limited to the spread between one and six month forward rates or $(2.77–2.75) 10,000,000 = $20,000,[22] which is believed to be manageable by most banks. Table 1 gives a simple example of how our Belgian trader's forex positions could be in $/£ and $/DM.

Note that for both currencies:

"long (asset) positions(+) = short (liability) positions (−)"

if one ignores the maturity of the contract involved. For sterling, the reader will verify that our trader would hold a square position since

£10 million (long/asset) − £10 million (short/liability) = 0

---

[22] Disregarding the time value of money — a net gain if the forex gain comes first or a loss if the forex loss comes first.

SPECULATING FROM A COMMERCIAL BANK'S TRADING DESK: WHEN CITIBANK IS NOT QUITE A HEDGE FUND À LA GEORGES SOROS[23]

As the reader will recall our Belgian trader made a simple bet that the pound sterling would survive current speculative pressure and would not devalue in the next 12–18 months. Turning this bet into a profitable trade involved buying pound sterling forward (going long pound sterling) at rates as low as $2.69 = £1 for maturities ranging from 9 to 18 months. The reader may wonder how could the forward rate fall below the floor spot rate and trade at a discount when the spot exchange rate is limited to fluctuating within a tunnel closely monitored by the Bank of England? It has to do with the interest rate differential between dollar and sterling; as the Bank of England defended the $2.80 = £1 parity, it increased interest rates from 4.50% to 7.50% to encourage short-term capital inflow, which in turn pushed up the spot dollar price of sterling (see Figure 2 which charts US and UK interest rates in 1964–1965). As the interest rate differential widened, it drove the forward rate to a deeper discount (see Box C): for example, as UK interest rates increased from 4.50% in September 1964 to 7.50% in

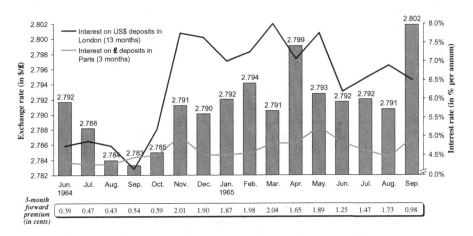

Figure 2 $/£ exchange rate vs. US and UK interest rates (1964–1965).

---

[23] In 1992, Soros — through the Quantum hedge fund that he controlled — speculated that the pound sterling would drop from the European Monetary System — that is would devalue from its fixed rate against the German mark and other European Union currencies, which made up the European Monetary System. Through large scale forward sale of pound sterling Soros made a huge speculative gain in excess of $1 billion when sterling did devalue on September 16, 1992. Of course, Soros was not constrained by the square position requirement that our Belgian trader operated under as hedge funds can make any speculative bets they so wish.

Box C. *Valuing Forward Exchange Rates and the Interest Rate Parity Theory.*
Forward exchange rates are not subjected to Central Bank price limits (as spot prices are) and are primarily determined by interest rates according to the theory of Interest Rate Parity. Consider the example of Fidelity Investment money market mutual fund's treasurer (MMMF), who has to invest $100 million for the next 360 days. According to the MMMF's charter, the funds should be kept in very low-risk securities — say US one year treasury note yielding 4% and/or UK treasury notes known as gilt of similar maturity yielding 6%; the higher yield in sterling is enticing ($2 million of additional interest income would be earned) but assumes that the spot exchange rate between dollar and sterling will remain steady at $2.80. Otherwise, the interest rate differential may be partly or fully wiped out by a sterling devaluation of up to 2%.

Thus our treasurer would compare the yield on a domestic investment (no credit risk and no currency risk), which would return $100,000,000(1+.04) = $104,000,000 with the higher yield on a sterling-denominated investment. Specifically to take advantage of the higher UK yield, our treasurer will

(1) *purchase spot sterling in the amount of $100,000,000/2.80 = £35,714,000;*
(2) *invest at the rate of 6% to receive in 360 days £35,714,000 (1+ .06) =£37,857,000;*
(3) *secure the dollar value of the sterling investment by selling forward both principal and interest income at the forward exchange rate F = 2.7475 and be guaranteed to receive in 360 days £37,857,000 × 2.7475 = $104,012,000.*

In effect the comparison between the two investment options will determine where the funds will be invested: in this case, there is a small advantage to investing in sterling. More generally, if the return on covered investment in sterling is somewhat higher short-term funds will migrate from New York to London thereby exercising upward pressure on the US interest rate and the spot dollar price of £1 while putting downward pressure on the UK interest rate and the forward rate until both investment options are equal: this state of equilibrium is also known as Interest Rate Parity.[24] More formally the theorem of Interest Rate Parity establishes a very simple relationship between domestic (i) and foreign (i*) interest rates, the spot (S) and forward (F) rates:

$$(1 + i) = (1/S) \times (1 + i^*) \times F \quad or \quad F = S(1 + i)/(1 + i^*)$$

and the reader should understand that even though tight limits may be imposed on the spot exchange rate the interest rate differential $i-i^*$ will determine the forward rate, which in equilibrium would settle at F = 2.80[(1 + 0.04)/(1+0.06)] = 2.7472, which is below the floor set for the spot exchange rate of 2.78.

---

[24] The reader will note that Interest Rate Parity does not mean equality of nominal interest rates but equality of nominal interest rates adjusted for the cost of a forward cover against exchange risk.

October 1964 (see bottom row of Figure 2 for actual discount rates) while US interest rates stayed steady at 4.25% the forward rate fell from

$$F = \$2.78 \times [(1 + .0425)/(1 + .0475)] = 2.77 \text{ in September 1964}$$

to

$$F^* = \$2.78 \times [(1 + .0425)/(1 + .0750)] = 2.69 \text{ in October 1964.}$$

Clearly the more UK interest rates spiked, the lower forward sterling dropped and the more attractive our Belgian trader speculative gamble became. However, the square position reporting constraint will not allow our Belgian trader to go long sterling for hundred of millions as it would raise a red flag for everyone to see.

Here is the loophole exploited by our Belgian trader which allowed him to conceal his speculative bet that the pound sterling would not devalue. Recall that our trader had purchased 360 days forward pound sterling at $2.69 thereby creating a pound sterling long/asset position, which had to be neutralized by a short/liability position of matching amount (but of mismatching maturity). Otherwise his large pound sterling asset position would have undoubtedly attracted Citibank comptroller's attention. To balance his long and long-dated pound sterling position our trader had — to satisfy the square position requirement — to sell pound sterling (short) to create an offsetting liability position. Of course the amount had to be matching but forward contract maturities would be mismatched as our trader sold sterling 30 and 60 days forward (while buying 270 and 360 days forward) thereby reporting a square position at all time.

For the first 30 days, no cash-flow losses would be reported; at the maturity of his first sterling liability position (he had sold sterling forward at $2.77 for delivery on October 30, 1965), he would deliver £100 million and receive $277 million; however, the £100 million had to be purchased at $2.78 or higher (since sterling had not devalued) which meant a cash flow loss of at least £1million, which presumably would be aggregated with other transactions on that day. Having liquidated his short sterling position, our trader would now be reporting a net sterling asset position which required him to immediately sell sterling forward again on a short-term maturity to balance out his sterling long-term forward contract position. Presumably our trader would roll over his short-term liability contract every time his short-term forward contracts expired incurring cash flow losses equal to the difference between the forward rate (at a deeper and deeper discount as UK interest rates increased) and the prevailing spot rate on that day (always at or above the floor of $2.78 since the pound sterling had not devalued). With sterling interest rates increasing throughout the fall of 1964, the position was rolled over at less and less favorable forward rate, which in turn led to increasing losses when the forward sales contract were cash settled at maturity. However, as long as the pound did not devalue he would stand to benefit handsomely from his long asset position as long as the losses incurred on the short positions were kept small. More formally our Belgian trader was hoping that

Losses on sterling short sales < Gains on sterling long purchases.

Our trader's speculative scheme was lopsided: sterling long purchases had a reasonable chance of delivering a big win but the sterling short sales were also bound to generate sizeable losses and the trader had no way of knowing with certainty whether the gains would outsize the cumulative losses. The only assurance that the trader had was that the longer-term sterling discount would be deeper proportionally than the shorter-term discount since the yield curve tends to be steeper than a 45% line for short-term maturities, which means that annualized one year interest rate is higher than six-month, three month or one-month annualized interest rates. In other words, the 360-day sterling discount would be deeper than 12 times the one month sterling discount. In fact only if the spot price stayed steady and interest rate differentials stayed constant over the 12 month period had the speculative gamble a chance to better than break even — that is 12 times the one month cash-flow loss due to rolling over the one month forward contract would be less than the 12 month cash-flow gain due to settling the pound sterling long position. In effect, the Belgian trader could not be sure that the cash flow losses that were inevitably accumulated on the sterling short sales would be more than recouped by the forward sterling purchases.

HASTY AND COSTLY CONCLUSION

Our trader never got a chance to bring to closure his creative speculative scheme. Indeed the pound sterling did not devalue and at least his sterling long position would have paid off in due time but he was never allowed to find out. Sometimes in the spring of 1965, Walter Wriston — then head of Citibank's foreign operations — was alerted by

> "a friend of his, Paul Jeantly, a partner in the British firm of Samuel Montague, then one of the world's largest gold dealers. Jeantly was concerned about Citibank's forex operations. He told Wriston that his firm, Montague, had a $100 million contract coming due the following week with Citibank's Belgian branch. "I almost dropped my teeth", Wriston said, "because that was ten times the contract a branch that size could possibly have."[25]

---

[25] Zweig, op. cit. p. 175.

Shortly thereafter the comptroller's department exposed the Belgian trader and unwound the outstanding positions at unfavorable current spot and forward rates as it is often the case with the forced liquidation of large scale speculative positions.

THE MORAL OF THE STORY

Losing close to 10% of Citibank's entire annual worldwide consolidated profits because of a rogue trader's ineptitude in the Belgian branch was indeed a humbling experience — especially at a time when the bank was readying itself to issue $250 million of subordinated convertible debt.

Lesson #1: Require Narrative of Daily Transactions. For each trade, the responsible trader should spell out clearly the nature of the underlying transaction: who are the end-users of the forex products? Presumably a commercial bank is working mostly with corporations; any other counterparties should raise questions. Here, it is critical to keep the forex dealing function clearly separate and independent from the accounting/control function also known as the back office. The forex trader executes his trades, keeps a daily log, and writes trade tickets which are entered by the accounting/control department. This latter department will in turn verify each trade against a broker or counterparty to validate and ensure accuracy of the transaction. More recently, many commercial banks have established a risk department, which will compute the trading gains/losses associated with the book of outstanding contracts.

Lesson #2: Monitor Each Trader by Requiring Daily Breakdown of Transactions. Require a breakdown of aggregate positions by tenor/maturity with each counterparty: even though a matched aggregate position should keep the bank reasonably safe, it hides speculative schemes as the one discussed in this chapter, which are contrary to the mission of the bank's trading desk. A separate entity within the bank akin to a hedge fund and engaging in proprietary trading could be envisioned but should be established under a different charter and different rules of engagement. Many investment banks have such separate departments and many of them are very profitable.

Lesson #3: Enforce Trading Loss Limits. Establish trading loss limits by forcing a daily "*marking-to-market*" of each outstanding contract. This would be typically done by the risk department in cooperation with the accounting/control department. What is today a widespread practice was ignored in the 60s. Because forward contracts are tailor-made contracts and are not continuously traded unlike currency futures "*marking them to market*" would require their valuation at the close of every business day. This can be readily done through the Interest Rate Parity theorem. For example, a 12-month forward contract on sterling purchased on September 1 at $2.73 may be worth only $2.7250 on September 2 if UK interest rates are increased. If our trader has an outstanding position of £100 million, the marking-to-market would translate into a paper loss[26] of

$$£100,000,000 \ (2.73 - 2.7250) = -\$500,000.$$

By establishing a trading loss limit of say $250,000 on a given trader, the back office would have caught early the speculative scheme and further trading activities would be actually frozen until proper accounting of the position was made available. This is a far more effective way of keeping a lid on the bank's overall exposure than the square position requirement, which can hide all kinds of contrived transactions which — in turn — may or may not have large cash-flow loss implications.

QUESTIONS FOR DISCUSSION

1. Knowing that the currency trader was on straight salary — that is he would not be paid any commissions nor bonus — what were his motivations to speculate?
2. Given that the pound sterling did not devalue until 1967 explain what would have been the end result of the Belgian trader's speculative scheme if the bank had let it ride until maturity. Detail timing and amount of cash-flows.
3. Why are forward exchange rates not necessarily trading within the prescribed bands of fluctuation as established under Bretton Woods? Under what scenarios would forward rates remain within such bands?
4. Do you believe that trading rooms within large commercial banks should be forbidden to engage in directional trades?
5. Under what conditions would you allow trading rooms to engage in directional trades?

---

[26] Until the forward contract is liquidated, no cash-flow would be incurred hence the reference made to a paper loss.

BANK NEGARA MALAYSIA

Using all the resources a Central Bank commands — privileged information, unlimited credit, regulatory power, and more — Malaysia's Bank Negara became the most feared trader in the currency markets. By trading for profit, Bank Negara committed apostasy against the creed of central banking.

Gregory Millman[27]

Bank Negara — Malaysia's central bank — reported on March 31, 1994 staggering foreign exchange losses of Malaysian Ringgit M$ 5.7 billion (equivalent to $2.1 billion), which followed an even larger loss of M$9 billion in 1992 ($3.3 billion). Jaffar bin Hussein — Bank Negara's long serving governor — was forced to resign on April 1, 1994 the day following the disclosure of the mammoth foreign exchange losses. Under normal central banking practices, such losses would have been the result of costly and legitimate but unsuccessful attempts by Bank Negara's at stemming the rise of its currency due to speculative capital inflows (see Box A). Indeed, in January 1994, *The Economist* reported that Bank Negara had declared war on "currency speculators," who were buying Ringgits in anticipation of its appreciation. *"But as the world's foreign exchange dealers well know, Bank Negara has long been a big punter in the currency market itself. In the last two years, its boldness has been matched only*

---

[27] Millman, G. *The Vandals' Crown* (Simon & Schuster, 1995), p. 226.

Box A. Central Banks' Intervention in Currency Markets. *Central banks gener-*
ally act as guarantor of their national currency's stability. To keep their currency
stable central banks will intervene in their own currency markets to stem too
steep a rise/fall in the value of their national currency. They will do so by buying
their own currency (selling foreign reserves such as dollars or yens) to prevent
a devaluation or selling their own currency (buying foreign reserve currencies)
to slow down the rise of their own currency. For example, if speculators were
to buy spot Ringgits at say M$2.50 = $1, *Bank Negara by selling Ringgits for*
dollars would accumulate dollar reserves. As capital inflows are successfully
bidding up the Ringgit, Bank Negara becomes dollar-rich, which may worth now
only M$2.40 = $1 *thereby incurring a foreign exchange loss when reserves are*
measured in its national currency. Many Asian central banks — most notably
Japan, China, and Taiwan — have experienced similar losses over the years.
Bank Negara's debacle was a different story!

---

by its incompetence."[28] Indeed, as early as 1988, Jaffar[29] had announced that to the
traditional goals of providing safety and liquidity in managing its foreign exchange
reserves, Bank Negara henceforth would add "*profit optimization and market exper-*
tise,"[30] which soon became a code word for currency speculation.

WHAT IS CENTRAL BANKING ALL ABOUT?

A country's central bank is generally charged with managing its national economy's
money supply to ensure monetary stability (in the form of low inflation) and to nurture
orderly economic growth. In so doing, it is expected to instill confidence in its country's
financial system. In times of crisis, it may act as lender of last resort to private sector
banks facing bankruptcy to stem panic and prevent systemic risk. Closely related to
its domestic economic mandate is the central bank's responsibility of ensuring the
country's international payments through orderly intervention in the foreign exchange
market whether the currency is pegged to the dollar, a basket of currencies or simply
allowed to float. Central banks are generally public institutions but maintain their
independence from their respective national governments: this is certainly the case
with the US Federal Reserve system, the Bank of England or the recently established

---

[28] Anonymous, Asian currencies: Malaise. *The Economist* (April 9, 1994), pp. 82–83.

[29] Jaffar — before becoming Governor of Malaysia's central bank — had served as head of
Price Waterhouse's Malaysian operations (he was an accountant by profession) and CEO of
Malayan Banking (Malaysia's leading commercial bank), where he had commanded respect
and admiration for his wise and prudent leadership.

[30] Shale, A. Bank Negara shrugs off forex fiasco. *Euromoney* (December 1993), pp. 49–51.

European Central Bank. Most emerging market countries' central banks, however, are still very much under the control of their national government.

> *"Bank Negara clearly chose to be a central bank with a difference: by trading for profit, Bank Negara committed apostasy against the creed of central banking. Instead of working to ensure global financial stability, Bank Negara repeatedly shoved huge sums of money into the most vulnerable market situations in order to stabilize exchange rates for its own profit ... Bank Negara's market speculation was so egregious that one American central banker said, 'if they tried this on any exchange in the world they'd go to jail'. However in the unregulated currency markets, there were neither police nor jailers. The only rule was the rough justice of the vandals, and it was this rule that eventually bought Bank Negara down."*[31]

BANK NEGARA AS A MACRO-HEDGE FUND

As a custodian of its national currency — the Malaysian Ringgit — Bank Negara maintained a steady peg against a basket of currency, which weighted heavily the US dollar and the Japanese yen by enforcing a narrow band of fluctuations of $\pm 2.25\%$ around the M\$'s par value of M\$2.60 $=$ \$1. Furthermore, Bank Negara maintained selective exchange controls on capital account transactions thereby further strengthening its exchange rate regime.

In the summer of 1992, as Britain was mobilizing its resources to maintain its participation in the European Exchange Rate Mechanism (ERM) or exchange rate fixity (it had just increased short-term interest rates from 10 to 12% with a promise of a further increase to 15% if necessary), Bank Negara made a huge speculative gambit that indeed the Bank of England would successfully withstand the onslaught of speculative attacks (see Box B). It is totally unheard of to have the central bank of a major South-East Asian nation taking large scale speculative positions in currency markets for reasons that are totally unrelated to the safe husbanding of its own national currency. In effect by outright speculation on the future of the pound sterling, Bank Negara had morphed into a hedge fund of a special kind — one owned by a sovereign nation rather than wild-eyed capitalists! In its shameless pursuit of speculative profits, Bank Negara lost \$3.16 billion when Britain dropped out of the ERM and allowed the pound sterling to float freely. Ironically Georges Soros's Quantum Fund — another, albeit legitimate, macro-hedge fund — read the announced increase in short-term interest rates to 15% as a measure of desperation by the Bank of England and promptly sold forward on September 16, 1992 \$10 billion worth of pound sterling. Soros made

---

[31] Millman, op. cit. p. 229.

> **Box B. The European Monetary System (EMS) and the European Exchange Rate Mechanism (ERM).**[32] *Launched in 1979 by the European Economic Community (the predecessor of the European Union), the EMS resurrected on a regional basis the old Bretton Woods system of pegged exchange rates (see Box A in Citibank chapter). A zone of quasi exchange rate stability (ERM) was to be achieved by establishing a grid of cross-exchange rates, based initially on the definition of bilateral par values among the seven "core" EMS currencies.[33] Indeed a matrix of 21 tightly managed exchange rates with fluctuations limited to ±2.25% around central rates functioned reasonably well over the life of the EMS (1979–1999). The EMS also floated as a bloc against other major currencies such as the US dollar and the Japanese yen. Somewhat surprisingly over its 20 year existence the EMS achieved a remarkable degree of exchange rate stability, despite a number of par value re-alignments brought about by divergent national interest and inflation rates. In August 1992, heavy speculative pressures led Italy and Britain to withdraw from the EMS. In 1999, the European Monetary Union and the single currency dubbed the Euro were launched. Britain opted not to join the Euro.*

a profit of $1 billion: he had wagered correctly that sterling would drop out of the ERM and depreciate sharply. Soros became known as the man who broke the Bank of England!

HOW DID BANK NEGARA SPECULATE?

In the months leading up to the ERM crisis of August 1992, Bank Negara was buying pound sterling forward for delivery in 90 or 180 days with US dollars and German marks. The forward rates were at a significant discount against then prevailing spot rates reflecting the high short-term interest rate in the United Kingdom at 12% (with a promise to increase them to 15%) as the Bank of England was attempting to shore up the value of its currency.[34] Bank Negara was expecting that the spot rate at time of delivery (90 or 189 days later) would remain steady and that the forwards would

---

[32] Jacque, L.L. *Management and Control of Foreign Exchange Risk* (Kluwer Academic Publishers, 1996)

[33] The seven founding member nations of the EMS were Belgium, Britain, France, Germany, Italy, Luxembourg, and The Netherlands. Subsequently Spain, Portugal, Denmark, Sweden, and Finland joined the EMS.

[34] The reader will recall that forward rates are determined by interest rate differential through the interest rate parity theorem (see Box B in Chapter 2): as the Bank of England was defending its currency, it had to push up short-term interest which drove the forward DM–£ to a discount (Germany kept its interest rate constant).

be closed at a profit. Indeed, it was supporting the pound sterling — not speculating against it — although its ulterior motives were less than altruistic. For example, if 90-day forward pounds sterling could be purchased at DM2.95 = £1 when the current spot rate stood at DM3.10 = £1, the forward would be closed at a spot rate of DM3.10 (or at least above DM2.95) as long as the pound did not drop out of the EMS. When the pound exited the ERM and nosedived by 30%, the long forward positions had to be closed at a huge loss. Assuming that the pound collapsed to DM2.40 = £1, the speculative gambit would have amounted to buying sterling at DM2.95 and selling at DM2.40 — a loss of DM.55 per pound. Bank Negara was rumored to have accumulated sterling long positions in the range of £20–25 billion and ended up losing $3.16 billion.

Part II

FUTURES

Part II

FITTINGS

AMARANTH ADVISORS LLC

Speculators may do no harm as bubbles on a steady stream of enterprise. But the position is serious when enterprise becomes the bubble on a whirlpool of speculation. When the capital development of a country becomes a by-product of the activities of a casino, the job is likely to be ill-done.

John Maynard Keynes (1936)

Hedge funds are often associated with Wall Street excesses and capitalistic greed. Indeed outsized compensations for hedge funds managers — in the billions rather than the millions as in the case of T. Boone Pickens take-home pay of $1.4 billion in 2005 — routinely capture headlines in the financial press. When disaster strikes hedge funds, it is also of outsized magnitude as with the demise of Amaranth Advisors LLC, which announced on September 20, 2006 a loss in excess of $5 billion. Reportedly, the losses were due to massive bets placed on natural gas futures and they were incurred over a relatively short period of three weeks. When "margin calls" from the New York Mercantile Exchange (NYMEX) came knocking at Amaranth's door, only liquidation of the hedge fund $9 billion in assets could clear the slate. Unlike the much publicized debacle of Long-Term Capital Management (see Chapter 15), which reverberated throughout financial markets around the world, Amaranth's demise hardly caused any ripples and, in very short order, its losing portfolio was taken over by J.P. Morgan Chase and the Citadel Hedge Fund. It had set an all time record in the annals of global derivative debacles and yet the massive losses were absorbed painlessly by the global financial system. Was it the calculated yet daring risk-taking predicated on expert knowledge of the inner workings of the natural gas market which drove Amaranth to fail? Or was it foolhardy and reckless bets placed on the weather by ill-disciplined traders, who believed that they could repeatedly beat the market by taking mammoth futures positions in the natural gas market? From the perspective of the US consumer' best interests how could the NYMEX allow one player to dominate and therefore manipulate the market without enforcing position limits? More generally, should regulatory agencies control futures markets more tightly?

THE RISE AND FALL OF AMARANTH ADVISORS LLC

Amaranth Advisors LLC was established in 2000 as a "multistrategy" hedge fund (see Box A) and was named after an imaginary flower that never fades. In the galaxy of the hedge fund industry, Amaranth's declared strategy would allow it to invest in about any market without restriction on position limits, leverage, or use of exotic derivative instrument. Initially, with approximately $600 million in capital, Amaranth

---

Box A. What Are Hedge Funds? *Hedge funds are unregulated pools of money, which are aggressively managed with a great deal of flexibility. In fact, hedge funds are anything but "hedged" or safe and are not meant for the faint-hearted investor. Like mutual funds, hedge funds are financial intermediaries, which channel savings into productive investments thereby seeking to protect capital and to deliver a hefty rewards to high net worth individuals, pension funds, endowments, and other investors who entrusted their money. Unlike mutual funds, which are tightly regulated in the simple investment strategies they are legally allowed to pursue, the fees their managers can collect and the reporting requirements they must abide by, hedge funds can pursue complex strategies which includes heavy borrowing, using all sort of derivative products, short selling and do all the above in almost total secrecy with minimal disclosure requirements. There is no limit on the fees that hedge fund managers can pay themselves (15 − 30% of profits) although, in some cases, fees will be waived when losses are incurred and not recouped — sometimes known as "high water marks." In the more direct language of Cliff Asness of AQR Capital, "Hedge funds are investment pools that are relatively unconstrained in what they do. They are relatively unregulated (for now), charge very high fees, will not necessarily give you your money back when you want it, and will generally not tell you what they do. They are supposed to make money all the time, and when they fail at this, their investors redeem and go to someone else who has recently been making money. Every three or four years, they deliver a one-in-a-hundred-year flood."[35]*

---

[35] *The New York Magazine*, April 9, 2007.

was going to rely on more traditional and not terribly original arbitrage strategies targeting convertible bonds[36] and merger stocks.[37]

In the early going, the fund delivered enviable returns of 29% in 2001, 15% in 2002, and 21% in 2003. In early 2004, with convertible bond arbitrage failing to deliver double-digit returns, Amaranth redirected its strategy toward more promising activities: indeed, as early as 2002, Amaranth had started to pay attention to energy markets and had hired several Enron[38] traders. Brian Hunter — the hero turned villain in the Amaranth saga — joined the firm as a natural gas trader in 2004 and was shortly thereafter promoted to be the co-head of the fund's commodities group. By 2005, approximately 30% of Amaranth's capital was earmarked to energy-related arbitrage activities:

> *"The fund had hired a couple of former Enron energy traders to build an Energy Arbitrage Desk. Energy arbitrage opportunities can also take a number of forms due to the significant amount of available "Energy" products. A generic geographical arbitrage can be trading the difference of price in a given commodity either in the same location or in a different geographical location. Other arbitrage opportunities include Grade arbitrage which encompasses trading the difference in price of two related crude oil commodities such as the spread between West Texas Intermediate and Brent crude. Generally these arbitrage opportunities are created by fundamental news affecting production and inventory. In addition trades may be on the perceived volatility of crude oil and other crude products such as gasoline, jet fuel and heating oil and/or the correlation between one another. These views have been expressed through calendar spreads.[39] In addition deep-out-of-the-money call options are purchased as a cheap way to take advantage of price shocks. Leverages ranges from 5 to 8 times."[40]*

Brian Hunter, a Canadian national, was 32 years of age when he joined Amaranth Advisors LLC. Early on, he had trained in physics and applied mathematics at the

---

[36] Convertible bonds are combination of a straight bond paying a coupon at below market interest rate combined with a call option on the firm's stock issuing the bond. Amaranth would buy the convertible bond and sell short the underlying stock.

[37] Merger arbitrage refers to investing in stocks which are rumored to be possible targets of merger, acquisition, or restructuring: Amaranth would typically buy long the target firm's stock and sell short the acquirer's.

[38] Enron was an energy conglomerate which diversified into the trading of energy products and their derivatives. It collapsed in 2001 after a massive fraud was exposed.

[39] Calendar spreads, futures, and options on natural gas and how Amaranth used them for speculative purposes are explained in the next section.

[40] JP Morgan Chase, CP Leveraged Funds Due Diligence, Annual review, Bates No. JPM-PSI 0007031, cited in Senate Subcommittee report, June 25, 2007.

University of Alberta. For the prior eight years, Hunter had applied his quantitative skills to disciplined trading in natural gas futures and options first at TransCanada Corp — a Calgary-based pipeline company — which was expanding its activities into gas trading. When Deutsche Bank offered better pay for the same kind of work plus the mystique of Wall Street, Hunter moved to the hub of international finance — New York City.

Daring bets on natural gas futures first paid off for Hunter and his employer with significant profits in 2001 and 2002. The year 2003 first showed handsome profit but finished on a sour note with a loss of $51 million, which Hunter blamed on Deutsche Bank's faulty trading platform and market misbehaving — understand unanticipated and adverse — natural gas price movements. Denied his yearly bonus, Hunter left Deutsche Bank and sued his former employer.

Amaranth, which was the first hedge fund to constitute an energy trading group after the demise of Enron, hired Brian Hunter. Rick Maounis, the CEO of Amaranth, apparently knew of Hunter's rollercoaster performance at Deutsche Bank but found *"nothing that made us uncomfortable."*[41] Gutsy bets on natural gas placed before Hurricane Katrina struck delivered $1 billion in profit to Amaranth at the close of 2005: Brian Hunter became a hero on Wall Street and gained tremendous bargaining power with his employer. Not surprisingly, Amaranth's star-trader was allowed to move his gas trading team back to his native Calgary (Canada) — some two-thousand miles away from Amaranth's headquarters in Connecticut (USA). After generating $3 billion in profit by August 2006, Hunter lost $5 billion in September 2006, which precipitated the liquidation of the fund. In Rick Maounis' words *"what Brian is really good at is taking controlled and measured risk"*[42]...! Somehow "hedging" in the name "hedge fund" had been left out....

To better grasp the nature of Amaranth's speculative activities in the natural gas market, we first sketch the rapid transformation of the US natural gas industry, how natural gas derivatives came into being as part of this transformation and how hedge funds such as Amaranth could put them to work.

GENESIS OF NATURAL GAS DERIVATIVES

Once upon a time, the US natural gas industry (see Box B) was tightly regulated with rigid price control from the wellhead (supplier) to the burner-tip (consumer): the regulator's objective was to protect the consumer against damaging price fluctuations while

---

[41] Davis, A. How giant bets on natural gas sank brash hedge fund trader, *Wall Street Journal* (September 19, 2006).
[42] Davis, A. op. cit.

Box B. The US Natural Gas Industry. *Natural gas accounts for nearly a quarter of the US domestic energy consumption. Its consumption pattern is seasonal with demand for residential heating (about 20% of total consumption) peaking in winter months but troughing during the summer. Other users — mostly industrial (30%) and commercial (14%) — maintain a fairly constant demand throughout the year. This imbalance between seasonal demand and fairly constant supply is managed though extensive underground storage of natural gas starting late in the spring and carrying through late summer. Prices also follow a seasonal pattern, falling when demand ebbs off and storage of excess gas supply begins (early summer) and rising when demand starts exceeding supply in the early winter months and de-stocking starts (see Figure 1). Domestic US demand for gas is not fully met by domestic production and 15% of its needs is imported mostly from Canada through pipelines. Unlike Europe, liquefied natural gas (LNG) plays a minimal role in the US gas equation, which means that the US gas market is relatively isolated from the world gas market. Major infrastructural investments would be needed to handle large scale importation of LNG from Northern Africa and the Middle East, which would smooth seasonal cycles in natural gas prices. In this respect, the gas industry is markedly different from the domestic US oil industry, which is closely integrated with the global oil industry.*

---

providing adequate supplies at fair prices. However in the 1970s — with two oil price shocks shaking the energy industry — an acute shortage of natural gas developed and Congress enacted the Natural Gas Policy Act of 1978, which unshackled the industry, effectively forcing price deregulation at the wellhead while freeing interstate natural gas transportation. With the progressive deregulation of the natural gas industry came the development of a spot market for natural gas (transactions which provide for immediate delivery); it created a forum where commercial interests could match their needs which were not already taken care of by long-term price contracts. During the 1980s, increasing natural gas price volatility in the spot market accompanied the transformation of the industry and naturally led to increased trading in over-the-counter hedging products such as forward and swap contracts in natural gas. In 1990, standardized contracts on gas futures and options were introduced by the New York Mercantile Exchange to allow various parties to cope with price uncertainty — a pattern that had characterized the oil industry a decade earlier.

A PRIMER ON SPECULATING IN NATURAL GAS DERIVATIVES

Most of Amaranth aggressive speculative bets were placed on natural gas derivative products. There are three principal strategies to consider: the simplest one is to take

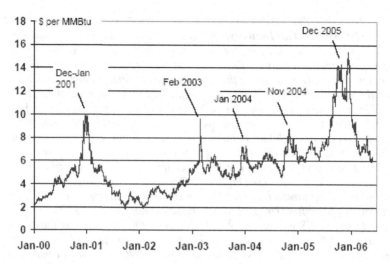

Figure 1 Recent winter price spikes NYMEX natural gas futures 1st month contract. Reprinted from US Senate Permanent Committee on Investigations (Committee on Homeland Security and Governmental Affairs), Excessive Speculation in the Natural Gas Market (June 15, 2007) p. 55.

futures position on a particular contract month, the second one is to combine two different contract month futures in what is generally referred to as *intra-commodity calendar spread* and, last but not least, is to buy or sell put and call options on gas futures. We consider the mechanics of each strategy next before reviewing month by month how Amaranth played the natural gas market before running the fund into the ground during the month of September 2006.

Speculating with One Contract Month at a Time. In January 2006, the Katrina and Rita hurricane disasters of the prior fall had propelled gas futures prices to an all-time high and Amaranth believed that a mild winter was setting the stage for a precipitous decline in near-term futures prices (see Box C). Accordingly, it started to build a growing position in March 06 futures contracts by "selling the contract short." By the end of January, Amaranth had sold nearly 40,000 March 06 futures contracts. Amaranth's anticipation was that by expiration date (last day of February 06 for a March 06 futures contract) those March 06 contracts would have lost in value against their initial sale price and that it would be able to close its position at a profit.

Let us review the mechanics of a successful short sale by considering the sale on January 12 of 1,000 March 06 futures contract at $9.00 per MMBTU. This means that each contract was worth $10,000 \times \$9 = \$90,000$ and 1,000 futures contract would thus amount to a $90 million position. If by February 12 the same March 06 futures contract is worth only $7.50, Amaranth would simply buy the 1,000 March futures contract to close its short position thereby netting a profit of $1,000 \times 10,000 \times (\$9.00 - \$7.50) = \$15$ millions. The actual profit will be actually somewhat smaller as Amaranth would

> **Box C. Gas Futures.** *A gas future contract is an agreement between two parties which calls for the seller to deliver to a buyer — at a price agreed to when the contract is first entered into — a specified quantity of gas at a designated date and place. One of the key features of futures contract is that they are standardized in terms of amount and delivery dates and are traded in a centralized market place such as the NYMEX at publicly disseminated prices: for example a March 09 gas future trades on the NYMEX for 10,000 million (MM) of British Thermal Units (BTU) at a price (P) quoted in dollars per MMBTU: thus the actual price of one natural gas contract is P × 10,000. If a March 09 contract trades at $7.71, it means that the contract is worth 10,000 × $7,71 = $77,100. Contracts mature every month in the last business day prior to the contract month of expiration: a March 09 natural gas futures contract will expire on the last business day of February 09. Physical delivery takes place at the Sabine Pipe Line Co's Henry Hub processing plant in Louisiana[43] at a more or less constant flow over the entire contract month. Standardization is meant to minimize transaction costs, enhance the liquidity of the contract, and allow for anonymous trading. The Exchange clearinghouse also plays an important role in eliminating counter-party risk since it interposes itself between the two sides of every trade and guarantees fulfillment of the futures contract terms.*

have been required to post a margin (set at 12.5% of notional value) or collateral with the New York Mercantile Exchange thereby incurring the opportunity cost of these funds at the interest rate of say 8% for 1 month (or 1/12 of one year):

$$Net \ speculative \ profit = Futures \ sale \ price - Futures \ purchase \ price$$

$$- \ Opportunity \ cost \ of \ margin$$

$$Net \ speculative \ profit = 1,000 \times 10,000(\$9.00 - \$7.50)$$

$$- \ \$90 \ million \times 0.125 \times 1/12 \times 0.08 = \$14.925 \ million.$$

This assumes further that the margin posted by Amaranth would stay constant throughout the two-month period. This may not necessarily be the case: should futures price continue to climb Amaranth's position would become "out-of-the money," which means to be in a loss position and NYMEX would require a larger margin (known as a margin call) to protect itself against the loss that Amaranth would incur should it decide to close its position.

For such speculation to turn a profit, Amaranth would have to be convinced that the March 06 futures would be mispriced, which in turn begs the question: mispriced in respect to what? Under normal circumstances futures prices should be related to current spot price through a simple relationship reflecting the "cost of carry." For example, on

---

[43] This delivery point was chosen because it stands at the intersection of 12 pipeline systems.

January 12, 2006, arbitragers have the choice between buying future natural gas futures for delivery in 45 days[44] at $F_{0;\text{March }06}$ or buying spot at S_0 and holding natural gas in a storage tank for 45 days. They would incur storage costs "s" (including insurance cost) for 45 days as well as the opportunity cost "i" of tying up the fund for buying the gas in the first place[45]:

$$F_{0;\text{March }06} = S_0(1 + s + i).$$

This valuation formula would indicate that the future price should always be higher than current spot prices — a relationship known as "contango." More often than not the actual futures price is below (not above) the spot price — a relationship known as "backwardation" and which is clearly counterintuitive. Explaining backwardation requires the notion of a significant convenience yield "c" of holding physical gas that reduces the cost of carry. In fact in energy markets — oil and gas — futures price are very often below — rather than above — spot prices which simply reflect that the convenience yield of holding physical natural gas or oil exceeds the cost of carry:

$$F_{0;\text{March }06} = S_0(1 + s + i - c).$$

As a numerical illustration, let us consider that $S_0 = \$9$, $s = 0.0024$, $i = 0.0132$ and $c = 0.03$, March 06 futures contract will stand at

$$F_{0;\text{March }06} = 9(1 + 0.0024 + 0.0132 - 0.03) = 8.879$$

which shows the often observed situation of "backwardation." More generally, the convenience yield will reflect tightness of supply and limited availability of storage and would be highest at the end of the winter season before de-stocking starts. At that point in time natural gas futures should revert back from the counter-intuitive position of "backwardation" to their more normal state of "contango."

Speculating Through Calendar Spreads. Amaranth would now combine a short/sale with a long/purchase position of two different contract months. The calendar spread favored by Amaranth was a winter/summer spread whereby it would sell October or November 06 futures and purchase January 07 futures in equal amounts. In a way, such a spread constitutes a quasi-hedge,[46] which would reduce considerably the margin requirements set by NYMEX and the Intercontinental Commodity Exchange

---

[44] There 18 days left in January plus 27 days in February until the futures contract matures = 45 days.

[45] Storage costs s and interest cost i are expressed in percentage terms per \$1 of investment for the 45-day period.

[46] It would not be a perfect hedge because futures prices do not move in a linear fashion but NYMEX and ICE would allow Amaranth to consolidate offsetting positions. From Eqs. (1) and (2) futures prices are a function of convenience yields which — unlike interest rates and storage costs which are quasi-invariant over time — will fluctuate according to availability of storage space and seasonality of demand.

(ICE),[47] which, in turn, would allow Amaranth to establish considerably larger positions. For speculation to be successful with a winter/summer spread, Amaranth would have to believe that the differential in futures prices was mispriced by the market — i.e., October 06 futures were overpriced and/or that January 07 futures were underpriced. Let us assume that on May 12, 2006, October 06 futures and January 07 are trading at $7.55 and $9.25, respectively and that two months later the same futures contracts are now worth $7.25 and $9.80, respectively. The short position on one October 06 contract yields a profit of $0.30 while the long position a profit of $0.55 for a total gain of [$0.55 + $0.30] × 10,000 = $8,500. The spread itself had increased from $1.70 up to $2.25. The reader will note that the two futures contracts price did not move in lock-step fashion, that is, the October contract declined by $0.30 while the January contract increased by $0.55. Since futures price are directly linked to the spot price and the cost of carry — which should remain quasiconstant — the reason has to be traced to convenience yields which are diverging. The October convenience yield increases as storage space becomes scarcer before winter starts (premium for owning physical gas) whereas the convenience yield starts to decline in winter months as storage space becomes plentiful.

When the mispricing corrects itself, the spread widens and Amaranth generates a profit. Here again mispricing has to be established against a benchmark and the speculator has to answer the question: what is the benchmark pricing of a spread? By definition, a spread is the price differential on the same underlying commodity — here natural gas — over two maturity dates. Since we already know how to price each futures contract independently, the spread can be valued on May 12, 2006 as[48]

$$F_{0;\text{Jan }07} = S_0(1 + s + i - c) \tag{1}$$

$$F_{0;\text{Oct }06} = S_0(1 + s^* + i^* - c^*) \tag{2}$$

$$\text{Spread}_0 = F_{\text{Jan }07} - F_{\text{Oct }06} = S_0(s - s^* + i - i^* + c^* - c).$$

Since storage costs and interest rates are relatively stationary, the spread is driven by movement in the spot price S_0 and changing convenience yields.

Speculating Through Options. Buying options on natural gas futures is far less speculative than outright long or short positions through futures contract (see Box D). Amaranth built a portfolio of call options in the summer of 2005. Natural gas prices had fallen as low as $7 per MMBTU and out-of-the-money December 05 call options at strike price of $12 were very cheap with premium at $0.50. In effect by purchasing call options at such a high strike price Amaranth was forecasting a violent hurricanes season followed by a cold winter, which would bring about severe production and delivery

---

[47] ICE is an internet based trading platform for over-the-counter commodity derivatives.

[48] Storage (s^*) interest rate (i^*) and convenience yield (c^*) are defined in percentage of $1 of natural gas for period of "carry" from March 12, 06 to the delivery day of Oct. 06 gas futures.

> **Box D. Options on Gas Futures:** *a call option gives the holder the right without the obligation to buy a gas futures at a price set today (exercise price) for delivery on the future maturity date of the underlying contract. To acquire this right, the option buyer will pay an upfront cash premium, which is cheap if the option is deep out-of-the-money (strike price considerably higher than current price). If on delivery day the price of the future contract exceeds the strike price, the call option will be exercised and the option holder will take delivery of the gas future contract, which can be sold immediately at a profit or held for future appreciation until the futures contract itself expires. Conversely, if on expiration of the option on futures, the price of the futures contract remains below the exercise price the option will expire worthless and the option holder's loss will be limited to the upfront cash premium*

disruptions. Gas shortages would lead to much higher prices. When Katrina struck in the fall of 2005 and a cold winter snapped, December 05 natural gas futures skyrocketed to $15 per MMBTU and Amaranth netted a $1 billion profit. Call options were exercised by taking delivery of December 05 futures contract, which could be readily sold for $15 per MMBTU or a profit of six times the option premium paid upfront.

THE ALCHEMY OF SPECULATION THROUGH NATURAL GAS FUTURES

Were Amaranth and its star trader building their speculative bets on the basis of proprietary insights about the inner working of the natural gas future markets? Could they count on access to superior weather forecasting services? Were weather derivatives

> **Box E. What are Weather Derivatives?** *They are financial instruments, which can be used to mitigate the adverse impact of weather conditions on a firm's activities. A farm or a power company may hedge against a poor crop or a lower demand for power due to a cooler summer than expected. Unlike other commodities derivatives, the underlying index such as number of heating degree days (HDD) or cooling degree days (CDD) has no intrinsic value. In 1999, the Chicago Mercantile Exchange introduced the first exchange traded weather futures and option contracts. A typical HDD contract's value would be based on the difference between daily temperatures and 18 degree Celsius in 18 US cities over a month during the period November to March and would pay $100 times the cumulative HDD over that month. A futures price for a particular month could be construed as a market consensus as to weather pattern — mild winter or cold winter...*

(see Box E) guiding some of these bets or was it all old fashioned "seat of the pants," gut feeling, and intuition-driven speculative strategy?

Behind any aggressive speculation strategy stands a fundamental belief that "one can beat the market repeatedly" — not just some of the time but most of the time. This runs contrary to the "Efficient Market Hypothesis" according to which futures price are the best predictors of future spot prices. More formally, futures prices as quoted today on January 12, 2006 (time 0) — of say the March 06 futures price $F_{0;\text{March }06}$ — are equal to the expected value E of the random variable ($\sim$), which models the future spot price $S_{\text{Feb }27,06}$ of natural gas for physical delivery on the last day of expiration of the March 06 contract which happened to be February 27:

$$F_{0;\text{March }06} = E[\tilde{S}_{\text{Feb }27,06}]$$

This forecasting model will work "on average" when it is repeatedly used. On a case-by-case basis, the forecast may overshoot or undershoot the actual spot price but error terms will algebraically sum up to zero — in other words it cannot be used as a basis for profitable speculation.

The converse approach to forecasting is based on large-scale econometric forecasting models, which can also provide natural gas futures forecasts. Typically, elaborate modeling of market supply and demand factors for natural gas would allow for contingent price forecasts. On the supply side, domestic production forecasts, projection of imports from Canada and overseas through Liquefied Natural Gas, storage capacity and level of inventory would be all carefully incorporated. On the demand side, level of economic activity, cross price elasticity of substitute sources of energy (especially relevant for power plants and industrial users) and weather forecasts would be the key clusters of explanatory variables. The resulting forecast is typically delivered in a contingent format whereby the user can build his/her assumptions about weather patterns, other energy markets, etc … as inputs into the forecasting model to get a price forecast.

A more focused forecasting approach is to rely on extrapolation of recent price pattern as captured by winter/summer spread. A recent study by Chincarini[49] shows that the winter/summer spread as played by Amaranth had performed well historically: back-testing Amaranth spread strategy as of August 31 over the period 1990–2003 the study finds a significant positive average return of 0.74% per month (8.96% annualized) with minor losses in down years. Figure 2 shows annual returns for the period 1990–2003 assuming that Amaranth's 2006 strategy had been replicated with one major qualification though: the tests simulated small positions in the various contract months — unlike Amaranth's massive positions amassed in 2006.

---

[49] Chincarini, L. Natural gas Futures and Spread Position Risk: Lessons from the Collapse of Amaranth Advisors LLC (working paper, 2008).

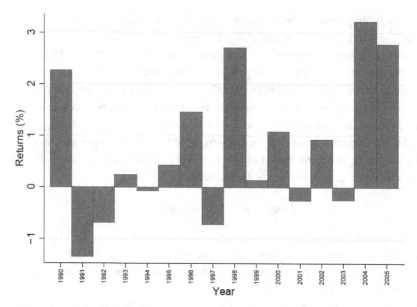

Figure 2   Back-testing calendar spread speculation. Reprinted from Chincarini (2008), p. 17.

As the author note, this would be comforting information to build a trading strategy on such past trends provided that the past can be counted on to repeat itself. However the natural gas world with Amaranth now looming so large on its derivatives market decidedly looked a lot different than before the hedge fund had entered the industry: past structural relationships could not be counted on to hold and would need to be reconfigured — in short, the future could not be reliably extrapolated from the past.

THE STORY UNFOLDS: AMARANTH SPECULATIVE
ASSAULT ON NYMEX

In the aftermath of Amaranth's debacle, the Senate Permanent Committee on Investigations launched a major investigation into the demise of the hedge fund (thereafter referred to as The Senate Report).[50] Based on trading data provided by NYMEX, ICE, and Amaranth itself, the report reconstituted in details the Fund's daily activities. It documents beyond any doubt how the massive positions that Amaranth progressively amassed had a distorting impact on gas futures prices. In this section, we summarize

---

[50] United States Senate Permanent Committee on Investigations (Committee on Homeland Security and Governmental Affairs), Excessive Speculation in the Natural Gas Market (June 15, 2007), thereafter referred as the " Senate Report."

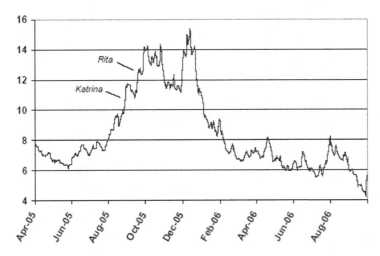

Figure 3 Natural gas futures prices, 2005–2006 next month contract, NYMEX. Reprinted from Senate Report, p. 55.

the key finding of the report and retrace the chronology of Amaranth speculative assault on NYMEX until it crashed.

Simple Shorting: January–April 2006. The mildest month of January on record convinced Amaranth traders that natural gas winter and spring futures prices which had peaked at $15 per MMBTU in December 2005 would continue their rapid decline in early 2006 (see Figure 3). Indeed levels of natural gas production, which had been severely curtailed by Katrina and Rita in early fall 2005, had recovered faster than anticipated with new on-shore wells coming on stream (Figure 4). In early 2006, gas storage tanks had higher level of inventories than at any time in the previous five years and would continue to do so for most of the year (see Figure 5). Consequently, Amaranth amassed 30,000 March 06 contracts finishing the month of January with a portfolio of 40,000 contracts. The Fund was shorting the March 06 contract — that is selling the contract at an average of $8 per MMBTU — anticipating to be able to close its position subsequently by buying it back at a price below $8. During the month of February 06, as March 06 contract were nearing expiration, Amaranth rolled/shifted its short position onto April 06 contracts effectively extending its bet that excess gas supply would continue to drive down near month futures prices.[51] In Figure 6, long

---

[51] Rolling over the March 06 short positions became necessary as they approached expiration. Rather than taking on physical delivery of natural gas Amaranth would close its outstanding March 06 positions by buying back those contracts. Simultaneously it would re-establish its position by selling short the next available contract month which was April 06. The closing of the March 06 contract position would result in net cash-flow gain or loss depending on how March 06 futures price had evolved.

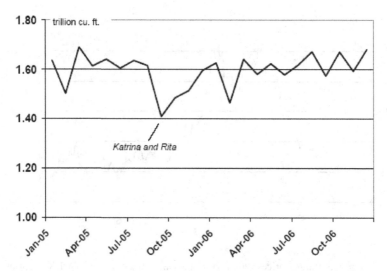

Figure 4   U.S. natural gas, monthly production. Reprinted from Senate Report, p. 54.
Note: See the dramatic drop in natural gas production in September 2005 when Katrina and Rita
struck. Production had returned to normal levels by January 2006.

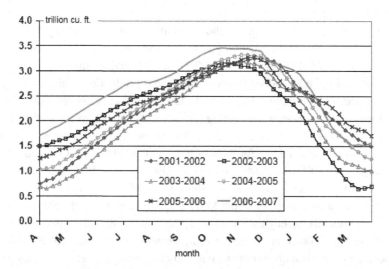

Figure 5   Natural gas in storage, by year. Reprinted from Senate Report, p. 55.

positions as of January 31 and February 28, 2006 in number of contracts are measured
along the positive/upper part of the vertical axis; conversely short positions are shown
on the negative/lower part of the same vertical axis; most contracts were held on the
NYMEX and were subjected to timely disclosure and position limits; only a small
percentage of overall trading was carried out on ICE, which is totally unregulated.

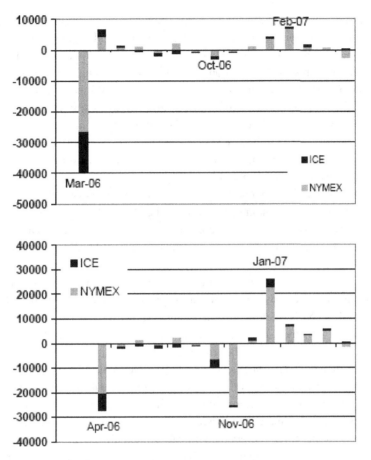

Figure 6 Amaranth's outstanding futures positions on January 31 (upper panel) and February 28, 2006 (lower panel). Reprinted from Senate Report, p. 60.

From Shorting to Buying Calendar Spreads. As a mild winter curtailed demand and Amaranth convinced itself that the natural gas glut — as evidenced by the rising level of inventories in storage tanks — would weigh heavily on futures price it started to build its position in November 06 and January 07 contracts. The speculation strategy was predicated on twin assumptions: (1) a continuing slide in natural gas prices from February 06 all the way to the heating season which starts in late October — hence Amaranth short-selling the November 06 futures contracts and (2) a perking up of winter gas prices as the heating season got underway — hence going long/purchasing the January 07 contracts.

As discussed earlier, the combination of a short November 06 contract with a long January 07 constitutes a calendar spread — referred to as the January/November spread, which became the mainstay of Amaranth speculative strategy until its collapse in September 06. By the end of February 06, Amaranth had built a position of 25,000 contracts in both months. Meanwhile March trading activities showed a continuation of shorting near month with the April 06 position rolled over into June 06 contracts and additional position building in the November 06/January 07 spread with some of the November 06 short positions being shifted to October 06 contracts.

On the face of it, there was nothing particularly bold nor daring about leveraging one's view that natural gas futures were likely to turn measurably more expensive in the winter months — sometimes referred to as an uneducated bet on the weather! What was unusual about Amaranth love affair with natural gas and not widely known — at least initially — to other market participants was the relentless hoarding of futures contract, which resulted in massive holdings. As early as February 06, Amaranth positions accounted for 70% of NYMEX open interest in the November 06 natural gas futures and 60% for the January 07 contract — a pattern that continued well into the summer months (see Figure 7).

Overall positions in adjoining contract months — most notably October 06 futures — were also built up by Amaranth resulting into a sizeable share (ranging from 30% to 45%) of NYNEX open interest in winter contract months (October through March) as shown in Figure 8. Equally revealing is the doubling in 2006 of natural gas futures open interest as compared to the prior three years: in fact, Amaranth's open interest in 2006 was higher than NYMEX entire total open interest in 2003, 2004, and 2005 when physical gas production in 2006 was not markedly different from previous years.

Inevitably the question that comes to mind is how such massive positions would impact futures prices. A simple comparison of the November 06/January 07 spread with prior years' similar spread is very damming for Amaranth as it reveals its doubling and a considerably more volatile spread in 2006 as compared to prior years (Figure 9).

The reader will recall that the calendar spread was a combination of a January 07 long position with a November 06 short position. As a massive buyer of the January contract (therefore bidding up its price) while a massive seller of the November contract (therefore driving down its price), Amaranth was deepening the differential between futures prices and therefore driving up the magnitude of the spread. This acquisitive policy delivered initially outsized gains for Amaranth, which reported $1 billion in profit at the end of April 2006: in May, as liquidity evaporated, the market took it all back:

> *"The box that Amaranth built and found itself inside of — buying up the market, bidding up the prices, and then finding a lack of other persons to sell those positions to — had detrimental consequences for other market participants too.*[52] *As a trader told the subcommittee "Bad news travel fast in the industry. You can't lose a billion*

---

[52] Senate Report, op. cit p. 75.

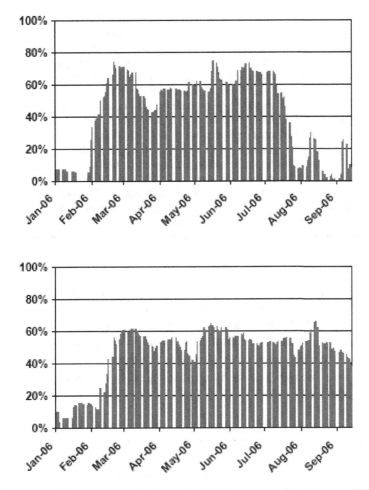

Figure 7 Amaranth's gas contracts for November 2006 (*upper panel*) and January 2007 (*lower panel*) as % of NYMEX open interest. Reprinted from Senate Report, pp. 62–63.

dollars and not have a lot of people not find out about it. No one else could have taken positions of this size."[53]

Instead of unwinding some its oversized futures position, Amaranth instead decided to add to them. June and July transactions indicate that a substantial enlargement of all existing positions with a most noticeable January 07 long position of 80,000 contract — the equivalent of the entire US residential gas consumption during

---

[53] Senate Report, op. cit. p. 76.

Box F. What is Open Interest? *It is the measure of all outstanding contracts for a given futures month. For example, if for the January 07 contract, open interest stands at 85,000 it means there are 85,000 contracts that were sold (and therefore bought), which are outstanding for that month. It is a "stock" gauge as opposed to daily activities in a given futures contract, which are more akin to a "flow" gauge. Open interest does not correspond to physical trading in natural gas. In fact, it is largely decoupled from the physical trading of natural gas as 99% of all outstanding contracts will be liquidated before expiration. Clearly Amaranth, by controlling a large percentage of open interest would have had a determinant role in the current price level. It would also have a major impact on futures price depending upon whether and how it decided to dispose of it. Should Amaranth decide to dispose of a large block of January 07 contract by selling its long position, it would drive down prices significantly — depending upon the extent of the sale. Conversely, should Amaranth dispose of its short November 06 position by buying it back to close its position, it would drive up the November futures prices.*

---

that same month (Figure 10). To spike further its otherwise gargantuan portfolio, Amaranth added the March/April spread by accumulation in short order 60,000 March 06 long contracts and 80,000 April 06 short contracts. Unlike other spreads which tend to move in unison, the March/April spread is especially volatile because March concludes the winter heating season (with destocking of natural gas coming to an end) and April opens the summer (with re-filling of storage tank starting); it is known as the "widow-maker" bet!

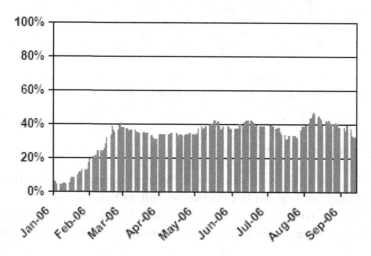

Figure 8   Amaranth's open interest in natural gas contracts for winter months 2006–2007. Reprinted from Senate Report, p. 68.

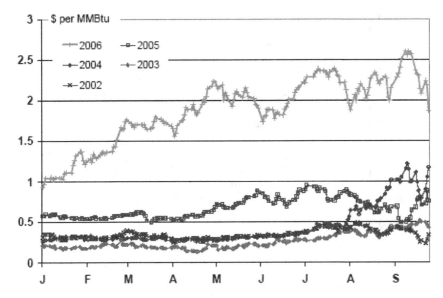

Figure 9 January/November futures price spreads 2002–2006. Reprinted from Senate Report p. 70.

Collapse. As the hurricane season was coming to an end and natural gas supplies remained plentiful, the winter/summer price spread started to narrow. Soon futures prices were collapsing with mammoth margin calls from NYMEX and ICE knocking at Amaranth's door. On August 30, margin requirements stood at $944 million and in short order mushroomed to $3 billion by September 8. As Amaranth's cash position was rapidly dwindling, it sought an exit strategy. Hectic negotiations with possible saviors forced Amaranth to disclose sensitive information about its portfolio to other participants in the market including the Houston-based rival energy fund Centaurus. Amaranth collapse had been almost avoided by a rescue plan that the fund had negotiated with Merrill Lynch and Goldman Sachs, which would have received $250 million and $1.85 billion in exchange for taking over "toxic trades" from its books. On September 18, 2006, JP Morgan-Chase which was Amaranth clearing broker with NYMEX refused to release collateral and margin funds to allow for the rescue plan to proceed on the grounds that too many futures positions would have been left unsecured. On September 20, JP Morgan-Chase and the Citadel group took over Amaranth's distressed portfolio of natural gas futures and forced its liquidation. By January 07, both were benefiting handsomely from their rescue operation with JP Morgan-Chase reporting a profit of $725 million. Amaranth is suing JP Morgan-Chase for having refused to turn over collateral and margin funds in a timely manner thereby forcing the fund liquidation.

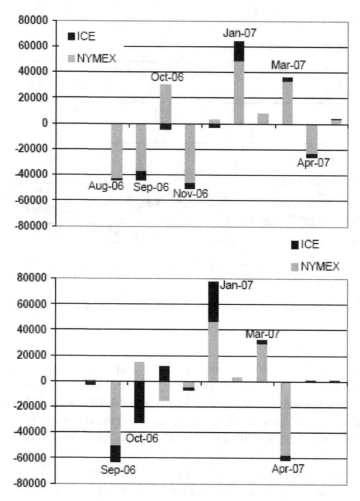

Figure 10   Amaranth's outstanding futures positions as of June 29 (upper panel) and July 26, 2006 (lower panel).

RISK MANAGEMENT AT AMARANTH

Hedge funds are in the business of taking calculating risks with the intent of outperforming markets averages. Risk management procedures are critical to this effort. On the face of it, Amaranth was very thorough in implementing a sound risk management system whereby each trading desk was paired physically with a risk manager (as many as 12), who monitored on a daily basis the metrics of risk performance. Value-at-Risk and stress tests of each position under adverse scenarios with special focus on the largest short or long positions were carefully scrutinized.

> **Box G. Value-at-Risk (V@R).** *Value at risk is an attempt at providing a summary statistic measuring in a single number the total risk of a portfolio of financial assets. History has it that the CEO of JP Morgan had asked his staff to provide him with one single number at 4:15 pm everyday of the risk faced by the bank for the next day. He was served with Value at Risk. "We are x percent certain that we will not lose more than L dollars in the next N days." In other words V@R estimates the maximum loss L in dollar terms over a target horizon (N days) with a given probability x; it answers in pseudoscientific terms the difficult question "How much are we likely to lose?" Amaranth was apparently satisfied that it could not lose more than $1.33 billion with a probability of 99% over the next 20 days. To arrive at such a compellingly simple statistic, a major effort at estimating past volatilities and correlations between each component of the portfolio is critical. Because of the historical nature of the data used in estimating V@R how far back in time should time series extend will impact the reliability of the metrics.*

The integrity of this otherwise sound process was severely compromised when the Fund's star gas trader Brian Hunter physically moved his team to Calgary (Canada) — about 2,000 miles from Amaranth's headquarters in Connecticut (USA). The risk manager attached to the natural gas book stayed behind at Amaranth headquarters in Connecticut. In theory, at least, the power of the internet and quasi-instantaneous communication via emails should have eliminated geographical distance as a hurdle to effective reporting and auditing. Other derivative debacles discussed in this book would indicate otherwise. Of primary concern to a hedge fund such as Amaranth would be market risk, liquidity risk, and funding risk. A detailed analysis and gauging of each type of risk as of August 31, 2006 is provided by Chincarini[54]:

- **Market risk**: using historical data from natural gas futures time series over the period 1990–2006, Amaranth's Value-at-Risk was calculated at $1.33 billion for the next 20 days. It meant that assuming that the natural gas derivatives portfolio remained unchanged over the next 20 days (that is until the day the fund was liquidated) the most that it could lose was $1.33 billion with a probability of 99.9%. In actuality, Amaranth losses under an invariant portfolio would have been $3.295 billion. Please note the expression "would have been" instead of "were" in the previous sentence: this reflect the fact that Amaranth, during the first 20 days of September 06, continued to trade thereby altering daily the configuration of its portfolio. To be able to make a meaningful comparison between what V@R estimated the risk to be and what the actual number turned out to be, we would have to hold Amaranth's portfolio frozen as of September 1, 2006. Clearly, from $1.33 billion to $3.295 billion the margin of error is huge. Hardly a close call! How could V@R be so wrong? Is the metric

---

[54] Chincarini, op. cit.

itself flawed? or was the historical data used in estimating V@R unreliable? Much of the answer has to do with liquidity risk.

- **Liquidity risk**: at its simplest, a liquid market for natural gas futures would be a market that would have allowed Amaranth to exit any of its position without jerking market prices out of alignment. The best approach to avoid liquidity risk is to maintain market positions, which are minor when compared to open interests or daily trading activities: 10% is a safe rule of thumb. As was abundantly illustrated in the previous section, Amaranth built mammoth positions in most futures contracts and had been warned repeatedly by NYMEX for violations of position limits. Amaranth was simply looming too large on the natural gas futures market horizon not to distort historical price and volatility patterns which served as a basis for estimating the parameters upon which V@R is calculated. In fact, marking to market of Amaranth's position throughout 2006 most likely overstated the cash value of the fund. As Vince Kaminsky, a risk management expert who protested chancy trades while at Enron corporation, noted

> "It is dangerous to take giant positions in relatively shallow markets which certain months are in gas futures.... This is a typical mistake of inexperienced and aggressive traders ... Mr. Hunter seemed to have a position that everyone knew about ... the markets are very cruel and can stay irrational longer than you can stay solvent".[55]

THE MORAL OF THE STORY

Lessons for Investors: investing in hedge funds is not for the faint-hearted. Pension funds, university endowments, billionaire investors, and other likely investors in hedge funds are all savvy investors, who will dedicate a limited part of their investment portfolio to such enticing opportunities: they do so knowingly and at their own perils. The search is for risk adjusted returns in excess of what market indices would yield — sometimes referred to as the "alpha" return — in excess of the "beta" market return. Commodity hedge funds have certainly become fashionable of late. For, investors, simple questions should be centered around the fund's basic investment philosophy, its trading team, and record as well as efficacy of the risk management system in place. Diversification of the fund's portfolio and relative positions to markets' outstanding open interests in the case of traded commodities or financial contracts should be clearly monitored as they may be indication of excessive concentration in shallow markets. Last but not least, marking-to-market of commodity futures positions may appear to be a relatively straightforward exercise under normal market conditions: in reality, under

---

[55] Davis, A., op. cit.

"abnormal" conditions, exiting excessively large positions — as Amaranth attempted on several occasions — may happen at prices that are quite different from pre-trade levels. This process clearly distorts a realistic valuation process and misleads investors as to the real performance and riskiness of their investments.

Lessons for Commodity Traders: the hectic pace of feverish activities in a trading room leaves little time for elaborating grand strategy and thoughtful consideration of the "big picture." Traders suffer from tunnel vision and immediate term scheming about their next trade. How much consideration did Amaranth gave to the fact that many of its positions in the natural gas future markets accounted for more than 50% of open interests on NYMEX and — when all positions are consolidated — more than 100%. The larger the position, the more treacherous the exit. Amaranth traders ignored liquidity risk: their risk managers should have enforced tight position limits as a percentage of open interest — perhaps with a ceiling at 12.5% to insure smooth exit when necessary.

Lessons for Policy-Makers and Regulators: commodity derivative markets perform an important economic function by enabling an efficient transfer of risk bearing from market participants least equipped to bear risk to market participants best equipped to bear risk. Speculators have an important role to play as offsetting parties to commercial producers and distributors of natural gas in search of a price hedge. However outsize positions controlled by one entity will distort price and volatility patterns, which in turn will distort the risk allocation process and may end up causing harm to end-consumers. NYMEX lapsed in its watchdog capacity when it failed to enforce the simple rule of maximum position of 12,000 contracts for any-one market participant. As illustrated in Figures 7 and 8, Amaranth was not slightly above the ceiling but several times over the limit with positions on specific contract dates in excess of 100,000. When NYMEX finally pressured Amaranth to comply with position limits, Amaranth simply moved its position to ICE which has no position nor any reporting requirement. Clearly, disclosure requirements and position limits should be extended to ICE — what is referred as closing the "Enron loophole." As one of several institutional end-users of natural gas, the Municipal Gas Authority of Georgia testified to the US Senate subcommittee that it incurred unnecessary hedging cost of $18 million over actual spot market prices for the winter season 2006–2007, which ultimately had to be passed on to consumers. This abnormal hedging premium can be directly attributed to excessive speculation and market manipulation by Amaranth and others.

POSTSCRIPT

"Twice bitten but never shy," Brian Hunter — within months of having almost single-handedly caused the demise of Amaranth Advisors LLC — was raising $600 millions to launch Salengro, a hedge fund dedicated to speculation in energy commodities which would have reconstituted the Amaranth trading team. The publication of the US Senate Report on Natural Gas Speculation on June 25, 2007 put his project on hold: instead he was forced to defend himself in several legal actions/investigations initiated by the CFTC. According to the periodical Canadian Business, *"Boston-based Peak ridge did enroll Brian Hunter in launching a new energy fund but could not quite bring itself to use his name; the most it could do was to announce its partnership with a "top-tier industry trader with a history of exceeding market benchmarks."*[56]

Questions for Discussion

1. Compare the US gas and oil industry. Would you expect natural gas prices to be more volatile than oil prices?
2. How do you explain the seasonal pattern of natural gas prices?
3. What are the principal reasons which lead Amaranth LLC Advisors to its collapse?
4. As an investor in a natural gas hedge fund, which information would you monitor on a periodic basis?

---

[56] Watson, T. The trials of Brian Hunter, *Canadian Business* (March 3, 2008), p. 64–74.

METALLGESELLSCHAFT

The price of an article is charged according to difference in location, time, or risk to which one is exposed in carrying it from one place to another or in causing it to be carried. Neither purchase nor sale according to this principle is unjust.

St. Thomas Aquinas, c. 1264

Per ardua ad astra (through difficulties to the stars)

In the annals of financial debacles that rocked the 1990s, Metallgesellschaft (MG)'s loss of $1.3 billion was the first case of "derivatives malpractice" to bring a giant industrial firm to the brink of bankruptcy. In December 1993, Metallgesellschaft reported massive losses at its US oil subsidiary — Metallgesellschaft Refining and Marketing (MGRM) — which were traced to mammoth oil derivatives positions estimated at 85 days of Kuwait oil production (160 million barrels of oil). The oil derivatives positions were rumored to be the necessary hedging counterpart of an ambitious marketing program whereby MGRM had offered its US customers long term price guarantees on the delivery of petroleum products. Only a massive $1.9 billion rescue package mounted by as many as 150 German and international banks staved off bankruptcy for Metallgesellschaft, long known as a conservative blue-blood pillar of the German industrial establishment. Yet, it was not fraud as in the case of Barings SA, nor lax operating controls as in the case of Sumitomo, nor entrapment as in the case of Procter & Gamble. Rather it was a case of daring financial engineering based on somewhat tenuous assumptions about the inner working of oil markets that were ill-communicated and ultimately not shared between the audacious (possibly reckless) American "child" and its conservative German "parent."

73

THE METALLGESELLSCHAFT DEBACLE

Metallgesellschaft is a large German industrial conglomerate with activities not only in the old world of mining and smelting non-ferrous metals — where it is best established — but also in the newer world of engineering, commodity trading and financial services. With sales of DM26 billion in 1993 (approximately $16 billion) on total assets with book value of DM17.8 billion ($10 billion) and a workforce of 43,000 employees Metallgesellschaft was truly one of the jewels of industrial Germany. As it is often the case in the German bank-centered financial system, MG was relatively closely held with 65% of its stock owned by only seven institutional investors with Deutsche Bank and Dresdner Bank playing a dominant role as both shareholder and creditor of the firm.

Metallgesellschaft's Foray in the North American Energy Market. MG's US oil subsidiary had grown significantly between 1989 and 1993 — largely as a result of its 49% purchase of the oil exploration firm Castle Energy. To facilitate Castle Energy transformation into a refiner MGRM committed to purchasing 46 million barrels per year from Castle Energy at guaranteed margins for up to 10 years above the oil spot price (spot oil price is the price at which oil can be bought or sold for immediate delivery — see Box A). To further strengthen its supply and trading capability MGRM invested in a storage and transportation network. As part of this new strategy MGRM had also hired, in 1991, W. Arthur Benson away from the commodity trading firm Louis Dreyfus Energy as a ploy to spearhead its foray in the North American energy market. Benson — who brought with him as many as 50 traders and others executives from Louis Dreyfus Energy — did not wait long before introducing novel energy derivatives products to a market which for the most part had to make do with energy futures (see Boxes B and C) contracts of very short term maturity.

In the early nineties, marketing research led MGRM to believe that independent oil & gasoline distributors/retailers were ill-equipped to weather surges in the spot oil prices and that it was uniquely positioned to provide — for a fee — this much needed long-term insurance coverage against oil price risk. Accordingly, in 1992, as part of its strategic effort to build up its position in the North American energy trading and distribution business, MGRM embarked on an aggressive marketing program by offering long-term price guarantees for up to 10 years on deliveries of gasoline, heating oil and diesel fuel.

More specifically, MGRM targeted independent or quasi-independent service stations which were pitted in a losing war against major oil refiner-owned service stations

---

[56] OPEC was first established as the world oil cartel in 1960 and currently includes twelve members: Iran, Iraq, Kuwait, Qatar, United Arab Emirates, Saudi Arabia, Libya, Algeria, Ecuador, Venezuela, Nigeria, and Angola. Collectively it controls about 2/3 of known oil reserves and

> **Box A. The Oil Market.** *Until the early seventies the oil market was relatively stable with price tightly controlled by the Organization of Oil Exporting Countries (OPEC).*[56] *In fact there was not much of an oil market as crude oil was directly sold through long term agreements between oil rich countries and major globally integrated oil companies such as Exxon, British Petroleum, Royal Dutch Shell... also known as the Seven Sisters. The dramatic oil price increase triggered by the first oil embargo of 1973 encouraged energy conservation and the development of non-OPEC oil reserves most notably in the North Sea and the former Soviet Union. Soon, as demand contracted and oil supply expanded, a surplus of crude oil started to undermine the official OPEC-determined price. By the late seventies, OPEC was starting to lose its monopolistic grip on oil prices as national quotas were increasingly difficult to enforce and Saudi Arabia relented on its role of swing producer and price stabilizer. Oil companies naturally started to rely increasingly on the spot market for an ever larger percentage of their total supplies. By the mid eighties, more than two-third of global oil procurement was sourced from the spot market; the remaining one third of total oil transactions were now locked into contracts of much shorter duration. This led in turn to greater price volatility for crude and refined petroleum products which soon fostered the establishment of futures markets in petroleum products.*

because they had to face their full exposure to oil price risk.[57] By September of 1993 MGRM had committed to supplying 160 million barrels of gasoline and heating oil products over the following 10 years at fixed prices. These forward contracts (see Box B) were indeed a welcome innovation for the energy distribution industry.

Hedging the Unhedgeable. MGRM's challenge was simple: it had committed to delivering millions of barrel of oil to independent distributors at fixed prices ranging between $24 and $27 per barrel (approximately $3–$5 per barrel over currently prevailing spot prices) depending upon the type of petroleum product over a 10 year period (1993–2003). It was *"short oil"*[58] for the next ten years. Somehow it had to create a "long" position in oil products of matching amount and maturity — hopefully at a somewhat lower price than the forward sale price so as to lock in positive profit

---

accounts for approximately one-third of world oil production. By setting national semi-annual oil quotas for its members which reflects global demand for oil and likely production by non-OPEC oil exporters, it seeks to influence world oil prices.

[57] Krupels, Ed. Re-examining the Metallgesellschaft affair and its implications for oil traders, *Oil & Gas Journal* (March 26, 2001).

[58] To be "short" oil means having committed to making a future oil delivery (or holding an oil liability exposure). Symmetrically, being "long" oil means having committed to taking future delivery of oil (holding an oil asset exposure).

Box B. What are Forward Contracts? *A forward oil contract is a commitment to buy or sell a certain quantity of oil on a certain date in the future (maturity of the contract) at a price (forward oil price) agreed upon today when the contract is signed. For example on September 30, 1993 MGRM could sell oil at $25 per barrel in the amount of 10 million barrels (BL) for delivery in 10 years. On September 30, 2003 MGRM would deliver BL.10 million and receive $250 million regardless of the spot value of oil on delivery day; if oil is worth $45 the buyer would obviously benefit from the forward contract having paid $25 per BL. and generating a profit BL.10 million ($45 − $25) = $200 million. Conversely, MGRM would incur a $200 million loss had it not hedged its forward oil sale. Clearly it is important to emphasize that a forward contract when signed is an exchange of irrevocable and legally binding promises (with no cash changing hands) obligating the two parties to going through with the actual transaction at maturity and delivering oil for dollar (or vice versa) regardless of the state of the world — that is the prevailing spot oil price.*

---

margins. To do so MGRM built a very large short-term[59] position in oil futures (see Box C), which established a "long"/asset position in oil of matching amount to the "short"/liability position to be hedged — albeit of a *mismatching* maturity. As these near-term futures contract matured they would be rolled over with a new stack of near-term futures. This is the hedging strategy known as "stack and roll" discussed in the next section. However the combination of steadily declining spot oil prices with a changing relationship between near-term futures and spot prices for most of 1993 resulted into mounting cash-flow losses when MGRM rolled over its stack of near-term futures. These losses eventually totaled nearly $1.3 billion and nearly bankrupted the parent company.

Calamitous Exit. MG had to negotiate a $1.9 billion bailout from its bankers in exchange for a major restructuring plan that cut at the core of MG's manufacturing, mining and trading activities. Needless to say the large futures position was to be unwound in short order. MG's equity had lost more than half of its market capitalization with its stock price falling from a high of DM427 in November 1993 to a low of DM216 in February 1994. Bankruptcy had been avoided but only narrowly so. As many analysts have wondered, how does one go about losing $1.3 billion by hedging? Was MGRM an unlucky hedger caught off-guard by adverse and abnormal oil price movements in the pursuit of an ill-devised strategic plan? Or was MGRM a reckless speculator that

---

[59] The reader will note that short-term position in oil does not mean being "short" oil. The two concepts are entirely different: the first one refers to the tenor of the contract and the second to the liability nature of the position.

> **Box C. Oil Futures.** *The trading of energy futures started in 1978 with heating oil futures on the New York Mercantile Exchange (NYMEX), followed by the introduction of crude oil and unleaded gasoline futures in 1983 and 1985 respectively. An oil future contract is an agreement between two parties which calls for the seller to deliver to a buyer at a price agreed to (when the contract is first entered into) a specified quantity and grade of oil at a designated futures market such as the NYMEX. One of the key feature of futures contracts is their standardization: for example a crude oil future trading on the NYMEX is defined in unit of 1,000 barrels of West Texas Intermediate (with sulfur content and gravity to be specified); it is quoted in dollars per barrel and matures every month in the 3rd business day prior to the 25th calendar day of the delivery month. Standardization is meant to minimize transaction costs and enhance the liquidity of the contract. Contract standardization also differentiates futures from forwards which are tailor-made contracts meeting the precise needs of the two parties signing the contract (see Box D).*

shrouded a questionable oil price strategy in the garb of a prudent albeit naïve hedging strategy?

THE "LONG AND SHORT" OF HEDGING IN THE OIL MARKET

As a result of its far-sighted marketing gambit MGRM was selling forward oil contracts with physical oil deliveries staggered over a ten year period (see Figure 1). Although negotiated forward contracts showed a hefty positive margin against current spot prices there was no guarantee that that future spot oil prices would remain low. Thus the uncertainty of future spot prices required MGRM to design a grand scheme that would lock in profit margins. Failure to do so would amount to outright speculation. Could

> **Box D. What is Different Between Forward and Futures Contracts.** *Both contracts allow the buyer and seller to agree on the price, date and amount of oil to be delivered. Forwards are tailor-made contracts negotiated directly by the two parties and generally do not require any posting of collateral or margin to guarantee their execution: counterparty risk or the risk that one party will default is an issue. Futures are standardized contracts in terms of amount, delivery date and grade and are continuously traded. They require the posting of a margin with the Exchange with which they are contracted. Futures contract are marked-to-market daily and any losses will be drawn from the margin account. If margin account is drawn down the Exchange will require the futures contract holder to replenish the margin account (so called margin calls) or, otherwise, the futures contract will be liquidated: as such futures contract are immune to counterparty risk.*

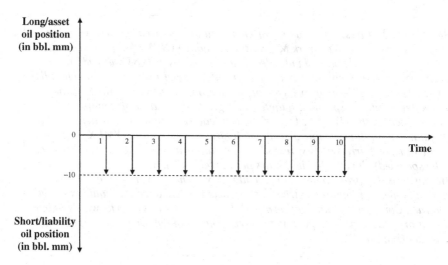

Figure 1 Unhedged "short" oil positions years 1–10.

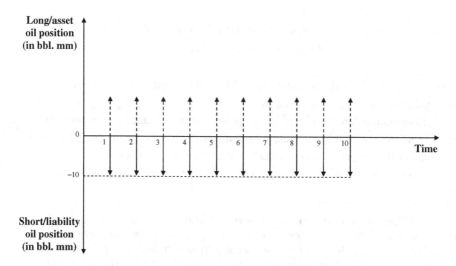

Figure 2 Hedged oil positions years 1–10.

MGRM pull it off? Let us review the hedging strategies which were available to MGRM:

Forward Hedge. The textbook approach to hedging a strip of long-dated short oil positions would be to buy oil forward contracts in matching amount and maturities (see Figure 2). For example, if MGRM had sold 10 millions barrel (BL) of oil to Federated Heating Oil — an independent oil and gasoline retailer in New England — at

$25 for delivery in 2003, MGRM would want to lock in a forward purchase contract at less than $ 25 — say $21. At delivery, in 2003, MGRM would net a cash-flow gain of BL10 million ($25 − $21) = $40 million. Of course, if the oil price risk were hedged, MGRM's success would still depend on both parties to the purchase and sale forward contracts to hold their side of the bargain (counterparty risk). On maturity day, oil had to be delivered to MGRM (by a third party) (forward purchase contract) and a large check from Federated Heating Oil had to be cashed by MGRM (forward sale contract). Unfortunately, there is not much of a market in oil forwards with maturities extending beyond 18 months which is precisely why MGRM was developing this new venture.

"Ex-Ante" Physical Storage also Known as "Synthetic" Forward Contract. The safest approach to hedging price risk on its forward contract would have been for MGRM to purchase physical oil on the spot market and store it until the forward contract called for its delivery. The cost of such a strategy is known ex-ante and can be computed simply on a per unit of energy product as follows:

Cost of a synthetic forward purchase of one barrel of oil $F_{0;10}^*$

today for delivery in 10 years

= Purchase cost of oil today at the spot price of S_0

+ annual cost of physical storage s for 10 years per $ of oil

+ annual percentage opportunity cost i of tying up the cost

of purchasing oil and paying storage

or

$$S_0(1 + s + i)^{10} = F_{0;10}^* \tag{1}$$

which should be compared to the forward/futures price $F_{0;10} = 25$ contracted with end-users now for delivery in 10 years.

For example, if the dollar spot price of oil is $S_0 = 20$, annual dollar storage cost per dollar of oil is $s = 0.01$ and the opportunity cost of capital is $i = 0.06$, MGRM could create a 10-year synthetic forward contract by storing physical oil for 10 years at a total cost of:

$$F_{0;10}^* = 20(1 + 0.01 + 0.06)^{10} = 39.34. \tag{1 illustrated}$$

Theoretically the forward rate which adjusts the spot price for the all-inclusive "cost of carry" should be higher than the spot price — a relationship known as "contango"; however, most of the time, the forward/futures price of oil is below the spot price — a counter-intuitive relationship known as "backwardation" and rationalized as a "convenience yield" that participants in the oil market attach to holding the physical product (see next section for further discussion).

Unfortunately, physical storage is expensive and Edwards and Canter (1995) estimate that if storage costs were higher than \$.0733 per barrel/per month this strategy would have resulted in a net loss for MGRM. In fact, all inclusive storage costs were closer to \$.24 per barrel per month (for an annual cost of \$3) not to mention that physical storage space is also severely limited.

Opportunistic Physical Storage. Conversely MGRM could have waited for time t at which the oil spot price S_t would fall below the break-even price S_t^* at which the cost of physical carry becomes affordable to lock in the physical storage hedge. Going back several years it would have been possible for MGRM to tabulate the probability of S_t falling below S_t^*, where this latter time-dependent break-even spot price is determined by the arbitrage relationship and by solving for S_t:

$$S_t(1 + s + i)^{T-t} = F_{0;T} \quad \text{with } t < T = 1, 2, 3, \ldots, 10. \tag{2}$$

Clearly the break-even spot price will increase as t approaches T with the cost of carry progressively declining. For instance, assume that after three years the spot price of oil, S_3, has dropped to \$12, buying and storing physical oil for the remaining $10 - 3 = 7$ years would then cost

$$12(1 + 0.01 + 0.06)^{10-3} = 19.27 \tag{2 illustrated}$$

which is clearly less than the forward rate of $F_{0;10} = 25$ that MGRM has contracted with Federated Heating Oil.

Synthetic Storage or "Stack and Roll" Hedge. MGRM would open a *stack* of futures contracts ("long"/asset oil position) for short maturities (presumably one month) matching in amount (but not maturities) its "short"/liability oil positions over the long term (see Figure 3). When the futures contracts came to maturity they were *rolled* over (renewed) after having been cash-settled. The new long futures positions were then reduced by the amount of the actual flow delivery that took place in the prior period.

The effective cost of hedging the forward purchase price of oil through a "stack and roll" strategy can be explained into two parts: (1) the effective all-inclusive forward purchase cost of oil and (2) the rollover cost of cash-settling the stack of futures contract at the end of each period; it should be noted that part 2 is an integral part of (1). We will analyze them in turn over a two period horizon:

(1) *Effective cost of oil forward purchase*: at time $t = 0$, MGRM buys a one period futures contract at

$$F_{0;1} = S_0(1 + s + i - c) = S_0 + b_0 \tag{3A}$$

where c is the "convenience yield" and $b_0 = F_{0;1} - S_0$ is known as the basis.

At time $t = 1$, MGRM would sell/settle its futures contract at S_1 (thereby incurring a gain/loss of $F_{0;1} - S_1$) and re-stack/roll its futures position by buying a new one-period

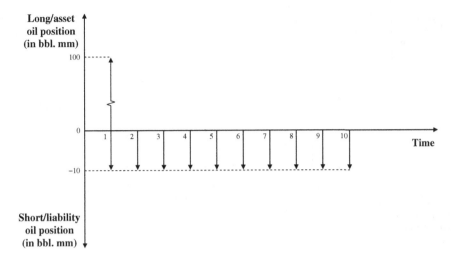

Figure 3   Stack futures in year 1 to hedge short position years 1–10.

futures contract at

$$F_{1;2} = S_1 + b_1. \tag{3B}$$

Thus at the end of the first period MGRM would have locked in a purchase cost of[60]:

$$F_{0;1} - S_1 + F_{1;2} = S_0 + b_0 - S_1 + S_1 + b_1 = S_0 + [b_0 + b_1]. \tag{4}$$

Since for each of the first two periods the basis b_0 and b_1 is tantamount to the cost of carry (see Eq. (1)), MGRM was creating a synthetic storage hedge where the *total* carrying/storage cost was the sum of *synthetic* carrying/storage cost (the basis) for periods 1 and 2. To the extent that oil markets tend to be in backwardation (negative basis) most of the time, MGRM had put into place a plausible hedging policy which seemed to guarantee a hedged oil purchase price below the forward sale price contracted by MGRM.[61] In the next section we will present empirical evidence that oil

---

[60] The cash flow cost of this hedge would be incurred progressively as short-term futures are cash-settled and rolled over and would, therefore, be realized a lot sooner than the maturity of the long-dated forward contract entered by MGRM.

[61] In sum, at the end of 10 periods, MGRM would have bought a futures position for

$$F_{0;1} - S_1 + F_{1;2} - S_2 + \cdots + F_{9;10} \tag{4A}$$

which by substituting Eqs. (3A) and (3B) into Eq. (4A) can be rewritten as

$$S_0 + b_0 - S_1 + S_1 + b_1 + \cdots - S_9 + S_9 + b_9 \tag{4B}$$

and readily simplified to

$$S_0 + [b_0 + b_1 + b_2 + \cdots + b_9]. \tag{5}$$

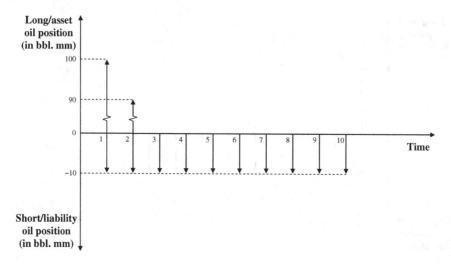

Figure 4   Stack and roll.

markets are more likely to be in backwardation that in contango and that, on average, the cumulative backwardation discount would exceed the contango premium over long periods of time.

(2) *Cash-flow cost of rolling futures stack*: a favorable hedging cost does not say anything about the actual cash-flow gain or loss generated by cash-settling a stack of futures contracts and rolling them over from period to period (see Eq. (4B)). This — as we will shortly discover — turned out to be the Achilles' heel of MGRM's daring hedging architecture. In effect, at the end of the first period, MGRM will cash settle the stack of futures at the spot price of S_1 incurring a cash-flow cost defined as the difference between the sale price S_1 and the purchase price of $F_1 = S_0 + b_0$:

$$S_1 - F_1 = (S_1 - S_0) - b_0. \tag{6}$$

Clearly it would be difficult for MGRM to know ex-ante whether the absolute change in the spot price $S_1 - S_0$ would be larger or smaller than the basis b_0 (positive contango or negative backwardation). In Table 1 we consider the different cases that MGRM confronted ex-ante by combining contango or backwardation (basis b) with absolute price changes $S_1 - S_0$. Under a consistent situation of backwardation MGRM stood a 75% chance of generating cash flow gains on its stack of "long" near-term futures (bottom row of Table 1 shows that — in three out of four situations — cash-settling of futures stack would be cash-flow positive). Overall — assuming the oil market being equally likely to be in contango or backwardation — MGRM should over time simply break-even on cash-settling its stacks of futures hedge contract (four out of a total of eight cells in Table 1 show a cash flow gain).

Table 1 Cash flow gain/loss from hedging through "stacking and rolling" oil futures (see below).

Oil market in	Spot price increases		Spot price decreases	
	<Basis	>Basis	<Basis	>Basis
CONTANGO (basis > 0)	LOSS	GAIN	LOSS	LOSS
BACKWARDATION (basis < 0)	GAIN	GAIN	GAIN	LOSS

For all practical purposes, MGRM was starting to implement the "synthetic storage" policy introduced above.[62] On the next and every settlement date, MGRM rolled over forward its futures positions, month after month, after having decreased it by the amount of physical oil products delivered (see Figure 4).

NUMERICAL ILLUSTRATION OF "EBBS & FLOWS" UNDER A "STACK & ROLL" HEDGE

The cash-flow implications of the "stack and roll" hedge described above are certainly not obvious and takes some painstaking effort to fully comprehend. This section works out numerically two of the eight different scenarios identified in Table 1 in order to illustrate with simple numbers how MGRM could have gone so wrong so fast.

Scenario 1: Backwardation with oil price decline overshooting backwardation discount. Let us consider a simple illustration (see Table 2) and assume that on September 1, 1993 ($t = 0$) MGRM sells forward 100 million barrels of diesel fuel (short position) at $23 per barrel for delivery in equal installment over the next 10 years starting on September 1, 1994 ($t = 1$). The current spot price is $S_0 = 20$ and one year futures are in backwardation at $F_{0;1} = 19.5$ — the rate at which MGRM will purchase at $t = 0$, 100 million barrels of diesel fuel to create an asset/long position of matching amount but of mismatching maturity. One year later, at $t = 1$, the spot price of oil has declined to $S_1 = 17.5$. MGRM will cash settle its futures position incurring a cash-flow loss of 100 million $(17.5 - 19.5) = -\$200$ million; however, MGRM will incur a cash-flow gain of $+\$55$ million on the first installment of 10 million barrels to be physically delivered since BL10 million $(23 - 17.5) = +\$55$ million (see Table 2). In sum, MGRM incurs a cash-flow loss of $-\$200$ million $+ \$55$ million $= -\$145$ million. Worth emphasizing is that in the early years of this scheme — as illustrated in this

---

[62] For the purpose of this paper forward and swap contracts are functionally equivalent to futures contracts (except for margin calls) on the same products for a one to one hedge.

Table 2 Oil price decline overshoots backwardation discount.

Maturity	0	1	2
Oil prices			
Spot (in US$)	20	17.5	15.5
Forward (in US$)	23	23	23
Futures (in US$)	19.5	17	
Outstanding short/liability oil position (in Barrels mm)		10	10
Outstanding long/asset oil position (in Barrels mm)		100	90
Cash flow on physical delivery (in US$ mm)		55	75
Cash flow on rolling futures (in US$ mm)		*−200*	*−135*
Net cash flow loss (in US$ mm)		−145	−60

scenario — the large stack of near-term futures could generate massive rollover losses while profits on the actual physical delivery of oil products are smaller and would be staggered over 10 years.

On September 1, 1994 MGRM will now re-stack and roll the remaining 90 million barrels ($t = 1$) at the new futures rate of $F_{1;1} = 17$. One year later the spot price has further declined to $S_2 = 15.5$ resulting in a cash flow loss on cash settling the futures contract which is not linked to the physical delivery of 10 million barrels — in the amount of BL 90 million $\times$ (15.5 − 17) = −$135 million. On the 10 million barrels to be physically delivered, MGRM further nets a cash flow gain of BL10 million $\times$ (23 − 15.5) = $75 million for a net cash-flow loss of −$60 million.

Clearly, this scenario would put heavy cash-flow stress on MGRM early on even, though actual oil deliveries would have been made at a significant profit. Interestingly, even when the futures market is consistently in backwardation MGRM would incur massive losses when the spot price declined every period in excess of the backwardation discount. MGRM had clearly hoped for a backwardation scenario with the spot oil price declining more slowly and undershooting the backwardation discount or even better appreciating. Unfortunately, the oil market swung to contango in 1993 while spot oil prices were declining precipitously: we turn to this situation next.

Scenario 2: Oil market in contango and spot price decreases undershooting contango premium (basis). As under the first scenario MGRM sells forward 100 million barrels of diesel fuel (short position) at $23 per barrel for delivery in equal installment over the next 10 years starting on September 1, 1993 ($t = 0$). The current spot price is $S_0 = 20$. The current one year future price stands at $F_1 = 22$ and is in contango (positive basis). One year later at $t = 1$ the spot price of oil has decreased to $S_1 = 18$. MGRM will cash-settle its futures position incurring a cash-flow loss of BL 100 million $\times$ (18 − 22) = −$400 million but with an additional gain on the actual

Table 3   Oil price decline undershoots contango premium

Maturity	0	1	2
Oil prices			
Spot (in US$)	20	18	16
Forward (in US$)	23	23	23
Futures (in US$)	22	19	
Outstanding short/liability oil position (in Barrels mm)		10	10
Outstanding long/asset oil position (in Barrels mm)		100	90
Cash flow on physical delivery (in US$ mm)		10	70
Cash flow on rolling futures (in US$ mm)		*−400*	*−270*
Net cash flow loss (in US$ mm)		−390	−200

10 million barrels to be physically delivered of BL 10 million $(23 - 22) = \$10$ million for a total cash flow loss of $-\$400$ million $+ \$10$ million $= -\$390$ million.

On September 1, 1994 MGRM will now "re-stack" the remaining 90 million barrels ($t = 1$) at the futures rate of $F_{1,2} = 19$. One year later the spot price has further decreased to $S_2 = 16$ resulting into a cash flow loss on cash settling the futures contract which are not linked to the physical delivery of 10 million barrels — in the amount of BL 90 million $(16 - 19) = -\$270$ million. On the BL 10 million to be physically delivered MGRM further nets a cash flow gain of BL 10 million $(23 - 16) = +\$70$ million. For a total cash flow loss of $-\$270$ million $+ \$70$ million $= -\$200$ million (Table 3).

Under both scenarios, adverse movements in the oil spot price resulted into massive rollover losses on the stack of futures contracts. These losses dwarfed the more distant, time-deferred profits on actual physical delivery of petroleum products. Under normal hedging conditions when the "naked" position and the hedge are matched in amount and maturity the cash flow gains and losses offset each other and this abnormal situation would not happen. With a "stack and roll" hedge of short-term maturity to neutralize long-dated oil positions MGRM experienced violent short-term pain while gains were slowly coming and steadily realized. Clearly when the "child's" pain became unbearable the "parent" had to put the "child" out of her misery . . . .

THE "MESSAGE IS IN THE ENTRAILS": EMPIRICS
OF THE OIL MARKET (1983–2002)

The success of MGRM's synthetic storage hedging policy was predicated on cumulative backwardation/discount exceeding the contango/premium. This section presents

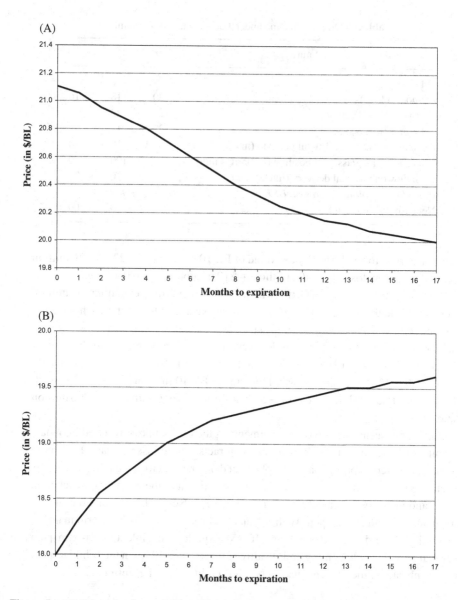

Figure 5   (A) Example of a market in backwardation (as of 21 August, 1992). (B) Example of a market in contango (as of 20 August, 1993).

empirical evidence indicating that oil markets are indeed in backwardation more often than they are in contango. Let us recall that in forward markets, if the forward price curve is upward-sloping, it is called a "contango" market; a market with a downward sloping forward curve is in "backwardation". Figures 5A and B show examples of a market in backwardation (as of 21 August 1992) and contango (as of 20 August 1993) respectively: to be specific, in Figure 5A the spot rate stood at $21.10 per barrel and all forward rates (maturities ranging from 1 to 17 months are shown below the spot price — the so-called backwardation relationship. An inverse contango relationship is shown in Figure 5B.

Under normal circumstances futures market should be in contango since the "cost of carry" (storage and financing cost) arbitrage formula prices futures at a premium vis-à-vis the spot/cash price. As pointed out earlier backwardation is unusually common in oil futures markets, however, and is generally interpreted as due to convenience returns associated with holding physical oil.

Extending the Historical Analysis. While it is common, backwardation is not necessarily a consistent phenomenon in oil futures markets. To gain a better grasp of the market dynamics that MGRM was confronting in 1993 we juxtaposed historical (1983–1992) with forward looking (1992–2002) data as if MGRM had been allowed to execute on its grand strategy: we establish that the historical patterns of backwardation that emerged was relatively steady and consistent with the notable exception of the year 1993.

Figures 6A–C give the monthly pattern of backwardation for crude oil, heating oil and gasoline futures. Monthly percentages of backwardation are given separately for the periods 1983–1992 (bars in grey) and 1992–2002 (bars in white). Each monthly bar simply indicates the percentage chance that over the corresponding period the futures market would find itself in backwardation. Generally, backwardation was stronger in the first period than in the second period for all three oil product categories.

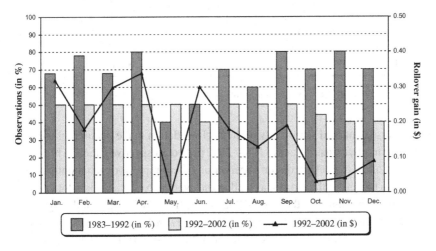

Figure 6-A Average monthly crude oil backwardation.

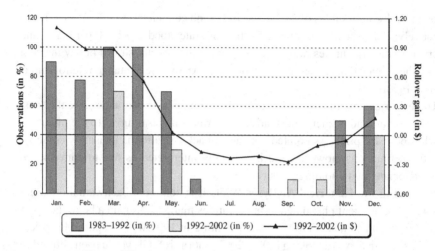

Figure 6-B   Average monthly heating oil backwardation.

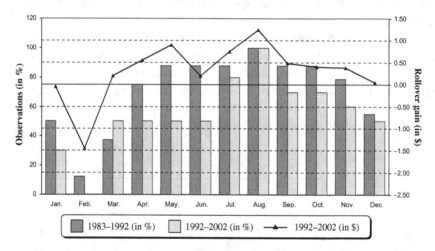

Figure 6-C   Average monthly gasoline backwardation.

There is also a marked seasonality to the backwardation in the heating oil market and gasoline markets, across the entire 1983–2002 period. Respective panels in Figure 6 gives the percentage of backwardation observations (bar graph) for each month in the sample (read to the left of the figure), as well as the average backwardation dollar gain (line graph) in each month for the 1992–2002 period (read to the right of the figure).

One can readily observe that heating oil futures are *rarely if ever* in backwardation in the summer months (June through October when consumption is low), while gasoline futures are *most likely* to be in backwardation during approximately the same period when consumption is high. Crude oil seasonality is not as marked, but contango pricing

---

Box E. Optimal Hedge Ratio. *A hedge ratio is the ratio of the "long" position that MGRM was taking in buying a stack of near term oil futures to the size of the portfolio of long-dated "short" delivery contracts. The simplest approach is to use a unitary hedge ratio whereby gains/losses on the hedge contracts offsets exactly the losses/gains on the underlying oil position. Because hedging is aiming at the more ambitious goal of minimizing the variance in the value of the firm rather than the narrow sub-objective of eliminating gains or losses on a specific transaction, a "minimum variance hedge ratio" — sometimes referred as optimal hedge ratio — is preferred. A minimum variance hedge ratio can be shown to be equal to the covariance between the return on the portfolio to be hedged and the return on the hedge itself divided by the variance of the return on the hedge.*

---

does seem more likely at the end of the year. This seasonality may reflect the impact of seasonal demand pressures on near term deliveries.

It is worthy of note that while the percentage of backwardation observations in the period 1983–1992 was generally higher than in the period 1992–2002, both samples generate the same conclusions regarding seasonality of pricing relationships.

Quintessential Backwardation. Backwardation is important for both locking in a positive margin on actual oil delivery called for by the forward sales that MGRM had entered into (see Eq. (4)) as well as rolling over the stack of futures hedge (see Eq. (5)). Over an extended period and under conditions of uninterrupted backwardation, a rolling stack will generate rollover gains with a probability of 75% (see Table 1 for a taxonomy of all situations). Furthermore, the backwardation characteristics of these futures markets appear to be significant and enduring. Thus, any "stack and roll" futures hedging strategy would be expected to capture some of those rollover gains — which may explain MGRM management's strategy to expand the hedge from a *minimum variance to a one-to-one hedge ratio* (see Box E).

IF ONLY MGRM HAD BEEN ALLOWED TO ROLL
THE DICE[63]

In 1993, when MG came to be on the brink of bankruptcy it forced its US subsidiary to abort its grand marketing gambit. In this section we play the devil's advocate and ask the question: what would have happened had MGRM been allowed to follow through and execute on its marketing gambit? With the benefits of hindsight and actual prices we recreate as faithfully as possible the actual transactions called for by MGRM's marketing gambit.

---

[63]Evans, R. J. and L. L. Jacque. When a hedge is a gamble: An empirical investigation (1993–2002) of Metallgesellschaft's high stake debacle, in the *Financier*, vol. 11/12, 2004–2005.

Our simulation of MGRM's rolling futures stack and forward deliveries is based on the following assumptions:

(a) A 160 million barrel equivalent futures position (in actuality 55 million barrels in exchange-traded futures and 105 million barrels in over-the counter forwards) was established mid-March 1993 to match delivery obligations for the same volume of oil products (gasoline and heating oil).

(b) The cash cost of establishing the position was assumed to be the required margin deposit (assumed 50% of face value) for the 55 million barrels in futures contracts, as opposed to the nominal value of the entire derivatives position.

(c) The futures position was distributed proportionally to the limits that the New York Mercantile Exchange (NYMEX) had imposed on MGRM: 25 million barrels of crude oil (46%), 15 million barrels of heating oil (27%), and 15 million barrels of gasoline (27%) for the total of 55 million barrels.[64]

(d) The delivery price had been fixed at $3 above the spot price for heating oil and gasoline on the day the futures position was established.

(e) The simulation is run for the 10 year period 1993–2002 to match the delivery schedule that MGRM had put in place.

The Cash Flow Roller-Coaster 1993–2002. Cash flows from the hedged delivery structure are divided into two streams: gains and losses from the physical delivery obligations, resulting from the difference between futures-hedged purchase prices and fixed sale prices for delivery are shown in Figure 7. Monthly cash flows are shown separately (shaded grey) from cumulative cash-flows. Clearly — if left to its own device — MGRM would have profited handsomely from its marketing gambit in spite of losses in the period 1999–2001.

The second stream of gains or losses from rolling over the futures positions are shown in Figure 8. When oil prices declined sharply early on in mid-1993 and unexpectedly moved from backwardation into contango MG's Supervisory Board had to react on the presumption that MGRM's strategy was precipitating the firm into bankruptcy. The abrupt termination of MGRM's hedging program and hasty liquidation of deep-in- the money forward supply contracts was certainly questionable but must have been the toll that the syndicate of lenders-of-last-resort extracted from MG.

The fixed delivery prices were $26.88 per barrel (63.99 cents per gallon) for heating oil and $27.78 per barrel (66.14 cents per gallon) for gasoline. With an initial $3–$5 premium over initial spot prices included in the fixed delivery prices, deliveries were usually made for a gain (see Figure 8). Gains and losses experienced substantial

---

[64] Culp C. L. and M. H. Miller, Metallgesellschaft and the economics of synthetic storage. *Journal of Applied Corporate Finance*, 7(4) (Winter 1990), p. 64.

(1992–2002)

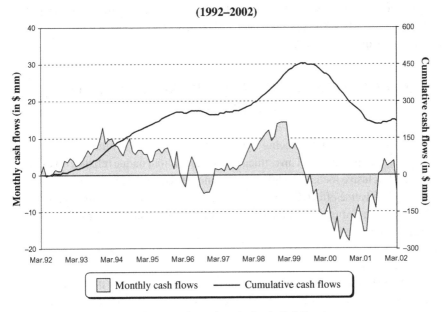

Figure 7   Cash flows from hedged oil deliveries.

(1993–2002)

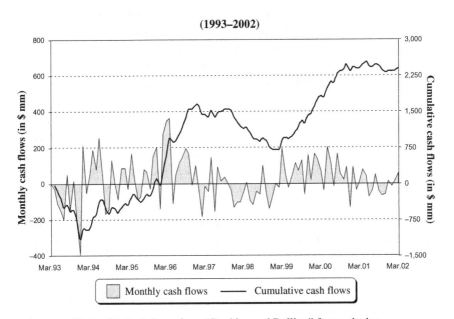

Figure 8   Cash flows from "Stacking and Rolling" futures hedge.

long-run variance, ranging from −$17.00 to $16.19 per barrel with a standard deviation (σ) of $8.24 in the 1993–2002 period, and from −$18.32 to $14.87 with $\sigma = \$7.72$ in the ten years from 1992–2002.

WHEN A HEDGE IS A GAMBLE: WAS MGRM HEDGING OR SPECULATING?

At its core, hedging is about reducing the volatility of the firm's value to insure an orderly funding of operating and investment activities without undue reliance on external financing. Exclusive focus of hedging on minimizing the variance of the firm's value may neglect the adverse effect that hedges with different maturities could have on the volatility and timing of cash-flows. However ingenious the "stack and roll" hedging might have been in terms of locking the net cost of long term delivery contracts it exacerbated the variability of the firm's initial cash-flows which may have proven worse than no hedge at all.

Of Perfect Hedge and Variance Minimizing Hedge Ratios. MGRM engaged in a *"one-for-one"* or "barrel for barrel" hedge whereby the entire amount of its "short" but longer-dated oil position was hedged through a near-term stack of futures. This, on the face of it, appears as the textbook definition of a "perfect hedge" if one disregards the fact that the maturity structure of the long and short positions were grossly mismatched. Hedging is however not about the complete elimination ("one-for-one" hedge) of price risk. Rather, it is about minimizing the variance of the hedging firm's value which typically results into a hedge ratio well below one (see Box E). Furthermore the maturity mismatch between long-dated forward delivery contract and near-term stack of futures called for a further downward adjustment in the hedge ratio — referred as "tailing" the hedge: quite simply the present value of gains/losses on a 10 year forward contract is considerably smaller that the present value of a 30–60 day futures contract. In other words, a "barrel-for-barrel" hedge was an overkill and highly speculative as it increased the firm's exposure to oil price risk. Various estimates[65] put the optimal hedge ratio between 0.50 and 0.75 for a 10-year monthly annuity of oil deliveries.

Not surprisingly, the speculative one-to-one hedge ratio coupled with the maturity mismatch between the very short term of the stack of futures and the long term delivery contracts staggered over a 10-year period significantly increased the variance of

---

[65] Edwards, F. R. and M. S. Canter. The collapse of Metallgesellschaft: Unheadgeable risks, poor hedging strategy, or just bad luck, in *The Journal of Futures Markets*, 15(3), 211–264 (1995); Pirrong, S. C. Metallgesellschaft: A prudent hedger ruined, or a wildcatter on Nynex, in *The Journal of Futures Markets*, 17(5), 543–578 (1997).

cash-flows which in turn exposed MGRM to funding and liquidity risk. The stack of near-term futures was bound to exacerbate the volatility of MGRM cash flows which was going to be slowly compensated by the staggered physical delivery of petroleum products.

More generally, it is very revealing to read in a MGRM business plan that hedging was construed as an adjunct to generating abnormal profits[66]:

> As is well documented in standard textbooks, a hedge is said to be perfect when the gain (or loss) in the cash market is totally offset by the loss (or gain) in the futures market. However, it is important to recognize that if a hedge program is carefully designed to "lock in" a favorable basis between spot and futures prices at the most advantageous time, **hedging can generate profits which can substantially enhance the operating margin.** Our proposed risk management program not only protects the plump profit margins with a minimum amount of risk from the spot market, **but also offers us an opportunity for extraordinary upside profit with no additional risk.**

It seems that MGRM designed its hedge with a view to generating abnormal profits (see emphasis added in above quote) while hedging was meant to take a back seat — hardly the mindset of a firm intent on minimizing exposure to oil price risk. How could MGRM honestly believe that rolling over a stack of near futures could be at once a good speculative investment and a good hedge? As one observer notes[67]:

> As MGRM added to its stack of near-month futures it was not trying to decrease its risk it was trying to multiply its bet on backwardation.

Assuming that the "stack and roll" hedging strategy had, on the surface, profitably eliminated price risk by creating a synthetic forward contract it had, in fact, created at least two additional kinds of risks, namely rollover cash-flow risk and funding/liquidity risk should rollover cash flow losses become occasionally very large.

MGRM AS A MARKET MAKER?

The potential impact of MGRM's mammoth positions in the oil futures market remains ambiguous. This simulation has assumed that oil prices and the term structure of futures prices are exogenous factors, uninfluenced by the market activities of MGRM. This

---

[66] Cited in Mello, Anthony S. and J. E. Parsons. Maturity structure of a hedge matters; lessons from the Metallgesellschaft debacle, *Journal of Applied Corporate Finance*, p. 115 (Spring 1995), p. 115.

[67] Mello, op. cit. p. 117.

may not necessarily have been the case, however. Edwards and Canter (1995) argue that
MGRM's position represented *only* 20% of open-interest — but where they suggest that
a position representing 20% of open interest is not enough to have a market-making
impact, others would suggest that in fact the oil futures market entered a contango
phase in 1993 in part *because* MGRM opened its enormous positions. Indeed, as soon
as MGRM closed its positions the oil futures market swung back to backwardation.
Worth noting is that while an average day of trading in the oil futures pit will generate
a volume of 15,000–30,000 futures contracts, MGRM was rolling over up to 55,000
contracts a month. Edwards & Canter (1995) are perhaps being overly sanguine when
suggesting that counterparties could not exert any pricing leverage over MGRM, or
that MGRM bid up the price of second-month futures every time it tried to roll over
its futures stack.

Nevertheless, contango markets are more likely to occur when spot prices are
falling,[68] which was precisely the case in the second half of 1993. Without being able
to control for the effect of falling prices on the shift in the basis, it is impossible to
determine to what degree MGRM's financial strategy may have actually contributed
to its own undoing through adverse market-making effects.

THE MORAL OF THE STORY

Lesson 1: History Does not Necessarily Repeat Itself. Beware of linear extrapolation.
Much of this daring scheme was predicated on extrapolating into the future past trends
characterized by an oil futures market consistently in backwardation. Humans have
a tendency to project into the future what they have experienced in the past — at
their own peril. Evidence from other speculative markets such as soybeans and copper
which had exhibited backwardation in their futures market for longer periods than
the oil market indicated that this relationship can be abruptly discontinued i.e. futures
market may revert to contango.[69]

Lesson 2: Do Not Ignore Worst-Case Scenarios. It is ironic that the pseudo-
hedge designed by MGRM and amounting to a notional value in excess of $3 billion
(twice the equity value of its parent MG) would not trigger a careful review of what
would happen under the most adverse scenario. More specifically, MG's supervisory

---

[68] The percentage change in spot price from month $t-1$ to t shares the same sign as the basis
60% of the time, a result with a confidence interval of greater than 95%.

[69] Statistical evidence is provided for the soybeans and copper market by Edwards, F. R. and
M. S. Canter. The collapse of Metallgesellschaft: Unhedgeable risks, poor hedging strategy, or
just bad luck, *Journal of Applied Corporate Finance*, (Spring 1995) pp. 95–97.

board should have raised two related questions: "how much could MG lose? and 'how much was MG likely to lose?" Neither question are necessarily easy to answer. The first question is typically addressed with the help of stress-testing and multiple scenario analysis while the second is gauged by the more sophisticated Value-at-Risk metric.

Stress-testing and multiple scenario analysis are simple methodologies for probing a doomsday scenario also known as "Black Swans" or "outlier" events. Stress-testing emphasizes one non-controllable variable which, by necessity, would have to be the spot price of oil. Multiple scenario analysis allows to schematize states of the world built on two or more key non-controllable variables. The combination of whether the futures market is in contango or in backwardation and whether the spot oil price is increasing or decreasing would be a powerful combination. Table 1 provides an exhaustive taxonomy of such bi-dimensional scenarios. For each scenario it is possible to design a worst case sub-scenario based on monthly oil prices corresponding to worst roll-over losses over the last 10 years. Unfortunately for MG, not much attention was given to probing worst-case scenarios or conservative stress-testing of the hedging scheme. When oil prices declined sharply early on and unexpectedly moved into contango MG's Supervisory Board had to react on the presumption that MGRM's strategy was precipitating the firm into bankruptcy. Judging from its awkwardness in dealing with MG's Chairman, the supervisory board had no understanding of the intricate speculation that MGRM had wrapped under the guise of a conservative hedging policy.

Lesson 3: Failure of Governance. Board of Directors are not expected to get involved in day-to-day management of the firm. However they are supposed to set clear strategic objectives and risk tolerance guidelines for the firm within which policies will be formulated. Senior management must also insure that such policies be woven into the fabric of the firm's daily operations. MG's Board of Directors should have been kept appraised and intimately involved with such a strategic shift that its subsidiary was undertaking. When one recalls that MG had faced a long term liquidity crisis of its own, starting as early as 1988, which had required a net debt increase of DM4.4 billions and three equity issues of DM1.21 billions, it is only fair to surmise that MG's level of risk aversion should have been high. The increased level of risk taking by MGRM was ill-measured both in absolute terms and in relation to MG's overall risk profile. Poor communications between the impulsive "child" and the cautious "parent" were compounded by the lack of financial engineering expertise at the board level which meant that the hard questions were never asked of MGRM. The abrupt termination of MGRM's hedging program and hasty liquidation of deep-in- the money forward supply contracts was certainly questionable but such must have been the price that the lenders-of-last-resort syndicate extracted from MG.

Bibliography

Culp, C. L. and M. H. Miller. Metallgesellschaft and the economics of synthetic storage. *Journal of Applied Corporate Finance*, **7**(4), 62–76 (Winter 1995).

Culp, C. L. and M. H. Miller. Hedging in the theory of corporate finance: A reply to our critics. *Journal of Applied Corporate Finance*, **8**(1), 121–127 (Spring 1995).

Edwards, F. R. and M. S. Canter. The collapse of Metallgesellschaft: Unhedgeable risks, poor hedging strategy, or just bad luck? *The Journal of Futures Markets*, John Wiley & Sons (New York, NY), **15**(3), 211–264 (May 1995).

Evans, R. J. and L. L. Jacque, When a hedge is a gamble: An empirical investigation (1993–2002) of Metallgesellschaft's high stake debacle in the *Financier*, 11/12, 2004–2005.

Hilliard, J. E. Analytics underlying the Metallgesellschaft hedge: Short-term futures in a multi-period environment. *Review of Quantitative Finance and Accounting*, **12**(3), 195–219 (1999).

Marthinsen, J. *Risk Takers: Uses and Abuses of Financial Derivatives* (Pearson Addison-Wesley, 2005).

Mello, A. S and J. E. Parsons. Maturity structure of a hedge matters: Lessons from the Metallgesellschaft debacle. *Journal of Applied Corporate Finance*, **8**(1), 106–120 (Spring 1995).

Pirrong, S. C. Metallgesellschaft: A prudent hedger ruined, or a wildcatter on NYMEX? *The Journal of Futures Markets*, John Wiley & Sons (New York, NY), **17**(5), 543–578 (August 1997).

Questions for Discussion

1. Compare the theory of Interest Rate Parity with "cost-of-carry" valuation formula.
2. Why should futures commodity markets expected to be in contango?
3. What was the nature of risk(s) faced by MGRM and had it planned to manage it?
4. What were the key assumptions necessary to ensure that the "stack-and-roll" hedging strategy devised by MGRM be successful?
5. Was MGRM speculating or hedging?

SUMITOMO*

At fault may be a culture that lavishly rewards traders who takes risk but not the people who are supposed to supervise them.

David Hale

On June 13, 1996 Sumitomo reported a staggering loss of $2.6 billion due to copper trading activities on the London Metals Exchange. Sumitomo — one of the largest and oldest Japanese trading companies — laid the blame unambiguously on its former chief copper trader Hamanaka Yasuo: *"These transactions were made solely by Yasuo Hamanaka himself. Hamanaka abused Sumitomo's name, and continued on with such unauthorized trading."*[70] The losses had apparently accumulated over a period of several years and one wonders how the cash-flow trail of trading losses could go undetected for so long: was Hamanaka truly acting alone? Or was Sumitomo engaged in a grand scheme of copper price manipulations and using Hamanaka as a scapegoat when found out?

The venerable House of Sumitomo traces its origins to the late 16th century when its founder Sumitomo Masatomo learned silver and copper smelting techniques from western traders. A century later the firm had expanded into banking and money-changing when it discovered the Beshi copper mine. Four centuries later Sumitomo Corporation was still deeply involved in the copper business (now trading rather than mining) with a star trader who had established the firm as the dominant global copper trader. Copper indeed accounted for one third of Sumitomo's turnover and somewhat less of its profits. Sumitomo was rumored to be twice as large as the next copper trader

---

[70] In the words of Tomiichi Akiyama — President of Sumitomo.

Box A. The London Metal Exchange (LME). *The LME dominates global trade in industrial metals (copper, tin, zinc, lead, nickel, and aluminum). In copper alone the LME was seven times bigger than the largest US futures market trading in copper — the COMEX known today as NYMEX. The LME was established in 1876 at a time when "Britannia ruled the waves" and London was truly the hub of international commerce and finance. Its primary function was originally to allow metal mining and trading firms to hedge the price risk of their cargo through forward contracts. Because physical delivery occurs on forward contract maturity the LME is both a cash and forward market unlike US commodity futures where physical delivery almost never takes place. For that reason the LME trades mostly 90-day forward contracts and any contract up to 90 days with specific delivery dates rather than specific contract months as it is the case for futures contracts US style. Only spot/cash and 90-day forward contract price are reported daily even though there are up to 60 delivery dates outstanding at any point in times. Margin requirements are similar to those found in US futures market but are enforced less stringently.*

The relationship between cash and forward prices follows the cost of carry formula (forward price = spot price + cost of carry due to warehousing, insurance and financing) when demand is slack (market is in contango-forward price above spot) but is in backwardation when supply is tight (forward price below spot).

---

and its star trader had won the nickname of "Mr. five percent" for allegedly controlling five percent of worldwide copper trading. The star trader had a name — Hamanaka Yasuo — dubbed "The Hammer" as a play on his name and his ability to hammer the market. Hamanaka had joined the firm in 1970, was assigned to the non ferrous metal division in 1975 and shortly thereafter was sent to the London Metal Exchange (LME) to learn the ropes of the trade (see Box A). Back in Tokyo, Hamanaka managed to stay in the same nonferrous metals division — never assigned to any rotation in other departments of the firm as it is the norm in large tentacular Japanese corporations: by 1983, Hamanaka was trading 10,000 metric tons of copper a month.

WAS SUMITOMO MANIPULATING COPPER PRICES?

Price manipulation is generally defined as *"the elimination of price competition in a market for cash commodities and/or futures contracts through the domination of supply or demand, and the exercise of that domination to intentionally produce artificially high or low prices."*[71] Such price manipulations can be primarily effected through the physical commodity market to create an artificial shortage usually in conjunction with

---

[71] Johnson, P. M. Commodity market manipulation, *Washington and Lee Law Review*, 38, 1981, p. 730.

futures market positions and is then known as "cornering" the market. If the price manipulation is limited to building up positions in futures and forwards it is referred as a "squeeze."

A simple example illustrates how combining a corner with a squeeze can benefit the manipulator. Assume that the 90 day forward copper price is $1,850 per metric ton (mt): by cornering the physical/cash market through steady purchases of physical copper our manipulator will drive the spot price of copper artificially higher to $2,000/mt thereby insuring that upon delivery it will net a profit of

$$\$2,000/\text{mt (cash sale)} - \$1,850/\text{mt (forward purchase)} = \$150/\text{mt}.$$

Apparently Sumitomo was doing both — accumulating sizeable amount of physical copper (corner) and being long copper forwards (squeeze): there is evidence that the steadily rising price of both spot and forward copper over the period 1993–1995 was Sumitomo's doing. Of course when copper prices finally collapsed in the spring of 1996 Sumitomo lost on both counts. As the Financial Times reported as early as August 3, 1993

> *"Mr. Yasuo Hamanaka, the senior manager responsible for Sumitomo Corporation's copper trading operations, has been described by many London Metal Exchange traders as the single most powerful man in the copper market. So it is not*

Box B. Silver Price Manipulations and the Demise of the Hunt Brothers.[72]
The manipulation of silver prices in 1979–1980 remains the greatest heist of all times perpetrated against a futures market. At one point the three Hunt brothers (billionaires in their own right) and their co-conspirators (Saudi speculators) controlled a silver stockpile worth $14 billion which drove the price of an ounce of silver from $5 (January 1979) to a all-time high of $50 (January 21, 1980) before it collapsed. The conspiracy proceeded on both the cash front (corner) — where the Hunt brothers amassed considerable amount of physical silver which was kept off the market — and the futures front (squeeze) where they accumulated gargantuan positions. By requiring physical delivery of futures contracts as they came due they were able to extract huge profits from the unsuspecting contract holders obligated to deliver physical silver now scarce and therefore very expensive. When finally the regulators (CFTC and futures exchanges) decided to burst the speculative bubble they forced liquidation-only trading whereby futures traders could no longer establish new positions and were restricted to closing existing positions. Futures prices collapsed as margins requirement were increased: on March 19, the Hunt brothers defaulted on their margin calls and would be forced several years later to declare bankruptcy.

---

[72] Kolb, R. W. and J. A. Overdahl. *Futures, Options and Swaps* (Blackwell, 5th edn, 2007), pp. 61–63.

surprising that his name has been mentioned most frequently in discussions about the 'squeeze' threatening to create turmoil on the LME market in September and October 1993. One trader said yesterday that Sumitomo had reached a position where if it were October today, it would control all the LME stocks." There has been other widespread suggestions that the copper market is being manipulated to boost the price even though stocks in LME warehouses are at a 15-year peak."

Similarly rumors of hoarding physical copper by Sumitomo confirmed the "corner" leg of its price manipulation — specifically it was reported in 1993 that most of the 39,000 mt of copper warehoused at Long Beach (California) had been sold to Sumitomo which would have amounted to no less than 20% of the entire worldwide copper stockpile held in LME warehouses! Empirical evidence of copper price manipulation for the period 1991–1996 is provided by Gilbert who concluded that

"Hamanaka succeeded for a considerable time but only at the price of increasing his physical position and thereby making his activities obvious to the regulators. It was pressure from these sources which resulted in his removal from trading, allowing successful speculative attacks in June 1996."[73]

ALARM BELLS

Was Hamanaka manipulating the copper market single-handedly? Were Sumitomo senior managers simply looking the other way as long as copper price manipulations seemed to deliver steady profits? Two early warning signals seem to indicate that Sumitomo was indeed complicit. As early as 1991, a London metal broker — David Threlkeld — received an usual request from Hamanaka: would they issue a back-dated invoice in the amount of $350 million for copper trades which never took place. Instead of obliging his client Threlkeld formally complained with the LME which in turn sought clarification from Sumitomo. Whatever investigation was initiated by Sumitomo it failed to uncover any wrongdoing by Hamanaka and the matter was dismissed on the grounds that the request for an invoice had been motivated by tax filing reasons. In 1993, plummeting copper prices sent Hamanaka's copper trading losses soaring. To cover part of the cash-flow drain, Hamanaka borrowed $100 million from ING Bank by forging the signature of his senior managers: again Sumitomo became aware of the fraud, initiated an internal audit but failed to take any action.

---

[73] Gilbert, C. L. *Manipulations of Metals Futures: Lessons from Sumitomo* (working paper: University of London, 1996).

DEBACLE

After repeated inquiries by the Commodities Futures Trading Commission and the Securities and Investment Board about abnormal copper trading activities Sumitomo finally relieved Hamanaka from his trading duties: hedge funds which had correctly read into Sumitomo's copper price manipulations saw in Hamanaka's "promotion" an opportunity to finally unleash speculative attacks on Sumitomo's large physical and futures holdings: from May to June 1996 copper prices dropped from $2,700 to $2,000 in about four weeks.

POSTSCRIPT

In June 1996 Hamanaka confessed to his fraudulent activities. In March 1997 a Tokyo court found him guilty on four counts of forgery and fraud and condemned him to eight years in jail. Sumitomo for its part paid a fine of $150 million to the United States' Commodities Futures Trading Commission and $8 million to the United Kingdom's Securities and Investments Board[74] to settle charges of copper price manipulations. In 1999 unrepentant Sumitomo filed suit against Merrill Lynch, UBS, Credit Lyonnais Rouse and Morgan Stanley for compensatory damages in an amount exceeding $2 billion for aiding and abetting its rogue trader: the outcome of these legal actions remains undisclosed to the public.

---

[74] Both agencies regulate commodities and financial markets in the United States and the United Kingdom, respectively.

Part III

OPTIONS

ALLIED LYONS

It is part of wise men to preserve themselves today for tomorrow, and risk all in one day.

Cervantes

Allied-Lyons — better known for its teabags and its teacakes than for its forays into the currency market — announced on March 17, 1991 a stunning $269 million foreign exchange loss (approximately 20% of its projected profits for 1991). Facing a sluggish economy, its treasury department had developed a sophisticated scheme that gambled not so much on the *absolute* level of the dollar/sterling exchange rate as on its *volatility*. This gamble was achieved through a combination of currency options known as *straddles* and *strangles* that in this particular case would have produced profits had the exchange rate turned out to be less volatile than the option premium implied.

This ingenious scheme was elaborated at the beginning of the 1990–1991 Gulf War when the relatively high price of options (due to heavy buying from hedgers and uncertainty about the duration of the war) convinced Allied-Lyons that it was propitious to place an attractive short-term bet that dollar-sterling exchange rate volatility would subside as soon as hostilities started. However, when the Allies launched their air offensive against Iraq, the initial uncertainty as to the outcome of the war did not reduce exchange rate volatility — at least not soon enough for Allied-Lyons to see its speculative gambit succeed. Indeed, it took another month for the ground offensive to appease the foreign exchange market by which time it was already too late for Allied Lyons: it had been forced by its bankers to liquidate its option positions at a great loss.

As *The Economist* recalls humorously, Allied Lyons' love affair with foreign exchange is neither a new one nor is it a fortunate one[75]:

> *Once upon a time there was a fuddy-duddy British company call J. Lyons. It ran teashops and made cakes to sell in them. It also made money. Then the latest scions of its two ruling families got ambitious. Lyons rushed out to buy business abroad, borrowing in strong currencies to do it. In 1978, tripped up by its foreign-currency errors, Lyons dropped its teacakes all over the floor.*
>
> *In rushed a friendly helper — Allied Breweries — to pick them up, and soon a new Allied-Lyons was doing nicely, still selling fuddy-duddy things like buns and beer. Then came the go-go 1980s, and Allied expanded, not least into up-market spirits like Canadian Club whisky, part of the Hiram Walker group which it bought in 1986: less fuddy-duddy, but still good, familiar business.*
>
> *In with Hiram Walker, though, came its chief executive, Clifford Hatch, who became Allied's finance director. No fuddy-duddy he Mr. Hatch's financial whizzos knew more exciting things to sell: the dollar, short, for example.*
>
> *Alas for Mr. Hatch, the dollar has been climbing like a rocket these past few weeks, and those who were caught short of it have been feeling like some earthling strapped to the stick. On Tuesday Allied-Lyons announced that £150 m ($269 m) had gone up in forex-dealing smoke, and that Mr. Hatch — a vigorous critic of City short-termism, curiously — would be going with it.*

How could the treasury department of a respectable company such as Allied-Lyons embark on a speculative gambit involving complex financial engineering without the blessing of its board of directors? Had the Treasury Department become a profit center? What was its true mission?

A NEW MISSION FOR ALLIED LYONS TREASURY DEPARTMENT

A large multinational food and drink conglomerate such as Allied Lyons exposes itself through its worldwide manufacturing and distribution activities to foreign exchange *transaction and translation* risk. *Transaction exposure* results primarily from exports sales or imports purchases on credit that Allied Lyons consummates with foreign parties. For example, a shipment of 100,000 bottles of Canadian Club Whisky to Japan would create a 90-day 500 million yen-denominated account receivable which Allied Lyons may decide to hedge should it be concerned by the possibility of the yen depreciating between the time of shipment (when the receivable is booked) and actual payment time — 90 days later.

---

[75] *The Economist*, Oops, again (March 23, 1991, p. 90).

Furthermore, multinational corporations such as Allied Lyons are required to report to their shareholders on a quarterly basis their worldwide performance from both the parent firm and their foreign operations in the form of simple statistics — consolidated earnings and the much awaited and studied earning-per-share. *Translation exposure* arises from the practice of periodically consolidating (aggregating) parent's and affiliates' balance sheets and income statements. Unfortunately for the firm's controller — the individual in charge of this task — foreign subsidiaries prepare their results in the currency of the country in which they operate — for example Yen for a Japanese subsidiary, different from the parent's currency such as the pound sterling for a United Kingdom-domiciled multinational corporation. It means that their results will have to be converted/translated from the foreign currency into the parent company's currency — typically the currency in which the firm's stock is listed and traded. Because exchange rates may have changed since the last translation, the multinational corporation's net worth may increase or decrease: this risk is rooted in the translation exposure resulting from foreign affiliates' ongoing operations. With major operations in the United States, the dollar figured prominently on Allied Lyons portfolio of both transaction and translation currency exposures.

Allied Lyons' treasury department would — in the normal course of business — be charged with hedging the company's stream of foreign currency revenues/costs such as receivables, payables or dividends (transaction exposure) as well as the value of foreign subsidiaries' net worth (translation exposure) against foreign exchange surprises. With "long or short" positions in several foreign currencies such as US dollar, Japanese yen, German mark, Korean won, French franc … Allied Lyons would sell/buy forward[76] the foreign currency at risk thus locking in their pound value. Currency options — for a fee known as the "option premium" — would also allow Allied-Lyons to hedge against downside risk while appropriating the profits from foreign currency potential appreciation (see Box A).

In the mid 1980s, Allied Lyons acquired Hiram Walker's spirit business whose heir, Chairman and CEO Clifford Hatch, became one of Allied Lyons' directors and, in 1987, its finance director. Hatch, born into wealth and used to authority and autonomy, moved promptly to re-organize the finance department asserting its independence from Sir Derrick Holden-Brown, Allied Lyons' autocratic and paternalistic Chairman. His treasury team was now five men strong and led by newly appointed Mike Bartlett — a former Eurobond trader with Credit Suisse First Boston. Confident enough of his trading savvy to audaciously navigate the high seas of the turbulent foreign exchange market, Bartlett went on record in November 1989 in an article published in the Treasurer:

---

[76] Hedging with forward contracts is widely discussed in Part I of this book and the reader is referred to chapters on Showa Shell and Citibank for specifics.

Box A: Currency Option Contracts. *A currency option gives the buyer the right (without the obligation) to buy (call contract) or to sell (put contract) a specified amount of foreign currency at an agreed price (strike or exercise price) for exercise on (European option) or on/before (American Option) the expiration date. For such a right, the option buyer/holder pays to the option seller/writer a cash premium at the inception of the contract. A European option whose exercise price is the forward rate is said to be at-the-money; if it is profitable to exercise the option immediately (disregarding the cash premium), the option is said to be in-the-money; and conversely, if it is not profitable to exercise the option immediately, the option is said to be out-of-the-money. As expected, "in-the-money" options command a higher premium than "out-of-the-money" options for the simple reason that — if exercised immediately — they would yield a cash profit. When held to maturity, the option will be exercised if it expires "in-the-money" and abandoned if it expires "out-of-the-money." Currency options can be negotiated over-the-counter with features (face value, strike price, and maturity) tailor-made to the special needs of the buyer, who is responsible for evaluating the counterparty risk (that is, the likelihood of the option writer delivering if the option is exercised at maturity). Of practical interest is the trade-off between strike price and premium: the further "in-the-money" the strike price is, the more expensive (i.e., the higher premium) the option becomes and conversely. Standardized option contracts available from organized exchanges such as the Philadelphia Exchange Market are practically devoid of counterparty risk, since the appropriately capitalized Exchange Market stands as the contract's guarantor of last resort; however, the option buyer is limited to a relatively small set — in terms of currency and delivery dates — of ready-made products directly available "off the shelf".*

"We wanted to hedge a long sterling position in a trendless market. We thought of buying sterling puts, but volatility was at an all time high so instead we sold sterling calls ...." As we will discover in the next section *writing/selling* — rather than *buying* — options is inherently speculative. The cautious task of hedging against currency risk had surreptitiously morphed into taking more daring bets on exchange rates. Interestingly, Allied Lyons reported £3 million in foreign exchange profits for the year closing in March 1988, £5 million for 1989 and £9 million by 1990 which, as Euromoney notes, compares favorably with giant oil company British Petroleum's £23 million in foreign exchange profits for the same period.[77] De facto Allied Lyons's treasury had become a profit center. Bartlett reported to Hatch — the Finance director — who reported to the Board of Directors. Had the new vocation of the treasury department been truly blessed by the Finance department and the company board of directors?

---

[77] Brady, S. Allied-Lyons deadly game, *Euromoney* (April 1991).

A PRIMER ON CURRENCY OPTIONS: WAS ALLIED LYONS HEDGING OR SPECULATING?

To make sense out of hedging or speculation with currency options, the reader needs to be introduced to the basics. As early as June 1989 Bartlett was hedging a long sterling position with put options. The risk faced by Allied Lyons was a pound depreciation (dollar appreciation) which would reduce the dollar value of its pound long position.[78] The natural way for Bartlett to hedge Allied Lyons long pound position with currency options would have been to buy a put on sterling: it marries the benefits of protection against a depreciating pound by allowing the hedger to sell pounds at the strike price which establishes a floor value for the position. Should the pound appreciate rather than depreciate the hedger would simply abandon the option and sell the pounds on the spot market at the higher rate. This flexibility comes at a cost — the so called option premium. Instead Bartlett was writing call options on the pound sterling: was this still hedging or true speculation? To answer this question with some degree of precision, let us review the mechanics of buying and writing put and call options for hedging or speculation purposes.

Hedging with Put Options. Consider the purchase on September 1, 1989 of a 90-day European sterling put option maturing on November 30, 1989, with strike price $E(90) = \$1.48$ and premium $p(0) = \$0.02$. The holder of such a sterling contract has the option (the right without the obligation) of selling sterling on November 30 at the strike price of 1.48 if the spot rate on November 30 denoted as $S(90)$ makes it advantageous to do so. Specifically, if the spot exchange rate turns out to be higher than 1.48 on November 30, the option holder would rather sell sterling on the spot market and simply abandon his put option with a total loss no larger than the *future* value of the premium paid on September 1, 1989. This is shown in Figure 1 as the horizontal portion to the right of point A on line (1) which sketches the terminal profit/loss (vertical axis) of the put option as a function of the spot exchange rate prevailing 90 days hence, $S(90)$, and measured on the horizontal axis.

For an exchange rate less than 1.48, the option holder will exercise his put option so as to profit from the difference between the spot rate and the exercise price. His cash profit equals the difference between the spot purchase price of one pound at less than 1.48 and the sale price at 1.48 (exercise price) and is portrayed by the 45 degree line starting at A. At first, the cash profit simply recoups the cost of the option premium. Perhaps most importantly, at no point is the buyer of the put option exposed to losing

---

[78] Buying a put on pound sterling is the same thing as buying a dollar call option which Allied Lyons would do to hedge a dollar short position perhaps due to dollar denominated payables. The discussion follows the same approach as taken by Bartlett.

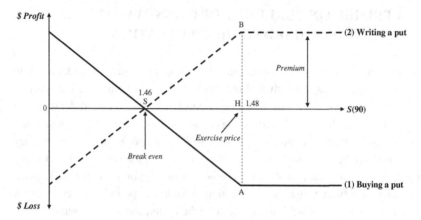

Figure 1   Buying and writing put options.

more than the upfront cash premium. Thus the payoff to the option holder can be summarized as follows:

for $S(90) \geq E(90)$:   Payoff $= -p(0) \cdot (1 + i_{US}) = -\$0.02(1 + .06/4) = -\$0.02$

for $S(90) < E(90)$:   Payoff $= [E(90) - p(0) \cdot (1 + i_{US})] - S(90)$

$$\text{Payoff} = 1.48 - 0.02 - S(90) = 1.46 - S(90)$$

where $i_{US} = 0.06/4$ is the opportunity cost[79] to the option buyer of tying up the premium for the life of the option. The intersection point $S(90)^*$ (break-even) at which the option holder is starting to make a profit in excess of the upfront premium can be readily found by setting the payoff equal to zero:

$$S(90)^* - [E(90) - p(0) \cdot (1 + i_{US})] = 0$$

$$S(90)^* = 1.48 - 0.02 \cdot (1 + (0.06/4)) = 1.46.$$

Thus the break-even spot rate is simply the strike price minus the future value (that is adjusted for the cost of money) of the option premium.

Consider now that Allied-Lyons is long sterling and wishes to hedge with a currency option: a put option will allow the hedger to protect his long sterling position at the minimum strike price rate (minus the future value of option premium) while allowing Allied Lyons to partake in the upside potential due to the possible appreciation of the pound. Figure 2 shows how to aggregate the naked long sterling position (line 1) with the put option (line 2) to yield the hedged profile shown on line 3.

---

[79] An annual interest rate of 6% becomes a quarterly rate (90 days) 6% × 90/360 = 1.5% or 0.015.

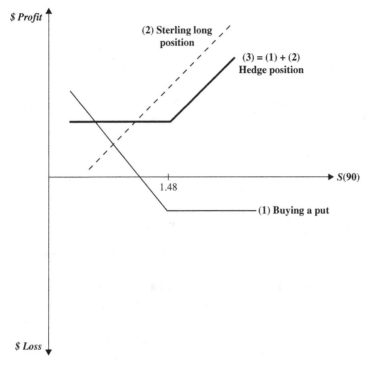

Figure 2   Hedging with put options.

Writer of a Put Option. For every purchase of a put option the buyer has to find a seller willing to write the option. For a cash premium $p(0)$ collected upfront the writer of a put option commits to buying pounds at the strike price $E(90) = 1.48$. Should the pound appreciate beyond the strike price the buyer of the put option will abandon the option and the put option writer will keep the option premium. If the spot price $S(90)$ at maturity of the option were to depreciate below 1.48 the option buyer will exercise his option forcing the option writer to buy spot pound at the exercise price of 1.48. The option writer will incur a cash loss of $1.48 - S(90)$. As the spot price depreciates further and further away from the exercise price his losses will deepen. His payoff (the dotted line (2) in Figure 1) is symmetrical to the option buyer's payoff since, combined, they have a zero-sum gain (disregarding transaction costs). In other words, what the option holder loses, the option writer keeps (option premium for $S(90) \geq 1.48$ shown as AH = BH) in Figure 1, and what the option holder gains, the option writer loses (for $S(90) < 1.48$). The reader will also note that the option writer faces *unlimited* losses when the option is exercised, whereas his gains are limited to the option premium. In Figure 1, the reader will note that the option premium (shown as the distance of the horizontal portion of the put option profile to the origin along the abscissa, AH or

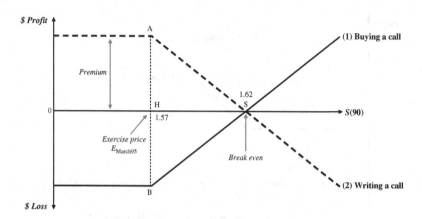

Figure 3   Buying and writing call options.

BH), is equal to the distance HS between the exercise price and the break-even rate (disregarding interest costs).

Hedging with Call Options. Consider the purchase on June 1, 1989, of a 90-day sterling call option with exercise price $E(90) = 1.57$ per pound and premium $p(0) =$ $0.05. The holder of such call option has the right to purchase sterling on August 31 at the strike price of 1.57 if it is advantageous to do so. Specifically, if the spot exchange rate turns out to be less than 1.57 on August 31, the option holder would rather purchase sterling on the spot market if he were indeed in need of sterling or else simply abandon his call option with a total loss no larger than the *future* value of the premium paid 90 days earlier. In Figure 3 the reader can see the horizontal portion to the left of point B on line (1) which sketches the terminal profit/loss (vertical axis) of the call option as a function of $S(90)$ measured on the horizontal axis. For an exchange rate in excess of 1.57, the option holder will exercise his call option so as to profit from the difference between the spot rate and the strike price. His cash profit equals the difference between the current sale price of one pound on the spot market at a rate higher than 1.57 and the exercise price at 1.57 (exercise of call option) and is portrayed by the 45 degree line starting at A. At first, the cash profit simply recoups the cost of the option premium. Perhaps most importantly at no point is the buyer of the call option exposed to losing more than the upfront cash premium. Thus the payoff to the option holder can be summarized as follows:

for $S(90) \leq E(90)$: Payoff $= -p(0) \cdot (1 + i_{US}) = -0.05(1 + 0.06/4) = -0.05$

for $S(90) > E(90)$: Payoff $= S(90) - [E(90) + p(0) \cdot (1 + i_{US})]$

$\qquad\qquad\qquad$ Payoff $= S(90) - (1.57 + 0.05) = S(90) - 1.62$

where the quarterly interest rate $i_{US} = 0.06/4$ is the opportunity cost to the option buyer of tying up the premium for 90 days (the life of the option). The intersection point

$S(90)^*$ (break-even) at which the option holder is starting to make a profit in excess of the upfront premium can be readily found by setting the payoff equal to zero:

$$S(90)^* - [E(90) + p(0) \cdot (1 + i_{US})] = 0$$

$$S(90)^* = 1.57 + 0.05 \cdot (1 + (0.06/4)) \simeq 1.62.$$

In Figure 3, the reader will note that the option premium (shown as the distance of the horizontal portion of the call option profile to the origin along the abscissa, AH or BH) is equal to the distance HS between the exercise price and the break-even rate (disregarding interest costs).

Writer of a Call Option. For a cash premium $p(0)$ collected upfront the writer of the call option commits to delivering pounds at the strike price $E(90) = 1.57$. Should the pound depreciate below the strike price the buyer of the call option will abandon the option and the call option writer will keep the option premium. If the spot price $S(90)$ at maturity of the option were to appreciate beyond 1.57 the option buyer will exercise his option forcing the option writer to deliver spot pound at the exercise price of 1.57. The option writer will incur a cash loss of $1.57 - S(90)$. As the spot price appreciates further and further away from the exercise price his losses will deepen. His payoff (the dotted line (2) in Figure 3 starting at A) is symmetrical to the option buyer's payoff since, combined, they have a zero-sum gain (disregarding transaction costs). In other words, what the option holder loses, the option writer keeps (option premium for $S(90) < 1.57$ shown as AH = BH) in Figure 3, and what the option holder gains, the option writer loses (for $S(90) > 1.57$). The reader will also note that the option writer faces *unlimited* losses when the option is exercised, whereas his gains are limited to the option premium shown as the distance of the horizontal portion of the call option profile to the origin along the abscissa, AH or BH and equal to the distance HS between the exercise price and the break-even rate (disregarding interest costs).

From Buying Puts to Writing Calls. The reader will recall that Bartlett had publicly announced his game-plan — no secret here! "... *We thought of buying sterling puts, but volatility was at an all time high so instead we sold sterling calls....*" We just explained how buying a put option to cover a sterling long position is a perfectly legitimate hedging policy. Is selling or writing sterling call options a clear-cut speculative move? Given the existence of the long sterling position writing a call option on sterling is known as writing a *covered* call. Let's see how the two positions stack up.

By writing *naked* (uncovered) call options on sterling, Bartlett clearly speculated since he accepted an up-front payment (premium) in exchange for an unlimited loss if sterling were to appreciate against the dollar. (See line (1) in Figure 4.) However it would stand to reason that if the *call option writer* were to hold an asset position in sterling (line (2)), he would have effectively covered his selling a naked call option — hence the reference to writing a *covered call* option. In fact, this is misleading, since a covered call option is nothing more than writing a *naked put* option on sterling as illustrated in Figure 4 by line (3) which is constructed as the graphical sum of lines (1)

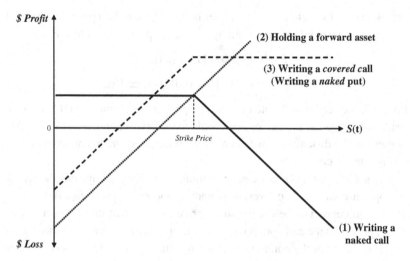

Figure 4   Writing a covered call option.

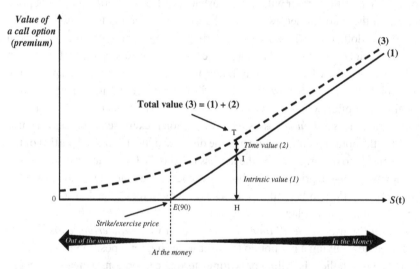

Figure 5   Value of a sterling call option prior of maturity.

and (2). Under the pretense of writing a covered call option to hedge a sterling long position Bartlett was indeed speculating.

The reader may be intrigued by Bartlett's reference to the high volatility of the dollar-sterling rate: it has to do with the complicated matter of valuing options. As explained in Box B one of the drivers of an option value is the volatility of the underlying exchange rate: the more volatile the more valuable the option becomes. Bartlett was taking advantage of the fact that the high volatility in the forex market was making options expensive and therefore by writing call options Bartlett was cashing in high

Box B. Valuation of Currency Options. *The option premium paid by the buyer to the writer can be broken down into two basic components: intrinsic value and time value.*

The intrinsic value refers to the difference between the exercise price of the option E(90) and the spot exchange rate S(t) with 0 < t < 90. Whenever the spot price of the underlying currency exceeds the exercise price of a call option, it stands to reason that the call option holder can make a profit by buying the currency at the exercise price and selling it at the prevailing spot price. Conversely, the option writer will seek fair compensation by charging a premium that is at least equal to the difference between the spot price and the exercise price:

$$\text{Intrinsic value of a call option} = S(t) - E(90).$$

The time value component of the option premium refers to whatever amount option buyers are willing to pay above and beyond the option's intrinsic value. Since options are in a sense a bet on the volatility of the underlying currency, the longer the time remaining until expiration of the option (90 − t) the more likely it is that the spot price will exceed the exercise price. Conversely, as the option expiration date draws closer, the option's time value will decline very sharply.

In Figure 5 the value of the premium of a sterling call option prior to maturity is shown as a function of the prevailing spot exchange rate. The option's intrinsic value, line (1), is (a) zero when the option is out-of-the-money (to the left of the exercise price E(90)), (b) equal to the difference between the spot rate and the exercise price when the option is in-the-money (to the right of the exercise price). The time value is shown as the difference between the total value, line (3), and the intrinsic value, line (2). It demonstrates that the value of an option is always larger than its intrinsic value provided that there is time left until expiration (t < 90). Clearly, at expiration (t = 90), the value of an option is its intrinsic value, since there is no time value left.

premia (see Figures 6 and 7 for an illustration of the Dollar-Pound Sterling exchange rate and exchange rate volatility).

SELLING VOLATILITY: ALLIED-LYONS "DEADLY GAME"[80]

Emboldened by steady and significant profits in their foreign exchange trading activities in 1989 and 1990, Allied Lyons' treasury embarked on a trading binge. Bartlett went on record asking *"how can we put volatility to work on our portfolio."*[81] Thus, rather than taking a directional view of the exchange rate — up or down — Allied Lyons played on a bet that volatility in the dollar-pound exchange rate was going to subside as soon as the Allies offensive was launched against Iraq (see Figure 7).

---

[80]We provide a simplified description of how Allied Lyons' option strategy combined with poor risk management procedures led to this debacle.

[81] Brady, S.: ibid, p. 24.

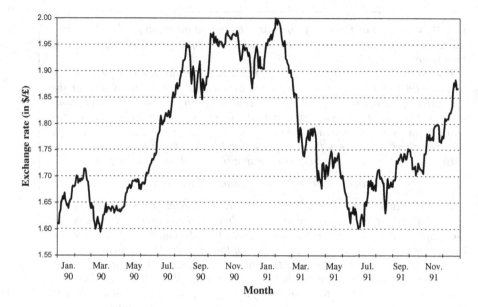

Figure 6   Daily exchange rates (in US $/£).

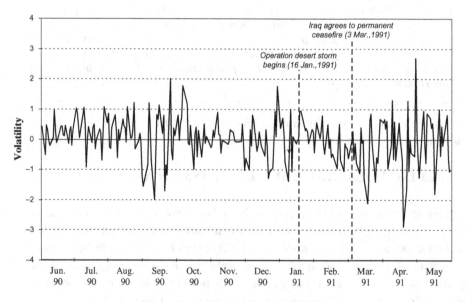

Figure 7   Daily volatility for US $/£.

By betting on volatility understand that the spot price had been fluctuating wildly over a short period of time. Allied Lyons wagered that the spot price was soon going to become far steadier or less volatile. Since option premia are closely linked to the volatility of the underlying exchange rate, at high volatility option premia were expensive; dampened volatility would bring premia down. Whatever option combination Allied Lyons had sold/written at a high price it was counting on being able to close its positions by buying them back at a much lower price thereby netting a sizeable profit. Indeed options — when appropriately combined — can provide lucrative results on specific volatility scenarios.

Most appropriate to plays on volatility are options strategies known as *straddle, and strangle*. Allied-Lyons wrote a large portfolio of put and call options combined in the mold of the above two option strategies. The key word is "wrote" (rather than bought) put and call options. In so doing Allied-Lyons collected hefty option premia hoping that these options would never be exercised if held to maturity or would be bought back at a lower price before maturity. If Allied-Lyons guessed wrong and the options were to be exercised Allied Lyons would face very large losses. Now let us turn to the specifics of the "deadly game" that Allied-Lyons chose to play.

Straddle. Buying a *straddle* is the simultaneous purchase of one put and one call option at the same exercise price and maturity. This strategy is especially attractive when one anticipates high exchange rate volatility but is hard-pressed to forecast the direction of the future spot exchange rate. Allied-Lyons was actually selling straddles on the premise that exchange rate volatility was going to subside and would stabilize at

---

Box C. Volatility and the Value of Options.Volatility is difficult to measure. It is usually proxied by the standard deviation of past exchange rate fluctuations. This approximation, in turn, assumes that exchange rates follow a lognormal probability distribution. Historic (ex-post) volatility is not necessarily a reliable predictor of future (ex-ante) volatility whereas implied volatility (derived from the options market price) captures the market consensus. Practically, as volatility rises, option premia should increase and vice versa. This approximation, in turn, assumes that exchange rates are well enough behaved to follow a lognormal probability distribution model. Implied volatility at any given point in time can be extracted from current option prices by solving option pricing models for volatility since all the other parameters are known. However one should keep in mind that option prices are themselves set by traders who feed into the option valuation models their own subjective measure of volatility — itself based on some measure of past volatility.

a low rate. Consider the following market situation faced by Allied Lyons on January 15, 1991 and how it constructed the writing/sale of a straddle.

Written: 1/15/91
Assume: 90-day maturity
Call strike: $1.95/£   *Put strike*: $1.95/£
Call premium: $0.027/£   *Put premium*: $0.0313/£.

Let us now sketch with precision the building blocks of a straddle strategy — that is the writing of a call and put option on pound at the same strike price of $1.95 = £1

Writing of a Call. For a cash premium of $0.027 collected on January 15, 1991 Allied Lyons would commit to delivering one pound at the strike price of $1.95 = £1. If the spot price were to remain below the strike price of 1.95 the option would not be exercised and Allied Lyons would keep the option premium. Should the exchange rate appreciate above the strike price Allied Lyons would have to deliver pounds at the cost of $1.95. These pounds would have to be purchased at a higher spot rate. The more expensive the pound gets the higher the losses incurred by Allied Lyons. Line (1), in Figure 8, sketches the payoff profile from the writing of a call option. Allied-Lyons makes a profit equal to the premium ($0.027) at any spot rate up to the strike price of $1.95 since the call option would not be exercised. Beyond $1.95 the profit line is downward sloping. However, between $1.95 and $1.977 (strike price + premium) the premium is at least partially covering losses due to the movement of the exchange rate. At $1.977 the loss due to spot price movement is exactly equal

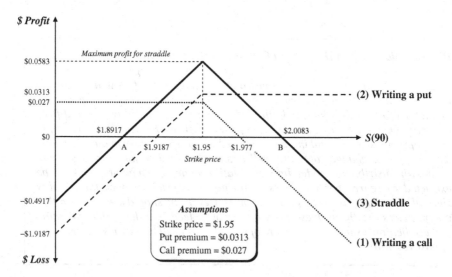

Figure 8   Writing a straddle.

to the premium. This is the break-even point. Beyond $1.977 Allied-Lyons incurs ever-increasing loss.

Writing of a Put. For a cash premium of $0.0313 Allied Lyons would commit to buying pounds at the strike price of 1.95. Line (2) in Figure 8 sketches the payoff profile from writing a put. Until the strike price of $1.95, the buyer will exercise his option to sell pounds at $1.95. Allied-Lyons will incur a cash flow loss in this range due to the fact that it must buy pounds at $1.95 and can only resell them at the lower spot price. Losses will be incurred up until $1.9187 (strike price — premium) where the loss due to spot rate movements equals the profit from the premium. Beyond the strike price of $1.95 the option will not be exercised and Allied-Lyons retains the full premium of $0.0313 per pound transacted

Plotting the Straddle. Writing the straddle is the bundling of a put and a call shown in Figure 8 as the graphical sum[82] (3) of a call (1) and put (2). Please note the pyramid top (in bold) of a straddle where Allied Lyons nets a profit. Of interest are the break-even exchange rates A and B within which Allied-Lyons makes money because of very low volatility and outside of which it incurs deepening losses because of increased volatility.

To figure out the spot rates at which the straddle will cross the x-axis (the break-even points), we simply add/subtract the *sum* of the call and put premia to/from strike price.

Break-even A: $S(90)^A$ = strike price − (call premium + put premium)

$S(90)^A = 1.95 - (0.027 + 0.0313) = 1.8917$

Break-even B: $S(90)^B$ = strike price + (call premium + put premium)

$S(90)^B = 1.95 + (0.027 + 0.0313) = 2.0083.$

Therefore, when the spot rate is below $1.8917 or above $2.0083, Allied-Lyons will lose money and the loss is literally unlimited should the spot exchange rate fall way below $1.8917 or appreciate well above $2.0083. Conversely, within the same range, when volatility is low, Allied-Lyons stands to gain. Its maximum profit comes when the spot rate is exactly equal to the strike price of $1.95. At that point neither option will be exercised. Therefore Allied-Lyons suffers no loss due to currency movement and it retains the full amount of both premia, equal to $0.0583 per £ transacted.

In this case, Allied-Lyons decided to write straddles because it believed that once hostilities began in the Persian Gulf, the current volatility of the US dollar vis-à-vis the British pound would subside. If this were the case, Allied-Lyons would keep most of the premia which were substantial since they were writing deep-in-the-money options.

---

[82] Referring to Figure 8 graphical sum of lines 1 and 2 shows for each exchange rate (horizontal axis) the algebraic sum of gains/losses for lines 1 and 2 on the vertical axis.

That meant that it would have been favorable for the option buyer to exercise those options immediately. However, the buyers could not do so because these were European options, which could only be exercised *on* the expiration date. The risk for Allied-Lyons was that if volatility remained high, it was exposed to unlimited losses. This is indeed what happened.

The pound was high when the options were written but most importantly the high volatility due to the uncertain outcome of the Persian Gulf war made the options expensive. By writing call and put options Allied Lyons was able to collect rich premia. Clearly Allied-Lyons thought that the expected decrease in volatility would result in cheaper option premia which would allow Allied-Lyons to buy back the same options it had sold at a high price much more cheaply.

Writing a Strangle. It is another speculative strategy based on volatility and which combines the writing of calls and puts. The main difference with a straddle is that the strangle combines out-of-the-money puts and calls at *different* strike prices. Correspondingly, the options are cheaper and the premia collected lower than in the case of straddle built on at-the-money put and call options. It is less speculative than a straddle because, as we can see in Figure 9, there is a wider band over which there is some profit. The downside is that, because of lower risk, the premia earned are lower.

Written: 1/15/91

Assume: 70 day maturity
Call strike: $2.00/£   *Put strike*: $1.90/£
Call premium: $0.0104/£   *Put premium*: $0.0116/£.

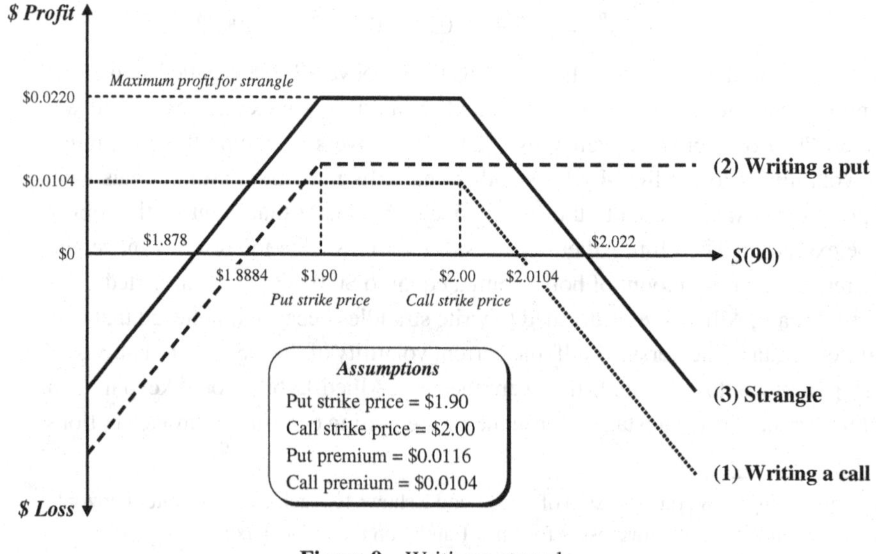

Figure 9   Writing a strangle.

We first plot the payoff profile of writing a call as shown by line (1) in Figure 9. The break-even is $2.0104 (strike price of $2.00 + premium of $0.0104) beyond which Allied — Lyons starts incurring increasing losses. In the same way, we plot the writing of the put (shown as line (2) in Figure 9) where the break-even point is $1.8884 (strike price of $1.90–premium of $0.0116). The payoff of the strangle itself is shown by line 3 as the graphical sum of line 1 and line 2: the maximum profit per pound sterling $0.0220 = $0.0116 + $0104 is received as long as the exchange rate $S(90)$ remains within the range of $1.90 to $2.00 (low volatility and small change in the absolute value of $S(90)$). The strangle remains profitable as long as $S(90)$ remains within the break-even exchange rates of $1.878 = $1.90 − ($0.0104 + $0.0116) and $2.022 = $2.00 + ($0.0104 + $0.0116). Outside that range the strangle results into mounting losses.

ALARM BELLS ARE IGNORED AS THE STORY UNFOLDS

As early as the summer of 1989, the Bank of England had alerted Sir Derrick of suspicious foreign exchange dealings initiated by Allied Lyons' treasury. An inquiry was opened and several meetings between the Bank and Clifford Hatch took place but it was concluded that no corrective actions were needed. By September 1990 alarm bells were ringing again, this time at the instigation of Peat Marwick — Allied Lyons' auditor — which pointed out a deficient reporting system and indicated that the treasury department had breached the £500 million exposure limit.[83] Repeated requests from Sir Derrick to close down currency positions were either ignored or delayed when in mid February 1991 Allied Lyons could have exited its position for as little as £10 million loss.

Indeed, after appreciating moderately in late January and early February 1991 the pound embarked on a precipitous descent from February 21 when it stood at $1.96 onwards. By March 4, the pound fell below the break-even rate of 1.89 at which point the straddle started to be out-of-the money. On March 16, when National Westminster bank finally closed the book, the pound stood at $1.79. The hoped for scenario of a combined lower volatility and non-varying exchange rate (staying close to the strike price of 1.95) had not materialized. On March 18, 1991 the pound stood at $1.7895 when National Westminster abruptly closed down Allied-Lyons' option positions. The cash loss for each straddle would amount to 1.89 − 1.79 = $0.10 per pound which was approximated to a notional position of £1.5 billion. The loss was due principally to put options exercised by buyers and reduced by the combined revenue of put and call option premia collected by Allied Lyons.

---

[83] Allied chiefs to go after £147 million loss, *The Times* (May 4, 1991).

Last, it is important to emphasize why Allied Lyons was writing European options. A European option is one that must be exercised on the expiration date while an American option can be exercised on or before the expiration date. Because the options were written so deep in the money, it would have been favorable for the buyer to exercise them immediately had the options been American rather than European style. Allied-Lyons expected the exchange rate relationship to change little over time and being able to force buyers to hold onto the options until the end of the period was essential in order to reap maximum profit.

THE MORAL OF THE STORY

Lesson 1: Failure to Set a Clear Mission for Treasury as a Profit Center. A company's treasury department is charged with two principal tasks: (1) procuring financing at the lowest possible cost of capital with financing running the gamut from short-term suppliers' funding in the form of account payables to medium and long term bank loans of capital market debt and, (2) hedging risk by limiting the firm's exposure to exchange rate and interest rate risk. Neither funding nor hedging are profit-making activities *per se* since the goal of financing is to minimize costs while hedging is all about minimizing risks. And yet many corporations have in the last 25 years redefined the mission of their treasury operations to turn them into profit centers. With the overhauling of the treasury function and its changing of the guard as early as 1987 Allied Lyons' treasury seemed to have morphed into a *de facto* profit center without ever articulating clearly the risk-return profile within which it could operate. As alluded to earlier, Allied Lyons had reported increasingly significant profits from foreign exchange trading and success clearly emboldened its treasury to pursue high stakes currency gambits. Profits came with the firm taking on sizeable speculative positions to which the governance of the firm seemed to acquiesce. Unfortunately, there was no charter prepared by treasury, supported by the finance director and debated before being blessed by the Board of Directors. Speculation within the treasury was no secret and the alarm bells did ring on a number of occasions without any formal attempt by senior management to rein in the treasury's activities

Lesson 2: Failure to Control. Most trading rooms within large industrial or financial institutions have reporting guidelines in place with tight position limits. Allied Lyons claimed to have had position limits of £500 million which were easily circumscribed by Bartlett and his acolytes. Position limits are actually not enough and should be superseded by far more effective *trading loss limits* which can be enforced by a *"marking-to-market"* of each outstanding forward contract or currency option. Because forward contracts and over-the-counter currency options are not traded continuously — unlike currency futures —*"marking them to market"* would require careful valuation at the close of every business day. This can be readily done through the Interest Rate Parity theorem or option valuation models as presented in the appendix to this chapter. Each trade, when executed, should be recorded via a trade ticket with the "back-office" accompanied by its rationale. Presumably an industrial corporation such as Allied Lyons should primarily trade currencies paired with real transactions — that is transactions having to do with imports/exports of goods or services. This is known as the legitimate activity of managing transaction or translation exposures. Speculation — if tolerated as part of profit center mandate — should have been closely supervised with stress-testing of pessimistic scenarios accompanied by value-at-risk analysis and measurement. Unfortunately, at Allied Lyons overly lax controls allowed currency traders to build an overall speculative position in excess of £1.5 billion which bore no relationship to the scope of its international operations.

Lesson 3: Failure to Report. These were sizeable transactions which should have been continuously scrutinized by senior management (possibly at the board level) outside the treasury department. What to report, when to report and to whom to report are often ill addressed by large organizations. A breakdown of aggregate positions by tenor/maturity is necessary to avoid creative yet noxious speculative schemes (see Citibank's case in Chapter 3). Reporting should be on a daily basis and reach not only Treasury's senior management but also the very governance of the firm.

Lesson 4: Failure to Audit. Given the complexity and multitude of transactions flowing through a trading room, systematic audits are a vital complement to reporting. Auditing should be internal and external to the firm and based on principles of independence between the auditor and "auditee." Trade tickets are the informational foundation on which auditors will be able to uncover illicit transactions when they reconcile trades recorded by the "front" and "back" offices. But any transaction engages a counter-party: establishing channels of communications with such independent parties — typically the trading rooms at banks — is a critical adjunct to this process. In fact in several instances of major derivative malpractices — including the case of Showa Shell — the plot was uncovered through counter-parties which had commented on abnormal trades.

APPENDIX: PRICING CURRENCY OPTIONS

A warning to the reader: this short appendix is mathematical because of the complex nature of option pricing. The reader will find the second half of the appendix more accessible where the "greeks" are introduced.

Currency options can be priced by modifying the Black–Scholes stock option valuation model. Garman and Kohlhagen proposed a valuation model for a currency call option with exercise price $E(T)$:

$$p(0)^c = [F(T) \cdot N(d_1) - E(T) \cdot N(d_2)]e^{-\lambda T}$$

where

$$d_1 = \frac{\ln(F(T)/E(T) + (\sigma^2/2)t)}{\sigma\sqrt{T}}$$

$$d_2 = d_1 - \sigma\sqrt{T}$$

where $p(0)^c$, $F(t)$, and $E(t)$ are respectively the forward rate and exercise price for maturity t and $e^{-\lambda T}$ is the continuous discounting factor. Furthermore, t is the time before expiration (in years or fraction thereof); λ is the risk-free interest rate expressed on a continuous compounding basis; σ is the standard deviation of the continuously compounded annual rate of change of the exchange rate (proxy for the volatility of the underlying asset) generally approximated by calculating the standard deviation of $\ln[S(t)/S(t-1)]$ over T observations and multiplying correspondingly by T; finally, $N(d)$ is the probability that a deviation less than d will occur in a normal distribution with a mean of zero and standard deviation of 1 (given d, this can be readily found from any standard normal probability table).

It should be emphasized that this currency valuation model assumes that changes in the exchange rate follow a log-normal distribution with constant variance, whereas empirical studies indicate that exchange rate changes tend to follow a longer-tailed probability distribution model than does the log-normal distribution.

For the option buyer, it is important to understand how the value of the option responds to the spot exchange rate. For the buyer of a call option, the *delta* coefficient (or hedge ratio) is defined as the percentage change in the price of the option premium for a 1% change in the value of the exchange rate. This is indicated in Figure 5 by the slope of the tangent to the premium curve shown as line (3). When the spot exchange rate is at the money, the delta coefficient is equal to 0.5. As the spot exchange rate grows larger than the exercise price, i.e., the option becomes in the money, its delta increases asymptotically toward 1. Conversely, when the spot exchange rate falls below the exercise price, i.e., the option becomes out of the money, its delta tends asymptotically towards zero.

Since option values are largely built on the volatility of the underlying asset, we should briefly mention the *vega* coefficient. It is defined as the sensitivity of the option premium to a 1% change in the volatility of the underlying asset. Volatility, of course, is difficult to measure. It is usually proxied by the standard deviation of past exchange rate fluctuations. This approximation, in turn, assumes that exchange rates are well enough behaved to follow a normal probability distribution. *Historic* (ex-post) volatility is not necessarily a reliable predictor of *future* (ex-ante) volatility whereas *implied* volatility (derived from the options market price) captures the market consensus. Practically, as volatility rises, option premia should increase and vice versa.

ALLIED IRISH BANKS

It's very clear now that this guy targeted every control point of the system and systematically found ways around them, and built a web of concealment that was very sophisticated.

Michael Buckley, CEO of Allied Irish Banks

On February 6, 2002, Allied Irish Banks (AIB) disclosed that its US subsidiary Allfirst Financial Inc. had incurred a staggering loss of $691 million. The loss was traced to foreign exchange trading activities conducted by its currency trader John Rusnak. It was later revealed that the currency losses started as early 1997 and had been fraudulently concealed by the rogue trader from the senior management of the bank. The loss was significant enough to cut Allied Irish Banks' 2001 consolidated earnings by 60% and deplete the bank's capital by 10%.

However creative Mr. Rusnak may have proven to be, one cannot help being mystified by how hundred of millions of cash-flow losses could escape the bank's close scrutiny over a period of five years. This chapter reconstructs the loss-making forex trading activities conducted by Rusnak and the elaborate scheme, which allowed him to conceal actual cash-flow losses from auditors.

RUSNAK AND CURRENCY TRADING AT ALLFIRST

Allied Irish Bank's entry in the North American market was relatively recent: its initial partial acquisition of the regional bank Maryland Bancorp dated back to 1983 and became a fully owned subsidiary in 1989 when it was renamed Allfirst. AIB believed that Allfirst's management was strong and therefore extended a good deal of autonomy to its foreign subsidiary. Still AIB felt it important to appoint one of its own senior executives David Cronin as Allfirst treasurer: Cronin was indeed an experienced banker who had started his professional career as a currency trader in Dublin at the Central Bank of Ireland later overseeing AIB currency trading operations with as many as 50 traders: de facto his reporting proved to be of a dual nature with all the ambiguity it implied for the control relationship between Allfirst and AIB.

In 1989, when Cronin joined Allfirst, there was no currency proprietary trading (see Box A) as the bank's activities focused on serving the bank's customers which included some major corporate clients such as Black & Decker with significant international dealings; it was a fee-based activity with very minimal exposure to risk for Allfirst. From his days at AIB in Dublin Cronin knew that there was money to be made from more aggressive foreign exchange trading: shortly thereafter, in 1990, a currency trader was hired to build up proprietary trading at Allfirst. After a short tenure he left the bank and Cronin looked again for an experienced currency trader. Enter John Rusnak who had worked as a currency option trader with First Fidelity Bank in Philadelphia (1986–1988) and Chemical Bank (1988–1993). Rusnak claimed that sophisticated currency option trading would be far more profitable than directional currency trading — that is taking one-way bets on currencies such as the Japanese yen or the Deutsche mark; by running a large currency option book hedged in the cash and forward markets Allfirst would be able to generate consistent arbitrage profits while avoiding exposure to speculative positions on one way currency bets. Rusnak was hired and would join the bank in July 1993.

We explain in the next two sections what directional currency trading means and how hedging a book of currency options can deliver steady arbitrage profits before we return to our story. This pedagogical detour will serve as a primer on currency forwards and options and facilitate the reader's understanding of the elaborate and deceitful speculative scheme that John Rusnak had designed.

Box A. Proprietary Trading. *Proprietary trading is trading activities initiated by a bank with its own capital (as opposed to agency trading undertaken with the bank customers' money on its behalf). Proprietary trading desks are similar to hedge funds except that they are nested within financial institutions and operate in parallel to traditional investment banking activities such as issuance of stocks and bonds, mergers & acquisitions and other advisory activities. Like hedge funds proprietary trading relies on strategies such as index arbitrage, currency arbitrage, merger arbitrage, volatility arbitrage or outright directional specu-lation on foreign exchange rates as in the case of Allfirst. Proprietary trading generally generates hefty but volatile profits and is considered as riskier than more traditional banking activities. Commercial banks usually do not engage in proprietary trading: Allfirst was an exception and did so on a limited scale.*

GAMBLING ON CURRENCIES WITH
FORWARD CONTRACTS

Speculating in the Forex market can be carried out either through outright spot[84] transactions or more complex forward contracts:

(1) *Spot speculation* consists of buying a currency — say the yen — perceived to be cheap (undervalued) in terms of another currency say — the US dollar, holding it until it appreciates and selling it at a higher price later. With the anticipation of a dollar depreciation (yen appreciation) speculators would buy spot yens (sell dollars), wait out its appreciation before buying back dollars at a much cheaper rate (fewer yen needed to buy one dollar): for example assume that the dollar is expected to depreciate over the near-term from ¥117 to ¥111 = $1.00; $1.00 buys ¥117 before the depreciation but only ¥111 are now needed to buy back one dollar after the depreciation. Thus the round trip would consist of the following sequence of transactions: $1 buys ¥117 which then buy back ¥117/111 = $1.05 for a cash profit of $1.05 − $1.00 = $0.05 if one disregards the time value of money. Funds however would be tied up for the entire duration of the (unknown) speculative period and financial cost would have to be incurred if the funds had to be borrowed: this indeterminate interest burden tied to the cost of carry would limit speculation through the spot market for John Rusnak since it would have immediate cash-flow implications and would have to be sanctioned by the treasury department.

(2) Alternatively, one can *speculate with a forward contract* (see Box B) which by its very nature does not tie up cash and is therefore a good deal more discreet. To take a numerical example, consider the following situation prevailing on September 30,

---

Box B. What Are Forward Contracts? *A forward exchange contract is a commitment to buy or sell a certain quantity of foreign currency on a certain date in the future (maturity of the contract) at a price (forward exchange rate) agreed upon today when the contract is signed. Clearly it is important to understand that a forward contract when signed is an exchange of irrevocable and legally binding promises (with no cash changing hands) obligating the two parties to going through with the actual transaction at maturity and delivering the respective currencies (or cash settlement) regardless of the state of the world — that is the prevailing spot exchange rate on delivery day. Unlike a futures contract entered with an organized exchange forwards are over-the-counter tailor-made contracts which do not require the posting of a margin nor are they subjected to daily marking-to-market.*

---

[84] Spot transactions refer to the sale or purchase of a foreign currency for immediate delivery — within one or two business days.

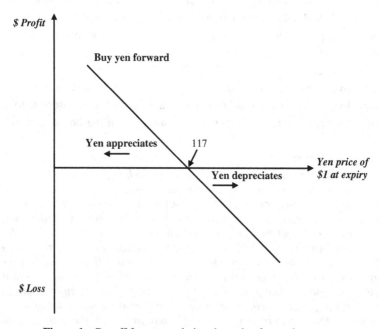

2000: yen can be purchased forward at ¥117 for delivery in 6 months on March 31, 2001 while we expect the dollar to depreciate on the spot market below the current spot rate of ¥117 = $1 to say ¥111 = $1. If John Rusnak bought forward ¥10 billion at ¥117 and proved to be right in his expectation of the spot price falling to ¥111 on March 31, 2001 he would deliver ¥10 billion/117 = $85.47 million now worth ¥10 billion/111 = $90.09 million for a profit of $90.09 million − $85.47 million = $4.62 million[85] — a nice return on an investment of — yes −$0.00, ... (Figure 1 portrays $ profit on the upper half of the vertical axis when the exchange rate on delivery day falls to the left of forward rate at ¥117 = $1) Now of course — if he bets wrong and the dollar had appreciated to say ¥124 our trader would still be obligated to deliver ¥10 billion/117 = $85.47 millions, receive ¥10 billion worth now only ¥10 billion/124 = $80.65 million for a loss of $4.82 million (see Figure 1 to the right of forward rate). As it turned out the yen depreciated steadily over the period 1996–1998 (see Figure 2) during which John Rusnak was consistently buying the yen forward on the premise that the yen would appreciate. By the end of 1997 Rusnak had accumulated a trading loss of $29 million.

Figure 1   Payoff from speculating through a forward contract.

---

[85] $100 million buys ¥11.7 billion but it takes only ¥11.1 billion to buy back $100 million for a profit of ¥600 million or 600 million/111 = $4.62 million.

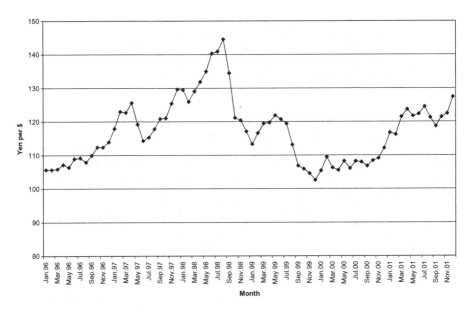

Figure 2 Yen/dollar exchange rate 1996–2001.

ARBITRAGING THE FORWARD AND OPTION MARKET: THE INTERNATIONAL PUT-CALL PARITY THEOREM

John Rusnak had claimed that he could build a currency options book which would allow the bank to reap steady gains by arbitraging the option and forward market. This would certainly have been a very low or no risk method of generating steady but small profits. This trading methodology is rooted in the powerful arbitrage relationship which binds the option market to the forward exchange market. To understand this arbitrage relationship known as the international put-call parity theorem consider that a 90-day forward yen purchase contract can always be replicated by simultaneously buying a 90-day European yen put and selling a 90-day European yen call option (see Box C for an introduction to currency options) at the same strike price assumed to be $E(90) = ¥117$ per dollar.

Indeed by combining the purchase of a yen put option (portrayed as line 1 in Figure 3A) with the writing of a yen call option (line 2 in Figure 3A) at the same exercise price $E(90)$, one effectively (or synthetically) sells forward yen at the options' premium-adjusted exercise price (line 3 in Figure 3A which is the "graphical sum" of lines 1 and 2). Thus, in the option market it is easy to create synthetic forward contracts whose price can be readily compared to prevailing rates in the forward market. This fundamental relationship between the option and forward markets drives the constant

---

Box C. What Are Currency Options? *A currency option gives the buyer the right (without the obligation) to buy (call contract) or to sell (put contract) a specified amount of foreign currency at an agreed price (strike or exercise price) for exercise on (European option) or on/before (American option) the expiration date.[86] For such a right, the option buyer/holder pays to the option seller/writer a cash premium at the inception of the contract.*

A European option whose exercise price is the forward rate is said to be at-the-money; if it is profitable to exercise the option immediately (disregarding the cash premium), the option is said to be in-the-money; and conversely, if it is not profitable to exercise the option immediately, the option is said to be out-of-the-money. As expected, "in-the-money" options command a higher premium than "out-of-the-money" options. When held to maturity, the option will be exercised if it expires "in-the-money" and abandoned when it expires "out-of-the-money."

Of practical interest is the trade-off between strike price and premium: the further "in-the-money" the strike price is, the more expensive (i.e., the higher premium) the option becomes and conversely. Standardized option contracts available from organized exchanges such as the Philadelphia Exchange Market are practically devoid of counterparty risk, since the appropriately capitalized exchange stands as the contract's guarantor of last resort; however, the option buyer is limited to a relatively small set of ready-made product directly available off the shelf.

---

arbitrage activity between the two markets and is known as the "put-call forward exchange parity."

Indeed the same amount of yen can be immediately purchased on the forward market at the prevailing market forward rate of $F(90) = 120$ (line 4 in Figure 3B). However, the synthetic forward contract created by selling a call and buying a put at the same strike price will be slightly different from the strike price.[87] It will reflect the cost due to the difference between the premium $p(0)^p = 8$ paid, for buying the put, and the income generated from writing the call, $p(0)^c = 5$. Accounting for the fact that this difference is paid (received) when the option contract is entered into rather than exercised, the total cost or terminal value of buying synthetically the foreign currency forward is:

$$F(90)^* = E(90) - [p(0)^p - p(0)^c] \cdot (1 + i_{us}) = 117 - (8 - 5) \times 1.015 \simeq 114$$

(1a)

---

[86]The terminology of American vs. European option does not refer to the location whether the options are traded. Both European and American option contracts are traded on both continents, as well as in the Far East.

[87] Figure 3B shows the strike price of both options equal to the synthetic forward rate. This is a simplification due to the fact that the graph assumed both put and call premia to be identical — which would not be the case in reality.

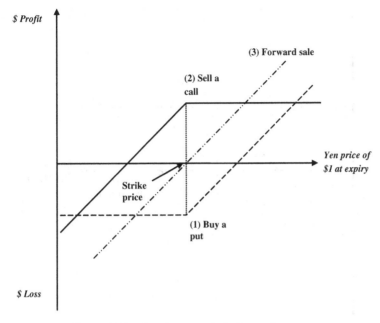

Figure 3(A) Creating a synthetic forward contact.

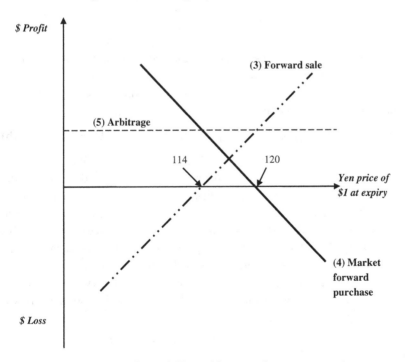

Figure 3(B) Arbitrage profit.

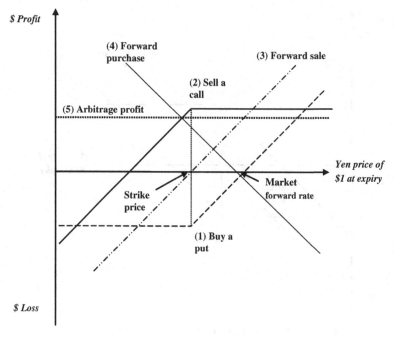

Figure 3(C)   International put-call parity.

where $i_{us} = (6\%) \times 1/4 = 1.5\%$ is the interest rate over the 90-day period (or $90/360 = 1/4$ year) period. Thus, by buying forward yens at the cheaper market rate of $F(90) = 120$ and buying back dollars at the stronger synthetic price given by the Eq. (1a) of ¥114 = $1 the arbitrager is generating a *risk-free* profit of[88]

$$F(90) - E(90) + [p(0)^p - p(0)^c] \cdot (1 + i_{us}) = 120 - 114 = 6 > 0 \qquad (1b)$$

shown as line (5) (line (3) plus line (4)) in Figure 3C. This disequilibrium will set arbitrage forces into motion as the price of the put option is bid up and the price of the call option is bid down until the risk-free profit disappears and *parity* prevails. As arbitragers purchase yen at the market forward rate of $F(90) = 120$, its rate will be driven up. Simultaneously, by selling at the higher synthetic forward rate $F(90)^* = 114$, arbitragers will depress its level, thereby forcing inequality (1b) toward equality. Such discrepancies tend to be small and short-lived as trading desks equipped with powerful computer software are continuously monitoring rates. Discrepancies will be arbitraged away in a few seconds and quasi-parity between the option and forward markets will

---

[88] $1 buys ¥120 but it takes only ¥114 to buy back the initial $1 leaving a profit of ¥6 per $1 transacted.

soon prevail. Small profits though can be steadily accumulated at almost zero-risk. Rusnak had sold himself as a skillful currency trader who could generate profits through continuous arbitrage at very low risk for Allfirst. History proved otherwise!

THE ART OF CONCEALMENT

Almost from day one of his tenure as a currency trader at Allfirst, John Rusnak started to speculate on the yen appreciation through old-fashioned forward contracts — precisely the kind of proprietary trading he had belittled when he first interviewed for the position of currency trader. Of course the steady yen depreciation delivered nothing but embarrassing foreign exchange trading losses. However Rusnak's lack of creative trading insights was compensated by cunning deceit. The challenge for Rusnak was to find a reliable method of concealing mounting trading losses in the hope of buying himself time until the unlucky streak of losses would reverse itself.

As is customary in these circumstances John Rusnak would execute his trades, keep a daily log and write trade tickets which were entered by the back office in the bank's accounting system. Allfirst's back office would then confirm each trade independently with the bank's counterparty. Thus confirmation would have to come from the other side of the trade — typically a Japanese bank in the case of speculating on yen forwards. This is part of the usual reporting and monitoring process that one would expect to find in the trading operations of a commercial bank. Allfirst's Treasury unit responsible for overseeing this process was comprised of three departments:

(1) "*Front office*" or Treasury Funds Management was responsible for funding, interest rate risk management, investment portfolio management and global trading. Global trading itself was divided between interest rate derivatives and foreign exchange trading — each activity being staffed by a managing director and assisted by a trader. Rusnak was managing director for foreign exchange trading and focused on proprietary trading while supervising a currency trader responsible for Allfirst's corporate customers.

(2) "*Back Office*" or Treasury Operations was responsible for processing, booking, confirming and settling foreign exchange and currency derivatives trades. Any proprietary trading initiated by Rusnak would have to clear the back office by the close of the day.

(3) "*Middle Office*" or Asset and Liability Management and Risk Control would report on traders' compliance with Allfirst's guidelines on trading limits, counterparty credit and value-at-risk. Rusnak's trades would have to satisfy the boundaries imposed by the above metrics.

Phase I: Bogus Options. In or about 1997 Rusnak had entered in several unidirectional speculative trades through yen forwards which were rapidly turning sour. To conceal losses and the size of his positions Rusnak fictitiously booked bogus pairs of yen currency options. Specifically Rusnak would enter combinations of put and call options on the yen with the same strike price and exactly offsetting premia but very different maturities: he would write one day deep-in-the-money put options (amounting to a liability for the bank) while buying longer-dated call options also deep-in-the-money (thereby creating an asset). The one day put option would have — under normal trading circumstances — generated sizeable cash-flow premium income when first written and should have been exercised by the option buyer at a considerable cash-flow cost to the bank (one day later) more or less wiping out the premium income collected the day before. The longer-term call option would have been expensive to purchase but when exercised would have yielded significant speculative gains. The ruse was for Rusnak to bully a junior staff member in the back office in accepting the principle that for pairs of options whose combined premia was zero (no net cash transfer) there was no need to get independent confirmation. He — John Rusnak — would provide proper trade confirmation and the back office would not need to chase independent confirmation. Besides, the back office's staff would have to get confirmation in the middle of the night (Japanese counterparties in Tokyo are 15 hours ahead of Baltimore) and Rusnak did not want to impose selfishly on his esteemed colleagues! Once entered into the system the one day put option would lapse (with no red flag triggered by the bank's internal control system) and the option premium would stay on the book. The valuable deep-in-the money call option would be the only one left standing providing at expiry the cash-flow income meant to recoup the initial option premium paid and offset the cash-flow losses due to yen forward sale.

Interestingly the back office did not catch on to the fact that there is not such a thing as a put and a call option at the same strike price commanding the same premium especially when their maturities are so different: if the put option is deep-in-the-money and expensive the call option will be deep-out-of-the-money at the same strike price and relatively inexpensive. Furthermore the combination of an out-of-the-money short position in yen (forward contract) combined with a yen call option shows a hedged position in the form of a put option on the yen. Figure 4 illustrates how to aggregate the forward yen sale contract (line 1) at the rate of ¥117 with a call option at a strike price of ¥117 (line 2) which amounts to buying a put option (line 3) — sometimes known as a covered call which would not provide the offsetting asset necessary to neutralize the yen forward sale liability position.

Phase II: Writing Deep-in-the-Money Options. As Rusnak's trading activities grew, Allfirst's Treasury became concerned that the meager profits it generated were not justified by the extensive use that it made of the bank's balance sheet and capital

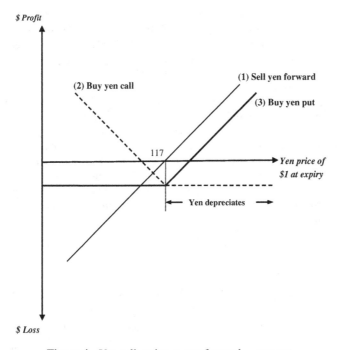

Figure 4 Yen call option + yen forward = yen put.

(see Box D). From a cost accounting perspective the currency trading desk had to be properly assessed for the use of Allfirst's balance sheet without which it could not trade: starting in January 2001, an internal bank memo noted that as gross currency trading profits nearly doubled from $6.6 to $13.6 million, when adjusted for the cost of capital tied, its net profit contribution only increased by $1.1 million. Interestingly, at a time when the back and middle offices were being deceived by Rusnak mounting losses, the treasury did seize on the bank's misallocation of capital. Rusnak in fact was directed to reduce its use of the bank's balance sheet — that is he was asked to curtail drastically his proprietary currency trading activities.

Rusnak — never at a loss for creative stratagems — started shortly thereafter to develop his own capital base to allow for continued trading activities: he sold five deep-in-the money yen put options for the modest amount of a $300 million premium! As Rusnak put it to one of his counterparties *"I have come to you with a problem, we need to outsource our balance sheet funding."*[89]

---

[89] Promontary Financial group and Wachtell, Lipton, Rosen & Katz also known as the "Ludwig Report". *Report to the Board of Directors of Allied Irish Bank, plc, Allfirst Financial Inc. and Allfirst Bank Concerning Currency trading Losses* (March 12, 2002), p. 13.

> **Box D. Basel II and Capital Charges for Proprietary Trading.** *In June 2004,
> the Basel Committee revised yet again the original Basel Accord first signed in
> 1992 which purported to level the global playing field for financial institutions
> by mandating standard capital adequacy ratios (CARs). By requiring adequate
> and consistent capitalization of financial institutions worldwide the Basel Accord
> meant to strengthen the global financial system. The revised Basel Accord specif-
> ically required risk-based capital charges to protect financial institutions against
> credit risk, market risk and operational risk. With rapidly growing proprietary
> trading at many investment banks the Basel Accord had already been amended in
> 1996 to add a charge for market risk: the trading book (proprietary trading) had
> to be segregated from the banking book (traditional lending) and would require a
> special capital charge based on the marked to market value of outstanding over-
> the-counter derivatives such as currency forward or option contracts as held for
> instance by Allfirst.*

Deep-in-the-money put options simply means that the strike prices were well
above the current spot rates, which indicated a strong probability that upon expiration
said put options would be exercised by the option buyer — in other words the option
seller Rusnak would incur a sizeable loss. However upon selling said options Rusnak
would receive a large upfront cash premium which allowed him to vastly expand his
proprietary trading activities which had been severely limited by the balance sheet
constraint that Allfirst's treasury had imposed on its currency trader. More specifically,
the cash raised also allowed Rusnak to settle on loss-making directional trades that
were accumulating. For example, in February 2001, Rusnak entered into an option
contract with Citibank whereby it sold a yen put option at a strike price of ¥77.37 for
an upfront cash premium of $125 million.[90] Since the spot price on the day of selling
the put option stood at 116 yen to the dollar it would require the dollar to depreciate
by at least 35% for the option to expire unexercised. For any rate above ¥77.37 to the
dollar Citibank would exercise its option at a considerable loss for Rusnak.

More generally it should be further noted that writing deep-in-the money options
is a form of short-term financing whose cost is tied to the differential between the strike
price and the spot exchange rate on the day of expiration. Should the spot exchange
rate on the day of expiration be above or at the strike price the put option would expire
unexercised and Rusnak would effectively benefit from zero-interest financing and
would not have to repay the principal. Conversely, should the option expire in the
money — spot rate lower than strike price — the interest cost would be equal to the
differential between the strike and spot exchange rates.

---

[90] Burke, S. Currency exchange trading and rogue trader John Rusnak (Unpublished working
paper: Villanova University, 2004), p. 11.

As Rusnak was writing deep-in-the-money options he was creating large liabilities for the bank which had to be neutralized: Rusnak resorted to his old stratagem of writing a one day bogus put option paired with purchase of a longer maturity call option for the same premium and identical strike price with the same counterparties he had written actual put options. The one day bogus put option would immediately expire unexercised and leave in Allfirst's system the bogus purchased call option seemingly offsetting the writing of the actual put option.

WHEN ALARM BELLS ARE IGNORED

In March 2000, AIB (Allfirst's Irish parent company) group treasurer Ryan received an inquiry from Citibank about a large settlement in excess of $1 billion on the prime brokerage account which had been opened by Rusnak in late 1999. The payment was due in early April and Ryan duly asked one of his staff members in Dublin to investigate with Allfirst on the transaction. Apparently the lead was channeled through Allfirst's middle office: the request though came with a qualifier — it had to be carried out "discreetly." The response came that the net settlement was in fact a small credit rather than a debit for Allfirst because Citibank owed more than a $1 billion to Allfirst. One has to wonder why the investigation had to be carried "discreetly"; it would seem that a $1 billion dollar question would warrant a direct face-to-face discussion (not necessarily confrontational) with the currency trader directly responsible for the prime brokerage account with Citibank. One also has to wonder why would Citibank enquire about a gross settlement when the net settlement was a negligible amount.

In late May 2001, a market source brought to AIB's attention the very heavy foreign exchange trading conducted by the bank's North American subsidiary Allfirst. The warning did not make specific reference to any given trade nor to any given individual. A call was placed to Allfirst's treasurer for clarification. The response came back in the form of a forceful and categorical denial of any unusual activities:

> *To bring closure to our conversation earlier today about foreign exchange turnover, I confirm that we have had no unusual or extra-large transactions in the last two weeks with counterparties locally or in London. Our daily average turnover in this period was $159 million .... To the extent that someone who spoke with you has anxieties with respect to our activities it could be explained by our concentration of turnover with two institutions i.e. Citi and Bank of America. We transact 90% of our dealings via "Prime" clearing accounts with these banks. This is done to minimize counterparty exposure using a monthly netting program. It is ironic that initiatives to minimize one risk can understandably be misinterpreted as giving rise to another."*[91]

---

[91] Burke, S. op. cit. pp. 23–24.

In fact AIB had earlier and very official information about Rusnak's outsized currency trading activities: Allfirst's 10K filing in 1999 and 2000 made reference to Allfirst's notional currency trading being in the billions. As early as 1997 an internal memo prepared for AIB group treasurer indicated that *"Allfirst's average foreign exchange option book is $1 billion nominal ... Rusnak, Allfirst option trader was accountable for 95% of Allfirst's forex trading ... and that about 100 transactions are dealt with per day approximately 80% are speculative (proprietary trading) and 20% corporate driven."*[92] AIB chose to ignore these repeated warnings.

An internal audit unveiled a significant weakness in Allfirst's treasury controls whereby the back office failed to obtain prices from an independent source for validating foreign exchange transactions. In a sad case of being "penny wise and pound foolish" Allfirst's back office chose to save $10,000 by forgoing a direct feed from Reuters. Instead foreign exchange rates were to be downloaded from Rusnak's Reuters terminal into his personal computer's hard disk drive and then fed into a database on the shared network making it accessible to the front, back and middle office. This arrangement was in direct violation of the core principle of separation of duties between front and back offices. Rusnak had insisted that the Reuters feed be first accessible to him so that he would have direct access to the rates necessary to monitor his Value-at-Risk and prevent him presumably from breaching trading limits he was subjected to. Not surprisingly, a subsequent audit of the foreign exchange rates spreadsheet provided by Rusnak to the back office on a routine basis turned out to be "corrupt": the cells for the yen and euro — the two currencies Rusnak favored in his trading — had been tampered with. Rusnak had used manipulated rates to disguise the real outcome of many of his trades to his advantage.

Years of covert trading and deceit all unraveled when a supervisor in the back office inquired about two currency trade tickets for which confirmation seemed to be lacking. "Pairs of offsetting options did not require independent confirmation" he was told by a back office staff member. The supervisor insisted that all trades required independent confirmation and pairs of currency options were no exception; he also noticed that option pairs did not quite offset each other because of different expiration dates. However insistent the supervisor may have been he did not really follow up with the back office clerk until, in January 2002, he noticed yet again another pair of currency options which also lacked proper independent confirmation. This time the supervisor ordered a review which promptly turned out as many as 12 unconfirmed trades. Counterparties were duly contacted and failed to confirm the trades. Finally, when confronted, Rusnak left written confirmation of the trades on the desk of a back office employee. The staff of the back office found the documents to be suspicious: indeed they proved to be fake documents that Rusnak had forged on his personal

[92] Burke, S. op. cit. p. 23.

computer by importing the logo of alleged counterparties to be able to print forged confirmation of his trades. Rusnak never returned to the bank and went missing until his arrest by the FBI.

THE MORAL OF THE STORY

Lesson # 1. Failure to Control. At its simplest the mechanics of daily reporting and control of trading activities between the "front" and "back" office work as follows: the currency trader executes his trades, keeps a daily log and writes trade tickets which are entered by the back office into the bank's accounting system. This latter department will, in turn, verify independently each trade against a broker or counterparty to validate and ensure accuracy of the transaction. It will then settle the trade. Independent confirmation is really the backbone of the control process. The "middle" office or risk department will then compute the daily trading gains/losses associated with the book of outstanding contracts and compare it with daily trading limits.

In order to implement such a control system commercial banks put great emphasis on enforcing a foolproof rule book and charge the back office with implementing it. However the best administrative guidelines will never fully discourage an inventive trader from circumventing them. Allfirst's control process failed both the letter and spirit of its intent.

The Letter. The back office ignored one of its basic responsibilities: to get proper and independent confirmation directly from the counterparty rather than the trader himself. Since the bank is trying to get independent confirmation of what its front office's trades are it stands to reason that it should not rely on the trader itself to get confirmation. The back office should apply a healthy dose of mistrust to the front office questioning the letter as well as the spirit of each rule.

The spirit of the trader's activities was also ignored: it is not enough to seemingly follow the rules, the trader should be asked to provide a simple narrative allowing for each transaction to be put in an understandable strategic context. No one questioned the rationale of Rusnak's booking pairs of bogus options with the same strike price with different maturities. Nor was the writing of actual deep-in-the-money yen put options ever challenged by the middle or the back office. Raising $300 million in option premium should have caught someone's attention — it did not.

Lesson # 2: Failure to Follow the Cash Flow Trail. Financial accounting documents can be easily misleading. Realized and unrealized amounts (in a cash-flow sense) are commingled and the practice of not marking-to-market outstanding foreign exchange contracts only exacerbates the confusion. Attention is wrongly given to the income statement rather than to the cash-flow statement or how else could Rusnak fool for so long the accounting and the auditing staff of the bank? Over-the-counter trades — unlike standardized exchange traded products — are not subject to margin calls. Attaching a margin account to the currency trading desk and treating every single

over-the-counter currency trade as if it were exchange traded would have forced the
bank to follow the cash-flow trail rather than the accounting trail of Rusnak's currency
trades. Eventually the bank started in 2001 to charge Rusnak for his usage of its balance sheet which was a commendable attempt to rein in its currency trader's reckless
activities: a margin account would de facto have achieved the same goal while forcing
the transparency and discipline of a cash-flow account.

Lesson # 3: Failure to Break the "Routine Chain." When all else fails, rotating
employees and enforcing consecutive vacation rules will unveil elaborate and fraudulent concealment schemes. US laws require that traders take 10 consecutive days of
vacation off from trading activities every year. The intent of the law is clearly that
someone else would take over temporarily the activities of the trader on leave and
thereby facilitate the uncovering of fraud. Apparently Allfirst did not enforce the law
and Rusnak never strayed away from his trading desk. In fact, Allfirst equipped Rusnak with Travel Bloomberg software so that he could trade from home or on vacation
allowing him to exercise uninterrupted control over the currency trading desk.

EPILOGUE

In January 2003, Rusnak — after pleading guilty to one count of bank fraud as part of
a plea bargain — was sentenced to spend $7\frac{1}{2}$ years in jail and to pay $1,000 per month
for five years following his release. Allfirst Chairman Frank Bramble and President
and CEO Susan Keating left the bank or resigned in the spring of 2002. AIB went on
to sell Allfirst to M&T Bank Corporation for $3.1 billion. The deal closed in April
2003 and gave AIB a 22.5% interest in M&T Bank Corporation thereby retaining a
presence in the North American banking market.

The landmark Sarbanes–Oxley Act (SOA) became law in July 2002: amongst
its many provisions for strengthening the governance of US public corporations SOA
called for dramatically increased accountability of corporate management with respect
to auditing of financial reports and the maintenance of strong internal controls. Singled out were segregation of duties in the treasury office especially as they apply to
the division of labor between the front and back office as well as job rotation ... the
reader will recall how Rusnak was able to bully back office staff members in forsaking
independent confirmation of his trades not to mention that Rusnak stayed in the same
position for more than seven years.

Bibliography

Creaton, S. and C. O'Clery. *Panic at the Bank: How John Rusnak Lost AIB
$691,000,000* (Gill & Macmillan, 2002).

Promontary Financial group and Wachtell, Lipton, Rosen & Katz also known as the "Ludwig Report". *Report to the Board of Directors of Allied Irish Bank, plc, Allfirst Financial Inc. and Allfirst Bank Concerning Currency trading Losses* (March 12, 2002).

Questions for Discussion

1. Why are deep-in-the-money currency options more expensive than out-of-the-money options?
2. How was Rusnak able to conceal the trail of cash-flow losses on his forward speculation?
3. Explain why entering pairs of put and call options at the same strike price for identical premia should have raised a red flag with the back office.
4. Explain how the international currency option put-call parity model can be used for arbitrage purposes.
5. Would Rusnak have been able to deceive Allfirst if he had speculated through exchange-traded currency futures and options instead of over-the-counter instruments?
6. Compare John Rusnak's modus operandi with Nick Leeson (Barings).
7. What is the cost of financing when funds are raised by writing deep-in-the money options?

BARINGS

But to tell the truth, Sam, I had sort of made up my mind to keep out of speculation since my last little deal. A man gets into this game, and into it, and into it, and before you know it he can't pull out — and he don't want to.

Frank Norris, *The Pit: A Story of Chicago* (1902)

On February 25, 1995, shocking news rocked the City of London. The venerable House of Baring was on the verge of collapse. The Sunday Times headlines bannered:

Queen's bank near collapse in £400 m loss. Bank desperate to find buyer after losing $600 m in derivatives trading.

Reportedly, a rogue trader, in the far away Singapore branch had built massive positions in Nikkei 225 index futures, Japanese Government Bond futures and euro–yen futures. Losses had accumulated over time since 1992 without being found out. The Bank of England had attempted a financial rescue package but without success and Baring was placed under administration before being acquired by the Dutch financial conglomerate ING for the symbolic value of £1.

How could a fresh-faced trader fool for so long the oldest and one of the savviest merchant banks in the City? The saga of Barings' demise is the explosive combination of sophisticated fraud and ill-devised speculation on derivatives coupled with faulty risk management procedures which were sloppily enforced. We open this chapter by briefly sketching the antecedents of Barings and the rise of its detractor.

143

THE RISE AND FALL OF THE HOUSE OF BARINGS

The oldest merchant bank in the City of London traces its roots as far back as 1763 when John and Francis Barings & Co. was established in London by father and son who hailed from a family of German immigrants. The merchant house initially involved itself in the textile trade and the international commerce of raw materials such as copper, indigo and cochineal. Having developed a network of agents in foreign hubs of commerce Francis Barings started to realize that financing trade was far more lucrative than trading itself. By guaranteeing that the supplier would be paid by the buyer who may be domiciled in a foreign country half-way around the world Barings would facilitate international commerce and de facto provide credit. Barings became known as one of the first "acceptance house" in the City thereby marrying trading with banking into what later evolved into merchant banking.

Barings also developed close working relationships with governments raising as much as £770 million for the British government between 1793 and 1815. In 1803, it masterminded the acquisition of the Territory of Louisiana on behalf of the United States from the French by raising $15 million in London and Amsterdam — admittedly the real estate deal of the second millennium! The fact that France was at war with Britain and that Napoleon would use the sale proceeds to finance his war efforts did not seem to matter. The Duke of Richelieu — prime minister of King Louis XVIII of France — paid Barings the ultimate accolade by famously declaring in 1818: "*There are six great powers in Europe : England, France, Prussia, Austria, Russia and The Barings Brothers*". As the City of London rapidly grew to become the hub of international trade and finance Barings Brothers & Co. continued its meteoric rise: for example, by the mid-nineteen century Barings had underwritten one third of all shares and bonds issued by US railway companies.

In 1890 however, Barings met its fate in a near-death encounter as a result of its reckless underwriting of a £10 million stock and debentures issue for the Buenos Aires Water Supply and Drainage Company Ltd. Barings had sent the money to Argentina before the stock and bond issues — supposed to finance the large infrastructural project — had been successfully completed. Facing an acute liquidity crisis Barings had to borrow massively to honor its obligations. The Bank of England came to the rescue by establishing a guarantee fund which would eventually raise £17 million with most of the City's prominent merchant banks contributing; the House of Barings escaped bankruptcy but only narrowly. The Barings family was stripped bare of its fortune. It was a traumatic and humbling experience for the venerable institution; however the firm wasted no time in re-engineering itself as Barings Brothers & Co. Limited — the important change being of course "limited" and a newly found cautious attitude toward risk in general and large scale infrastructural projects in emerging markets in particular.

The end of World War I sharply curtailed the global reach of the City of London which was no longer the preferred port of call for foreign governments and foreign firms raising funds through debentures and stock issues — an activity which had long benefitted Barings in the form of underwriting commissions. As a result, Barings suffered a reversal of fortunes and retreated from international finance: it reoriented itself towards more domestic corporate finance, restructuring and advisory activities in mergers and acquisitions such as the high profile £200 million hostile bid by ICI for Courtauld in 1961.

It was not until the seventies that Barings re-entered international finance and emerging markets — a move that paralleled the rising tide of privatization and deregulation which was sweeping financial markets around the world. Beyond core merchant banking activities Barings greatly widened the scope of its asset management franchise by becoming in 1975 the co-manager of the $170 billion petrodollar reserves of the Saudi Arabian Monetary Authority. In 1981 it underwrote a £100 million bond issue on behalf of the World Bank: was Barings rediscovering its roots? Somehow Barings' resurgence on the world stage of international finance favored Asia — principally Hong Kong, Japan and Singapore rather than Latin America and Argentina which had been at the core of the firm's fortunes for a good part of the 19th century.

The Big Bang which re-launched the City of London as one of the principal hubs of international finance shook the somewhat sheltered and staid world of British broking in stocks and gilts.[93] The cozy family arrangement between British merchant banks and brokerage houses was soon jerked by the "en force" entry of US, continental, and Japanese banks and brokerage firms. Barings made the adjustment in what looked at the time as a timid foray in the broking business. It acquired the far-eastern arm (15 employees) of a mid-size brokerage firm and — with it came — a "force de la nature" in the person of Christopher Heath who was to head the newly formed Barings Far East Securities Ltd (BFES). BFES soon became a major contributor to Barings overall profits and Heath the highest paid merchant banker in the City at £5 million in 1986. Heath and his team were riding the fortunes of the roaring Tokyo Stock Exchange having mastered the world of Japanese Eurobonds with warrants.[94] Thus, brokerage and agency businesses developed rapidly next to the merchant banking side of Barings and indeed soon overshadowed the parent merchant bank. Two cultures — trading and brokerage on one hand and more conservative merchant banking on the

---

[93] Gilts are British treasury bills and bonds.

[94] Warrants are long dated call options on the stock of the firm issuing the Eurobond. They give the warrant holder the right to buy the eurobond issuer's stock at a set price — known as the strike price. If the stock price rise above the strike price warrants become valuable and will be exercised. Since the 1980s were a period of explosive stock price appreciation warrants — attached to low yielding debentures — were very attractive securities.

other — cohabited uneasily, jealously and suspiciously of one another and fostered an organization with ill-defined and confusing lines of reporting between far-flung Asian operations and their London-domiciled parent. Ultimately it was in this context of organizational ambiguity and ill-natured and ill-nurtured control systems that a Nick Leeson could thrive, cajole and deceive peers and senior colleagues for close to three years before bringing the House of Barings down in a calamitous bankruptcy: unlike the rescue of 1890 this time the Bank of England failed to engineer a bail-out.

ROGUE TRADER

Nick Leeson came from humble origins. Born in Watford (East London) from a working class family (his father was a self-employed plasterer and his mother a nurse), Nick Leeson did not attend a privileged public school (the name in England for private prep schools) nor did he graduate from Oxford or Cambridge. Barely equipped with six "O" levels (he did get an A on the math "O" level but failed the "A" level exam in math[95]) from Parminter comprehensive school a university education was not in the cards. Instead Leeson decided to apply to a number of banks in the City of London. In the summer of 1985, he went to work as a clerk for Coutts & Co.'s banking division in their Lombard Street branch; Coutts & Co. was a smaller bank which catered to the wealthy and higher echelons of British society. In 1987 Leeson moved to Morgan Stanley where he continued to work in the back office, now specializing in futures and options settlement: still performing relatively menial clerical tasks but at least being initiated into the mysterious world of financial derivatives which, in the mid-1980s, was in the process of propelling the financial services industry to a new level of explosive growth and groundbreaking innovation.

As part of Barings Securities effort to shore up its back office operations Leeson was hired by its settlement department in July 1989 on a salary of £12,000. In 1990, as Barings Securities' Jakarta operations struggled to keep up with the explosive growth of trading activities and associated paperwork, Leeson was chosen along with four other settlement specialists to trouble shoot the Indonesian back office quagmire. First stationed in Barings' Hong Kong office — which oversaw the Indonesian office — Leeson was successful in unlocking the bottleneck. Back in London as of September 1991, Leeson was asked to investigate an apparent case of fraud involving futures and options trading between a client and an employee of the bank; allegedly, the

---

[95] "O" and "A" levels stand for ordinary and advanced level examinations in different subjects. O levels are taken in the penultimate year of high school and A levels in the last year. Five O and three A levels are required to gain admission to university.

> **Box A. Front and Back Offices.** *A bank's back office settles trades and accounts. In the old days, prior to the establishment of central clearance corporations each transaction would involve the physical delivery of a stock, bond or derivative product in exchange for payment by check to cover the cost. Back office is often contrasted with front office operations — the more glamorous and lucrative side of the bank — with involves sales, trading and research. In the late eighties Barings Securities had experienced explosive growth in its brokerage activities mostly in Japan and other emerging Asian markets. Its back office was still in its infancy and ill-equipped to deal with the front office explosive growth.*

employee had used the client's account to trade on a proprietary basis until margin calls unraveled the scheme: did Leeson get any idea from this incident which bears an uncanny resemblance to the mega-debacle which was yet to come? In any event, he was asked to take over responsibility of the settlement of Japanese futures and options trades which undoubtedly proved to be a golden but lethal educational experience for Leeson. By then, Leeson had established himself as a trusted employee with valuable expertise in back office operations (see Box A) as they applied to the world of futures and options: Leeson had made it known that he was more than ready for a change confiding to one of his superiors *"I have a low boredom threshold. I do not want to be a settlement clerk forever."*[96]

The break came in the form of a posting to Singapore in April 1992 where Barings had decided to open an office dedicated to futures and options trading.[97] Leeson's new responsibilities were to head the newly-formed subsidiary's settlement operations but also to be its floor manager on the Singapore International Monetary Exchange (SIMEX) where an increasing volume of trading on Japanese futures and options was migrating because of lower cost and more consumer-friendly circumstances. This extraordinary blunder of entrusting the same individual with front and back office responsibilities seeded the collapse of the House of Barings. As it turned out, the new Singapore operations soon became an unmitigated success and Leeson was on an ego trip which must have damaged his psyche for good. Recounting a usual day on the frenzied floor of the SIMEX Judith Rawnley described very vividly the regal aura

---

[96] Fay, S. *The Collapse of Barings* (W. W. Norton, 1996), p. 77.

[97] Barings had been operating in Singapore since 1987 as Barings Securities focusing on the Stock Exchange but with no direct activities on the SIMEX. Indeed its futures and options trades were cleared through Chase Manhattan. By 1992 Barings had applied for clearing membership on the SIMEX and purchased three seats on the exchange. With burgeoning activity in futures and options it made good sense to avoid paying commissions to a third party.

around Leeson:

> *"Nick walked swiftly across the floor to his own booth which sported a wilting Union Jack. Even in their rush, his colleagues and fellow SIMEX traders took time to greet him. He was after all one of the most pivotal figures on the exchange. Out on the street, Nick was just another expat businessman, but on the SIMEX floor he was KING. Barings accounted for a high proportion of the market's turnover and Nick had an overriding influence on the market. Rival traders constantly monitored his positions to see how the market might move against them."*[98]

In February 1992, shortly before his posting to Singapore, Leeson had applied for a trading license in the City of London to the Securities and Futures Authority (FSA) — a requirement for anyone involved in trading securities or managing portfolios. As part of a routine check of his application the FSA discovered that Leeson had failed to report a judgment against him in the small amount of £2,426 entered by the National Westminster Bank. Christopher Sharples, the FSA Chairman, recalls:

> *"We didn't reject his application. We simply pointed out that he had been untruthful in terms of the application form — honesty is a very important part of licensing in the financial services industry — and referred it back to Barings for them to decide what to do. They withdrew it without another word and that was the end of it. Leeson was in Singapore very shortly after that....If he'd admitted to it, given some justification and if he'd repaid his debts and cleared the county court judgment, the likelihood is that, subject to probably a probationary period when he'd been told to be under special supervision by someone else at Barings, he'd have been given a license."*[99]

ARBITRAGE

It all started with innocuous and rather lame arbitrage activities in Nikkei 225 stock index futures (see Box B) between the Tokyo Stock Exchange (TSE) and the Osaka Stock Exchange (OSE). In the early nineties most of Barings' derivatives trading activities had been carried out in Japan. Its chief trader, Fernando Gueler, a Californian with a Harvard degree in Economics, had spotted recurring pricing anomalies between the cash (TSE) and the futures market (OSE) for Japanese stocks. By buying the basket of stocks making up the Nikkei 225 index and carrying it until the maturity of the ready-made Nikkei 225 index futures Gueler had de facto created a "home-made" Nikkei

---

[98] Rawnsley, J. H. *Total Risk: Nick Leeson and the Fall of the Barings Bank* (Harper Collins Publishers: New York City, 1995), p. 11.
[99] Rawnsley, J. H. op. cit. p. 80.

Box B. What is a Nikkei 225 Index Futures? *A stock index futures is a futures contract based on the value of a stock market index such as New York's Dow Jones 30 or Tokyo's Nikkei 225 which are defined by a basket of representative stocks. It is no different in design from any other futures contract based on commodities or currencies except that a stock index futures is cash-settled, i.e., does not require physical delivery of each stock in the index which would be cumbersome and costly to do. Clearly the underlying security is more complex since the index is based on the value of a basket of stocks which needs to be unambiguously measured at any given point in time. A representative set of stocks of a given stock market are combined in an index to provide a summary statistic of price movement in said stock market with reference to a base period when the index level was arbitrarily set — generally at 100. The Nikkei 225 index is defined as the value of 225 blue chip stocks traded on the Tokyo Stock Exchange.[100] Futures on the Nikkei 225 index are standardized contracts whose terms (amount, maturity) are agreed today for delivery at some future date (one business day before the second Friday of the contract months — March, June, September, or December). Futures contracts are worth ¥500 times the value of the Nikkei 225 index (in the case of Singapore International Monetary Exchange) or ¥1000 times the value of the Nikkei 225 index (in the case of Osaka Stock Exchange). For example, if the Nikkei 225 is at 20,000 one futures contract on the SIMEX would be worth ¥500 × 20,000 = ¥10,000,000 and ¥1000 × 20,000 = ¥20,000,000 on the OSE.*

---

225 index futures contract. If the "home-made" futures was slightly cheaper than the "ready-made" OSE-traded futures a small profit was generated by purchasing the "home-made" and selling the "ready-made" index futures. This is known as arbitraging the cash/futures market.

As an illustration assume that the Nikkei 225 index is made up of two stocks only: Honda trading at ¥16,000 and Sony trading at ¥4,000. The index — being price-weighted — is worth ¥10,000 if it is constructed as a "home-made" index by purchasing 1 Honda share and 1 Sony share for a value of $[1 \times ¥16,000 + 1 \times ¥4,000]/2 = ¥10,000$. This amount is also known as the cash value of the index contract. Note that Honda stock accounts for $¥16,000/[¥16,000 + ¥4,000] = 75\%$ of the index cash value on that particular day. Similarly Sony stock would amount to

---

[100] Different weighting schemes can be used for defining the value of a stock index: (1) arithmetic average of each component stock price weighted according to the firm's market capitalization as in the case of the Standard and Poor 500 index, (2) arithmetic average of each component stock price weighted according to stock price (more expensive stock are weighted more heavily than cheaper ones regardless of the size and market capitalization) such as the Dow Jones 30 or the Nikkei 225.

25% of the index cash value on that same day. Assuming that the index futures matures in 60 days, the cost of financial carry of the home-made constructed index at an annual rate of 4% (or 0.04 × 60/360 for two months) will push up its cash value to ¥10,000 (1 + 0.04 × 60/360) = ¥10,067. If the index futures trades on the OSE at ¥10,110 the cash/futures arbitrage will yield a risk-free profit of ¥10,110 − ¥10,067 = ¥33 per contract as arbitrageurs simultaneously buy the cash and sell the futures: at maturity of the futures contract they simply net the difference between the cash-and-hold of the home-made index and the value of the futures contract. As arbitrageurs are hard at work, price discrepancies will be short lived as buying cash stocks to construct the index will exercise upwards pressure on their price while selling the futures contract will bring its price down. Computer programs can automatically replicate the Nikkei 225 index and trigger trading as soon as price discrepancies between the cash and the futures market appear. Gueler would soon include the Singapore International Monetary Exchange (SIMEX) as an alternative market with which to arbitrage the cash/futures market: Nick Leeson, newly anointed as Barings' chief and only trader on the SIMEX, would become the point man for the arbitrage trading program.

In the same spirit, arbitrage is also about taking advantage of price differentials in the same product in two different geographical locations or exchanges. Arbitrageurs will closely monitor prices on both exchanges and will act as soon as price discrepancies appear, buying where it is a bit cheaper and selling simultaneously where it is slightly more expensive. This can all be done at the speed of the internet which is almost instantaneous. As long as the product is indeed the same on both exchanges, arbitrage is a profitable yet quasi-riskless activity — provided that the price differential is not entirely eaten up by transaction costs. The Law of One Price[101] will ensure that such price differentials are indeed short-lived as market participants will relentlessly arbitrage away such discrepancies. If the Nikkei 225 September futures trades at ¥13,444 on the OSE but only ¥13,441 on the SIMEX, arbitragers will enter in offsetting trade buying on the SIMEX at ¥13,441 — thereby pushing up the index price — while simultaneously selling on the OSE — thereby driving down the price there. The arbitrageur will generate a profit of ¥13,444 − 13,441 = ¥3 per contract transacted minus whatever transaction cost are associated with the purchase and sale. This will all happen at the speed of light as computer programs are actually doing the work. Arbitrage is indeed a powerful force which moves financial markets ever closer to quasi perfect integration by eliminating price discrepancies.

---

[101] The Law of One Price holds that the same security however it is constructed and wherever it is traded must have the same price. Should price differences arise arbitragers will immediately buy the security where it is slightly cheaper and sell where it is more expensive bringing about One Price.

Slim margins on arbitrage transactions make it a very low profitability business which requires large volume to make it worthwhile. To energize these arbitrage activities, Nick Leeson gave it a boost of "insider trading": whenever a large trade would come to Barings' in Singapore Leeson had noticed that he could count on an upwards price movement because SIMEX is a relatively small market; SIMEX also has a lower margin requirement on futures contracts than the OSE which makes it a popular exchange with offshore customers. Leeson would then immediately buy the Nikkei 225 index futures on the OSE (eventhough the price may be slightly higher) fully expecting that the trade on the SIMEX will bring about a price increase in excess of the differential between the SIMEX and the OSE. Leeson would then resell the OSE futures to Barings' customer in Singapore — a type of arbitrage transaction known as "switching". Assume that before the large trade comes in, Nikkei 225 index futures are trading at 19,001 on the SIMEX and 19,003 on the OSE. A large order comes to Baring to purchase 5,000 futures on the SIMEX. Leeson would immediately purchase 5,000 futures on the OSE at 19,003. As expected the large order drives futures price up on the SIMEX to 19,020. Leeson resells OSE purchased futures to his Singapore client at 19,020 netting an arbitrage profit of $5,000 (19,020 - 19,003) = ¥85,000$. Clearly, Leeson benefited from Barings' customer trade beyond a simple commission by riding on the insider' information embedded in the trade to generate an arbitrage profit without giving the customer the benefit of the cost saving. When a trader trades ahead of a client order it is known as front-running and is against the rules. Leeson was effectively front-running on a different exchange which Barings apparently tolerated. Hardly ethical if apparently legal!

FROM HARMLESS ARBITRAGE TO LETHAL SPECULATION

Duplicitous arbitrage activities on the SIMEX introduced Nick Leeson to the fast moving and seductive world of speculation. Initially, Leeson started modestly with the purchase of Nikkei 225 index futures and the sale of Japanese Government Bond Futures. Curiously, at times, when the general sentiment was bearish on the Japanese economy, Leeson built positions in both securities clearly holding a contrarian[102] bullish view on the stock market and the bond market.

More specifically Leeson was speculating on the Nikkei 225 index futures by buying contracts with different maturities in the anticipation that the contract value would rise before the expiration date. Figure 1 sketches the yen value of one March 95

---

[102] Being bearish on the Japanese economy means expecting an economic slow down which would lower stock prices. By building long positions on Japanese stocks, Leeson was holding a bullish and therefore a contrarian view on the Japanese economy.

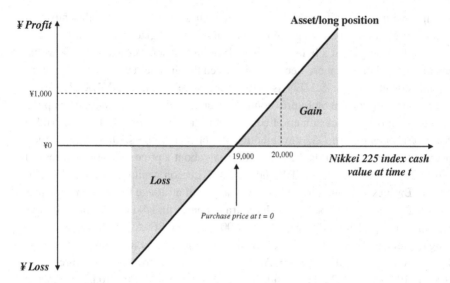

Figure 1   Profit loss profile of going long on Nikkei 225 index futures.

Nikkei 225 index futures as a function of the cash value of the index — assuming that the purchase price was 19,000. Slightly before expiration of the March 95 contract (time t), Leeson would net the difference between the purchase price $F_{0;\text{March 95}} = 19,000$ and the sale price $F_{t;\text{March 95}} = 20,000$ or a profit of $1,000 \times 500 = ¥500,000$ per SIMEX contract. Generally, if the Japanese stock market sees rising stock prices (bullish scenario) the Nikkei 225 index will gain in value (to the right of 19,000 on the horizontal axis of Figure 1) and "long" speculators will benefit from the difference in the index value (vertical axis on Figure 1). Conversely, should the Japanese stock market slide downward "long" speculators will incur a loss (left of 19,000 on the horizontal axis of Figure 1).

Clearly, Leeson had been very bullish on the Japanese stock market as evidenced by his consistently long positions on the Nikkei 225 index. This was — as pointed out earlier — a contrarian view against a broadly bearish consensus which held that — with an economy characterized by no growth and price deflation — the stock market could only head in one direction — down: when it did Leeson started to pile up cash losses. Early on losses had remained small — £2 million by the end of 1992 but £23 million one year later. In 1994, losses mushroomed to £185 million thereby greatly exceeding the Bank's overall profits for that year. The irreversible debacle really swept Barings in January and February of 1995 with losses reaching £827 million by February 27.

The unexpected Kobe earthquake on January 17, which caused a significant drop in the Nikkei 225 index from 19,400 to 17,800 led Leeson to sharply increase his futures position from 10,814 contracts on January 20 to 26,032 contracts on January 31 to

56,032 contracts by February 24. Incredibly, Leeson's long position in March 95 Nikkei 225 futures accounted for 49% of the contract open interests[103] and 24% of the June 95 contracts on SIMEX. However counter-intuitive this may appear this is actually a well documented behavior referred to as Gambler's ruin whereby a trader experiencing a large loss would double his position in the hope of recouping his losses — thereby digging himself into a deeper hole — rather than cutting his losses[104]:

> *Thus in finance, where many occupations are high-wired acts, the fear of falling is constantly in the background and sometimes can lure people in disastrous activities. Individuals can become gripped with a frantic panic and may try to conceal their losses, or double up their bets like crazed gamblers trying to punt their way out of their mounting debts. This is the classic gambler's fallacy.*

As his losses were mounting, Leeson was aggressively increasing his positions — in his own words[105]:

> *I felt no elation at this success. I was determined to win back the losses. And as the spring wore on, I traded harder and harder, risking more and more. I was well down, but increasingly sure that my doubling up and doubling up would pay off… I redoubled my exposure… as the market soared in July 1993 my position translated from a £6 million loss back into glorious profit….*

On January 30, the Nikkei did rebound partially and temporarily by 700 points which would have allowed Leeson to exit his long position at no loss. Figure 2 sketches over the period January 1–February 27, 1995 (horizontal axis) the cumulative losses on Nikkei 225 futures as they rapidly increase (measured on the right hand-side vertical axis of the figure) while the Nikkei 225 fell (measured on the left hand-side vertical axis). By February 27, the Nikkei has fallen precipitously to 15,500 and Leeson's Nikkei 225 index futures positions skyrocketed to 60,000 contracts.

While buying Nikkei 225 index futures, Leeson was also selling Japanese Government Bond futures. The motivation for selling JGB futures short was that Leeson expected long term interest rates in Japan to increase thereby driving down bond prices (see Box C). This was clearly inconsistent with a bullish view on the Japanese

---

[103] Open Interest represents the number of futures contracts outstanding at a particular time held by all market participants. It is a "stock" concept rather than a "flow" concept. There are open interest figures for each contract month of each listed contract. For the Nikkei 225, JGB and Euroyen contracts, the contract months are March, June, September and December.

[104] Brown, S. J. and O. W. Steenbeek. Doubling: Nick Leeson's trading strategy, *Pacific-Basin Financial Journal*, 9, 83–99 (2010).

[105] Op. cit. p. 89.

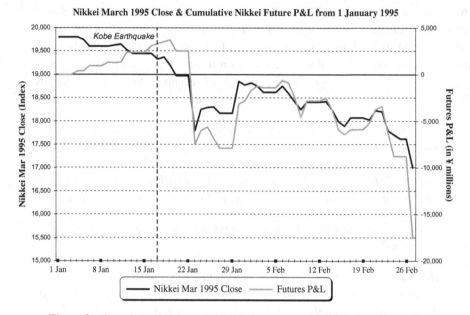

Figure 2   Cumulative losses on Nikkei 225 futures. *Source*: The Report, p. 60.

Box C. Interest Rates, Bond Prices and Japanese Government Bond Futures.
*Bonds are securities which pay a set annual or semi-annual interest or coupon
and repay principal at maturity. Bond prices are determined as the present value
of future periodic interest payments and principal repayment discounted at the
market interest rate for similar bonds in terms of credit risk and maturity. The discount rate that equates the present value of future interest payments and principal
repayment to the current value of the bond is the yield-to-maturity. As the level of
interest rates (discount rates) rise in the economy the value of bonds will adjust
downward and conversely lower interest rate will drive bond prices higher as
long as the credit quality of the bond remains unchanged. Japanese Government
Bond Futures are futures contract on the value of a 10,000,000 yen face value
notional long-term Japanese Government Bond with a fictional 6% coupon. If one
speculates that interest rates are going to rise one will sell Japanese Government
bond futures — say at 93% : as interest rates rise the price of bond futures will
fall to say 90% thereby netting the speculator 3% × 10,000,000 = ¥300,000.
Conversely, should interest rates fall, Government bond futures would rise to say
97% creating a loss for the speculator of 4% × ¥10,000,000 = ¥400,000.*

---

stock market as it is generally understood that lower (not higher) interest rates —
which encourage investment and prop up consumer demand by making consumer
finance more accessible — tend to drive stock prices higher. The opposite happened
as illustrated in Figure 3 which shows accumulating losses (measured on the right

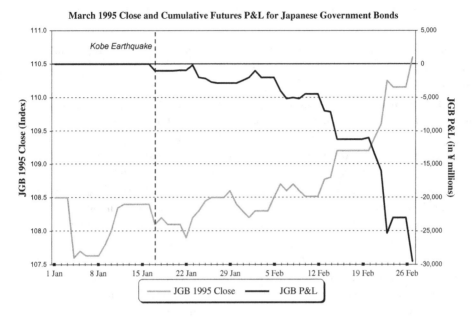

Figure 3 Cumulative losses on Japanese government bond futures. *Source* : The Report, p. 63.

vertical axis) and corresponding rising JGB futures prices (measured on the vertical left axis).

Bond futures prices hovered below 108.50% of par value until February 5, 1995 when they started to climb steadily up to 110.50%. Leeson's losses were negligible until January 15 when they started to accumulate as his short position eventually reached 26,079 contracts (a notional value of ¥260,079,000,000 or approximately $2 billion) or an astounding 85% of the open interest in the March 95 contract and 88% in the June 95 contract.

Thus far, we have explained how Leeson went about speculating with Nikkei 225 index futures and Japanese Government Bond futures. Any such trade would require the posting of sizeable cash margins with the respective SIMEX or OSE exchanges. Furthermore, any futures position which moved against Leeson — as many did — would trigger margin calls or, in other words, increasing cash contributions to these accounts. The practical question is: how was Leeson financing his speculative addiction without raising suspicion from supervisors and auditors? In large part, Leeson was able to build his speculative gambles by writing options and thereby collecting option premia. To get to the mechanics of Leeson's option trades we first review some basics about option trading before retracing Leeson's actual option trades on Nikkei 225 index futures and Japanese Government Bonds futures.

A PRIMER ON HOW TO SPECULATE WITH OPTIONS

To make sense out of speculation with stock index options the reader needs to be introduced to the basics of buying and selling/writing put and call options for speculative purposes.[106]

Put Options. Consider the purchase on January 14, 1995 of a March Nikkei 225 index European put option maturing on the last day of March 1995 with strike price $E_{March\ 95} = 19,000$ and premium $p(0) = ¥500$. The holder of such a contract has the option (the right without the obligation) of selling the index futures on March 31, 1995 at the strike price of 19,000 if the Nikkei 225 index futures price on that date makes it advantageous to do so. Specifically, if the value of the index futures $F_{March\ 95}$ turns out to be higher than 19,000 on March 31, the option holder would simply abandon his put option with a total loss no larger than the *future* value of the premium paid 75 days earlier.

This is shown in Figure 4 as the horizontal portion of line (1) to the right of point A which sketches the terminal profit/loss (measured on vertical axis) of the put option as a function of the futures index value $F_{March\ 31}$ on expiration day (measured on the horizontal axis). Should the index fall below 19,000 the option holder will exercise his put option so as to profit from the difference between index futures price and the

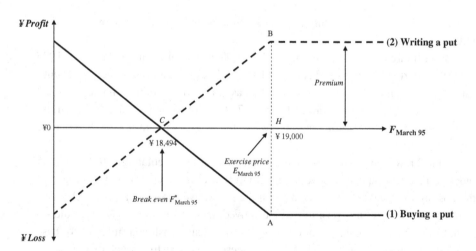

Figure 4   Payoff of put option on Nikkei 225 index futures.

---

[106] If the reader is already comfortable with his/her understanding of buying/writing stock index options he/she may skip this section and directly proceed to our discussion of selling volatility.

exercise price. His cash profit equals the difference between the spot purchase price of one Nikkei 225 index future at less than 19,000 and the sale price at 19,000 (exercise price): it is portrayed on line (1) by its 45 degree portion starting at A. At first, until the break-even point $F^*_{\text{March 95}}$, the cash profit simply recoups the cost of the option premium. Perhaps most importantly, at no point is the buyer of the put option exposed to losing more than the upfront cash premium. Thus the payoff to the option holder can be summarized as follows:

for $F_{\text{March 95}} \geq E_{\text{March 95}}$:

$$\text{Payoff} = -p(0) \cdot (1 + i_{\text{JAP}}) = -¥500[1 + 0.06/(365/75)] = -¥506.16$$

for $F_{\text{March 95}} < E_{\text{March 95}}$:

$$\text{Payoff} = F_{\text{March 95}} - E_{\text{March 95}} - p(0) \cdot (1 + i_{\text{JAP}})$$
$$= F_{\text{March 95}} - 19{,}000 - 500[1 + 0.06/(365/75)]$$

where $i_{\text{JAP}} = 0.06/(365/75) = 1.23\%$ is the opportunity cost to the option buyer of tying up the premium for the life of the option (75 days). The intersection point $F^*_{\text{March 95}}$ (break-even) at which the option holder is starting to make a profit in excess of the upfront premium can be readily found by setting the payoff equal to zero:

$$F^*_{\text{March 95}} - [E_{\text{March 95}} - p(0) \cdot (1 + i_{\text{JAP}})] = 0$$
$$F^*_{\text{March 95}} = 19{,}000 - 500(1 + (0.06/(365/75))) = 18{,}494.$$

Clearly speculating through the purchase of a put option is a very prudent way of making a bet on a downward moving stock market. The maximum loss is known ex-ante as the put option premium. By contrast writing, a put option is a very aggressive way of speculating that the stock market would not decline.

Writer of a Put Option. For every purchase of a put option the buyer has to find a seller willing to write the option. For a cash premium $p(0)$ collected upfront the writer of a put option commits to buying the Nikkei 225 index future at the strike price $E_{\text{March 95}} = 19{,}000$. Should the index appreciate beyond the strike price the buyer of the put option will abandon the option and the put option writer will keep the option premium. If the index price $F_{\text{March 95}}$ at maturity of the option were to depreciate below 19,000 the option buyer will exercise his option forcing the option writer to buy the Nikkei 225 index at the exercise price of 19,000. The option writer will incur a cash loss of $19{,}000 + p(0) - F_{\text{March 95}}$. As the index price depreciates further and further away from the exercise price his losses will deepen. His payoff (the dotted line (2) in Figure 4) is symmetrical to the option buyer's payoff since, combined, they have a zero-sum gain (disregarding transaction costs). In other words, what the option holder loses, the option writer keeps ($F_{\text{March 95}} \geq 19,000$ shown as AH = BH) in Figure 4), and what the option holder gains, the option writer loses ($F_{\text{March 95}} < 19,000$). Thus the option writer faces *unlimited* losses when the option is exercised, whereas his gains are limited to the option premium. In Figure 4, the reader will note that the option premium (shown as the distance of the horizontal portion of the put option profile to the origin along the abscissa, AH or BH), is equal to the distance HC between the exercise price and the break-even rate (disregarding interest costs).

Call Options. Consider the purchase on January 14, 1995, of a March 95 call option with exercise price $E_{\text{March 95}} = 19,000$ and premium $p(0) = ¥500$. The holder of such a call option has the right to purchase a Nikkei 225 index futures contract on March 31 at the strike price of 19,000 if it is advantageous to do so. Specifically, if the stock index future turns out to be less than 19,000 on March 31, the option holder would simply abandon his call option with a total loss no larger than the *future* value of the premium paid 75 days earlier. In Figure 5 the horizontal portion to the left of point B on line (1) sketches the terminal profit/loss (vertical axis) of the call option as a function of $F_{\text{March 95}}$ measured on the horizontal axis. Should the Nikkei 225 index futures be in excess of 19,000 the option holder will exercise his call option so as to profit from the difference between index price and the strike price. His cash profit equals the difference between the current sale price of one Nikkei 225 stock index futures at a rate higher than 19,000 and the exercise price at 19,000: it is portrayed by the 45 degree line starting at B. At first, the cash profit simply recoups the cost of the option premium. Perhaps most importantly at no point is the buyer of the call option exposed to losing more than the upfront cash premium. Thus the payoff to the option

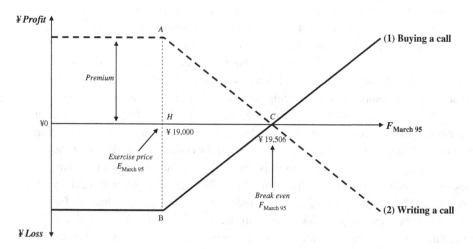

Figure 5   Payoff of call option on Nikkei 225 index futures.

holder can be summarized as follows:

for $F_{\text{March 95}} \leq E_{\text{March 95}}$:

$$\text{Payoff} = -p(0) \cdot (1 + i_{\text{JAP}}) = -¥500[1 + 0.06/(365/75)] = -¥506.16$$

for $F^*_{\text{March 95}} > E_{\text{March 95}}$:

$$\text{Payoff} = F^*_{\text{March 95}} - E_{\text{March 95}} - p(0) \cdot (1 + i_{\text{JAP}})$$
$$= F^*_{\text{March 95}} - 19,000 - 500[1 + 0.06/(365/75)]$$

where $i_{\text{JAP}} = 0.06/(365/75) = 1.23\%$ is the opportunity cost to the option buyer of tying up the premium for the next 75 days or life of the option. The intersection point $F^*_{\text{March 95}}$ (break-even) at which the option holder is starting to make a profit in excess of the upfront premium can be readily found by setting the payoff equal to zero:

$$F^*_{\text{March 95}} - E_{\text{March 95}} - p(0) \cdot (1 + i_{\text{JAP}}) = 0$$
$$F^*_{\text{March 95}} = 19,000 + 500[1 + 0.06/(365/75)] = 19,506.$$

In Figure 5, the reader will note that the option premium (shown as the distance of the horizontal portion of the call option profile to the origin along the abscissa, AH or BH) is equal to the distance HC between the exercise price and the break-even rate (disregarding interest costs).

Writer of a Call Option. For a cash premium $p(0)$ collected upfront the writer of the call option commits to delivering the Nikkei stock index futures contract at the strike price $E_{\text{March 95}} = 19,000$. Should the index decline below the strike price the buyer of the call option will abandon the option and the call option writer will keep the option premium. If the index price $F_{\text{March 95}}$ at maturity of the option were to appreciate beyond 19,000 the option buyer will exercise his option forcing the option writer to deliver the Nikkei stock index futures contract at the exercise price of 19,000. The option writer will incur a cash loss of $19,000 + p(0) - F_{\text{March 95}}$. As the futures index price appreciates further and further away from the exercise price his losses will deepen. His payoff (the dotted line (2) in Figure 5 starting at A) is symmetrical to the option buyer's payoff since, combined, they have a zero-sum game (disregarding transaction costs). In other words, what the option holder loses, the option writer keeps (option premium for $F_{\text{March 95}} \leq 19,000$ shown as AH = BH) in Figure 5, and what the option holder gains, the option writer loses (for $F_{\text{March 95}} > 19,000$). The reader will also note that the option writer faces *unlimited* losses when the option is exercised, whereas his gains are limited to the option premium shown as the distance of the horizontal portion of the call option profile to the origin along the abscissa, AH or

---

Box D. Valuation of Stock Index Futures Options. *The option premium paid by the buyer to the writer can be broken down into two basic components: intrinsic value and time value.*

Referring to the March 95 call option on the Nikkei 225 index the intrinsic value equals the difference between the exercise price of the option $E_{\text{March 95}}$ and the value of the futures index $F_{\text{March 95}}$. Whenever the spot price of the underlying index exceeds the exercise price of a call option, it stands to reason that the call option holder can make a profit by buying the index futures at the exercise price and selling it at the prevailing futures price. Conversely, the option writer will seek fair compensation by charging a premium that is at least equal to the difference between the futures price and the exercise price:

$$\text{Intrinsic value of a call option} = F_{\text{March 95}} - E_{\text{March 95}}.$$

The time value component of the option premium refers to whatever amount option buyers are willing to pay above and beyond the option's intrinsic value. Since options are in a sense a bet on the volatility of the underlying index futures, the longer the time remaining until expiration of the option (March 31−t) the more likely it is that the futures index price will exceed the exercise price. Conversely, as the option expiration date draws closer, the option's time value will decline very sharply.

In Figure 6 the value of the premium of a Nikkei 225 futures index call option prior to maturity is shown as a function of the prevailing index futures price. The option's intrinsic value, line (1), is (a) zero when the option is out-of-the-money (to the left of the exercise price $E_{\text{March 95}}$) or (b) equal to the difference between the spot index futures price and the exercise price when the option is in-the-money (to the right of the exercise price). The time value is shown as the difference between the total value, line (3), and the intrinsic value, line (2). It demonstrates that the value of an option is always larger than its intrinsic value provided that there is time left until expiration (t < March 31). Clearly, at expiration (t = March 31), the value of an option is its intrinsic value, since there is no time value left.

BH and equal to the distance HC between the exercise price and the break-even rate (disregarding interest costs).

Behind speculative bets through options are scenarios about the volatility of the Nikkei 225 index futures and how they relate to the complicated matter of valuing options. As explained in Box D one of the drivers of an option value is the volatility of the underlying asset. The more volatile the value of the underlying asset the more valuable the option becomes. Leeson was taking advantage of the fact that the high volatility in the stock market was making options expensive and therefore by writing put and call options on the Nikkei 225 index futures Leeson was cashing in high premia which he needed to fund his expensive "speculative addiction."

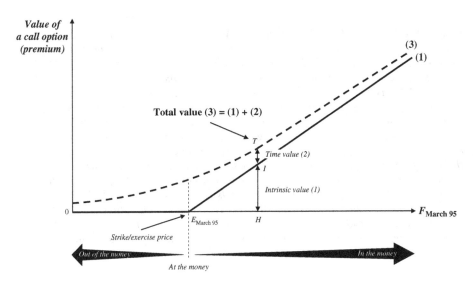

Figure 6 Value of a call option premium.

FINANCING MARGIN CALLS BY SELLING VOLATILITY

Confronted by gargantuan margin calls resulting from huge long positions on the Nikkei 225 index, Leeson started to write options on said index so as to generate sizeable premium income which would allow him to partially finance margin calls. Curiously and somewhat inconsistently, in addition to taking a directional view on the Nikkei 225 index — up in this case — Leeson was also betting that the volatility in the Nikkei 225 was going to subside and that its value would fluctuate within a narrow range (see Box E). Since option premia are closely linked to the volatility of the underlying index, high volatility means expensive option premia; conversely dampened volatility would bring premia down. Whatever option combination Leeson had sold/written at a high price he was anticipating to be able to buy them back at a much lower price provided that volatility had subsided — thereby netting a sizeable profit. Indeed options — when appropriately combined — can provide lucrative payoffs on specific volatility scenarios.

Most appropriate to plays on volatility are options strategies known as *straddle and strangle*. Leeson wrote a large portfolio of put and call options combined in the mold of the above two option strategies. The key word is that Leeson "wrote" (rather than bought) put and call options. In so doing Leeson collected hefty option premia hoping that these options would never be exercised if held to maturity or could be bought back at a lower price before maturity. If Leeson guessed wrong and the options

> **Box E. Volatility and the Value of Options.** *Volatility is difficult to measure. It is usually proxied by the standard deviation of past prices — in this case past prices of futures on the Nikkei 225. This approximation, in turn, assumes that prices of stock market indices follow a lognormal probability distribution. Historic (ex-post) volatility is not necessarily a reliable predictor of future (ex-ante) volatility whereas implied volatility (derived from the options market price) captures the market consensus. In generating such estimates one will have to decide what past time periods to use for observing prices as well as the frequency of the data. Volatility measured over the last five weeks with daily prices will be quite different from volatility gauged over the last five years using weekly prices. By contrast implied volatility at any given point in time can be extracted from current option prices by solving option pricing models for volatility since all the other parameters are known. However one should keep in mind that option prices are themselves set by traders who feed into the option valuation models their own subjective measure of volatility — itself based on some measure of past volatility.*

were to be exercised Barings would face very large losses. Now let us turn to the specifics of the "deadly game" that Leeson chose to play.

Straddle. Buying a straddle is the simultaneous purchase of one put and one call option at the same exercise price and with the same maturity. This strategy is especially attractive to option buyers when one anticipates high stock index volatility but is hard-pressed to forecast the direction of the stock market. Leeson was actually selling straddles on the premise that the Nikkei 225 index volatility was going to subside and that the Nikkei 225 would stabilize at a level around the options' strike price. Consider the following market situation faced by Leeson on January 14, 1995 and how he constructed the writing/sale of a straddle.[107]

Written:	1/14/95		
Assume:	March 95 option		
Call strike:	¥19,000	Put strike:	¥19,000
Call premium:	¥500	Put premium:	¥500

Let us now sketch with precision the building blocks of a straddle strategy — that is the writing of a call and put options on the Nikkei 225 index at the same strike price of 19,000.

Writing of a Call. For a cash premium of ¥500 collected on January 14, 1995 Leeson would commit to delivering one Nikkei 225 index futures at the strike price of

---

[107] This is a simplified numerical illustration: in reality for the same strike price put and call premia would be different.

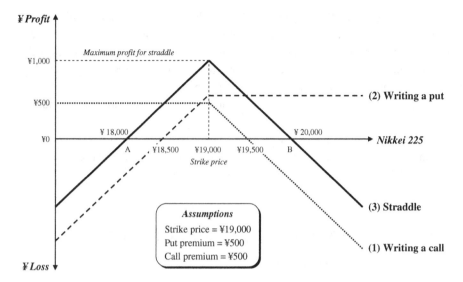

Figure 7 Payoff from writing a straddle.

19,000. If the stock index were to remain below the strike price of 19,000 the option will not be exercised and Barings keeps the option premium. Should the stock index rise above the strike price Barings will have to deliver the stock index futures at 19,000. These stock index futures would have to be purchased at a higher level. The more expensive the Nikkei 225 index gets the higher the losses incurred by Barings. Line (1), in Figure 7, sketches the payoff profile from writing a call option. Barings makes a profit equal to the premium ¥500 at any level up to the strike price of 19,000 since the call option would not be exercised. Beyond 19,000 the profit line is downward sloping. However, between 19,000 and 19,500 (strike price + premium) the premium is at least partially covering losses due to the movement of the stock index. At 19,500 the loss due to stock index movement is exactly equal to the premium. This is the break-even point. Beyond 19,500 Barings incurs ever-increasing losses.

Writing of a Put. For a cash premium of ¥500 Barings would commit to buying the Nikkei 225 at the strike price of 19,000. Line (2) in Figure 7 sketches the payoff profile from writing a put. Until the strike price of 19,000, the buyer will exercise his option to sell the Nikkei at 19,000. Barings will incur a cash flow loss in this range due to the fact that it must buy the Nikkei at 19,000 and can only resell them at the lower price. Losses will be incurred up until 18,500 (strike price − premium) where the loss due to the stock index movements equals the profit from the premium. Beyond the strike price of 19,000 the option will not be exercised and Barings retains the full premium of ¥500 per stock index transacted.

Plotting the Straddle. Writing the straddle is the bundling of a put and a call shown in Figure 7 as the graphical sum[108] (line 3) of a call (line 1) and put (line 2). Please note the pyramid top (in bold) of a straddle where Barings nets a profit. Of interest are the break-even exchange rates A and B within which Barings makes money because of small movements in the value of the Nikkei 225 (low volatility) and outside of which it incurs deepening losses because of large swings in the value of the index (high volatility).

To figure out the index prices at which the straddle will cross the x-axis (the break-even points), we simply add/subtract the *sum* of the call and put premia to/from the strike price.

Break-even A:

$$S^A = \text{strike price} - (\text{call premium} + \text{put premium})$$

$$S^A = 19,000 - (500 + 500) = 18,000$$

Break-even B:

$$S^B = \text{strike price} + (\text{call premium} + \text{put premium})$$

$$S^B = 19,000 + (500 + 500) = 20,000.$$

Therefore, when the stock index is below 18,000 or above 20,000, Barings will lose money and the loss is literally unlimited should the stock index fall way below 18,000 or appreciate well above 20,000. Conversely, within the same range, when volatility is low, Barings stands to gain. Its maximum profit comes when the stock index is exactly equal to the strike price of 19,000. At that point neither option will be exercised. Therefore it suffers no loss due to stock index movement and retains the full amount of both premia, equal to ¥1,000 per Nikkei 225 index futures transacted.

Writing a Strangle. It is another speculative strategy based on volatility which also combines the writing of calls and puts. The main difference with a straddle is that the strangle combines out-of-the-money puts and calls at different strike prices. Correspondingly, the options are cheaper and the premia collected lower than in the case of straddle built on at-the-money put and call options. A strangle is less speculative than a straddle because, as we can see in Figure 8, there is a wider range over which the seller/writer of a strangle makes a profit. The downside is that, because of lower risk, the premia earned are lower.

---

[108] Referring to Figure 7 graphical sum of lines 1 and 2 shows for each Nikkei 225 index level (horizontal axis) the algebraic sum of gains/losses for lines 1 and 2 on the vertical axis.

Written:	1/14/95		
Assume:	March 95 option		
Call strike:	19,000	Put strike:	18,500
Call premium:	400	Put premium:	¥400

We first plot the payoff profile of writing a call in the normal way. See line (1) in Figure 8. The break-even is 19,900 (strike price of 19,500 + premium of ¥400). In the same way, we can plot the writing of the put where the break-even point is 18,100 (strike price of 18,500 − premium of ¥400). See line (2) in Figure 8. Writing the strangle is the bundling of the call option (line 1) and the put option (line 2) and is shown by line 3 as the graphical sum of lines 1 and 2. Of interest are the strangle break-even points when the payoff line crosses the horizontal axis (premium income equals option losses):

Break-even A:

$$S^A = \text{put strike price} - (\text{call premium} + \text{put premium})$$
$$S^A = 18,500 - (400 + 400) = 17,700$$

Break-even B:

$$S^B = \text{call strike price} + (\text{call premium} + \text{put premium})$$
$$S^B = 19,500 + (400 + 400) = 20,300.$$

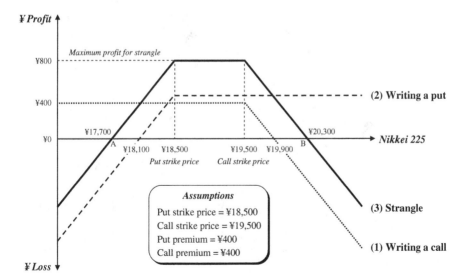

Figure 8 Payoff from writing a strangle.

Between the break-even points of 17,700 and 20,300 the strangle is profitable with maximum gains earned between the strike prices of the put and call option when neither option are exercised and Barings would collect the full sum of the put and call premia in the amount of ¥400 + ¥400 = ¥800.

Combining a Short Straddle with a Long Futures. Selling short straddles was meant to generate cash-flow premium income which Leeson could use to fund the margin required to write more straddles and to buy more Nikkei 225 index futures. Did Leeson have a master plan in combining both speculative strategies? Figure 9 sketches how the combination of one short straddle and one long futures results into writing a put option on the Nikkei 225 index at the strike price of the put and call options making up the straddle.

The most Barings could benefit from this combined strategy was capped at the premium income (to the right of 19,000) but at the cost of exposing itself to steeper bottomless losses (to the left of 19,000). Things would get worse if the combined strategy bundled more than one straddle with a long futures. Depending upon the ratio of straddles to futures, the upside potential of the long futures contract is diluted by the call option component of the straddle: the higher the ratio the less upward sloping (right of 19,000). Similarly — to the left of 19,000 — with the Nikkei index falling — the losses are steeper faster when the put option component of the straddle is combined with the losing component of the long futures contract.

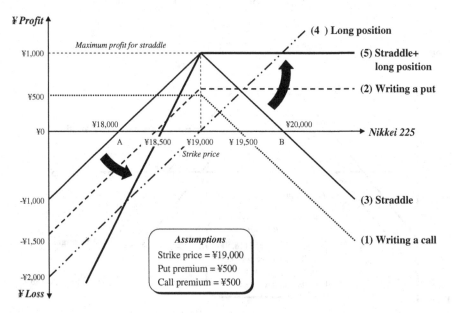

Figure 9   Combining a straddle and a long position.

Leeson's Master Plan. In the previous section we detailed the speculative positions on the volatile Nikkei 225 futures contract. Noteworthy was that at the beginning of 1995, Leeson's Nikkei position was minimal; it was not until the Kobe earthquake that Leeson went wild. His selling/writing of straddles and strangles had much to do with it. In November and December 1994 alone Leeson had sold/written 34,000 option contracts constructed as straddles and strangles. Premium income had been more than significant but the ultimate outcome of writing such option combinations had most to do with where the Nikkei would be at expiry. Most option strike prices were within a range of 18,500 and 20,000: as long as the Nikkei remained between the pre-Kobe earthquake range Leeson would hold on to some or most of the option premium income; outside the range option buyers would exercise their options and Leeson would experience possibly catastrophic losses. On January 17 the Nikkei stood at 19,350 and ended the week at 18,950 as the market seem to believe that the earthquake massive losses would soon be compensated by reconstruction activities. When the true extent of the destruction started to settle in the Nikkei fell precipitously to 17,950 on January 23. By January 27 Leeson had purchased 27,158 Nikkei 225 March 95 index futures which would eventually be doubled to 55,206 contracts by February 22. Equally damming for Leeson was the dramatic reversal of the option book with most positions now deeply out-of-the-money (see Figure 10 for cumulative losses incurred by the option book

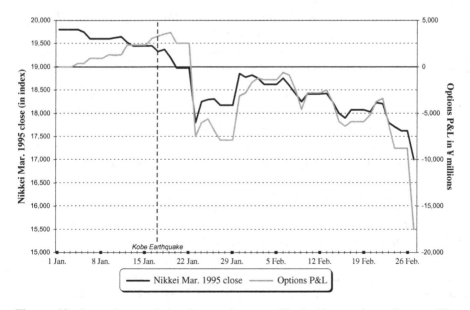

Figure 10 Leeson's cumulative losses due to selling/writing options. *Source*: The Report, p. 74.

(shown on right vertical axis) as a function of the Nikkei 225 measured on the left vertical axis). Leeson singlehandedly was attempting to shore up the Nikkei 225 to bring it back to the pre-Kobe earthquake range of 18,500–20,000 where his massive option books would expire in the money. When the Nikkei 225 refused to oblige "The Master of the Universe" had been humbled!

WARNING BELLS

How could the scale of Leeson's speculation go un-noticed and undetected for so long? Several warning bells did ring but were ignored. The first telling sign was the huge profits generated by simple arbitrage between the SIMEX and the OSE. The central paradigm of finance is the trade-off between risk and return: a very low risk activity such as arbitrage of stock index futures can only deliver parsimonious returns which made Leeson's performance abnormal and beyond comprehension. Simple benchmarking against other key players in the market would have signaled the obvious: no one made much money arbitraging Nikkei 225 index futures between the SIMEX and the OSE except for Nick Leeson. Many at Barings had questioned the relentless stream of profits that BFS consistently delivered. One referred to Leeson as a "turbo-arbitrager." An internal audit conducted over a two-week period in the summer of 1994 by James Baker purported to seek answers to *"some of the questions raised by such exceptional results: have the rules been broken to make these profits? Have exceptional risks been taken?"* And the auditors concluded that while the individual controls over BFS's system and operations are satisfactory, there is significant risk that the controls could be over-ridden by the General Manager (Leeson):

> *He is the key manager in the front and the back office and can thus initiate trans-actions on the Group's behalf and then insure that they are settled and recorded according to his own instructions."* Remarking that *"companies commonly divide responsibility for initiating, settling and recording transactions among different areas to reduce the possibility of error and fraud,"* it listed four duties that Leeson should cease: *"supervision of the back office team, check signing; signing off on the reconciliation activities at SIMEX and signing off bank reconciliation.*[109]

Approved in principle, these recommendations were never implemented. Second, but even more telling, were Leeson's repeated requests for funding which grew expo-nentially as his futures and options book flew off the chart. By and large Barings obliged the requests without questioning their rationale nor attempting systematic rec-onciliation with clients' records (see Table 1 for the actual amounts transferred by

---

[109] Cited in Rawnsley, J. H. *Total Risk* (Harper Collins, 1995), p. 155.

different units of the bank to BFS). Simple common sense should have told Barings that if Leeson's activities were so profitable, margin cash should have been returned from — rather than paid to — the SIMEX. Repeated margin calls simply meant that BFS's futures and options position were losing value.

In a related vein another incident should have raised eyebrows but did not : in late 1994, Leeson had failed to cover a £50 million shortfall in his margin account which he corrected by entering a fictitious trade in the CONTAC system — which was Barings' computerized system to maintain records of clients' trading positions. The fictitious transaction was for the writing of 2,000 lots of March 95 put options on Nikkei 225 futures which generated premium income sufficient to more than compensate for the margin account deficit. Pressed by its auditor Cooper & Lybrand to explain why it seemed that the actual cash premium had not been paid Leeson produced a forged document as evidence that the New York securities house Spear, Leeds & Kellog had indeed purchased the put options and that Citibank had credited the option premium to Barings. Scissors and paste were called into action to doctor the Citibank bank statement!

Another red light was flashed at Barings by no less than the SIMEX itself: in early January 1995, the Exchange alerted Barings to the scale of its operations and gave a detailed inventory of its position as of December 31, 1994. It also raised questions about the fact that BSL seemed to be directly financing the margin account of some of its clients which is in contravention of the law. Apparently, the correspondence was exchanged with Simon Jones — Regional Operations Manager for Barings Securities (distinct from Barings Futures) and never reached higher echelons of the bank in London.

THE ART OF CONCEALMENT

When Barings collapsed on February 27, 1995 it disclosed staggering notional positions of $7 billion on Nikkei 225 index futures, $20 billion on Japanese Government Bond futures and euro–yen interest futures and $6.68 billion on writing put and call options on the Nikkei 225 index futures for a total exposure of close to $35 billion. Most startling was the fact that all of these positions required sizeable cash margin deposits with the SIMEX and the OSE[110] when Barings' equity position was a paltry $615 million! Therefore the last piece of the puzzle that needs to be elucidated is, how

---

[110] The notional value of outstanding positions is misleading. A more reliable marked-to-market value of all contracts was probably closer to $1.5 billion — still close to three times Barings' equity position.

Table 1 Funding provided to Leeson's BFS.

Company	7 Jan. 94 £ millions	31 Dec. 94 £ millions	24 Feb. 95 £ millions
Barings Securities (London) Limited	7	13	105
Barings Securities Limited	33	142	337
Barings Securities Japan	(1)	66	300
Total	39	221	742

Source: Chew, L. *Managing Derivatives Risk* (Wiley, 1996), p. 229.

could such massive speculative positions be concealed for so long from the senior management of the bank as well as from successive internal and external auditors? When repeated and increasingly larger cash transfers to meet margin calls were requested by Leeson from various units of the Bank it seemed that all parties called upon acquiesced without raising questions (see Table 1). More specifically there are at least three core questions that need to be answered to understand the masterful deception that Leeson was able to engineer:

- How could Leeson report consistent trading profits when he was hemorrhaging speculative cash-flow losses?
- How could Leeson disguise massive speculative positions under the pretense of playing the quasi-riskless arbitrage game?
- How could Leeson keep the SIMEX at Bay?

Error Account 88,888. The instrument of deception was *Error Account* 88,888. The number 8 has special symbolic significance in the world of Chinese superstition and choosing a quintuple 8 to label the error account must have been a bad joke knowing what Leeson intended to do with the account. Error accounts are typically set up to handle trades that are miscommunicated, ill executed or disputed by the client. Such disputed trades are supposed to be resolved and closed out very promptly after the trade takes place with resulting gain or loss arising from the discrepancy lumped with the overall results of the brokerage unit. Naturally, error accounts were never meant to be used for active proprietary trading when only small profit or loss balances would be expected to be found in such account.

Error account 88,888 was opened in early July 1992 — very shortly after Leeson's arrival in Singapore: on July 8 of that year, Leeson gave specific instructions to have error account 88,888 excluded from all daily company reports sent electronically by BFS to London with the exception of the margin file (initial and maintenance margin by account and currency). Specifically, the "trade file" (trading activities of the day) and the "price file" (closing settlement prices) — which should have been reported to

London — were omitted. In Singapore, only the back office staff and some members of the trading team knew about error account 88,888. Since Leeson had hired and trained the clerical staff in charge of settlements it was relatively easy for him to keep the secret account under wraps — so much so that Barings senior management had no clue of the existence of error account 88,888 until February 23, 1995. Clearly Leeson's intimate experience with the settlement process of securities trading allowed him to manipulate the system: he had standing instructions for all trades flowing through account 88,888 that the printed bottom copy be shredded with the top copy destined to his personal records.

Fact versus Fantasy. How was Leeson able to report consistent trading profits when his speculative positions were generating consistent losses? The inquiry carried out by the Board of Banking Supervision (referred thereafter as the Report) shows the extent of the gap between aggregate reported and actual positions (see Table 2) keeping in mind that all reported and authorized positions were supposed to be matched (neither short nor long as shown in the "Reported" column in Table 3) since Leeson was engaged in risk-less arbitrage: in fact, the actual (and concealed) positions were either long on the Nikkei 225 or short on JGB or Euro–yen futures not to mention the option book and radically different from the reported (and fictitious) positions as shown under the "Actual" column in Table 3.

It concluded that the key instrument enabling the deception was the "cross-trade"[111] which explains how the maze of "crosses" allowed Leeson to inflate the results in *legitimate account* 92,000 while concealing the losses in *error account* 88,888[112]:

Table 2   Fact versus fantasy: Profitability of Leeson's trading activities.

Period	Reported	Actual	Cumulative actual[117]
1 Jan. 1993 to 31 Dec. 1993	+£8.83 million	−£21 million	−£23 million
1 Jan. 1994 to 31 Dec. 1994	+£28.529 million	−£185 million	−£208 million
1 Jan. 1995 to 27 Feb. 1995	+£18.567 million	−£619 million	−£827 million

Source: Report of the Board of Banking Supervision Inquiry into the circumstances of the collapse of Barings, Ordered by the House of Commons, Her Majesty's Stationery Office, 1995.

---

[111] According to the Report "a cross-trade is a transaction executed on the floor of an Exchange by just one member who is both buyer and seller. If a member has matching buy and sell from two different customers accounts for the same contract and at the same price he is allowed to cross the transaction (execute the deal). However, he can only do this after he has declared the bid and offer price in the pit and no other member has taken it up. Under SIMEX rules, the member must declare the price three times and a cross-trade must be executed at market price."

[112] Report of Board of Banking Supervision Inquiry into the Circumstances of the Collapse of Barings, Ordered by the House of Commons, Her Majesty's Stationary Office, 1995.

Table 3 Fantasy versus fact: Leeson's positions at end of February 1995.

Contract	Number of contracts[113] Nominal value in US$ amounts		Actual position in terms of percentage open interest of relevant maturity[116]
	Reported[115]	Actual[114]	
Futures			
Nikkei 225	30,112 $2,809 million	Long 61,039 $7,000 million	49% of March 1995 contract and 24% of June 1995 contract
JGB	15,940 $8,980 million	Short 28,034 $19,650 million	85% of March 1995 contract and 88% of June 1995 contract
Euro–yen	601 $26.5 million	Short 6845 $350 million	5% of June 1995 contract, 1% of September 1995 contract and 1% of December contract
Options			
Nikkei 225	Nil	37,925 calls $3,580 million 32,967 puts $4,100 million	

Source: The Report of the Board of Banking Supervision Inquiry into the Circumstances of the Collapse of Barings, Ordered by the House of Commons, Her Majesty's Stationery Office, 1995.

[113]Expressed in terms of SIMEX contract sizes which are half the size of those of the OSE and the TSE. For Euroyen, SIMEX and TIFFE contracts are of similar size.

[114]The actual positions refer to those unauthorized trades held in error account "88,888."

[115]Lesson's reported futures positions were supposedly matched because they were part of Barings' switching activity, i.e., the number of contracts shown was offset by an equal number of contracts on either the Osaka Stock Exchange, the Singapore International Monetary Exchange or the Tokyo Stock Exchange.

[116]Open Interest represents the number of futures contracts outstanding at a particular time. There are open interest figures for each contract month of each listed contract. For the Nikkei 225, JGB and Euroyen contracts, the contract months are March, June, September and December.

Barings Future Singapore (Leeson was general manager of BFS) entered into a significant volume of cross transactions between account 88,888 and account 92,000 (Barings Securities Japan — Nikkei and Japanese Government Bond Arbitrage), account 98,007 (Barings London — Japanese Government Bond Arbitrage) and account 98,008 (Barings London — Euroyen Arbitrage). Many of the crosses transacted by BFS appear to have taken place in the "post-settlement period," a period of three to five minutes after the official close where trading is allowed at the official settlement price. It is likely that Leeson chose this period as being one where other market operators were least likely to wish to participate in the transaction, which they were entitled to under the rules of SIMEX.

It appears that after the conclusion of the trade, Leeson would instruct the settlement staff to break down the total number of contracts into several different trades, and to change the trade prices thereon to cause profits to be credited to the "switching" accounts referred to above and losses to be charged to account 88,888. Thus while the cross-trades on the Exchange appeared on the face of it to be genuine and within the rules of the Exchange, the books and records of BFS, maintained in the Contac system (a settlement system used extensively by SIMEX members) reflected pairs of transactions adding up to the same number of lots at prices bearing no relation to those executed on the floor. Alternatively, Leeson would enter into cross-trades of smaller size than the above but when these were entered into the Contac system he would arrange for the price to be amended, again enabling profit to be credited to the "switching" account and losses to be charged to account 88,888."

The Money Trail. Mammoth speculative positions and recurring losses resulting from unsuccessful trades prompted repeated margin calls from SIMEX. Leeson could not lie to SIMEX the way he was able to consistently mislead BSL. Most requests for large cash transfers from BSL were made on behalf of clients' accounts required by SIMEX to meet margin calls. Leeson used the excuse that many of Barings customers resided in different time zones and that their checks took time to clear. Leeson also argued that large scale arbitrage between the SIMEX and the OSE necessitated the maintenance of large margins with both exchanges and that unfortunately gross positions on SIMEX and OSE could not be netted out.

The Treasurer of Barings Brothers and Co. — based in London — who was responsible for the entire group finance needs admitted that as early as 1993 differences between what BFS had requested and actual clients margin contributions could not be reconciled and that by mid-1994 the amount had grown to £100 million and by then

---

[117]The cumulative actual represents Leeson's cumulative losses carried forward.

had been accepted as a structural and irreconcilable discrepancies: they were carried on the bank's books as "loan to clients."

Fooling SIMEX. When internal controls fail the next line of defense should come from external parties — clearing houses for exchange-traded instruments or counterparties for over-the-counter contracts. To be in good stead with the SIMEX Leeson had to produce separate accounts for agency (trading on behalf of clients for commissions) and proprietary purposes (trading for the bank for profit) with proper margin requirements. The SIMEX adheres to a strict margining system known as "gross margining" whereby each client's account has to stand on its own — that is there was no netting allowed across different accounts managed by the same bank. More specifically infamous accounts 88,888 and 92,000 were set up as customers' accounts and could not be netted out for margining purposes which clearly complicated the relationship between the SIMEX and Leeson. According to the Report — from January 10, 1995 on — Leeson instructed BFS settlements staff to make adjustments between the two accounts to reduce the margin burden. The falsification of said accounts fooled SIMEX into remitting cash to BFS when it was owed money so much so that on February 23 it is estimated that BFS's margin account with SIMEX was short of at least £250 million. Leeson's masterful deception had worked his magic on SIMEX as well as it did with the House of Barings.

THE MORAL OF THE STORY: LEESON'S SEVEN LESSONS

Lesson #1: Enforce Division of Labor and Separation of Power Between Front and Back Offices. One of the golden rules of the securities and brokerage business is to segregate front and back office duties. Both desks should be staffed independently with frequent rotation at the back office to avoid collusion between the front and back office. The clerical responsibilities of the back office are focused on confirming, settling and recording the securities trades made by the front office. Most critical to these administrative responsibilities is the reconciliation of the details of each trade provided by the bank's counterparties and by the front office in terms of type of trade, price and amount of each transaction. Upon satisfactory verification, the back office will authorize payment and release of relevant securities. Such tight checks are meant to prevent unauthorized trading or criminal activities such as embezzlement. Because of the small scale of Barings' Singapore operations Leeson was allowed to run both front and back offices in spite of several warnings from successive auditors.

Lesson #2: Follow the Cash-Flow Trail. Trading futures and writing options leaves an indelible cash flow trace. When the futures contract is first bought or an option written the Exchange will ask for a margin; in the case of SIMEX it is set at 15% of the nominal value of the contract. Second, when the contract is "marked-to-market" at the close of each trading day any loss resulting from a drop in the cash value of the contract will be debited from the contract holder's margin account. A margin call will ensue whereby the contract holder will be asked to replenish the margin account to bring it back to the 15% of the notional value of the contract. Last, when the contract is liquidated or simply expires at a loss a cash outflow will immediately ensue. Senior management and auditors clearly lost the cash-flow trail early on. Reconciling the margin account against SIMEX and OSE records should be carried out by external auditors to the firm. Massive loan requests by Leeson for financing his margin account were met without much questioning of what the funds were specifically used for. When such a request exceeded the book value of Barings it would stand to reason that whoever authorized the transfer — and given the amount it had to be someone very senior within the firm — would want to investigate thoroughly the rationale for the request. Blind trust and naïve gullibility from Barings various echelons of management were just incredible!

Lesson #3. Understand Your Business. Warren Buffet is famously known — among other things — for investing only in businesses he understands. There is ample evidence that senior management on both the banking and securities broking side of Barings betrayed ignorance of the fundamental workings of derivatives market: *"A colleague once had a good position, where he had bought a very deep discount warrant on Hong Kong listed Guandgong Investments and had sold the underlying stock to create what was effectively a fully hedged long put position. But Peter Norris, chief executive of Baring Securities, called him from London and said that, as he thought Guandgong Investments was heading for a fall, the position should be closed out. My colleague was unable to explain that we would have made money if the stock price had fallen."*[118] All too often senior management at leading financial institutions is ill versed in the nuts and bolts of derivative products and financial engineering — relying on junior staff to deal with such technicalities. Board members and senior management would be well-served to school themselves into the guts of their business by attending training seminars which in 2–3 days can convey the essence of derivatives products, their valuation and how they can be configured in elaborate financial architecture.

Lesson #4: Analysis of Variance. As part of the financial planning and control process every unit within Barings would prepare a pro-forma income statement based on clear assumptions about the economic and business contexts within which the unit profit would be earned. When Leeson's unit reported 500% of his projected profit in 1994 — supposedly from arbitraging Nikkei 225 index futures between SIMEX and OSE — his

---

[118] "Barings' near death experience" in *Euromoney* (March 1995), p. 40.

supervisors should have asked questions about the unique reasons behind the abnormal results. Peter Barings declared that he was "pleasantly surprised"! Specifically analysis of variance is all about understanding differences between projected and actual performance/profit and tracing abnormal results to specific factors. Barings senior management was happy to take in the profits without asking too many embarrassing questions.

Lesson #5: Establish Trading Position Limits and Enforce Them Tightly. Leeson was allowed relatively small trading positions with some leeway to exceed them on an intra-day basis. Marking-to-market at the close of each business day should have been closely monitored for the proprietary trading book by senior management. Reconciliation with open interests with SIMEX and OSE should have provided validation of daily internal monitoring by external and independent sources but was never attempted.

Lesson #6: Monitor Open Interests. Exchanges should monitor carefully who are the key holders of open interests in their different products. Banks' senior management should also monitor open interest positions that their various trading operations may be responsible for thereby creating an external channel for auditing purposes. Sudden and dramatic change in positions in any given products by one prominent client should automatically trigger an investigation into the matter. Before the Bank's collapse Leeson was responsible for an amazing 49% of open interest in Nikkei 225 March 95 futures on SIMEX. The Exchange should keep channels of communications open with the trading entity itself — BFS in this case — as well as more senior overseers of BFS to be able to ascertain the veracity of the information obtained: traders should be held guilty of rogue behavior until proven innocent!

Lesson #7: Segregate Agency from Proprietary Trading. When the same trader executes orders on behalf of a bank's client (agency trading) and for the bank itself (proprietary trading) an obvious conflict of interest arises and the client is typically shortchanged. Proprietary trading should be ring-fenced from agency trading with each activity relying on its own separate trading desk and back office. Auditing and control mechanisms will be inherently different: agency trading is performed as a service to the bank's customer. The bank should not in principle be exposed to any risk if proper credit risk and account management are properly carried out. Proprietary trading, on the other hand, commits the bank's capital and careful control of traders' activities is vital: each trader should be subjected to tight position limits and daily reporting is an absolute necessity. Leeson was commingling both activities with no audit or control being carefully exercised on either one. Margin positions were combined and senior management had no clue which part belonged to agency or proprietary business. Position limits on futures positions for Nikkei 225 index, JGB and Eurocurrency futures were continuously flouted with no supervisory control mechanisms able to stop Leeson.

EPILOGUE

Had Barings rolled over its position for the remainder of 1995 it would have largely recouped its losses and come ahead. The Nikkei 225 index fell as low as 15,000 by midyear but closed the year above 19000. As it turned out, on March 5, 1995 ING bank — the Dutch financial conglomerate — agreed to purchase Barings wholesale for the symbolic value of £1 assuming the entire loss estimated at $1.4 billion: outstanding speculative positions were liquidated in short order just about when the Nikkei 225 index bottomed out thereby insuring maximum cash-flow losses.

On March 2, 1995, Leeson was arrested at the Frankfurt airport before being extradited to London and later to Singapore to stand trial. Condemned to a six years jail sentence, Leeson served four and a half year in the Singapore penitentiary. His autobiography "Rogue Trader" was published on the first anniversary of Barings' collapse and later turned into a film with the royalties going towards paying his legal fees. The disgraced ex-Barings trader soon became a media celebrity and was able to exploit his shameful past by appearing as a highly paid keynote speaker at conferences on fraud, operational risk and computer security. Leeson typically recounts how he brought down Britain's oldest merchant bank in 1995 under the title "Understanding the Barings Bank disaster from the man who caused it." Some would argue that in the name of rehabilitation Leeson has paid his dues, having served several years in a Singapore jail, lost his first wife and fought colon cancer. He has since recovered from cancer, rebuilt his life, remarried and is living in Ireland working as the commercial manager of Galway United football club when he is not busy on the conference and after-dinner speaking circuit.

Barings senior management barely accepted any responsibility, escaped criminal justice, never paid fines nor served a day in jail. Barings shareholders and bondholders lost their investment entirely.

Bibliography

Chew, L. *Managing Derivatives Risk* (Wiley, 1996), p. 229.

Fay, S. *The Collapse of Barings* (W. W. Norton, 1996).

Gapper, J. and N. Denton. *All that Glitters: The Fall of Barings* (Hamish Hamilton, 1996).

Ministry for Finance, Singapore. Barings futures (Singapore) Pte Ltd.: The Report of the Inspectors appointed by the Minister for Finance, 1995.

Rawnsley, J. H. *Total Risk: Nick Leeson and the Fall of the Barings Bank* (HarperCollins, 1995).

Report of Board of Banking Supervision Inquiry into the Circumstances of the Collapse of Barings, Ordered by the House of Commons, *Her Majesty Stationary Office*, 1995.

Stonham, P. Whatever happened at Barings: The Lure of Derivatives and Collapse, *European Journal of Management*, **14**(2), 167–175 (1996).

Stonham, P. Whatever happened at barings: Unauthorized trading and the failure of controls, *European Journal of Management*, **14**(3), 269–278 (1996).

Stoll, H. Lost barings: A tale in three parts concluding with a lesson, *The Journal of Derivatives*, 109–114 (Fall 1995).

Questions for Discussion

1. Why is arbitraging Nikkei 225 index futures between the OSE and the SIMEX unlikely to generate large profits? Were they any risks involved in these trades?
2. Explain the differences of speculating by buying vs. selling options on a stock index futures such as the Nikkei 225.
3. What is the difference between writing a straddle and a strangle? Are such trades speculative in natures and how do they compare to plain long or short positions on the Nikkei 225 index/
4. How was Leeson financing margins and margin calls on his futures' trading?
5. Do you believe that Leeson acted alone?
6. What should have been the role of the Board of Directors in monitoring Barings' derivatives activities?
7. Why was Barings rescued in the 1890 crisis but not in 1995?

SOCIÉTÉ GÉNÉRALE

*The urge to gamble is so universal and its practice so pleasurable that
I assume it must be evil.*

Heywood Broun

On January 24, 2008 at 8 am (Paris time) Société Générale (SoGen) announced in a terse press release that it had been the target of a fraud amounting to the modest amount of €4.9 billions ($7.2 billions). Ironically, the mother of all derivatives debacles had hit SoGen's equity trading desk — its inner sanctum for which the bank was most admired. Trading in SoGen's stock was suspended while the international financial community reeled in disbelief. A young trader Jerôme Kerviel was accused of building mammoth positions in stock index futures which he had hidden through fake offsetting trades. How could a junior trader fool the control systems of one of the most sophisticated bank? Why did he do it? Or was Kerviel made a convenient scapegoat for SoGen's acquiescence of one of its traders' reckless but highly profitable trades. The saga of wild speculation cloaked in deceit of what soon became "l' affaire Kerviel" is recounted next.

THE MAKING OF A ROGUE TRADER

Nothing predestined the villain of this story to perpetrating "financial terrorism" against one of the pillars of the French banking establishment. Jerôme Kerviel was born in a middle class family on January 11, 1977 in Pont L'Abbé — a small provincial town in western Brittany. His mother owned a beauty saloon and his father was a blacksmith

179

who also taught his trade part-time at a vocational school in Quimper. A serious student in the Lycée (French high school), Kerviel developed an early interest in finance and stock markets and received a high school diploma (Baccalauréat) with a specialty in Economics. Kerviel first aimed at the elite track in the French higher education system and prepared the "Concours" (entrance competition exam) for gaining admission to one of the "Grandes Ecoles" — the very competitive institutes which enroll approximately 1% of all French university students in Engineering, Business and Political Sciences and from which most French senior civil servants and business executives graduate. Kerviel first targeted the Institut des Etudes Politiques in Lille known for its strong curriculum in European and International affairs. Having failed to qualify, he had to settle for a more plebeian mass education at the public University of Quimper before transferring to the Institut Universitaire Professionalisé in Nantes where he earned a bachelor's degree in economics. During his last year of study he interned at one the local branches of SoGen in Nantes where he received high marks for his drive and dutiful behavior: he was encouraged to continue his studies so that he could apply for a full-time position. Kerviel heeded the advice by enrolling in the specialized masters' program in "Back and Middle Office Management for Capital Market Operations" at The University Lumière Lyon 2 which focuses on the clerical and administrative oversight of capital markets trading within financial institutions. The program was primarily taught by practitioners rather than academics and required an internship which Kerviel completed with Banque Nationale de Paris. Having graduated with a less than stellar "mention assez bien" (second class honor) Kerviel nevertheless was one of very few graduates of his class to be hired by a leading bank. Kerviel started to work for SoGen in June 2000 in the middle office at the Bank's headquarters in Paris-La Défense for the salary of €35,000.

SoGen is one of pillars of the French banking establishment whose roots go back to the mid-19th century when France was ushering into the era of modern capitalism. Société Générale was founded in 1864 by a decree from no less than Napoléon III *"pour Favoriser le Développement du Commerce et de l'Industrie en France"*[119] at a time when the French economy was undergoing fast-paced industrialization. Nationalized by General de Gaulle after World War II along other large commercial banks it was not until 1987 that SoGen was privatized again. To fully appreciate how devastating was "l'affaire Kerviel" one has to understand how large Société Générale today loom on the French finance and banking firmament:

> *"Société Générale may be best known as one of France's largest high street banks, but mention it to anyone in finance and another image comes to mind: its trading desks, populated by mathematically brilliant Frenchmen, capable of spinning gold*

---

[119] "To facilitate the development of commerce and industry in France."

out of the very raw cloth of algorithm and financial models. For the past 15 years SoGen has been to French banking what Goldman Sachs has been to Wall Street — a money making machine with a reputation for both mystery and arrogance. Chairman and CEO Daniel Bouton was the embodiment of his bank, a brilliant man given to lecturing his peers from atop his staggering profits. While other banks noodled around offering advisory advices and retail banking, Société Générale was off in the financial stratosphere, recruiting the cleverest graduates and letting them loose with the firm's own capital. Their activities were so recondite, even their bosses, let alone regulators, struggled to understand them.[120] "

Kerviel's initial assignment was of a clerical nature — working primarily in a support capacity on the equity derivatives trading desk's data base and computer systems. Performance evaluations by his superiors were generally positive singling out his "efficiency" in 2001, his "mastery of computer software" in 2002, "rigorous and independent" in his work in 2003 — in other words a model employee (Box A). The much coveted promotion to the front office finally happened in 2005 when Kerviel

---

Box A. Front, Middle, and Back Offices. *The **front** office refers to the actual trading activities of the bank such as taking of positions on various speculative markets — stock, bonds, currencies, commodities, and their derivatives. Trading is one of the very glamorous and much coveted activities at any financial institution and traders command considerable salaries and even more considerable bonuses.*

*The **back** office provides administrative and logistic support to the front office — most notably settling, bookkeeping and reconciliation of all transactions. It is also responsible for financing and payment of margins and margin calls, delivery of securities and ensuring that all activities are conducted according to applicable rules and regulations.*

*The **middle** office is charged with managing and controlling the different risks occasioned by various trading activities carried out by the trading desks including keeping track of each trader's gains and losses and enforcing position limits. It is responsible for computer systems' hardware and software and their security. In so doing it relies on the data — accounting and otherwise — provided by the front and back offices. Rogue traders such as Leeson (Barings) and Kerviel were first trained in back or middle offices before being promoted to trader. Neither of them could have hidden so effectively their fraudulent trades without an intimate knowledge of back and middle office computer-based bookkeeping and tracking systems.*

---

[120] Broughton, P. D. Tricks of the Trader: this junior French banker is taking the blame for one of the biggest scandals in history — but is he just a scapegoat for the recklessness of his bosses? *The Sunday Times* (February 15, 2009).

made its debut as an assistant trader. Kerviel received good marks as an "aggressive trader" in 2005, and "good at managing risks" in 2006 which were nuanced by "should take more vacations"[121] in 2006 and "must pay attention to operational risks" in 2007. In July of 2007 Kerviel was promoted to trader in the arbitrage trading desk of Delta One at a salary of €48,500 (approximately $65,000) plus bonus. Delta One is one of the several trading desks which make up Sogen market trading activities and is generally considered as low risk catering primarily for the bank's clients placing bets on plain vanilla stock market index futures. Ironically, Delta refers in options theory to the rate of change in the value of a derivative product for a one percent change in the value of the underlying asset: Delta One means a perfectly hedged position whereby a one percent loss in the value of the underlying is exactly compensated by a one percent gain in the value of the derivative. The Delta One trading desk with Kerviel on board at SoGen did not quite live up to its name!

FROM ARBITRAGE TO DIRECTIONAL TRADES

Banks' proprietary trading generally combine lower risk arbitrage activites with directional trades where the traders may take speculative positions with the bank's capital. Kerviel first assignment as a trader was to arbitrage turbo-warrants which are exotic options with "barriers" (see Box B). As it is often the case with proprietary trading, arbitrage is used in a somewhat loose sense since the trades do not involve an exact zero-risk combination of long/buy and short/sale positions of quasi-identical securities. In this instance, Kerviel would purchase a call option "down and out" on the DAX index (see Box C) at the strike price equal to the futures rate of say 8,000 for a cash premium of €50 with a down and out barrier at 7,750 and would "cover"[122] it by selling a DAX index futures. All this means is that if, at any point in the life of the option, the DAX index falls through the lower barrier the call option expires worthless. Because

---

[121] One of the golden rules of controlling traders is to force them to take at least 10 days of vacation every year to avoid the kind of elaborate fraud perpetrated by Kerviel. The idea is that if the trader is unable to access his trading accounts for a period of time during which someone else takes over, a fraudulent scheme would be aborted. The same issues dogged Barings and AIB whose rogue traders never went on vacations ... Ironically, France — which pioneered the 35 hour work week — takes its paid vacations very seriously: Kerviel was clearly an exception!

[122] Strictly speaking selling a DAX index futures for the same notional amount doesn't cover the purchase (long position) of a turbo call option on the same index for the same amount. However the trader did combine a long position with a short position on the same underlying security for the same amount and the same maturity.

Box B. Turbo Warrant. *Turbo warrants are long dated put or call options on stocks or stock market indices whose value at expiry is "path dependent." This means that at expiry the value of the turbo warrant will not only be a function of the value of the underlying security on that day but also of the path that the price of the underlying security followed during its life. This defining feature is an upper or lower barrier which if ever crossed during the life of the turbo warrant annuls the ability of the turbo warrant holder to exercise the call option at a subsequent point in its life. For example in the case of "down and out" call option on the DAX the turbo warrant would be de-activated — that is it would expire worthless — if at any point during the life of the turbo warrant the DAX index (underlying security) would hit the lower barrier. For bullish investors, turbo-warrants provides a highly geared instrument (hence the name "turbo") to speculate on the appreciation of the DAX index because its premium would be lower than for a plain vanilla call option (a plain vanilla option which costs more offers the same potential rewards as a turbo-option which costs less).*

---

the "down and out" call option restricts the flexibility of the option holder it is cheaper than a traditional option. Kerviel was mandated with this trade at a time of heightened stock market volatility which increased the likelihood of the DAX index crossing the lower barrier and de-activating the option thereby further lowering its cost. Kerviel

---

Box C. What is a Stock Index Futures? *A stock index futures is a futures contract based on the value of a stock market index such as New York's Dow Jones 30, Paris' CAC 40, Frankfurt's DAX or Eurostoxx whose value is itself determined by a basket of 50 European representative stocks. It is no different in design from any other futures contract based on commodities or currencies except that a stock index futures is cash-settled, i.e., does not require physical delivery of each stock in the index which would be cumbersome and costly to do. Clearly the underlying security is more complex since the index is based on the value of a basket of stocks which needs to be unambiguously measured at any given point in time. A representative set of stocks of a given stock market is combined in an index to provide a summary statistic of price movement in said stock market with reference to a base period when the index level was arbitrarily set — generally at 100.*[123] *Futures on a stock index are standardized contracts whose terms (amount, maturity) are agreed today for delivery at some future date (for example one business day before the second Friday of the contract month — March, June, September or December).*

---

[123] The index value is derived from individual stock prices. Different weighting schemes can be used for defining the value of a stock index: (1) arithmetic average of each component stock price weighted according to the firm's market capitalization as in the case of the Standard and Poor's 500 index, (2) arithmetic average of each component stock price weighted according to stock price (more expensive stock are weighted more heavily than cheaper ones regardless of the firm size and its market capitalization) such as the Dow Jones 30 or the Nikkei 225.

would also sell a futures contract at the strike price of the call option so as to reduce — but not eliminate — the risk of this trade.

- *Favorable scenario*: the DAX index falls through the lower barrier of 7,750 to 7,500. The call option expires worthless at a cost of €50. Kerviel closes the futures position by buying back the futures at 7,500 for a gain of $(8,000–7,500)−50 = 450$.
- *Unfavorable scenario*: the DAX appreciates to 8,250. The call option is in the money and can be exercised with a profit of $8250 − 8000 − 50 = 200$ since the option holder has the right to buy the DAX index at 8000 which he now can sell at 8250. The futures contract is closed at a loss of $8250 − 8000 = 250$. The net outcome is a loss of 50 which is the option premium.

In effect the bundling of "down and out" call option (line 1 on Figure 1) with a futures short position on the DAX index (line 2) was creating a "down and out" put option (line 3) on the DAX index.[124] SoGen had a downside exposure limited to the option premium (cheaper because a turbo rather than a plain option was used). Clearly Kerviel would be betting on a lower DAX index (directional trade) through a futures contract while neutralizing the downside potential (DAX appreciating above 8,000). For the trade to be attractive the option premium on the synthetic put option (already reduced by the fact that it is a turbo-warrant) would have to be slightly lower than the market

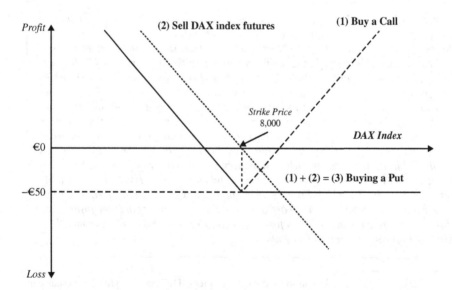

Figure 1   Buying a covered call option = buying a naked put.

---

[124] Figure 1 assumes that the "down and out" barrier is not activated.

price of a "down and out" put option. In sum the trade would exploit slight mispricing in the turbo-warrant market to create a very low risk directional trade on a downside bet on the DAX index.

The first signs of "deviant" trading appeared as early as July 2005 when Kerviel started to sell short Allianz shares for a nominal amount of €10 million which shortly thereafter generated a profit of €500,000 for the bank (see Box D). This was clearly a directional trade in direct contravention of his mandate as an assistant trader. Apparently Kerviel got mixed signals from his supervisor — a mild reprimand for breaching the ban on directional trades with a nod and a wink for the gain. Emboldened by what he understood to be a tacit approval for his speculative trades, Kerviel, for the next several months, continued to short other stocks such as Solarworld, Q-Cells, Nokia, Continental with aggregate positions rising to €140 million.

It was not until January 2006 that Kerviel shifted his focus onto futures on stock market indices — most notably the Frankfurt's DAX and the EuroSTOXX. By January 2007, Kerviel's short positions on DAX futures were still a modest notional €850 million but thereafter climbed to €2.6 billion (end of February), €5.6 billion (end of March) to peak at €28 billion on July 19, 2007. Kerviel's was convinced that the early reports of subprime mortgage foreclosures in the United States were to adversely impact European stock markets. Coincidentally and not unsurprisingly, the timing of Kerviel's emboldened speculative gambles coincided with the departure of his direct supervisor: for almost three months the position remained vacant and the

---

Box D. What is a Short Sale? *To sell a stock short Kerviel would first borrow the stock[125] and sell it immediately. Upon maturity of the loan — say 90 days later — Kerviel would have to return the stock to its rightful owner who lent it to SoGen in the first place. Kerviel would have to buy on the 90th day or sooner the stock at whatever prevailing price in order to return it to its owner and therefore close his short sale. For example assume that Kerviel borrowed Allianz shares and sold them immediately at the prevailing price of €95. Ninety days later — or sooner — to close his short sale Kerviel would purchase the same stock which now trades at say €80 thereby generating a net profit of €95 − €80 + €95 (0.04/4) = €16 where the last term accounts for the interest earned (at the rate of 4% for 90 days or 90/360 = 1/4 of a year) on the cash proceeds from the short sale. The cash proceed from the short sale would be deposited with the owner/lender of the stock. Typically a small amount of 1 or 2% would be added to the cash deposit should the value of the stock sold short to increase. Should Allianz shares to increase in value to say €110 Kerviel would close his short sale at a loss of €95 − €110 + €95 (0.04/4) = −€14.*

---

[125] The lender of the stock is getting a collateralized loan.

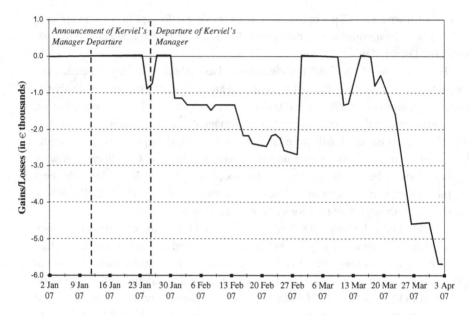

Figure 2 Date of Kerviel's manager departure (23/01/07) coincides with building of fraudulent and speculative positions on stock market indices. *Source*: Société Générale (Inspection Générale), *Mission Green: Rapport de Synthèse* (20 Mai 2008), p. 44.

supervisory responsibilities were assumed temporarily by the trading desk's senior trader (see Figure 2)

These short positions triggered massive losses through the first part of 2007 which were recouped in early August 2007 when they were unwound. Shortly thereafter Kerviel started to rebuild mammoth short positions on the same indices. The rollercoaster of trading gains and losses had shown massive losses reaching €3 billion in July 2007 before a dramatic reversal of fortune allowed Kerviel to climb out of the hole to finish the year with a profit which reached the staggering sum of €1.4 billion — half of SoGen's entire trading profits. Kerviel concealed most of his closing position by entering into eight offsetting but fake forward contracts for a notional amount of €30 billion thereby creating a fictitious offsetting loss of €1.357 billion and reporting a more reasonable €43 million[126] in net profit (see Figures 3 and 4). Kerviel asked for a bonus of €600,000 but was awarded only half of it on the basis that he was still a junior trader.

---

[126] The reported profit of €43 million are equal to: realized profit on stock index futures — fictitious and unrealized losses on fake forwards = €1.4 billion − €1.357 billion = €43 million.

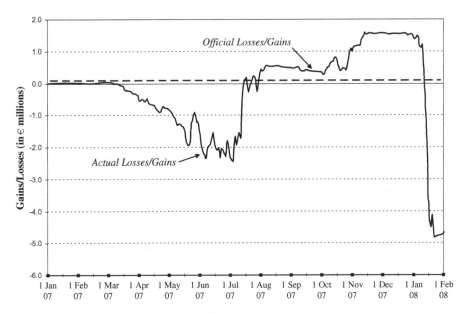

Figure 3 Kerviel's "actual" trading gains/losses are concealed to show a modest "official"gain (shown as dotted almost horizontal line). *Source*: Société Générale (Inspection Générale), *Mission Green: Rapport de Synthèse* (20 Mai 2008), p. 22.

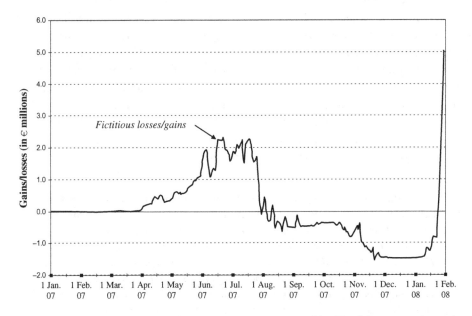

Figure 4 Estimated amount of fictitious gains/losses created by Kerviel to conceal actual losses/gains. *Source*: Société Générale (Inspection Générale), *Mission Green: Rapport de Synthèse* (20 Mai 2008), p. 22.

In early 2008, Kerviel rekindled his speculative gambit and rapidly built long positions on European stock market indices which reached €50 billions by mid-January.
His bet this time was that there would be no recession after all and that stock markets
would renew their ascent. The DAX however which had opened the year close to an
all-time high of 8,000 had lost close to 20% of its value by January 21: Kerviel's
positions were in free fall while SoGen was finally starting to ask pointed questions to
counterparties about some of his fraudulent forward contracts which had allowed him
to conceal his huge 2007 trading profits. Specifically, on January 17, compliance officers enquired about the Baader Bank listed as the counterparty on one of the forward
contracts. Kerviel replied that an error had been made and that the correct counterparty was in fact Deutsche Bank and provided documentation by forging two e-mails
which pretended to be confirmation from traders at Baader and Deutsche Bank.[127]
When confirmation from Deutsche Bank failed to materialize the alarm bells finally
rang. The Kerviel's gambit was about to unravel: the tip of the iceberg had finally been
sighted.

HASTY CONCLUSION

The compliance unit remained skeptical of the two e-mails produced by Kerviel and
when verification from Deutsche failed SoGen set up a crisis unit. The various heads
of trading could not comprehend why would a young trader set up a fictitious losing
trade for €1.357 billion. Somewhat embarrassingly for SoGen it had taken sometime
before calling competitor Deutsche to enquire about a phantom €30 billion trade. But
now there was no escaping the facts which were coalescing into a mammoth fraud.
When finally confronted by Jean-Pierre Mustier — SoGen head of all investment
banking activities — about his fictitious forwards Kerviel admitted *"Yes, it is true —
they are fictitious. But I invented this trade to offset the €1.4 billion in my 2007 profits.
I wanted to make you a surprise. I discovered a martingale on short-term DAX index
futures by toying with the market schedule of opening hours."* SoGen's inner circle

---

[127] On January 18, Kerviel forwarded two e-mails that were supposed to emanate from Baader
and Deutsche Bank: the first one from Deutsche Bank read *"Hi Jerôme, to confirm the trades
done with Baader have to be booked against me and not Baader. Keep me informed if you need
more details or you need to exercise them this month. Regards, C."*; the second came from
Baader *"Hi Jerôme, as discussed by phone, I fully understand the problem so you have to book
directly against Deutsche Bank London, the counterpart I crossed futures with. As a reminder
here are the trades to be booked. Christophe from Deutsche agreed on it as well and of course
this is to be netted by pair (in and out)"* in Delhommais, P.-A. Cinq Milliards en Fumée (Seuil:
Paris, 2008), p. 15.

of senior managers at the investment banking unit were dumbfounded by what they just heard. They were all high-powered "quants" and financial engineers — graduates from the elite French engineering schools: trading for them is a science played through rigorous mathematical models and equations — markets are anything but a casino. That Kerviel — who graduated from a third-tier university — may have uncovered the secret formula for winning consistently on futures and option markets was beyond comprehension. Very quickly the true extent of the monumental fraud was discovered and the web of Kerviel's trading activities for 2007 unmasked. When asked about whether he had resumed his speculative trades in 2008 Kerviel's nonchalant response was "a few but nothing major." As it turned out in the first two weeks of 2008 Kerviel had built another €50 billion of long positions which unfortunately were now showing a loss of €2.7 billion.

After consulting with his close lieutenants, Daniel Bouton decided to close or liquidate the bank's mammoth positions as early as economically feasible while abiding by market rules of not exceeding 10% of daily overall trading. That meant as early as the next morning of Monday, the 21th of January 2008. Bouton informed in guarded terms his board of directors after having — that same Sunday — consulted with the Governor of the Banque de France Christian Noyer and no one else. Neither President Sarkozy or his Minister of Finance Christine Lagarde were informed until after positions had been fully liquidated.

SoGen wanted to avoid any leak both within the bank and in financial markets at large to avoid a run on the bank's stock. The fear was that rival banks would seize on the opportunity to corner SoGen by selling aggressively the same stock index futures that SoGen had to unload thereby deepening the huge losses. SoGen proceeded with the speed of light. On that same Sunday afternoon (January 20) it summoned to its headquarters at La Défense its star trader, Maxime Kahn, who had made a personal fortune trading derivatives and who was especially experienced in arbitraging stock index futures against synthetic basket of stocks. Kahn was given sole responsibility to unload some €50 billion of outstanding stock index futures in 72 hours. SoGen set him up in a special office with all necessary computers and screens away from the main trading floor so that total secrecy could be maintained. Kahn himself was not told the whole story: instead the bank pretended that it had taken these positions on behalf of a client who now needed to unwind them as quickly as possible. In fact there was no client! It was a thankless task to be carried out with utmost secrecy in the most difficult of market conditions. Indeed the index futures positions were gargantuan with €30 billion on the EuroSTOXX index, €18 billion on the German DAX and €2 billion on the British Footsie. Most problematic was going to be the DAX futures positions which amounted to 140,000 contracts or the daily turnover on the German futures market.

WHEN ALARM BELLS ARE IGNORED

The "affaire Kerviel" raises at least three very perplexing questions (1) how can a trader subjected to daily trading limits and forbidden to engage in directional trades build speculative positions on several European stock index futures amounting to €50 billion? (2) How could a trader engaging in low-risk quasi arbitrage trading of turbo-warrants generate such off the chart results without raising eyebrows, and (3) How could — over the entire 2007 calendar year — a cash flow loss of €3 billion later reversed into a cash-flow gain of €1.4 billion go entirely undetected? Could a rogue and lone trader pull off the fraud of all times without any complicity from SoGen's higher echelons of management? Were SoGen's management and information systems so inadequate that a junior trader could single-handedly circumvent them over and over again? When all else failed an external inquiry from no less than the clearing house Eurex should have arisen suspicions.

Circumventing Trading Limits. Outright speculation on stock market indices would by necessity create large either long or short positions at the close of each trading day. Kiervel's trading desk (which included a total of eight traders) was subject to a daily overall trading limit of €125 million. Somehow Kerviel masterminded a complex scheme of offsetting transactions which fooled not only his direct supervisor and the manager of his trading desk — both of whom were the first line of defense in enforcing daily trading limits — but also SoGen's back and middle offices (see next section). Typically alarms bells should be set off both internally when the back office verifies counterparties and externally when clearing houses investigate positions which exceed open interest limits.

Tracking Performance. The basics of any performance evaluation system is to set an ex-ante goal for the results that Kerviel could conceivably generate through arbitraging turbo-warrants and to track them ex-post against actual results. When actual results — in the case of Kerviel a €55 million profit — are compared to budgeted profit of €3 million alarms bells should have rung loud and clear: variance analysis — understanding the reasons behind the huge gap between budgeted and actual results — should have led to an in-depth audit of Kerviel's trading activities.

Following the Cash-Flow Trail. The huge positions taken by Kerviel inevitably triggered large scale cash-flows movements requiring SoGen to post initial margins and answer subsequent margin calls. Indeed this is one important responsibility for the back office to insure that on a daily basis proper disbursement be made to each clearing house. Since the amounts involved on account of Kerviel's trading alone were often in excess of €1 billion one must wonder how could such huge cash flows be disbursed without sounding any alarm. Apparently the back office did not get a breakdown of cash flow payment by trader; therefore Kerviel's cash flows were diluted in the overall cash disbursements of the bank and were not directly traced back to him: however as Figure 5 illustrates, Kerviel's margin cash-flows accounted for an average of 25% of

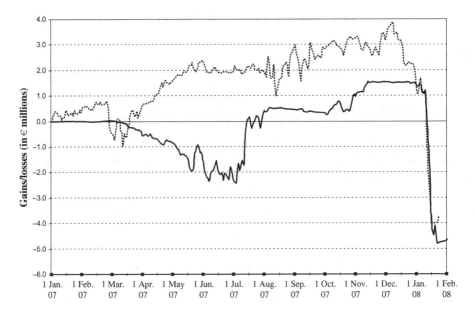

Figure 5 Total cumulated cash paid by SoGen to FIMAT (Frankfurt) as a dotted line vs. total cumulated cash paid on Kerviel's account to FIMAT as a continuous line. *Source*: Société Générale (Inspection Générale), *Mission Green: Rapport de Synthèse* (20 Mai 2008), p. 54.

SoGen's cash-flow movements with FIMAT alone and peaked at approximately 40% in late November 2007: clearly such huge cash-flows should have drawn attention. More perplexing is the fact that both Kerviel's direct supervisor and the manager of Delta One trading desk would each get a daily cash flow statement from each of their trader: it is hard to believe that neither of them over time became suspicious when Kerviel's mandate was market making and arbitraging turbo warrants!

External Alerts. On two occasions in November 2007, Eurex — Deutsche Borse's clearing house — contacted Kerviel's supervisor inquiring about the pattern of Kerviel trading in DAX futures. Most notably a specific question was raised about the purchase over a very short time interval of 2 hours of 6,000 contracts amounting to approximately €1.2 billion. SoGen simply forwarded Kerviel's answers without any further investigation. Surprisingly Eurex did not question the enormous positions in DAX futures that Kerviel was amassing: it clearly exceeded the mandatory ceiling of 12.5% of open interests that any market participant is supposedly limited to. At the height of the crisis Kerviel had an open position of €18 billion in DAX futures corresponding to approximately 90,000 contracts when the open interest for this contract hovers around 200,000 contracts: with 45% of all outstanding contracts Kerviel was clearly cornering the market and regulators were looking the other way!

THE ART OF CONCEALMENT

The repeated breach of trading limits was achieved by a complex strategy of rolling over fictitious trades. The first stratagem used by Kerviel was to book fictitious trades which would neutralize his fraudulent trades: since the reporting system focused on *net* daily trading positions — rather than *gross* positions — Kerviel was able to show a net position close to zero and therefore not arise any suspicions. To avoid the creation of a cash flow trail Kerviel chose to offset large stock index futures positions through over-the-counter forward contracts on the same stock market indices which — unlike futures — do not require the posting of cash margins. Such fictitious trades (like any other trades) would have to be confirmed with their counterparties and Kerviel would purposely choose transactions which would offer the latest settlement date (as late as 7 days) and thereby delay confirmation. One of the ruse that Kerviel would use was to define the counterparty as "pending" and/or internal to SoGen: for example, many of the fictitious trade would identify CLICKOPTIONS — a 100% SoGen owned subsidiary — as a counterparty knowing that in such cases confirmation is not necessary and that reconciliation of accounts amongst various units of the bank would only occur monthly. Kerviel would cancel the fictitious trade right before it would come to settlement and rebook it putting in place a deceitful but effective strategy of "fake and roll." The Green commission report commissioned by SoGen identified no fewer than 947 transactions of this type.

The second stratagem meant to muddle the cash flow trail was the booking of a pair of fictitious trades meant to create a fictitious loss or gain depending on the circumstances. For example, on March 1, 2007 Kerviel purchased 2,266,500 shares of SOLARWORLD at €63 and sold the same number of shares at €53 for a fictitious loss €22.7 million without creating a new position. To the extent that the back office scrutinized profit and loss statements rather than cash flow statements the paired trades would help conceal actual profits that Kerviel was generating on account of its speculative directional trades. The Green commission report identified 115 such transactions.[128]

THE MORAL OF THE STORY

Lesson #1. Failure to Control. At its simplest the mechanics of daily reporting and control between the "front" and "back" office of the bank's trading operations work as follows: the derivatives trader executes his trades, keeps a daily log and writes

---

[128] Société Générale (Inspection Générale), Mission Green: Rapport de Synthèse (2008): p. 24.

trade tickets which are entered by the back office into the bank's accounting system. This latter department will, in turn, verify independently each trade against a broker or counterparty to validate and ensure accuracy of the transaction. Independent confirmation is really the backbone of the control process. The "middle" office or risk department will then compute the daily trading gains/losses associated with the book of outstanding contracts and compare it with daily trading limits.

In order to implement such a control system commercial banks put great emphasis on a foolproof "book" of rules and then charge the back office with implementing it. However the best administrative guidelines will never fully discourage an inventive trader from circumventing them. SoGen's control process failed both the letter and spirit of its intent.

The letter. The back office ignored one of its basic responsibilities: to get proper and independent confirmation directly from the counterparty rather than the trader himself. Since the bank is trying to get independent confirmation of what its front office is dealing it stands to reason that it shouldn't rely on the trader itself to get confirmation. The back office should apply a healthy dose of mistrust to the front office questioning the letter as well as the spirit of the "book" of rule.

The spirit of the trader's activities was also ignored: it is not enough to seemingly follow the rules, the trader should be asked to provide a simple narrative allowing for each transaction to be put in an understandable strategic context and to be shown to be consistent with legitimate trading.

Lesson #2: Failure to Follow the Cash Flow Trail. Financial accounting documents can be easily misleading. Realized and unrealized amounts (in a cash-flow sense) are commingled and the practice of marking-to-market outstanding futures and option contracts only exacerbates the confusion. Attention is all too often wrongly given to the income statement rather than to the cash-flow statement. Tailor-made over-the-counter trades — unlike standardized exchange traded products — are not subject to margin calls. Attaching a margin account to each trading desk and treating every single over-the-counter forward trade as if it were exchange-traded would have forced the bank to follow the cash-flow trail rather than the accounting trail. Trading futures leaves an indelible cash flow trace. When the futures contract is first bought the Exchange will ask for a margin: in the case of Eurex it is set at 15% of the nominal value of the contract. Second, when the contract is "marked-to-market" at the close of each trading day any loss resulting from a drop in the cash value of the contract will be debited from the contract holder's margin account. A margin call will ensue whereby the contract holder will be asked to replenish the margin account to bring it back to the 15% of the notional value of the contract. Last, when the contract is liquidated or simply expires at a loss a cash outflow will immediately ensue from the margin account. Senior management and auditors clearly lost the cash-flow trail early on. Reconciling the margin account against Eurex records should be carried out by external auditors to the firm to avoid any tempering with the process by insiders.

Lesson #3: Failure to Establish Trading Position Limits and Enforce Them Tightly. Kerviel was allowed a relatively small trading position of €500,000 with some leeway to exceed them on an intra-day basis. Marking-to-market at the close of each business day should have been closely monitored for the proprietary trading book by senior management. Reconciliation of open interests with Eurex should have provided validation of daily internal monitoring by external and independent sources but was never attempted.

Lesson #4: Failure to Monitor Open Interests. Exchanges should monitor carefully who are the key holders of open interests in their different products. Banks' senior management should also monitor open interest positions that their various trading operations may be responsible for thereby creating an external channel for auditing purposes. Sudden and dramatic changes in positions in any given products by one prominent client should automatically trigger an investigation into the matter. Before the SoGen derivative debacle Kerviel was responsible for an amazing 40% of open interest in DAX index futures on Eurex. The Exchange should have kept channels of communication open with the trading entity itself — Delta One in this case — as well as with more senior overseers of Delta One to be able to ascertain the veracity of the information obtained: traders should be held guilty of rogue behavior until proven innocent!

Lesson #5: Failure to Break the "Routine Chain." When all else fails, rotating employees and enforcing consecutive vacation rules will unveil elaborate and fraudulent concealment schemes. US laws require that traders take 10 consecutive days of vacation off from trading activities every year. The intent of the law is clearly that someone else would take over temporarily the activities of the trader on leave and thereby facilitate the uncovering of fraud. Apparently, SoGen didn't enforce the law and Kerviel never strayed away from his trading desk for more than four days.

Lesson #6: Avoid Promoting Back or Middle Office Administrators to the Position of Trader. To orchestrate frauds on the scale of the one perpetrated by Kerviel required an intimate familiarity with the bank's back office modus operandi as well access to its computer systems. Short of being a brilliant computer hacker the next best training is to work for some length of time in the back office of the bank's trading operations. Kerviel did and so did Leeson. Both were suffering from inferiority complexes which compounded their propensity to prove themselves as part of the elite breed of star traders by gambling away the capital of their employer.

Lesson #7: Failure to Allocate Adequate Resources to Back and Middle Offices. SoGen was experiencing rapid growth and exploding profits in its proprietary trading activities and yet, failed to allocate commensurate resources to its control apparatus. SoGen's computer software system — known as Eliot — had been conceived in the mid-1990's to handle a volume of transactions of one-tenth of what it was in 2008.

In 2004, Bouton commissioned the computer control system modernization project Idea which was supposed to bring SoGen into the 21st century: launched with much fanfare this in-house ambitious €50 million project was marred with problems almost from its inception and was still in the design (rather than implementation) phase when the Kerviel debacle hit SoGen. Similarly the back office was overwhelmed by the volume of transactions as it failed to build up its manpower to provide adequate follow up on each trader's daily activities. Kerviel trades prompted several dozens of computer-generated red-flags which were almost never investigated. As Figure 4 illustrates the departure of his direct supervisor on January 23, 2007 emboldened Kerviel to test the control system's tolerance for deviant trading. It would seem that with the huge trading profits and bonuses paid out to traders Sogen may have been well-advised to set aside a small percentage — perhaps 10% — of its proprietary trading profits to double up on each trader with a "shadow" controller/auditor. Simple numerical goals for metrics such as headcount of "(back office + middle office staff)/front office traders" and "(gross volume of trading)/(total cost devoted to back and middle office)" would insure a balanced allocation of resources between front office activities and what is necessary to keep in place an adequate monitoring system.

POSTSCRIPT

Released with bail from prison on March 18, 2008 Kerviel was hired in late April as a trainee by Lemaire Consultants & Associates.[129] The firm is specialized in computer security and system development and should be able to put to good use the unique hacking talents of Mr. Kerviel who was called a "computer genius" by no less than Christian Noyer — the Governor of the Banque de France. Jean Veil, the lead lawyer for Société Générale commented that he was "delighted" that Kerviel had found gainful employment: "it means he will be in a position to start repaying the bank." With France's 35 hour work week it is not clear what life expectancy was being projected for Kerviel ... As a condition for his release however, Kerviel is not allowed to set foot inside a trading room nor involve himself in capital market activities which probably cap his earning potential!

On April 17, SoGen announced that Daniel Bouton would relinquish his responsibilities as CEO of the bank but would continue as the chairman of its board of directors. For Bouton this was the anticlimax of a meteoric career. The grandson of a railway gate-keeper, Bouton had won first prize in History at the Concours Général and graduated from Institut des Sciences Politiques and Ecole Nationale d'Administration — one of

---

[129] Clark, N. Société Générale's rogue trader finds a new job, *The New York Times* (April 26, 2008).

France's elite Grande Ecoles to become "Inspecteur Général des Finances" at the age of 23. After more than ten years as a senior civil servant Bouton was appointed CEO of SoGen which he transformed from a stodgy high street bank into a powerhouse in the field of derivatives trading.

Bibliography

Delhommais, P.-A. *Cinq Milliards en Fumée* (Seuil: Paris, 2008).

PricewaterhouseCoopers, *Société Générale: Summary of PwC diagnostic and analysis of the action plan* (23 May, 2008).

Société Générale (Inspection Générale), *Mission Green: Rapport de Synthèse* (20 Mai 2008).

Questions for Discussion

1. Compare a turbo-warrant with a plain option. Why would you expect the premium for a turbo-warrant to be lower than for a plain option?
2. What would be the impact of increased volatility of the DAX index on the value of call or put options on the index as compared to its impact on the corresponding turbo-warrant?
3. Where turbo-warrant get their name from?
4. Why was secrecy so important to the liquidation of SoGen's speculative positions?
5. Should liquidation of outstanding speculative positions have been staggered over a period of weeks or even months rather than 72 hours?
6. Should universal banks which combine commercial banking with investment banking be allowed to engage in proprietary trading activities?
7. Identify the three most compelling explanations as to why Sogen failed to stop Kerviel's fraudulent scheme.

Part IV
SWAPS

12
PROCTER & GAMBLE

A dog, used to eating eggs, saw an oyster; and opening his mouth to its widest extent, swallowed it down with the utmost relish, supposing it to be an egg. Soon afterwards suffering great pain in his stomach, he said, "I deserve all this torment, for my folly in thinking that everything round must be an egg."

The Fables of Aesop

On April 13, 1994, Procter & Gamble announced a one-time pretax charge of $152 million against net income. The loss resulted from the early closing of two seemingly innocuous leveraged interest rate swaps, which Procter & Gamble had entered into with Bankers Trust as a way of reducing financing costs. For a company with over $30 billion in sales which reported net income of $2.2 billion in fiscal year 1994, this noncash charge was hardly life threatening. And yet the episode — by pitting in a landmark lawsuit a blue-chip American multinational corporation against one of the pillars of the financial establishment — redefined the relationship between Main Street industrial firms and their Wall Street investment bankers. Indeed Procter & Gamble alleged that it had been played, manipulated, and deceived by Bankers Trust and initiated a lawsuit against the latter. The landmark lawsuit was settled out of court and allowed Procter & Gamble to pay a much reduced amount of $35 million. Bankers Trust which was then proudly proclaiming in one of its advertisement *"Risk wears many disguises. Helping you see beneath its surface is the strength of Bankers Trust"* saw its wings clipped and came out of this imbroglio with its good name tarnished and the "Trust" under a cloud.

Despondent shareholders were told by the humbled Procter & Gamble chairman that *"Derivatives like these swaps are dangerous and we were badly burned. We won't let this happen again."* Yet, one had to wonder how the giant consumer products multinational — best known for its marketing savvy in household names such as Tide, Crest or Pampers — would venture, lose its balance and stumble badly in the shifting sands of financial derivatives. After all, Procter & Gamble had a long running relationship with Bankers Trust which had resulted over time in the successful trimming of its financing costs. Why were these two leveraged interest swaps any different from past transactions? Had Bankers Trust — known for its creative financial engineering prowess — suddenly turned into an ogre devouring the lame and naïve manufacturing behemoth? Or was Procter & Gamble known for its savvy treasury operations simply turned into a sore loser after a long running winning streak? Before addressing these questions we first review in some details the infamous interest rate swaps which proved to be so toxic to Procter & Gamble.

HOW TO REDUCE FINANCING COSTS WITH LEVERED INTEREST RATE SWAPS

Since the early 1990s, Procter & Gamble had implemented a disciplined financing policy which achieved effective financing costs below the benchmark rate on 30 day average commercial paper.[130] At the core of this policy was the swapping of long term fixed rate debt into floating rate short term debt which allowed Procter & Gamble to capitalize on its wager that short term interest rates would continue to decline. In late October 1993, Procter & Gamble had approached Bankers Trust yet again about renewing an interest rate swap which was about to expire. Procter & Gamble sought to bring its cost of debt financing to 40 basis points[131] below the already low prevailing cost of about 3.25% on 30 day average commercial paper rate. Several proposals were submitted by Bankers Trust which were turned down one after the other by Procter & Gamble until a deal was finally reached in early November 1993. Bankers Trust proposed a tailor-made interest rate swap (see Box A) meeting its client's special requirement which offered floating rate debt at 75 basis points below commercial paper rate. However, the attractive cost of debt was predicated on interest rates remaining stable or declining further. Indeed there is "no free lunch" in financial markets and

---

[130] Commercial paper (CP) is an unsecured promissory note with a fixed maturity ranging from 1 to 270 days. CP is issued by large banks and corporations with strong credit ratings and is generally a cheaper source of short-term financing than bank financing. CP is largely bought by money market funds.

[131] One basis point is one hundredth of 1% — in this case 40 basis points are equal to 0.4 of 1%.

> **Box A. What are Interest Rate Swaps?** *Procter & Gamble had borrowed fixed rate 5 year debt at 5% and wanted to take advantage of the lower commercial paper market floating interest rate of approximately 3.25%. By entering into an interest rate swap with Bankers Trust, Proctor & Gamble would now pay the floating rate on commercial paper to Bankers Trust while receiving the fixed 5% interest payment with which it would meet its pre-swap fixed rate debt obligation. Each payment was based on a notional amount of $200 million. For all practical purposes — once the swap was in place — it is as if Procter & Gamble had borrowed short term floating rate commercial paper.*
>
> *The terms of an interest swap are set so that the present value of the "fixed interest cost leg" is equal to the present value of the "floating leg" so that neither party would gain or lose from entering into the swap. The value of the "fixed interest rate leg" is easy to compute since interest payment are contractually defined at the outset (see Box B on bond valuation) but valuing the "floating rate leg" is complicated by the problem of not knowing what future short term interest rates are going to be. By extracting forward interest rates from the zero-coupon yield curve it is possible to generate market-based forecasts of what those future short term interest rates are going to be. With that information it is possible to value the "floating rate" leg of the swap the same way it is done for the fixed rate leg of the same swap.*
>
> *The reader may wonder what are the motivations for two parties to enter in a swap. Proctor & Gamble wanted to free itself from the rigidity of fixed interest rate loan and take advantage of lower floating interest rates. The counter-party could be a Savings and Loan which lends at five year fixed rate to a AAA-rated construction company and is financed with floating rate CP: it would want to eliminate its exposure to interest rates (it lends at a fixed rate money that it borrowed at a floating rate) by locking its margin — swapping out of its floating rate debt into a five year fixed rate note. It would be a natural counterparty to Procter & Gamble and Bankers Trust would just play matchmaker. Interest rate swaps are used mostly to reduce the cost of financing as well as hedging a firm's exposure to interest rate movements.*

in order to achieve a reduction in its cost of debt Procter & Gamble had to take on some extra risk. Specifically it would have to be prepared to accept a higher cost of debt should interest rates misbehave and decide to rise instead of staying stable or continuing to decline. The actual swap that Procter & Gamble eventually agreed to was a far more complicated instrument than the plain vanilla swap described in Box A.

The Procter & Gamble — Bankers Trust Leveraged Interest Rate Swap. The agreed interest rate swap had a term of five years and a notional amount of $200 million (rather than the $100 million initially planned): for the first six months it called for Procter & Gamble to receive a fixed interest rate of 5.3% and pay to Bankers Trust a 30 day average CP floating interest rate minus 75 basis points (see Figure 1). For the

Box B. Bond Valuation. *Suppose Procter & Gamble issues a five-year bond at par with a face value of $1,000 paying an annual coupon of 5% (par value is the same thing as face value). A buyer of the bond will receive a coupon payment of $50 each year (5% of $1,000) for five years and recover the $1,000 principal at the end of the fifth year. If the bond is held to maturity the investor earns an annual rate of return equal to the 5% coupon rate because investing/buying the bond is equivalent to depositing $1,000 in a savings account, collecting an annual interest of 5% for five years and withdrawing the $1,000 at the end of the fifth year.*

Yield-to-Maturity. Assume now that Procter & Gamble issues the same five year 5% coupon bond below par, at $955. The bondholder paid only $955 but will receive the same $50 coupon for the next five years and recoup the bond principal value at its face value of $1,000. Clearly the expected return is higher than 5% since in addition to annual coupon payments the bond investor benefits of a capital gain of $45 equal to $1,000 minus $955 at the time of redemption. What is the expected return on this bond investment purchased at $955 and redeemed at $1,000 while paying $50 every year for five years? It is the rate — called yield to maturity (YTM) — that makes the bond price equal the present value of the bond's cash-flow stream. This polynomial equation can be solved with some difficulty by trial and error but effortlessly by a financial calculator or spreadsheet software:

$$955 = \$50/(1 + YTM) + \$50/(1 + YTM)^2 + \$50/(1 + YTM)^3$$
$$+ \$50/(1 + YTM)^4 + \$1050/(1 + YTM)^5.$$

The solution is YTM = 6.07%: in other words a bond investor buying the bond for $955 and holding it to maturity can expect to earn a yield of 6.07%. The yield is higher than the coupon rate of 5% because it takes into account the $45 capital gain earned at maturity when the bond is redeemed at par/face value of $1,000.

Bond Prices When Interest Rate Changes. Now assume that a year has passed since Procter & Gamble issued the five-year five percent coupon bond with face value of $1,000. The general level of interest rate paid on similar bonds (similarity being defined in terms of maturity and credit risk) has risen to 6%: what is the market value of our original bond? We know that whatever price it will fetch it should be such that it will be equal to the present value of annual coupon payments of $50 each and principal repayment of $1,000.

$$Bond\ Price = \$50/(1 + 0.06) + \$50/(1 + 0.06)^2 + \$50/(1 + 0.06)^3$$
$$+ \$1050/(1 + 0.06)^4 = \$965.$$

The lower price allows the investor to compensate the lower coupon payment (as compared to prevailing market interest rate) by a capital gain at time of redemption. Rising interest rates are driving bond prices down.

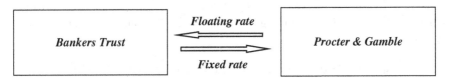

CP −75 bp (for the first six months)
Then CP −75 bp + swap spread* for 4.5 years

Figure 1   The Procter & Gamble — Bankers Trust interest rate swap.
Swap spread (set in six months time) = (98.5 [5 year CMT yield/5.78%]−30 year treasury price)/100.

remaining 4.5 years the rate would be set on May 2, 1994 (the six month anniversary of the signing of the swap) according to a complex formula which added a spread to the base interest rate set at (30 *day average commercial paper rate — 75 basis points*). Under the best circumstances the spread would be zero — a scenario corresponding to a stable or declining long term interest rate which meant that Procter & Gamble would effectively pay 30 day average commercial paper rate — 75 basis points. Otherwise — should longer term interest rates rise — the spread and therefore the floating interest rate would very quickly reach astronomical levels. Formally, the interest cost formula for Procter & Gamble was set as

Interest cost = interest cost on 30 day commercial paper − 75 basis points + spread

The first two terms of the interest rate formula were relatively innocuous — the spread was of course another story.

The "Formula from Hell." The spread formula which played havoc with Procter & Gamble interest costs is indeed a "brain-twisting" concoction and a testament to the creativity of Bankers Trust's "rocket scientists." It is defined as

$$\text{Spread} = \text{Max}\{0; [98.5 \times (5 \text{ year CMT yield})/5.58\%$$

$$- 30 \text{ year Treasury Bond price}]/100\}$$

Where:

- Five year CMT is the yield on the five year Constant Maturity Treasury note — a synthetic five-year bond interpolated from the US treasury securities yield curve.[132]

---

[132] The yield curve graphs the relationship between the yield on bonds of the same credit quality but of different maturities ranging from 30 days to 30 years. Because treasury bonds are quasi-free of default risk and are widely traded the yield curve for US treasuries is easy to graph and is most widely used.

This index provides a yield for a specific maturity even if no outstanding Treasury bond has exactly that fixed maturity.

- Thirty-year Treasury bond price is the midpoint between the bid and ask[133] prices on the 6.25% treasury bond maturing on August 15, 2023 — not including accrued interest.

In plain English the spread was linked to the difference between the *yield* on five year Treasury bond and the *price* of 30 year Treasury bond. Bankers Trust could have chosen a simpler yield or price differential of 5 and 30 year treasuries (innocuous and inelastic to changing interest rate level) but had reasons of its own to resort to a mismatched and contrived differential between yield and bond prices. One wonders whether the reason was simply to confuse the client with a complicated formula which cloaked the explosive spread in a veil of ambiguity! Recalling that yields and bond prices move in opposite directions when interest rates change (see Box B) the practical question to ask is which one of the yield and bond price will respond most to a change in interest rate. For example, a small interest rate hike by the Federal Reserve would result into a smaller increase of the five-year yield but a deeper decline in the 30 year bond price and would therefore exacerbate their differential on which the spread was based. In fact bonds with very long maturities are very sensitive to small change in interest rates — a concept generally known as duration.

Gauging Risk Through Numerical Analysis. To get a better sense of how the spread would respond to gradual interest rate increases Table 1 tabulates this relationship: the first column shows the five-year yield on CMT rising from the prevalent level of 4.95% — when the swap was signed — to 6.45%; the second column estimates the corresponding price of a 30-year bond assuming a parallel shift in the yield curve; the third column calculates the actual spread[134] and shows how it literally exploded with relatively minor change in interest rates; the fourth column computes the leverage embedded in the formula as the ratio of the *change in the spread/[corresponding change in five-year yield on CMT]* — in effect measuring the percentage change in the spread triggered by a one percent change in the five-year interest rate. With a leverage ratio at "*31 times*" the swap was indeed a leveraged interest swap as Procter & Gamble discovered the hard way. The fifth and last column shows the corresponding interest payments which Procter & Gamble would actually be required to make. The reader will no doubt be flabbergasted to see the penalty corresponding to the annual spread to

---

[133] In financial markets prices for securities such as bonds are set as the result of the interplay of buyers "bidding" and sellers "asking" prices. The bid-ask spread is simply the difference between buyers and sellers' prices.

[134] The spread had a floor of zero which effectively kept the interest rate at no less than 6 month CP — 75 bp even though the spread would be negative until the 5 year interest rate reached approximately 5.58% (see the first three lines in Table 1).

Table 1 Simulations on the Procter & Gamble's leveraged swap.

Five-year CMT[i] yields (%)	30-year treasury price (%)	Spread (bp)	Leverage[ii]	Net spread (bp)	$ Equivalent[iii]
4.95	103.02	−1905		−1830	$1.5 M
5.35 (+40 bp)	97.61	−644	31	−569	$1.5 M
5.55 (+60 bp)	95.07	−49	31	−124	$1.5 M
5.65 (+70 bp)	93.85	+243	31	+168	−$3.36 M
5.75 (+80 bp)	92.64	+535	31	+460	−$9.20 M
5.95 (+100 bp)	90.30	+1110	30	+1035	−$20.70 M
6.45 (+150 bp)	84.86	+2505	29	+2430	−$48.60 M

[i]Extra Dollar Payments due solely to spread Coming into Operation. (Assume that both five-year CMT yields and 30-year Treasury yields increase by the same amount, i.e., parallel shifts of the yield curve.)
[ii]Leverage is defined as change in spread as computed by formula triggered by corresponding change in the five-year fixed rate.
[iii]The dollar equivalent shows the incremental annual interest cost resulting from the spread minus 75 basis points. At 4.95%, 5.35%, and 5.55% the spread would be negative in effect zero because Bankers Trust had set a floor. Procter & Gamble would still reduce its floating rate by $0.0075 \times \$200$ million = $1.5 million.
Source: Chew, L. *Managing Derivative Risks: the Use and Abuse of Leverage* (John Wiley & Sons, 1996).

be added to the base interest rate rising from −$1.5 million to + $48.60 million when the five-year yield on CMT goes from 4.95% to 6.45%. That is an increase of only 150 bp — which under normal circumstances should translate into an increase of $3 million in interest payment — would in fact be magnified 16 times and result into an interest cost increase of $48 million. So much for the power of leverage!

As it turned out Procter & Gamble renegotiated the terms of the swap in January 1994: the locked in date for the spread was pushed back from May 4 to May 19 and the base interest rate was improved to *30-day average commercial paper rate — 88 basis points* but the spread itself remained unchanged. The additional 13-basis points would further reduce the annual interest payment for Procter & Gamble by $130,000 before taking into account the spread; however it would increase the uncertainty around the level at which the spread would be set for the remaining 4.5 years since it would take another 15 days before the level of the spread would be set. With interest rates rapidly moving upwards, in March 1994 Procter & Gamble decided to lock in early the value of the spread and therefore the terms of the swap for the remaining 4.5 years: the spread was set at 15% (1,500 basis points) which corresponded to a total loss in present value terms of $106.541 million. A loss of more than $100 million on a notional principal of $200 million was more punishment than Procter & Gamble was ready to bear.

Break-Even Analysis. Clearly Procter & Gamble took on significant exposure to interest rate movements: how significant was the exposure and did Procter & Gamble fully comprehend its extent? One approach is to ask by how much could the interest rate on five-year Treasuries (coupled with a parallel increase on 30 year treasuries yield) rise before the spread turn positive and therefore start eating away the 75 basis points subsidy. From Table 1 which shows the value of the spread for various increases in interest rates it appears that five-year interest rate would have to move up by 62 basis points before the spread would turn positive and 66 basis points when the spread would completely offset the 75 basis points subtracted from the average 30 day average commercial paper rate.[135] One wonders how such simple "back-of the envelope" analysis could have eluded Procter & Gamble's treasurer. It would seem that however complicated the spread formula may have appeared all was needed was a simple pocket calculator to compute the actual interest cost to Procter & Gamble under alternative interest rate scenarios — hardly rocket science!

Multiple Scenario Analysis. Simple break-even analysis as conducted above is predicated on a parallel shift of the entire yield curve when interest rates rise or decline. It is certainly a reasonable first approximation: however it misses out the fact that future states of the world are characterized by more than one variable. The spread embedded in the leveraged interest rate swap was driven by two key variables — yield on five-year treasuries and the price of 30 year treasuries. Typically both 5 and 30 year yield on treasuries would move in tandem when interest rates rise or decline but not necessarily to the same extent. For example, an increase in interest rates may increase the yield on five-year treasuries less than it does on 30 year treasuries thereby resulting in a steepening of the yield curve. Table 2 tabulates what the spread would have been under possible combinations of 5- and 30-year yield on treasuries: along the diagonal of the matrix are situations reflecting a parallel shift of the yield curve as interest rates rise. To the left of the diagonal the five-year yield increases faster than the 30-year yield on treasuries corresponding to an inversion of the yield curve while the rest of the matrix portrays a steepening of the yield curve.

EMBEDDED OPTIONS AND HIDDEN RISKS

Reverse Engineering. A closer look at the spread formula reveals an "option-like" pay-off profile for Procter & Gamble. Thus the leveraged interest rate swap that Bankers

---

[135] These are close approximation based on linear interpolation. A more sophisticated analysis by Smith (1997) based on duration finds similar results — 55.5 and 58 basis points respectively in lieu of 62 and 66 basis points.

Table 2 Multiple scenario analysis showing spreads for various combinations of 5- and 30-year interest rates.

5 year yields	30-year treasury yields						
	5.75%	6.00%	6.25%	6.50%	6.75%	7.00%	7.25%
4.75%	−0.2608	−0.2247	−0.1904	−0.1579	−0.1269	−0.0975	−0.0696
5.00%	−0.2182	−0.1821	−0.1478	−0.1152	−0.0843	−0.0549	−0.0270
5.25%	−0.1756	−0.1395	−0.1052	−0.0726	−0.0417	−0.0123	+0.0156
5.50%	−0.1330	−0.0969	−0.0626	−0.0300	−0.0009	−0.0303	−0.0582
5.75%	−0.0904	−0.0543	−0.0200	−0.0126	+0.0435	+0.0729	+0.1008
6.00%	−0.0478	−0.0117	+0.0226	+0.0552	+0.0861	+0.1155	+0.1431
6.25%	−0.0052	+0.0309	+0.0652	+0.0978	+0.1287	+0.1581	+0.1860
6.50%	+0.0374	+0.0735	+0.1078	+0.1404	+0.1713	+0.2007	+0.2286
6.75%	+0.0800	+0.1161	+0.1504	+0.1830	−0.2139	−0.2433	−0.2712
7.00%	+0.1226	+0.1587	+0.1930	+0.2256	+0.2565	+0.2859	+0.3138

Source: Smith, D. J. Aggressive Corporate Finance: A Close Look at the Procter & Gamble — Bankers Trust Leveraged Swap, *The Journal of Derivatives* (Summer, 1997), p. 71.

Trust had skillfully designed for the benefits of reducing Procter & Gamble's cost of capital was in fact the bundling of a plain vanilla interest rate swap with written put options on US Treasury bonds (see Box C). The reason why Bankers Trust would pay a yearly 75 basis points subsidy on the interest rate swap was simply that it was buying a put option on US treasuries from Procter & Gamble. Thus the 75 basis points were the option premium Procter & Gamble received for writing a put option on US treasuries. In exchange for the upfront cash premium Procter & Gamble gave Bankers Trust the right to sell a portfolio of 5- and 30-year treasuries at a strike price which was the portfolio price (given as the spread) when the interest rate swap was first entered into.

As long as US treasuries price increased (same thing as interest rates declining) — that is the spread remained negative (portfolio price stays above strike price) — Procter and Gamble would pocket the 75 basis points and the embedded options in the swap would expire unexercised (see Figure 2 line 1 to the right of the exercise/strike price). Thus Procter & Gamble upside potential gains from writing highly speculative put options were capped at 75 basis points. Should the spread turn positive (under a scenario of declining US treasury prices or rising interest rates) and the embedded options were exercised the losses shouldered by Procter & Gamble would rise exponentially because of the highly leveraged nature of the spread formula. Clearly the downside risks were abysmal and didn't seem to warrant the meager premium income which was the quid pro quo for writing put options on US treasuries.

Box C. Put Options on Interest Rates. *For every purchase of a 90 day put option on a 30 year bond (valued at B(90) at time of option expiry) the buyer has to find a seller willing to write the option. For example for a cash premium p(0) = 3 collected upfront the writer of a 90 day put option commits to buying 30-year Treasuries at the strike price of say E(90) = 91% (par value of the bond is 100%). Should bond prices rise — which is the same thing as interest rate/yield-to-maturity on 30-year bonds declining — beyond the strike price the buyer of the put option will abandon the option and the put option writer will keep the premium. If the bond price B(90) at maturity of the option were to depreciate below 91 (the same thing as interest rate rising) the option buyer will exercise his option forcing the option writer to buy the bonds at the exercise price of 91. The option writer will incur a cash loss of 91 − B(90). As bond price depreciates further and further away from the exercise price, his losses will deepen. His payoff (the dotted line (2) in Figure 2) is symmetrical to the option buyer's payoff since, combined, they are a zero-sum game (disregarding transaction costs). In other words, what the option holder loses, the option writer keeps (option premium for B(90) ≥ 91 shown as AH = BH) in Figure 2, and what the option holder gains, the option writer loses (for B(90) < 91). The reader will also note that the option writer faces unlimited losses when the option is exercised, whereas his gains are limited to the option premium. In Figure 2, the reader will note that the option premium (shown as the distance of the horizontal portion of the call option profile to the origin along the abscissa, AH or BH), is equal to the distance HC between the exercise price and the break-even rate (disregarding interest costs).*

Procter & Gamble was selling put "options-like" on 30-year treasuries. This was a bet predicated on the assumption that interest rate were going to fall — bond prices were going to rise, put options would expire unexercised and Procter & Gamble would keep the premium collected. When interest rates started to rise option buyers exercised their put options at the expense of the option writer — Procter & Gamble in this case.

The True Cost of Financial Intermediation. Unbundling the leveraged swap into (1) a plain vanilla interest rate swap and (2) a put option allows us to gauge the value of writing put options on US treasuries by replicating the strategy directly on the Chicago Board of Trade. Smith (1997) in a clever study asked two simple related questions: what would it take to generate $6.513 million in premium income[136] in November 1993 by writing put options on treasury bonds: the option premium was necessary for Bankers Trust to be able to reduce the cost of floating rate financing to

---

[136] $6.513 million is the present value (using a 5.30% discount rate) of the 75 basis points interest rate subsidy (notional amount of $20 million) on the ten semesterly payments provided by Bankers Trust to Procter and Gamble if put options expire unexercised (spread is at zero).

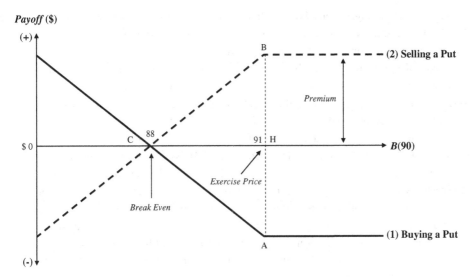

Figure 2   Writing put options on US treasuries.

Procter & Gamble below the average 30 day CP rate (a 75 basis points subsidy every six months). Second, what would have been the losses incurred by closing those option positions in March 1994. Of course it would have been difficult to replicate exactly the complicated play on put options embedded in the leveraged interest rate swap spread formula. The study showed that by writing put options on 15 year treasuries at a strike price set at-the-money the same premium income would have been generated but the losses would have been limited to $17 million.

Bankers Trust acted as an expensive intermediary between Procter & Gamble and the option market as the difference between Procter & Gamble overall loss of $100 million and the much lower cost of replicating the written options must have been Bankers Trust outsized profit. Lack of ingenuity and failure to understand what it was buying on the part of Procter & Gamble was exactly symmetrical to Bankers Trust ebullient creativity: the former paid dearly for it and Bankers Trust was handsomely rewarded for it. Clearly this was a time when profits were dwindling for plain vanilla swaps which are easy to understand, widely traded and very liquid. As dealers such as Bankers Trust saw their margins narrowing with readily available and standardized products such as plain vanilla interest rate swaps they started to develop new, more creative and at times very exotic products which were difficult for the customer to understand and close to impossible to replicate. Clearly these new proprietary products were considerably more profitable for the financial institutions which designed them and would offer high bonus potential to their front office/sales force. However these same products were highly leveraged and very risky for the customer and it would only be a matter of time before they would backfire: indeed when Procter & Gamble felt the sting it did not wait to seek redress through the court system for what it saw as unscrupulous dealing on the part of Bankers Trust.

Accounting Gimmickry. Although it seems difficult from a strict financial valuation perspective to justify Procter & Gamble choice of the over-the-counter (OTC) leveraged interest rate swap versus the direct bundling of a plain vanilla interest rate swap with exchange-traded options on treasuries it is nevertheless relevant to compare the accounting treatment of both strategies. One factor which would have militated in favor of Bankers Trust's leveraged OTC interest rate swap is that only interest payments would be recognized in the current income period whereas all gains/losses associated with quarterly (not daily) marking-to-market would be deferred until the maturity of the swap; the transaction itself would have been reported as a footnote and wouldn't have materially impacted Procter & Gamble's financial statements. By contrast, by selling exchange-traded put options Procter & Gamble would have had to recognize immediately the cash premium in full even though it would have much preferred to amortize it over the five year life of the underlying debt instrument; it would also have been required to post a margin and would have had to mark-to-market daily its option contracts.

LANDMARK LAWSUIT

As early as October 27, 1994 and even before paying a single cent on the swap gone sour Procter & Gamble filed a lawsuit against Bankers Trust on grounds of *"racketeering, fraud, misrepresentation, breach of fiduciary duty,*[137] *negligent misrepresentation and negligence."*[138] Procter & Gamble had been played by its trusted adviser; it was mad and Bankers Trust was going to pay reparations.

Sore Loser. Procter & Gamble had indeed benefited from a long standing and successful working relationship with Bankers Trust which had resulted in a steadily lower cost of financing than normal market conditions would have warranted. And Procter & Gamble was hardly a novice at using derivatives as its 1993 annual report disclosed derivatives positions in excess of $2 billion. Yet, Procter & Gamble had this old-fashioned notion that its banker should be looking after its best interest. After all,

---

[137] Fiduciary responsibility is a legal concept whereby one party (Procter & Gamble) engages in a relationship of confidence, good faith and trust with another party (Bankers Trust) from which aid, advice and protection is expected. Bankers Trust was a financial service provider to Procter & Gamble but not necessarily its agent.

[138] The Procter & Gamble Company, Plaintiff v. Bankers trust Company and BT Securities corporation, defendants, No. C-1-94-735, United States District Court of the Southern District of Ohio, Western Division.

it was not unreasonable of Procter & Gamble to rely on its banker for savvy advice and accurate price information on a transaction which was far more complex than previous ones had been. In its court filing against Bankers Trust, Procter & Gamble argued that[139]

> *it entered into the 5/30 swap because in response to its repeated questions, Bankers Trust had falsely assured that it would be protected against significant losses from rising interest rates because it could safely lock in its rates if interest rates began to rise. When rates did rise, Bankers Trust changed the rules, imposing on Procter & Gamble a lock-in interest rate calculated under a secret, proprietary, complex, multi-variable pricing model that it would not share and to this day has not shared with Procter & Gamble.*

Although complex in design the above discussion of the leveraged interest rate swap showed that it was relatively simple to gauge the extent of interest rate exposure that Procter & Gamble was willingly undertaking by writing put options. Did Procter & Gamble truly understand the architecture of the deal — that is that the reduced cost of financing was made possible by collecting a premium from writing put options on interest rates? And if it did, should it have known how to hedge its exposure and how expensive it would be to do so: "Caveat Emptor" or "Buyer Beware."

Mistrusting Bankers Trust. Half of all financial institutions have the word "*trust*" in their name and lavish on marble lobbies in their branches to nurture the confidence of their depositors and customers! If Procter & Gamble was not the unsuspecting and naïve player in high finance that it pretended to be, Bankers Trust was hardly the trusted adviser, honest broker and financial adviser that it claimed to be. In a melodramatic twist to the story, damaging taped conversations between two senior Bankers Trust officials were inadvertently released to the public domain and seemed to make the case for Procter & Gamble. Kevin W. Hudson a managing director for Bankers Trust and point-man on the sale of the infamous swap to Procter & Gamble was caught confiding in another Bankers Trust employee Alison Bernhard — vice-president in the same group.[140] Hudson bragged to Bernhard that the leveraged swap deal he had just closed would earn the bank an unheard of $7.6 million in profit. When Bernhard voiced her concern "*Do they understand that ... what they did?*" Hudson replied "*No, they understand what they did, but they don't understand the leverage, no.*" On February 4, when the Federal Reserve unexpectedly raised interest rates Hudson confided to Bernhard that Procter & Gamble had a loss of $17 million: "*are they dying*" Bernhard asked. "*They don't know*" replied Hudson and he added that Procter & Gamble never

---

[139] Chew, L. *Managing Derivatives Risks: the Use and Abuse of Leverage* (Wiley, 1996), p. 36.
[140] Cited in "High finance and office romance" by Carol J. Loomis, *Fortune*, November 27, 1995, p. 35.

Box D. Interest Rate Swap on Deutsche Mark (DM).[141] *Curiously, on February 14, 1994 Procter & Gamble entered into yet another highly leveraged interest rate swap involving a play on German interest rates. This happened to take place shortly after the Fed had increased interest rates which jeopardized the first outstanding leveraged interest rate swap. One has to wonder why Procter & Gamble wanted to dig itself into a deeper hole — this time by exposing a DM notional amount equivalent to $93 million to German interest rates. Presumably Proctor & Gamble already had a long term fixed rate DM denominated debt it wished to swap into floating DM debt. Procter & Gamble would borrow at a very favorable interest rate as long as interest rates would remain within a "wedding band" of 4.05% to 6.10%. More specifically for the first year of the swap Bankers Trust would pay a net 1% to Proctor & Gamble on the notional amount of $93 million. Thereafter the interest rate for the remaining 3.75 year of the swap would be set at 4.50% plus a premium equal to ten times the difference between the 4 year DM swap rate prevailing on January 16, 1995 and 4.50%.*

Unlike the US dollar interest rate swap, the DM swap offered tremendous upside potential saving of [4.50% − Prevailing DM swap rate] × $93 million × 10 should German interest rates fall below the 4.05% floor of the band or astronomical additional cost if interest rates crossed the ceiling of 6.10%. The factor of "10" built tremendous leverage in the transaction. For example if interest rates fell barely below the floor of the "wedding band" to 4% the savings to Proctor & Gamble would amount to 0.50 × $93 million ×10 = $4.15 million.

As it turned out US interest rates started to rise in early 1994 pulling along German interest rate: by the reset date of January 16, 1995 the DM swap rate had broken through the ceiling of the "wedding band" and Procter & Gamble was obligated to pay a spread of 16.40% which would translate to a total loss of $60 million over the life of the swap. Procter & Gamble's law suit was thereafter amended to include this second swap!

---

bothered to ask where it stood (and Bankers Trust certainly didn't volunteer to update its customer). In fact Hudson was in the process of selling Procter & Gamble a second leveraged swap denominated in Deutsche Mark (see Box D): "*Let me get the Deutsche Mark trade done first, then they can ask.*"[142]

Settlement. Most charges against Bankers Trust were dismissed by Judge Feikens who ruled that (a) the leveraged interest rate swap was not a security and

---

[141] There is limited information on this second swap. See Loomis, C. J. Untangling the derivative mess, *Fortune* (March 20, 1995) and Marthinsen, J. *Risk Takers: Uses and Abuses of Financial Derivatives* (Pearson Addison-Wesley: 2005), pp. 143–144.

[142] According to Procter & Gamble filing, Hudson had a good 1993 year, collecting a bonus $1.3 million on top of a $125,000 salary. On November 5, 1995 Hudson and Bernhard were married in Greenwich, Connecticut.

(b) that Bankers Trust had no fiduciary responsibility. However Judge Feikens did find:

> *the defendant had a duty to disclose material information to plaintiff both before the parties entered into the swap transactions and in their performance, and also a duty to deal fairly and in good faith during the performance of the swap transaction…. An implied contractual duty to disclose may arise where (1) a party has superior knowledge of certain information, (2) that information is not readily available to the other party and (3) the first party is acting on the basis of mistaken information.* "[143]

The ruling was crucial to Procter & Gamble because it cleared the way for a lawsuit on the grounds of common law fraud. The second ruling was indeed very disappointing to Procter & Gamble which had relied on Bankers Trust for financial expertise over the years, to whom it had disclosed proprietary information and with whom it generally had a long standing relationship of trust — all of which seemed to define a fiduciary responsibility owed by Bankers Trust to Procter & Gamble and which had been breached. The lawsuit was eventually settled out of court: the two swaps were not rescinded nor were punitive damages paid by Bankers Trust. But Procter & Gamble was vindicated to the extent that it was excused from 83% of all the monies owed to Bankers Trust and only paid $35 million in lieu of $157 million. Bankers Trust's good name had been irreparably damaged but it did not concede to any wrongdoing.

THE MORAL OF THE STORY

Lesson 1: Failure to Set a Clear Mission for Treasury as a Profit Center. A company's treasury department is charged with two principal tasks: (1) procuring financing at the lowest possible cost of capital with financing running the gamut from short-term suppliers' funding in the form of account payables to medium and long term bank loans or capital market debt and, (2) hedging risk by limiting the firm's exposure to exchange rate and interest rate risk. Neither funding nor hedging are profit-making activities per se since the goal of financing is to minimize the cost of capital while hedging is all about minimizing risks. And yet many corporations have in the last 25 years redefined the mission of their treasury operations to turn from cost centers into profit centers.

Lesson 2: Failure to Consider Worst-Case Scenarios. More specifically, Procter & Gamble's Board of Directors or its finance committee should have raised two related

---

[143] *Procter & Gamble, 1996 WL 249435* at p. 20 cited in Forster, D. M. The State of the Law after Procter & Gamble v. Bankers Trust, *Derivatives Quarterly* (Winter, 1996).

questions: "how much could Procter & Gamble lose from entering into a levered interest swap? and "how much was Procter & Gamble likely to lose?" Neither question is necessarily easy to answer. The first question is typically addressed with the help of stress-testing and multiple scenario analysis while the second is gauged by the more sophisticated Value-at-Risk metric.

Stress-testing and multiple scenario analysis are simple methodologies for probing doomsday scenarios or "outlier" events. Stress-testing emphasizes one non-controllable variable which, by necessity, would have to be interest rates and we showed in Table 1 that it was relatively easy to gauge the downside risk of entering in the leveraged interest rate swap proposed by Bankers Trust.

Multiple scenario analysis allows to schematize states of the world built on two or more key non-controllable variables. In this case the variables of choice were five-year yield on CMT and the price of 30-year treasuries. Their combination was tabulated in Table 2 showing how the spread would respond through a parallel shift or a steepening/inverting of the yield curves. It would have provided a useful complement to simple break-even analysis.

Lesson 3: Failure to Communicate. Board of Directors are not expected to get involved in day-to-day management of the firm. However they are supposed to be kept appraised and intimately involved with any strategic shift or undertaking that management at the parent or subsidiary level may undertake. If Procter & Gamble's treasury were to redefine its strategic mission away from minimizing financing costs to writing options on interest rates for speculative profits the Board of Directors should have known. Better the Board of Directors should review its options before deciding whether authorizing proprietary trading of interest rate derivatives is indeed appropriate for the firm.

Lesson 4: Failure to Report Leverage. It is likely that Procter & Gamble preferred an OTC tailor-made derivative transaction to exchange-traded products because presumably gains/losses could be staggered over the life of the instrument instead of being recognized in current income. Exchange-traded products have the merit of forcing the posting of a margin collateral marked-to-market on a daily basis and therefore imposing a reality check on their users. Corporate users of tailor-made derivatives would be well-served by developing an in-house reporting/control system which mimics the margining system used for exchange-traded products. Embedded risks as in the leveraged interest rate swap transaction entered into by Procter & Gamble would have surfaced early and the true degree of leverage exposed to its managers.

Bibliography

Chew, L. *Managing Derivative Risks: the Use and Abuse of Leverage* (John Wiley & Sons, 1996).

Forster, D. M. The state of the law after Procter & Gamble v. Bankers Trust, *Derivatives Quarterly* (Winter, 1996).

Marthinsen, J. *Risk Takers: Uses and Abuses of Financial Derivatives* (Pearson Addison-Wesley, 2005).

Smith, D. J. Aggressive corporate finance: A close look at the Procter & Gamble — Bankers Trust Leveraged Swap, *The Journal of Derivatives* (Summer, 1997).

Srivastava, S. Value-at-risk analysis of a leveraged swap, *The Journal of Risk*, 1(2).

Questions for Discussion

1. Would you consider Procter & Gamble treasury operations best characterized as a cost or a profit center? If Procter & Gamble were to choose Profit Center as a model for its treasury what should its charter include to avoid the embarrassing and costly debacle that it experienced?
2. Why would a spread formula built around the differential in yields or prices of 5- and 30-year treasuries be far less risky than the actual mismatched formula used by Bankers Trust?
3. Should Judge Feiken have ruled in favor of Procter & Gamble on the issue of fiduciary responsibility?
4. How could Procter & Gamble hedge its exposure to the interest rate risk embedded in the leveraged swap. Would you expect the approximate cost of such a hedge to be equal to, more than or less than the 75 basis points that Bankers Trust was generously paying to Procter & Gamble? How would your answer change as interest rates started to rise?

GIBSON GREETING CARDS

Caveat emptor (Buyer beware)

Gibson Greeting cards are more likely to conjure images of Santa Claus than being associated with Wall Street's daring and possibly unscrupulous financial engineers. The Cincinnati, Ohio-based manufacturer of consumer products specializing in greeting cards and wrapping paper had sales revenue reaching $547 million in 1993 with profits of $20 million that same year. Gibson's unlikely and traumatic foray in the world of arcane derivatives was motivated by the desire to reduce funding costs. In 1991, Gibson had raised $50 million in fixed rate debt: the coupon interest rate was set at 9.33% with repayment of principal staggered over the period 1995 to 2001. When interest rates started to decline, Gibson unfortunately found itself unable to prepay the bond issue because of a restrictive clause in its indenture.

Gibson next best option to take advantage of lower interest rate was to swap its fixed rate debt obligation into a variable debt which it did by executing in November 1991 two plain vanilla interest rate swaps with Bankers Trust[144] (see Box A in chapter on Proctor & Gamble for a definition of an interest rate swap). The two swaps had each a notional amount of $30 million with maturities respectively of two and five years. The two-year interest swap required Bankers Trust to pay Gibson six-month LIBOR and Gibson to pay Bankers Trust a fixed rate of 5.91%. The second swap with a maturity

---

[144] Chew, L. *Managing Derivatives Risk* (Wiley & Sons: Chichester, England, 1996), pp. 38–39.

of five years required Gibson to pay six month LIBOR to Bankers Trust while Bankers Trust would pay Gibson a fixed rate of 7.12%. The net of the two transactions was for Gibson to receive the difference between the two fixed interest rates of 1.21% in the amount of $30 million $(0.0712 - 0.0591) = \$363,000$ while LIBOR payments would cancel out. The net receipt would clearly reduce Gibson's original fixed interest rate of 9.33%.

In mid-July 1992 — ahead of the maturity dates on its swap agreements extending to November 1993 and 1996 — Gibson canceled the two swaps for a net profit of $260,000. It is not clear why Gibson decided to cancel its interest rate swaps since they provided significant cost relief on its original 9.33% bond issue at no risk to Gibson. Shortly thereafter, it initiated a "ratio swap" followed by a series of increasingly complex risky leveraged swaps with lingo names such as "spread lock 1 and 2, treasury-linked swap, knocked-out option, wedding band 3 and 6, etc."[145] Without getting into the intricacies of each transaction suffices to describe the first leveraged swap concluded between Gibson and Bankers Trust on a notional amount of $30 million, which called for a fixed interest payment of 5.5% from Bankers Trust to Gibson and a LIBOR-linked payment to Bankers Trust by Gibson: specifically Gibson would pay $LIBOR^2/6$. As long as LIBOR remains below 6%, the formula would be very favorable to Gibson (at 6%, $LIBOR^2/6 = LIBOR$) but beyond 6% the interest paid to be paid by Gibson would rapidly become costly (see Table 1).

Clearly, Gibson must have thought that it could beat the market and definitely believed that interest rates were relentlessly marching downwards. After initial profits, Gibson started to pile up losses when interest rates reversed their course in 1993. Gibson — which portrayed itself as being conservatively managed — claimed that it unambiguously communicated to Bankers Trust that its loss limit was at a maximum

Table 1   LIBOR

LIBOR (%)	$LIBOR^2/6$ (%)
3	1.50
4	2.67
5	4.17
6	6
7	8.17
8	10.67
9	13.50

---

[145] Chew, L. op. cited. See pp. 37–49 for an excellent discussion of the different exotic hyper-leveraged interest rate swaps that Bankers Trust was able to sell to Gibson Greeting Cards.

of $3 million. Unfortunately Gibson had to rely on Bankers Trust's valuation model to know exactly how much it was losing. Although an accurate picture of what actually happened was muddied by the chain link series of no less than 29 swap transactions or amendments between the two firms Bankers Trust started lying to Gibson at the end of 1992 — systematically under-reporting actual losses which caused Gibson to release inaccurate financial statements for 1992 and 1993. What is clear though is that as Gibson was being told of its deepening losses, it allowed itself to be persuaded to amend existing swap contracts into evermore leveraged ones. By early 1994 when it reached a loss of $17.5 million Gibson was told that the company's losses were "potentially without limit." Panicked, Gibson signed up for yet another amendment and a new leveraged interest rate swap capping its losses at $27.5 million but also holding the somewhat remote possibility that the loss could be reduced to $3 million. Incredibly it was Gibson's 29th transaction over a period of three years culminating in a $27.5 million loss when its previous year profit had been only $20 million. Bankers Trust for its part earned $13 million from transaction-related fees.

At about the same time Bankers Trusts proudly proclaimed in its advertisement *"Risk wears many disguises. Helping you see beneath its surface is the strength of Bankers Trust."* Gibson Greeting Cards' tale of deception and manipulation at the hands of Bankers Trust bears otherwise. Bankers Trust repeatedly misrepresented the fair value of Gibson swap positions. Most damming was the taped discussion by a Bankers Trust Managing Director of how he was "managing" the differential between the fair value of Gibson's swaps and what Gibson was told[146]:

> *I think we should use this (a downward market price movement) as an opportunity. We should just call the Gibson contract, and may be chip away at the differential a little more. I mean we told him $8.1 million when the real number was 14. So now if the real number is 16, we'll tell him that it is 11. You know, just slowly chip away at the differential between what it really is and what we're telling him.*

If there were any doubt as to Bankers Trust cynicism in its dealings with Gibson another incriminating taped conversation has a Managing Director saying

> *From the very beginning, Gibson just, you know, really put themselves in our hands like 96%... these guys have done pretty wild stuff. And you know, they probably do not understand it quite as well as they should... and that like perfect for us.*

The Commodity Futures Trading Commission and the Securities and Exchange Commission jointly fined Bankers Trust $10 million, which is a relatively modest

---

[146] The Commodity Futures Trading Commission Filing of Administrative Proceedings against BT Securities Corporation, a subsidiary of Bankers Trust company, in the connection with the sale of derivatives products, paragraph #12.

penalty when compared to the $13 million in fees that the bank earned from selling 29 different swaps to Gibson. Gibson, in turn, settled $6.5 million out of the $27.5 million in losses that it had accumulated. Bankers Trust was further directed to insure that its customers would understand the inner mechanics of leveraged transactions they entered into and would have access to truly transparent daily closing prices — thereby approximating as much as possible exchange-traded instruments.

In the end, Gibson rightly claimed that it had been repeatedly misadvised and misled by Bankers Trust in marking-to-market its outstanding swap positions and that the latter had breached its fiduciary duty vis-à-vis its client. Bankers Trust had consistently refused to share with its client its proprietary valuation models thereby depriving Gibson from the tools necessary to carry its own stress-tests. Gibson was nevertheless guilty of venturing in uncharted territories by entering in complex transactions that it did not fully understand.

ORANGE COUNTY

Neither a borrower, nor a lender be;
For loan oft loses both itself and friend,
And borrowing dulls the edge of husbandry.

William Shakespeare, *HAMLET*

Municipal finance conjures up images of cautious and conservative investment in safe low-yielding tax-free bonds. When Orange County declared bankruptcy in December 1994 after announcing a loss of $1.65 billion it sent shock waves through capital markets: the $1 trillion municipal bond market lost one percent of its value while other California municipal bonds (exclusive of Orange County) lost as much as 3–4% in value.[147]

At its simplest, the debacle of Orange County is the case of a public investment pool which was supposed to run itself conservatively as a money market mutual fund but somehow morphed into a hedge fund by leveraging itself to enhance the yield on its asset portfolio. The investment strategy worked for years with low or declining interest rates as long as the pool could borrow short term at lower interest rates than it could re-invest longer term at a higher interest rate. When interest rates reversed their course

---

[147] Municipal bankruptcies are relatively rare events. Chapter 9 bankruptcy filing was established during the depression for dealing with the special circumstances of local government: only 491 municipal bankruptcies were recorded between 1937 and 1994 and they involved small municipalities mostly in rural districts. To put the scale of municipal bankruptcies in a national economic context, it should be contrasted with a yearly average of 16,000 corporate bankruptcies, which were recorded in the 1980s.

and started to rise, the asset–liability maturity mismatch became unsustainable and Orange County was forced into bankruptcy. Clearly gullible county officials and poor governance allowed the Treasurer of Orange County to gamble the County taxpayers' money without reporting or accounting for the exposure of its portfolio to alternative interest rate scenarios. This chapter explains how a seemingly innocuous investment strategy in safe fixed income securities (the fancy names for various types of short term, medium term and long term bonds) engulfed Orange County finances into a Ponzi scheme which led to the loss of $1.65 billion for a portfolio of $7.5 billion.

MUNICIPAL FINANCE IN ORANGE COUNTY

The saga of the Orange County debacle is closely intertwined with the history of Robert Citron and his 24-year long tenure as the County treasurer and tax collector. In this capacity Robert Citron was responsible for the financial management of the County resources. In effect he supervised the collection of local (mostly real estate) taxes and their investment into safe and short-term securities before they would be disbursed for operating expenditures (such as paying salaries of police officers …) and capital improvements (such as building a swimming pool for one of the county high schools).

Proposition 13 and the New Municipal Finance Paradigm. Functioning as a county treasurer was a relatively straightforward task until the seeds of Orange County's demise were first sown fifteen years earlier: until 1978 the increasing cost of providing municipal services was generally met through real estate tax increases. The taxpayers' revolt in 1978 led California to vote the infamous Proposition 13 which imposed a straitjacket on property tax increases in particular and local government ability to raise taxes in general. In order to maintain the quality of municipal services, local governments found themselves in a quandary and became eager to generate non tax revenues to supplement tax revenues whose growth was now severely limited. This is the time when California relaxed the tight municipal financial management rules under which county treasurers could operate. Borrowing to invest in risky securities in order to enhance interest earnings to supplement tax revenues became possible and Robert Citron would rise to the occasion.

The Orange County Investment Pool (OCIP). It was the investment vehicle through which the county's tax revenues were put to work: in fact, a constellation of 189 different public entities such as thirty one cities, various school districts, water authorities, sanitation districts etc … — all domiciled in Orange County — entrusted their finances and channeled their investments through OCIP to Robert Citron. Some had to do it and others chose to do it; a number of them even borrowed in order to invest in OCIP. It made good sense to pool resources into a $7.5 billion mega-fund under centralized management to minimize management expenses: OCIP charged a management fee of 7 basis points or 0.07% (a basis point is one hundredth of one percent) — when a small fund would have spent 30 basis points — for a saving of $7.5 billion $(0.0030 - 0.0007) = \$17.48$ million per year. Just as retail investors pool their investment in mutual funds, municipalities domiciled in Orange County found it attractive to join the OCIP to have access to superior investment management and economies of scale in partaking of special opportunities only available to investors who can make larger investments.

Robert Citron's proven record as an asset manager was indeed so stellar that other California municipal agencies which were not domiciled in Orange County wanted to join the pool to piggy-back on its superior performance but were turned down. Robert Citron had delivered an average return of 9% during his tenure when the State of California could only earn 5–6%: Over the period 1991-1993 alone Robert Citron was credited to have earned an excess $500 million over the State of California investment performance.

From Hero to Villain. Robert Citron grew up in Orange County — the son of a medical doctor. He attended the University of Southern California first as a "pre-med" student before switching to Business Administration; however, he left the college several semesters short of having completed a bachelor's degree. After nearly a decade spent in the private sector as a consumer loan officer with the Century Finance Corporation Citron joined the tax collector's office of Orange County. In 1971, Citron ran for the elected position of tax collector and won. A democrat, Citron was reelected six times in a county which had grown to become staunchly republican. As a savvy investor who had delivered consistent and abnormally high returns on what was supposed to be low risk, short term fixed income investment Citron had built a strong popular base: Orange County taxpayers were certainly grateful for the additional income stream that Citron's savvy investment policy delivered when Proposition 13 had capped the County ability to raise taxes to fund higher expenditures. Indeed Citron's abnormal investment performance allowed the County to provide municipal services which would have had to be either curtailed or simply cut under normal returns.

Citron's achievements earned him national fame and recognition which inflated his ego to the point that Citron could not tolerate criticisms: for example, in 1993, to Goldman Sachs which had dared to criticize some of his decisions, Citron wrote back *"that Goldman does not understand the type of investment strategies that we are using. I would suggest that you not seek doing business with Orange County."*[148] The most serious assault however came from John Moorlach — a newspaper columnist and a cable TV host of the Costa Mesa Conservative Report — who challenged Citron in the June 1994 election. Moorlach — a Certified Public Accountant and a Certified

---

[148] Cited in Jorion, P. *Big Bets Gone Bad* (Academic Press, 1995), p. 8.

Financial Planner — was an informed opponent whose diagnosis of Orange County exposure to rising interest rates proved to be very prescient. Moorlach repeatedly pointed to the declining value of OCIP's asset portfolio which Citron refuted by arguing that these losses were "paper" losses which would not materialize as actual cash-flow losses as long as assets would be held to maturity. Moorlach's campaign attacks on Citron's highly leveraged and speculative investment strategy was grounded in sound financial theory and was echoed widely by the business press including the *Wall Street Journal* and *Derivatives Weekly* which called it "a scandal waiting to happen." Citron was in denial and resented the campaign as a personal attack: both republicans and democrats came to his rescue and the *Los Angeles Times* as well as the *Orange County Register* endorsed him: Citron was re-elected by a wide margin. Still, the electoral battle and intense scrutiny took a toll on Citron who according to his deputy Matthew Raabe "*turned into a very fragile man. He was an imposing and dominating figure all throughout the County for many, many, many years and by November 1994 he was this frail old man ....*"[149]

A PRIMER ON FIXED INCOME SECURITIES

Municipal investment pools such as OCIP are restricted to investing in fixed income securities. At it simplest, a fixed income security is a bond issued by a government, corporation or municipality which pays a fixed amount of interest every year until the bond matures when the issuer will pay back its full face value. It is called a fixed income security because interest payments and principal repayment are fixed in advance thereby guaranteeing the investor the return on his/her investment.

Credit Risk. "Fixed income" may turn out to be "less than fixed" for the unsuspecting investor if the bond issuer experiences difficulties in making interest payments or repaying principal in a timely fashion: this is what is called credit risk which may turn into unsavory surprises in the case of bond default. This is why bonds are graded by credit rating agencies such as Moody's or Standard and Poor's which study the likelihood that issuers will be able to pay in full both interest and principal when they are supposed to. When there is no doubt about the lasting financial health of the borrower the bond will receive the highest grade — an AAA in the case of Standard and Poor's or an Aaa in the case of Moody's. Lower grades such as BB or B simply signal that there is increasing doubt about the bond issuer's ability to fulfill their contractual payment obligations as enshrined in the bond's legal document. To complicate matters further a strong credit rating when a bond is issued is likely to change over the life of

---

[149] Jorion, P. op. cit. pp. 16–17.

the bond as the economic fortunes of the issuer evolve: a weakening of the issuer's financial health will typically translate into a credit downgrade when the likelihood of prompt interest and principal repayment in full diminishes.

Market Risk. The fixed face value of a bond at maturity nor the strong health of the issuer is any guarantee that the market value of a bond will remain fixed over its life. In fact bond values will almost always fluctuate with market interest rates. To understand how this works consider a five-year bond with a $1,000 face value paying 5% annual interest or $50 every year for the next five years when the $1,000 principal becomes due. Assume that one year after the bond issue, interest rates — because the economy is heating up — are now at 6% and our issuer — yet again in need of medium term funds — issues a new bond which offers an interest rate of 6%. Investors who had purchased the 5% coupon bond are stuck with a lower yielding bond paying only 5% when they could now get the higher interest income. They are foregoing, in an opportunity cost sense, $10 of income every year and the value of the original bond will have to fall to a level that is compatible with the new higher interest rate (see Box A). This is known as market risk. More generally the value of fixed income securities fall when interest rates rise and conversely rise when interest rates fall. Orange County was massively invested in fixed income securities and its investment strategy was strongly predicated on stable or declining interest rates as we will explain further in subsequent sections of this chapter.

Duration. The concept of market risk emphasized the sensitivity of bond prices to the level of interest rates in the economy. The maturity of the bond also plays an important role in this relationship: the longer the maturity of the bond the more sensitive — everything being equal — its value is to interest rates. Would a 10 year bond be twice as sensitive to a change of interest rate as a five-year bond or in other words would the 5% decline in the above example for a 1% interest rate translate into a 10% decline for a 10 year bond. Not quite — the reason being that the 10 year bond not only has a maturity twice as long as a five-year bond, it also has five additional intervening annual interest payments. Clearly maturity is an imperfect measure of this relationship. A better measure would take into account all payments — not only repayment of principal at maturity; it is known as duration. Like maturity it is measured in years. Duration will generally be shorter than maturity with one interesting exception: zero-coupon bonds — which pay no interest during their life and only principal at maturity — have a duration equal to their maturity. More specifically *"duration is a measure that seeks to answer the question, how long will it take to recover the market price, in present value terms, considering the average time required to collect all payments of principal and interest."*[150] For example a 30 year bond with interest payments (coupon)

---

[150] Jorion, op. cit., p. 29.

Box A. Bond Valuation. *Suppose Orange County issues at par*[151] *a five-year bond with a face value of $1,000 paying an annual coupon of 5% (par value is the same thing as face value). A buyer of the bond will receive a coupon payment of $50 each year (5% of $1,000) for five years and will recoup the principal of $1,000 at the end of the fifth year. If the bond is held to maturity the investor earns an annual rate of return equal to the 5% coupon rate because investing/buying the bond is equivalent to depositing $1,000 in a savings account, collecting an annual interest of 5% for five years and withdrawing the $1,000 at the end of the fifth year.*

    Yield-to-Maturity. Assume now that Orange County issues the same 5 year 5% coupon bond below par, at $955. The bondholder paid only $955 but will receive the same $50 coupon for the next five years and recoup the bond principal value at its face value of $1,000. Clearly the expected return is higher than 5% since in addition to annual coupon payments the bond investor benefits of a capital gain of $45 equal to $1,000 minus $955 at the time of redemption. What is the expected return on this bond investment purchased at $955 and redeemed at $1,000 while paying $50 every year for five year? It is the rate — called yield to maturity (YTM) — that makes the bond price equal the present value of the bond's cash-flow stream. This polynomial equation can be solved with some difficulty by trial and error but effortlessly by a financial calculator or spreadsheet software:*

$$955 = 50/(1 + YTM) + 50/(1 + YTM)^2 + 50/(1 + YTM)^3 + 50(1 + YTM)^4$$
$$+1,050(1 + YTM)^5. \qquad (1)$$

The solution is YTM = 6.07% : in other words a bond investor buying the bond for $955 and holding it to maturity can expect to earn a yield of 6.07%. The yield is higher than the coupon rate of 5% because it takes into account the $45 capital gain earned at maturity when the bond is redeemed at par/face value of $1,000.

    Bond prices when interest rate changes. *Now assume that a year has passed since Orange County issued the 5 year five percent coupon bond with face value of $1,000. The general level of interest rate paid on similar bond (similarity being defined in terms of maturity and credit risk) has risen to 6%: what is the market value of our original bond? We know that whatever price it will fetch should be such it will be equal to the present value of annual coupon payments of $50 each now discounted at the higher rate of 6% and principal repayment of $1,000.*

$$Bond\ Price = 50/(1 + 0.06) + 50/(1 + 0.06)^2 + 50/(1 + 0.06)^3$$
$$+1050/(1 + 0.06)^4 = 965. \qquad (2)$$

The lower price allows the investor to compensate the lower coupon payment by a capital gain at time of redemption. Rising interest rates are driving bond prices down. This is precisely the situation that Orange County's asset portfolio was confronting in early 1994.

---

[151] Issuing a bond at par means that the amount of money received is equal to the face value of the bond — value at which it will be repaid.

of 8% has a duration of only 11.76 years. More generally duration is a good measure of market price risk as it provides a reliable estimate of a bond's price change for a one percent change in yield: thus gains or losses due to interest rate changes can be readily computed as

Dollar gain/loss = duration × face value of bond × % increase (decrease) in yield.

Orange County's investment pool had an average maturity of only 1.4 years in October 1992 and yet its duration was 7.4 years when it went bankrupt. The reader may wonder why OCIP bond portfolio had a duration considerably longer than its average maturity: it had to do with its large investment in inverse floaters (discussed in the next section) which made OCIP hyper-sensitive to interest rate changes. With this information Jorion calculated that a 3% increase in interest rate would translate into a loss of

$$-\$1.6\,\text{billion} = 7.4\ \text{years} \times \$7.4\,\text{billion} \times (-0.03)$$

which is precisely the loss incurred by OCIP.[152]

ANATOMY OF ORANGE COUNTY ASSET PORTFOLIO

Before it went bankrupt Orange County entire investment pool totaled $20.5 billion — far in excess of the $7.5 billion core equity investment contributed to the pool by the 287 different entities: the difference resulted from aggressive borrowing by OCIP — an issue we will return to in the next section as leverage was one of the key component of OCIP successful investment strategy. But first we review in some details the key asset categories — as many as 206 different securities — which made up OCIP asset portfolio (see Table 1)

For the sake of simplicity Table 1 classifies the different assets in three different classes by increasing degree of market riskiness: cash, fixed income securities (including, collateralized mortgage obligations) and structured notes.

Cash. This account amounted to $645 million or less than 3% of the overall portfolio and would include money market accounts and overnight repurchase agreements (also known as repos): it had no exposure to interest rate fluctuations.

Fixed Income Securities. This category refers to any bond or note whose interest payment and principal repayment is fixed in advance. One of the key differentiating features of fixed income securities is the creditworthiness of their issuers.

Treasury securities. To finance the federal government budget deficit the US Treasury auctions off every month treasury securities ranging in maturities from 30 days to 30 years. Bonds (10–30 years in maturity) or notes (30 days to 10 years in maturity)

---

[152] Jorion, op.cit., p. 29.

Table 1 OCIP assets portfolio.

Type	Percentage	Book value	Market value	Loss	Market risk
Cash	3%	646,504,684			None
Fixed-Income	58%	11,857,330,590	11,032,143,453	825,187,000	Intermediate
Collateralized mortgage obligation	1%	228,536,168	222,431,070	6,105,000	Intermediate
Structured Notes					
Floating-rate notes	3%	588,000,000	556,643,093	31,357,000	Very low
Inverse floating-rate notes	26%	5,369,249,869	4,755,266,517	613,983,000	Very high
Index-amortizing notes	8%	1,699,030,670	1,549,044,495	149,986,000	Intermediate
Dual index notes	1%	150,000,000	134,919,100	15,081,000	Low
Total Assets		*20,538,651,981*	*18,896,952,413*		
Reverse repurchase agreements		−12,988,113,929	−12,988,113,929		
Net Value		*7,550,538,051*	*5,908,838,483*		

Source: Adapted from Miller, M. H. and D. J. Ross. The Orange County Bankruptcy and its aftermath: Some new evidence, *The Journal of Derivatives* (Summer, 1997), p. 53.

issued by the US government are the safest as their risk of default is the lowest of any fixed income securities: accordingly they pay the lowest coupon interest. OCIP had a relatively minor $310 million invested in such securities.

Agency securities. These bonds or notes are issued by agencies that are sponsored or guaranteed by the US government. In this category one finds The Federal National Mortgage Association (FNMA or "Fannie Mae"), the Government National Mortgage Association (GNMA or "Ginnie Mae") and the Federal Home Loan Mortgage Association ("Freddie Mac") which provides financing to the housing industry. The Student Loan Marketing Association affectionately known as "Sallie Mae" is the preferred lender to college and university students and would belong to this category. All three major agencies are formidable issuers in the fixed income markets and generally provide the cheapest financing for two major political constituencies: homeowners and students.

From an investor's perspective the key question is: are these securities as safe as US treasuries. Although there is a wide consensus that the US government would not allow the agencies to fail the guarantee is not an explicit one and the yield on such securities will be slightly higher than on US treasuries of the same maturity. The yield spread between two such securities gauges the differential in credit risk that is associated with agency securities: for example a GNMA five-year note in 1994 yielded 5.75% when a five-year Treasury note would offer a lower yield of 5.25% with the yield spread of 50 basis points capturing the somewhat lower credit status of Ginnie Mae as an issuer when compared to the US government.

Finally, various high grade bonds issued by private sector corporations, term repurchase agreements as well as mortgage-backed collateralized obligations were also included in the portfolio.

Overall fixed income securities totaled $12.1 billion or a little less than 60% of the overall portfolio. All securities in this asset class were exposed to interest rate fluctuations and a modest degree of credit risk. As long as interest rates remained stable or declined (which was Citron's bet) their value would remain unchanged or increase. Conversely should interest rate rise — as they started to do in early 1994 — the value of this asset class would decline. Under either scenario the gains or losses were unrealized (referred to as paper losses rather than actual cash-flow losses) as long as the securities were not liquidated. Held to maturity these securities would be redeemed at their par value without any loss of principal. However if "*marked to market*" during the course of their life (see Equation 2) these securities could exhibit significant losses in the case of rising interest rates and conversely gains could be made should interest rate decline.

Structured Notes. Unlike bonds which call for a fixed coupon payment, structured notes pay variable interest which are indexed to a key benchmark rate such as the London Interbank Offering Rate (LIBOR), the dollar-yen exchange rate, etc. . . . The index formula is what makes the interest payment a "derivative" of an underlying economic variable(s) via a more or less complicated but generally creative formula. This asset class included plain vanilla floating rate notes, inverse floaters, index-amortizing notes and dual index notes for a total amount of . . . . Of particular concern was the heavy reliance on inverse floaters (26% of asset portfolio) which constituted an aggressive bet on stable or declining interest rates.

Floating rate notes (*abbreviated as FRN and also known as floaters*). Interest payments on floating rates notes are defined as a function of a benchmark interest rate such as LIBOR plus a spread reflecting the credit risk of the issuer. The interest payment is floating/variable because it is reset periodically — usually every six month as the benchmark interest rate itself floats upwards or downwards. Consider for example a five-year $100 million floating rate note which pays LIBOR + 50 basis points for six months: if the six-month LIBOR on July 1, 1994 stood at 3.5% the FRN would pay on December 31, 1994 a semiannual interest (or 1/2 of one year) of

$$\$100 \text{ million } (0.035 + 0.005) \times 1/2 = \$2 \text{ million.}$$

The next interest payment covering the first six months of 1995 would adjust to the new LIBOR prevailing on December 31, 1994: assuming that LIBOR stood at 4% on December 31, 1994 the FRN would pay on June 30, 1995

$$\$100 \text{ million } (0.040 + 0.005) \times 1/2 = \$2.25 \text{ million}$$

and so on and so forth for the remaining eight semesters before the FRN would be redeemed. Because the coupon is reset every six months the value of the FRN is not exposed to changing interest rates — there is no market risk and in that sense FRNs are nearly as safe as cash as long as the issuer's credit risk remains steady.

Inverse Floating Rate Notes (also known as inverse floaters or reverse floaters). Reverse floaters pay an interest amount which is inversely indexed to the reference/ benchmark rate: it would increase when the reference rate decreases and conversely decreases when the reference rate increases. An example of an inverse floating rate note would be a $100 million note that pays a coupon at the rate of [7% − 6 month LIBOR] to be reset every six-months. Assuming LIBOR = 3% for the previous six-month period the inverse floater interest rate would be set at 7% − 6 month LIBOR = 0.07 − 0.03 = 0.04 and the coupon payment received would be

$$\$100 \text{ million } (0.07 - 0.03) \times 1/2 = \$2 \text{ million.}$$

If on the coupon payment day LIBOR has jumped to 4%, the coupon payment made at the end of the period would have fallen to

$$\$100 \text{ million } (0.07 - 0.04) \times 1/2 = \$1.5 \text{ million.}$$

Assuming that LIBOR at the end of the second six-month installment period has fallen to 2%, the inverse floating rate note would now receive a coupon payment of

$$\$100 \text{ million } (0.07 - 0.02) \times 1/2 = \$2.5 \text{ million.}$$

Inverse floaters are often leveraged whereby either or both the fixed and/or the floating rate of the coupon formula are multiplied by a factor of 2, 3 or 4.... Leverage would simply magnify upward or downward the change in the coupon amount paid as a function of the multiplier applied. For example, consider an inverse floater that pays 2 times fixed interest rate set at 6% minus three times LIBOR. For a five-year $100 million inverse floater the coupon paid would amount to

$$\$100 \text{ million } (2 \times 6\% - 3 \times 6 \text{ month LIBOR}).$$

For example under various interest rate scenarios the coupon payment would be computed as follows:

LIBOR $= 3\%$ Coupon payment $= \$100 \text{ million } (2 \times 0.06 - 3 \times 0.03)$

$$\times 1/2 = \$1.5 \text{ million}$$

LIBOR $= 4\%$ Coupon payment $= \$100 \text{ million } (2 \times 0.06 - 3 \times 0.04)$

$$\times 1/2 = \$0 \text{ million}$$

LIBOR $= 2\%$ Coupon payment $= \$100 \text{ million } (2 \times 0.06 - 3 \times 0.02)$

$$\times 1/2 = \$3 \text{ million}$$

LIBOR $= 1\%$ Coupon payment $= \$100 \text{ million } (2 \times 0.06 - 3 \times 0.01)$

$$\times 1/2 = \$4.5 \text{ million}.$$

The reader will have noted how in the case of the unleveraged inverse floater a 1% change in the variable rate in the formula triggers a 25% increase or decrease in coupon payment; with the leverage inverse floater the 1% change in LIBOR triggers a 100% increase or decrease in coupon payment.

Citron was clearly betting on declining interest rates and invested heavily in inverse floaters of the leveraged kind. Small decrease in interest rates would trigger generous increase in coupon payments and conversely increasing interest rates would quickly annihilate coupon payment. Even though the principal of such inverse floaters was never at risk as long as these notes were held to maturity a non interest paying note would be marked to market at a substantial discount akin to a zero coupon bond.

Index Amortizing Notes. This is a category of fixed income securities which repay principal according to a predetermined amortization schedule that is linked to a specific index such as LIBOR. As market interest rates increase and mortgage prepayment[153] rates decrease, the maturity of an Index Amortizing Note extends. Index amortizing notes are usually designed to behave similarly to a collateralized mortgage obligation with an embedded prepayment option. As rates decline and mortgage prepayment rates increase, the average life of an index amortizing note will contract. OCIP's portfolio included 8.3% of index amortizing notes.

---

[153] Mortgages — the staple instrument of long term consumer finance — generally give the borrower the right to prepay at any time with no question asked his debt: it is the so called prepayment option.

Dual-Index Notes. This is a category of structured notes whose coupon rate is determined by the difference between two market indexes such as the yield on a 15-year treasury note and 3 month LIBOR. A five-year dual-index note may have a fixed coupon rate of 7% for a brief period such as two years followed by a three year period at a variable rate set as the difference between the yield on a 5-year Treasury note and 1 month LIBOR. Dual-index notes have relatively low exposure to interest rates and they made up one percent of the overall asset portfolio.

OCIP AS A HEDGE FUND

Orange County was entrusted $7.6 billion to invest on behalf of its many constituents — municipalities, townships, school boards etc. When it declared bankruptcy in December 1994 its total assets exceeded $20.5 billions. As we shall explain, OCIP's vicissitudes came primarily from (1) leverage, (2) use of reverse repurchase agreements to fund its leveraged portfolio, and (3) investing in fixed income asset derivatives which proved to be far riskier than initially contemplated.

Leverage. As hedge funds generally do, Orange County used its assets as collateral to borrow an additional $12.5 billion in order to boost its yield above normal yields.

This is known as leverage — a widely used technique employed by corporations and banks alike. Leverage simply refers to borrowing in order to expand the scale of activities and is generally measured as the ratio of Total Assets (what you already own and generally referred as your "equity" –$7.5 billion in this case-plus what you borrow –$13 billion) divided by your "equity" or what you own. By general standards of leverage Orange County was at approximately 20.5/7.5 or a ratio of 2.7 to 1 — less than spectacular and certainly no cause for alarm. When Lehman Brothers declared

---

Box B. *What Are Hedge Funds?* *Hedge funds are unregulated pools of money which are aggressively managed with a great deal of flexibility. In fact hedge funds are anything but "hedged" or safe and are not meant for the faint-hearted investor. Like mutual funds, hedge funds are financial intermediaries which channel savings into productive investments thereby seeking to protect capital and to deliver hefty rewards to high net worth individuals, pension funds, endowments and other investors who entrusted their money. Unlike mutual funds, which are tightly regulated in the simple investment strategies they can pursue, the fees their managers can collect and the reporting requirements they must abide by, hedge funds can pursue complex strategies including borrowing heavily, using all sort of derivatives products, short selling and do all the above in total secrecy with no disclosure requirements. There is no limit on the fees that hedge fund managers can pay themselves (15–30% of profits) although, in some cases, fees will be waived when losses are incurred and not recouped — sometimes known as "high water marks."*

Table 2 Balance sheet of Orange County Investment Pool on 1 December, 1994 (Millions of Dollars).

Assets			Liabilities and equity	
Group 1: Assets exposed to interest			Short Term Debt $12,988.1	(63.2%)
rate risk	**(83.3%)**		Reverse repurchase agreements	
Inverse floaters $5,369.2	(26.1%)			
Fixed-income $11,857.3	(57.7%)			
Group 2: Other assets less				
or not exposed to interest				
rate risk	**(16.2%)**			
Cash $646.5	(3.2%)			
Collateralized Mortgage			Equity held by Investors	
Obligations $228.5	(1.1%)		$7,550.4	(36.8%)
Dual-index notes $150.0	(0.7%)			
Floating-rate notes $588.0	(2.9%)			
Index-amortizing				
notes $1,699.0	(8.3%)			
Total assets $20,538.5	**(100%)**		**Total liabilities and equity**	
			$20,538.5	**(100%)**

Source: Adapted from M. H. Miller and D. J. Ross. The Orange County Bankruptcy and its aftermath: Some new evidence, *The Journal of Derivatives* (Summer 1997), and Marthinsen, J. *Risk Takers* (Addison-Wesley, 2004), p. 167.

bankruptcy in September 2008 its leverage was in excess of 30 to 1. Of course Orange County was not supposed to be leveraged in the first place ... As long as Orange County was able to generate yields higher than its borrowing costs its equity base enjoyed spectacular return due to the leverage effect. Conversely, when interest rates reversed course leverage became very punitive and Orange County's own return on its equity dwindled drastically.

Let us turn to a numerical illustration of how leverage enhanced OCIP's yield performance. Assume that Orange County generates a yield of 5.50% annually on its portfolio of $7.5 billion. If Orange County borrows another $7.5 billion (leverage is now 2 to 1) and invests its total assets portfolio at 5.50% the impact of this indebtedness depends on the rate at which it borrows. Let us assume that Orange County borrows very short term at a rate of 4.00%. It can add 1.50% earned on the borrowed assets to its pre-leverage yield of 5.50% for a return of 7.00%. Leverage delivers a boost in yield of $[7.00\% - 5.50\%]/5.50 = 27\%$. Had Orange County borrowed $15 billion instead of $7.5 billion for a leverage of 3 to 1 the yield on its original portfolio would now reach $5.5\% + 1.5\% \times 2 = 8.5\%$ or a boost in yield of 55%. In other words leverage magnifies

---

Box C. Repurchase Agreements (Repos) and Reverse Repurchase Agreements.
*A repurchase agreement is the sale of a security (such as treasury bonds) with
an agreement (in the form of a forward contract) to buy it back at a set price on
a set date. The seller effectively gets a short term loan with the security being
sold serving as collateral. Because the value of the collateral is subject to credit
and market risk the seller will receive a little less than the market value of the
security — so-called "haircut" — thereby providing the lender a small safety
cushion. One of the advantage of repurchase agreement financing is that it is generally cheaper than unsecured bank financing. Reverse repos are for all practical
purposes equivalent to repos. The difference is that in reverse repo the borrower
(seller of the security used as collateral) is not a security dealer. A repo is the
inverse transaction where the borrower is a securities dealer. Because OCIP was
not a securities dealer its use of collateralized borrowing from a securities dealer
in the form of a repurchase agreement would be called a reverse repo.*

---

the unlevered yield that Orange County could deliver to its constituents. It worked as
long as OCIP could roll over its short term loan at consistently low interest rates; when
short term interest rates skyrocketed in 1994 from 5% to nearly 8% OCIP found itself
lending at a lower interest rate than what it was paying on its short term loans.

Risky Liabilities. Not being a licensed bank nor a Savings and Loans, Orange
County was somewhat restricted in how it could achieve the desired level of leverage
necessary to boost the yield on its original "equity" portfolio. The technique of choice
was the repurchase agreement (repo for short) whereby Orange County would pledge
its assets for a short term loan at the low rate of say 4.00% with which it would buy
additional fixed income securities yielding the higher rate of say 5.5%. Repos are
essentially collateralized short term loans (with maturities of 7, 30 or 90 days) which
would need to be continuously rolled over at expiration (see Box C). What OCIP
could do once it could do again: pledge the newly acquired fixed income securities to
borrow an additional $7.5 billion which in turn would be invested at the higher rate
of 5.50%. Critical to this leverage scheme was OCIP's ability to borrow consistently
at a lower rate than it would invest at. After all, any depository financial institutions
is — by charter — in the business of borrowing short at a low rate from its depositors
(typically very short term) and lending long to corporations or household which need
financing over longer terms and are ready to pay a correspondingly higher interest rate.

Leveraging the investment pool by borrowing through reverse repos was motivated
by the fact that such collateralized loans are very inexpensive: the cheaper the cost of
short-term financing the more beneficial leverage becomes. However funding through
repos is risky because the value of the collateral is itself exposed to market risk — that
is the market value of the pledged security is exposed to interest rate fluctuations. Let
us say that Orange County is pledging $100 million in five-year treasury notes with

coupon of 5.50% to borrow short term $100 million and the interest rate is set at 3% for one year. If one month into the loan the Federal Reserve Bank decides to increase discount rates by 50 basis points the value of the $100 million collateral will drop by 2.5% (bond prices decline when market interest rates rise): the lender now holds a collateral worth $97.5 million for a loan of $100 million and will ask the borrower to pledge an additional $2.5 million (also known as a collateral call and similar to a

---

Box D. Leverage as a Double-Edged Sword. *We showed earlier how leverage (borrowing to increase total asset portfolio) magnified the yield on the unlevered portion of the asset portfolio. We now consider how a 1% absolute increase or decrease in short term interest rate triggers an increase or decrease in the entire portfolio yield of ±25% thereby illustrating how vulnerable OCIP was to small changes in interest rates. For the purpose of this illustration OCIP is assumed to have borrowed $7.6 billion exactly doubling the size of its initial portfolio to $15.2 billion (leverage of 2 to 1); 50% is invested in five-year treasuries yielding 5.50% and 50% in inverse floaters paying (8.5% − repo rate). If the repo rate is 3% the inverse floaters yield 8.5% − 3% = 5.5%. Since the cost of the borrowed portion of the portfolio is also 3%, the total yield on the borrowed portion of the portfolio is 5.5% − 3% = 2.5%. The leveraged yield on the equity portion of OCIP's portfolio is therefore 5.5% + 2.5% = 8%.*

    Scenario 1: repo rate increase by 1%. *Assume that short term financing through repos cost 4% instead of 3%.*

- *OCIP' assets yield 5.50% on fixed income (50% of portfolio) but only 8.5% − 4% = 4.5% on inverse floaters (50% of portfolio) or a total of $0.50 \times 0.0550 + 0.50 \times 0.0450 = 0.0500$.*
- *OCIP' liabilities cost 4% (50% of total portfolio) while equity is free (50% of portfolio).*
- *The enhanced yield on the equity portion of OCIP's portfolio is now 5.50% + 0.50% = 6%.*
- *Change in yield induced by a 1% increase in short term debt financing (repo) triggered a reduction of $[0.08 − 0.06]/0.08 = −25\%$ for the unlevered portion of OCIP's assets.*

    Scenario 2: repo rate decline by 1%. *Assume that short term financing through repos cost 2% instead of 3%.*

- *OCIP's assets yield 5.50% on fixed income (50% of portfolio) but 8.5% − 2% = 6.5% on inverse floaters (50% of portfolio).*
- *The leveraged yield on the equity portion of OCIP portfolio is now 5.50% + 4.50% = 10%.*
- *Change in yield induced by a 1% increase in short term debt financing (repo) triggered an increase $[0.10 − 0.08]/0.08 = +25\%$ for the unlevered portion of OCIP's assets.*

margin call characteristic of a futures contract — see Box D). The borrower's portfolio is hit both ways: on the asset side his holding of $100 million in five-year treasury notes is showing a loss (unrealized as long as the notes are not liquidated) and, on the liability side, his shrunk collateral has to be topped up to satisfy the lender's collateral call. Orange County's assets (and therefore collateral) portfolio was "marked-to-market" regardless of the fact that it fully intended to hold its assets to maturity. Although Citron claimed until the very end that these losses were merely "paper losses" the required posting of additional collateral to satisfy lenders transformed these paper losses into cash-flow losses which — in turn — precipitated the liquidity crisis which ultimately forced Orange County into bankruptcy.

Risky assets. Of the several classes of assets which made up OCIP portfolio inverse floaters were singled out in our previous discussion as particularly toxic under an adverse interest rate scenario. By definition, inverse floaters reward investors when a declining interest rate triggers an increase in coupon payment. Because Citron had chosen leveraged or "supercharged" inverse floaters the change in coupon payments were magnified by the leverage factor (see Box D). With declining interest rates OCIP benefitted from enhanced yield which made Citron so popular with his constituents. When interest rates reversed course in early 1994 and started to rise, coupon payments on inverse floaters collapsed and precipitated a brutal downward marked-to-market adjustment in the value of said securities. Since these inverse floaters had been pledged as collateral for the repo financing their collapsing market value triggered collateral call by the lenders that OCIP was not in a position to meet because of its limited liquidity (see Box E).

DOUBLE JEOPARDY: HOW ORANGE COUNTY COLLAPSED

OCIP's balance sheet showed significant leverage: the original $7.6 billion of funds owned by Orange County and its many constituents served as a basis for borrowing another $13 billion primarily through reverse repos. This allowed OCIP to have access to short-term and relatively inexpensive financing. OCIP invested in longer term and higher yielding securities ranging from fixed income securities to structured notes including inverse floaters.

Under a scenario of stable or declining interest rates the "*hedge fund*" model delivered supercharged returns to Orange County as the liability side of the balance sheet was benefitting from cheaper and cheaper financing. The asset side also benefitted from lower interest rate — especially inverse floaters which were structured to magnify the inverse relationship to interest rate and therefore delivering higher yields. Other fixed income securities of longer-term maturities had locked in higher

> **Box E. Collateral Call.** *As interest rate started to edge upwards in early 1994 Orange County started to feel the squeeze of its leverage portfolio. As part of its reverse repo funding strategy it had pledged various fixed income securities whose marked-to-market value were being downgraded. For example a five-year 5% $100 million note purchased at par when issued (that is interest rate were at 5%) would be now worth significantly less when market interest rates increased to 6% or 7%. Lenders called on Orange County to post additional collateral to compensate for the reduced value of the asset that had been pledged — what is known as a "collateral call." Indeed Orange County went as far as issuing medium term notes in the spring of 1994 to precisely fund these repeated collateral calls. Investors were not told nor amused when they found out the hard way — when Orange County went into bankruptcy protection — what was the true reason for the bond issue.*

interest rate earlier on thereby widening the positive spread on the short term cost of financing.

Upward trending interest rates unraveled OCIP's leveraged investment strategy. Higher interest rates delivered a double blow to Orange County: in addition to a more expensive financing basis, the collateral for repos were being marked down. In other words lenders not only were charging higher interest rates but they were also making collateral calls — that is requiring OCIP to deposit additional capital to compensate for the shrinking value of pledged securities. On the asset side, fixed income securities were not generating higher income since they had locked in longer term lower yield at time of investment. Their market values were also adjusting downward, triggering the collateral call for repos. But, the real squeeze came from leveraged inverse floaters which were highly exposed to interest rates: with higher interest rates inverse floaters were no longer generating any interest income and were marked down accordingly. The combined squeeze of a negative rather than a positive interest spread combined with collateral calls on repos triggered by a significantly marked down value for the entire portfolio was the "double jeopardy" which forced OCIP into bankruptcy protection.

WAS FILING FOR BANKRUPTCY WARRANTED?

Seeking protection from creditors by declaring bankruptcy is generally warranted when test of solvency and liquidity fail to be met. On December 1, 1994, when Orange County publically acknowledged a $1.65 billion decline in the market value of its investment pool the net value of its portfolio was standing at $6.1 billion — hardly characteristic of insolvency. On the same day, Orange County had close to $650 million in cash — again hardly symptomatic of illiquidity. And yet the US Bankruptcy Court upheld

Orange County's decision to seek protection from creditors wanting to cash out from their investments and more specifically from reverse repo counterparties (investment banks) forcing collateral calls. Indeed the fact that "investment bankers declined to roll over or renew existing reverse-repurchase agreements in the amount of $1.2 billion"[154] panicked the county Board of Supervisors in seeking Chapter 9 bankruptcy protection.

A study by Economics Nobel prize laureate Merton Miller commissioned by defendant Merrill Lynch showed rather convincingly that had the investment pool not been liquidated and invested in money market funds but had — instead — stayed the course with its "hold-to-maturity" strategy OCIP would have avoided the cash losses that it reported; it would also have generated substantial net cash inflows and recovered $1.8 billion within 15 months — an amount which offset more than the loss declared on December 6, 1994. Unfortunately for Orange County, as it started to default on some payments, a number of lenders forced liquidation by seizing the collateral for immediate resale: out of a total portfolio of $20.5 billion, about $11 billion was liquidated without Orange County's consent for a realized loss of $1.3 billion.[155]

Ultimately, was OCIP in a position to forecast the course of interest rate when it decided to seek bankruptcy protection? Short term interest rates are dictated by Fed decisions and may be difficult to anticipate (see Figure 1). Analysis of yield curves may be helpful in forecasting medium and long-term interest rates but these are "unbiased" market based forecasts — that is, they forecast the mean of future interest rates without

---

Box F. Value-at-Risk (V@R). *Value at risk is an attempt at providing a summary statistic measuring in a single number the total risk of a portfolio of financial assets. History has it that the CEO of JP Morgan had asked his staff to provide him with one single number at 4:15 pm everyday of the risk faced by the bank for the next day. He was served with Value at Risk. "We are x percent certain that we will not lose more than L dollars in the next N days." In other words V@R estimates the maximum loss L in dollar terms over a target horizon (N days) with a given probability x; it answers in pseudo-scientific terms the difficult question "How much are we likely to lose?" Had Orange County generated consistent information about its V@R it would have known what to expect and may have been prompted to prepare for it.*

---

[154] Orange County Register, December 7, 1994, p. A19 cited in Miller, M. H. and D. J. Ross, The Orange County bankruptcy and its aftermath: Some new evidence, *The Journal of Derivatives* (Summer 1997).

[155] Jorion, P. Lessons from the Orange County bankruptcy, *The Journal of Derivatives* (Summer 1997), p. 65.

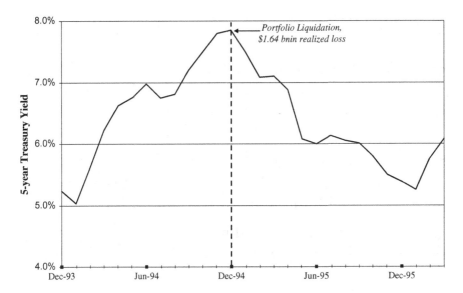

Figure 1 Path of interest rates.

Source: Jorion, P. Lessons from the Orange County Bankruptcy. *The Journal of Derivatives* (Summer 1997), p. 64.

revealing anything about the variance around the mean. Perhaps the more reliable information was to consider the Value-at-Risk of OCIP portfolio which indicated that as of December 1994 there was a 5% probability that over 1995 it would suffer another loss of $1.1 billion. That same statistical analysis also indicated that there was a 5% probability that OCIP could regain $1.3 billion. Orange County was in no mood to roll the dice (see Figure 2).

THE MORAL OF THE STORY

Lesson #1 About Managing Success When You Are an Elected Official. Failure to communicate the leveraged nature of his investment strategy made Robert Citron's demise all the more cathartic. With a stellar record of superior performance stretching over a period of 22 years Robert Citron had much to be proud of but consistently failed to diagnose the roots of his success. By explaining and communicating clearly and convincingly the premises behind his abnormal performance Citron would have been forced to wrestle with the weakness of his leveraged strategy. Simple financial management concepts such as V@R, stress-testing and asset–liability management should have been powerful educational tools for Citron to better grasp why his tenure was being so successful. Introspection and self-assessment are the best hedges against

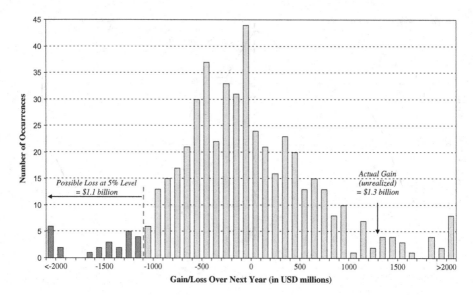

Figure 2 Distribution of possible gains and losses on OCIP annual returns over 1953–1994.
Source: Jorion, P. Lessons from the Orange County Bankruptcy, *The Journal of Derivatives* (Summer 1997), p. 64.

a blinding hubris. Part of this effort would have naturally led Citron to managing expectations better by clarifying reporting lines. Clearly Citron enjoyed his independence and the very limited accountability the Board of Supervisors subjected him to. His detractors consistently mocked him as someone who had limited knowledge and understanding of the world of high finance. Hubris may have blinded Citron but it is hard to believe that Citron could have fooled so many investment bankers and county supervisors for so long without a modicum of investment savvy and comprehension.

Lesson #2 about Governance. OCIP was for all practical purposes left to its own device as it was minimally overseen by a weak Board of Supervisors. It is certainly difficult to assert one's authority on a department enjoying a spectacular performance and led by a very popular treasurer in the person of Robert Citron. Overhauling its governance structure was indeed imperative. At the very least a charter defining clearly the investment objectives of the investment pool and what would constitute acceptable assets for investment purposes spelled out in terms of tenors, credit and market risk terms. Should leverage be tolerated and at what level: as discussed above leverage can be found at two levels: (1) directly, in terms of borrowing in order to increase the size of a total asset portfolio. If one believes in the mutual fund model OCIP would have been forbidden to use leverage to morph itself into a hedge fund and (2) indirectly, as leverage can be embedded in derivative investment products such as leveraged inverse floaters.

Should such toxic securities be prohibited or — at very least — severely limited? If moderate levels of leverage are allowed, clear and enforceable limits/threshold should be set.

An investment charter would also spell out the nature, timing and frequency of reporting and disclosure requirements to be made by the County Treasurer to the Board of Supervisors. Beyond reporting monthly or quarterly balance sheets, income statements and cash-flow statements key information on the risk profile of the pool in terms of Value at Risk and other risk metrics is critical. OCIP should also be required to stress-test its marked-to-market value under different interest rate scenarios.

Oversight of the investment pool activities is paramount. Electing or appointing a Board of Directors including a majority of independent and investment-savvy professionals without any conflict of interest with service providers is absolutely necessary. The Treasurer should be elected from a list of prescreened contenders with meaningful professional qualifications in the field of asset management: said individual and his/her team should be required to periodically enlist in executive education seminars on asset management and should abide to a term limit. Last but not least, independent auditors should be required to prepare detailed analysis of variance for each quarter between investment pool's planned goals and actual performance and asked to reach out to financial institutions which are service/product providers and/or counterparties.

Lesson #3 for Investing in Municipal Bonds. Retail or institutional investors who are inclined to invest in safe municipal bonds may want to engage in self-directed due diligence. The borrower's abnormal performance in the form of consistently superior yield should have been a red flag to any investor: indeed wide press coverage hailing Orange County's treasurer as an investment genius made the information widely available. The theory of finance has long established the robust relationship which exists between risk and return. As Citron was delivering high returns to his grateful constituents, higher level of exposure to risk had to be taken. Clearly credit rating agencies failed to ask this basic question and were willing to uphold a strong AA rating for OCIP's bond issues. Prudent investors would want to adhere to portfolio diversification and credit enhancement through bond insurance as guiding investment principles in municipal bonds. Reliance on credit ratings agencies may fail to unveil fundamental flaws such as leverage and over-reliance on derivatives-cum-fixed income securities. Access to publicly available reports issued by OCIP should have been enough to raise questions which — if remained unanswered — would have discouraged investors.

Lesson #4 About Regulating Municipal Finance. At both the state and federal level regulation should be enacted dictating explicit investment charters and governance mechanisms for managing municipal investment pools. Ironically, federal regulation covering various types of mutual funds has existed for many years protecting unsuspecting retail investors. Municipal investment pools should be obvious targets for such regulation with clear guidelines protecting agencies participating in such pools and investors financing them.

To strengthen further the protection of municipal finance, specific guidelines enacted as federal regulation should be forced on financial institutions selling sophisticated and complicated securities to treasurers of public entities such as Orange County. "Buyer beware" is legitimate when the buyer is a hedge fund or the Chief Financial Officer of a sophisticated multinational corporation but municipal finance officers should be handled with "kids' gloves."

EPILOGUE

Starting in February 1994, the Federal Reserve Bank initiated a series of interest rates hikes which ran counter to the stable-downward trending interest rate assumptions buttressing OCIP leveraged investment strategy. With $1.65 billion in losses and mounting collateral calls from investment houses, Orange County filed on December 6, 1994 for chapter 9 bankruptcy protection thereby preventing its creditors from seizing municipal assets such as schools, playgrounds or courthouses.

Default and Bankruptcy. Orange County defaulted on $110 million of notes that came due on December 8, 1994 which prompted a credit downgrade to "junk' status. The fear of a "domino" effect shook the world of California municipal finance with several counties found to be leveraged and therefore vulnerable to further interest rates hikes. Bankruptcy protection bought Orange County some time by pushing off the day of reckoning: on May 2, 1995 the US bankruptcy court endorsed the settlement of what was left in the investment pool: each participating institution in the pool received 77 cents on the dollar as a cash distribution of whatever investment they had in the investment pool. There were 189 institutions involved.

Lawsuits and Restitutions. In January 1995 Orange County filed a $2 billion lawsuit against Merrill Lynch on the ground that several of its brokers had willfully and deceitfully assisted the County in leveraging its investment portfolio and therefore bore responsibility for the major losses that ensued. In fairness to Merrill Lynch, it had assumed that it had protected itself by warning Citron in writing on three occasions about the investment pool exposure to rising interest rates: specifically it had spelled out that for every one percent increase in interest rate Orange County stood to lose $270 million. In his testimony Merrill Lynch's Mr. Stamenson declared that Robert Citron was hardly the neophyte that he professed to be "*I learned a lot from him, since he was doing reverse purchase transactions before I even knew what the term meant.*"[156]

---

[156] *The Economist*, Juicy (January 21, 1995), p. 74.

Merrill Lynch eventually agreed in June 1998 to settle for the modest sum of $434 million. Similarly Morgan Stanley, Dean Witter and Nomura Securities agreed to pay Orange County an additional $118 million. Ultimately Orange County was paid a total of $865 million through settling all the lawsuits which had also targeted its auditor KPMG and its law firm LeBeouf. In the final analysis, the 187 municipal investors in the Orange County investment pool recovered a significant amount of their initial 1994 loss.

Governance. The financial collapse of Orange County was a wake-up call to the State legislature and its executive branch as it was deemed that the solvency and creditworthiness of any local agency was paramount to the entire state's fiscal soundness. Deregulation was abruptly reversed and the SB 866 California State Legislation was signed into law by the Governor on October 12, 1995 which went into effect on January 1, 1996. The comprehensive reform set very tight operating guidelines for the County treasurer:

> *SB 866 specifies that the objectives of investing public funds are, first, safety of the principal, then the liquidity needs of the depositor, and, finally, achieving a return on the funds. Limits the amount that can be invested in reverse purchase agreements; prohibits investment in inverse floaters and other exotic securities; limits the length of term of investments on borrowed funds. Requires the Board of Supervisors to establish a county treasurer oversight committee; establishes educational qualifications for the county treasurer. Specifies rule for local agencies to enter and exit from county investment pools; Requires that local governments give adequate notice of withdrawals.*
>
> *SB 564 places requirements on local treasurers to provide the local governing boards and their oversight committees with an annual statement of investment policy, and to provide quarterly reports containing specified financial information.* [157]

Specifically, leverage was limited to 20% of the portfolio by restricting the use of reverse purchase agreements. Orange County itself went further than the letter of the law by banning leverage entirely and mandating that the investment pool be run as a money market fund. It also created a second oversight committee called the technical oversight committee which included outside financial experts from the private sector.

The road to recovery was remarkably short: the initial plan had planned to bridge the municipal finance abyss through a tax increase. But this was California — home to Disneyland and Proposition 13! Measure R — a tax increase of 1/2 of one percent was overwhelmingly defeated by angry voters in June 1995. In part this was due to the fact

---

[157] *Source*: Office of Senate Floor Analysis (1995), cited in Baldassare, Mark. *When Government Fails: the Orange County Bankruptcy* (University of California Press, 1998).

that Orange county residents had yet to feel the pain from the crisis since municipal services had been maintained. Orange County convinced reluctant investors to roll-over $800 million in short-term notes for another year, temporarily diverted infrastructure funds to meet emergency needs to continue providing necessary municipal services. One year later, after successfully issuing $880 million in 30 year municipal bonds, Orange County emerged from bankruptcy in June 1996. Moorlach, who had run a prescient campaign against Citron in early 1994, was appointed acting treasurer in March 1995. Robert Citron pleaded guilty to six felony charges, served eight months in a work release program and paid $100,000 in fine.

Bibliography

Baldassare, M. *When Government Fails: The Orange County Bankruptcy* (University of California Press, 1998).

Chew, L. *Managing Derivative Risks: The Use and Abuse of Leverage* (Wiley, 1996).

Jorion, P. *Big Bets Gone Bad: Derivatives and Bankruptcy in Orange County*. (Academic Press, 1995).

_____. Lessons from the Orange County Bankruptcy, *The Journal of Derivatives* (Summer 1997).

Marthinsen, J. *Risk Takers: Uses and Abuses of Derivatives* (Pearson Addison-Wesley, 2004).

Miller, M. H. and D. J. Ross. The Orange County bankruptcy and its aftermath: Some new evidence, *The Journal of Derivatives* (Summer 1997).

Questions for Discussion

1. Do you agree with the characterization that OCIP was run as a hedge fund?
2. Why are repurchase agreement (repo) a very inexpensive form of short term financing?
3. Comment on the maturity structure of OCIP assets and liabilities.
4. Explain how leverage was enabling OCIP to deliver significantly higher returns than other municipal entities in California.
5. Should municipal entities such as OCIP be forbidden to use leverage.

15
LONG-TERM CAPITAL MANAGEMENT

Traders and other undertakers may, no doubt, with great propriety, carry on a very considerable part of their projects with borrowed money. In justice to their creditors, however, their own capital ought to be, in this case, sufficient to ensure, if I may say so, the capital of those creditors; or to render it extremely improbable that those creditors should incur any loss, even though the success of the project should fall very short of the expectations of the projectors.

Adam Smith (1776)

The combination of precise formulas with highly imprecise assumptions can be used to establish, or rather to justify, practically any value one wishes ... Calculus gives speculation the deceptive guise of investment.

Benjamin Graham (1949)

Long-Term Capital Management (LTCM) was a hedge fund like no other. Its relentless delivery of low volatility outsized returns for the first four years of its existence was unparalleled. Its demise and near-collapse in the fall of 1998 was as calamitous as its rise had been spectacular. Indeed the world economy had very narrowly escaped the abyss but regulators failed to draw any lessons which would have avoided the current

245

crisis. At its apogee, in early 1998, with debt of $125 billion and off-balance sheet derivatives exposure in excess of $1 trillion piled up on a puny equity capital base of $4.7 billion Long-Term Capital Management had perfected financial leverage to a science. Unlike other derivatives debacles discussed in this book LTCM precipitous collapse stoked fear of systemic risk — that is of a domino effect engulfing the entire global financial system — so much so that the New York Federal Reserve Bank coerced fourteen major Wall Street firms — which were LTCM main creditors — to come to its rescue with a bail-out package of $3.6 billion. This chapter retraces the saga of the rise and fall of LTCM and exposes the alchemy of its phenomenal successes which also seeded its collapse.

WHAT ARE HEDGE FUNDS?

Hedge funds are unregulated pools of money which are aggressively managed with a great deal of flexibility. In fact hedge funds are not necessarily "hedged" or safe investment and are certainly not meant for the faint-hearted investor. The "hedge" misnomer is often traced back to the modest fund started by Alfred W. Jones in 1949 with $100,000 which he invested in common stocks "hedged" by short sales (see Box A). Like mutual funds, hedge funds are financial intermediaries which channel savings into productive investments thereby seeking to protect capital and to deliver hefty rewards to high net worth individuals, pension funds, endowments and other investors who entrusted their money. Unlike mutual funds, which are tightly regulated in the simple investment strategies they can pursue, the fees their managers can collect and the reporting requirements they must abide by, hedge funds can pursue complex strategies including borrowing heavily, using all sorts of derivatives products, short selling and do all the above in almost total secrecy with very limited disclosure requirements (see Box A). There is no limit on the fees that hedge fund managers can pay themselves (15–30% of profits) although fees will usually be waived when losses are incurred and not recouped — sometimes known as "high water marks." In sum,

> *"Hedge funds are investment pools that are relatively unconstrained in what they do. They are relatively unregulated (for now), charge very high fees, will not necessarily give you your money back when you want it, and will generally not tell you what they do. They are supposed to make money all the time, and when they fail at this, their investors redeem and go to someone else who has recently been making money. Every three or four years, they deliver a one-in-a-hundred-year flood."*[158]

---

[158] In the more direct language of Cliff Asness of AQR Capital cited in *The New York Magazine* (April 9, 2007).

Box A. Hedge Funds' Unorthodox Investment Strategies. *According to a recent report by Tremont Asset Flows Report (second quarter, 2005) more than two-thirds of the $1 trillion managed by hedge funds are accounted by four strategies*:

A *long-short equity hedge fund* (31%) *invests in common equity partially or fully hedged by short sales, futures or options thereby largely immunizing the fund returns from market price risk.*

An *event driven fund* (20%) *capitalizes on perceived mispricing of securities arising from significant events such as mergers, acquisitions, re-organizations and bankruptcies.*

A *macro-hedge fund* (10%) *places leveraged bets on currency, interest rates or commodities on the basis of its forecasting of geo-political trends or macro-economic events.*

A *fixed income arbitrage fund* (8%) *identifies temporary pricing abnormalities in bonds markets and arbitrage them away through leveraged convergence trades. See below detailed discussion of how LTCM turned this strategy into a money-making machine.*

THE RISE OF LONG-TERM CAPITAL MANAGEMENT

LTCM traces its roots to Salomon Brothers' bond arbitrage desk which had been run very successfully by John Meriwether until the 1991 bond scandal. A former star bond trader himself at Salomon, Meriwether had become vice-chairman overseeing Salomon's fixed income securities business until a bond trader by the name of Paul Mozer tried to corner the Treasury bond auction market by submitting fraudulently inflated bids. When the US treasury uncovered the ploy it threatened to ban Salomon from the Treasury bond market which nearly bankrupted the firm. John Meriwether — to whom the bond trader reported — was forced to resign after having been fined $50,000 by the SEC for failure to properly supervise its traders. LTCM was launched in early 1994 by the same John Meriwether who was bent on rebuilding its former Salomon bond trading operations from the different platform of a hedge fund. Not surprisingly Meriwether brought along several of high flying Salomon Brothers traders — most notably John Hillibrand and Eric Rosenfeld. To add to the fund's all star cast Meriwether also recruited two famous financial economists Myron Scholes and Robert Merton whose pioneering work had led the path to valuing options and who were to be awarded the 1997 Nobel Prize in Economic Science. David Mullins, a former vice-chairman of the Federal Reserve Bank was also made one of LTCM's founding partners (see Table 1 for a list of LTCM's key founding partners). By marrying academics' mathematical models with traders' market savvy and experience Meriwether

Table 1   LTCM partners.

John Meriwether	Former vice chair and head of bond trading at Salomon Brothers: MBA, University of Chicago.
Robert C. Merton	Leading finance scholar and Nobel laureate (1997); PhD, Massachusetts Institute of Technology (MIT); Professor at Harvard Business School.
Myron Scholes	Co-author of Black-Scholes option pricing model and Nobel laureate (1997); PhD University of Chicago; Professor at Stanford University.
David W. Mullins, Jr.	Vice Chairman of the Federal Reserve: PhD MIT; Professor at Harvard University.
Eric Rosenfeld	Arbitrage group at Salomon Brothers. PhD MIT; former Harvard Business School professor.
William Krasker	Arbitrage group at Salomon Brothers. PhD MIT; former Harvard Business School professor.
Gregory Hawkins	Arbitrage group at Salomon Brothers. PhD MIT.
Larry Hilibrand	Arbitrage group at Salomon Brothers. PhD MIT.
James McEntee	Bond-trader at Salomon Brothers.
Dick Leahy	Executive at Salomon Brothers.
Victor Haghani	Arbitrage group at Salomon Brothers. Masters in Finance, LSE.

was elevating the mystique of hedge funds to new heights. Indeed this unique line-up of expertise from Wall Street, academia and government proved to be a very successful ploy in raising capital from some of the most respected financial institutions (such as Merrill Lynch, UBS and Credit Suisse), a number of foreign governments (including the Bank of Italy and the Bank of China) as well as many high net worth individuals. On its first day of operation, LTCM had raised $1.3 billion in equity capital with $100 million contributed by its 16 founding partners. Minimum investment required stood at $10 million with a lock up period (no withdrawal) of three years. LTCM would collect an annual fee set at 2% of assets and keep 25% of profits. Investors certainly enjoyed the ride: LTCM delivered exceptional returns in the first four years of operations — 19.9% after fees in 1994, 42.8% in 1995, 40.8% in 1996, and 17.1% in 1997 (see Figure 1). Stellar performance had propelled the fund to $7 billion in equity capital at the end of 1997 when Meriwether decided to return $2.7 billion to its investors.

In truth, LTCM was more akin to a sophisticated bond trading house than a conventional asset manager for the wealthy. Michael Lewis, himself a former bond trader with Salomon Brothers turned best seller author with *Liar's Poker* was struck by the

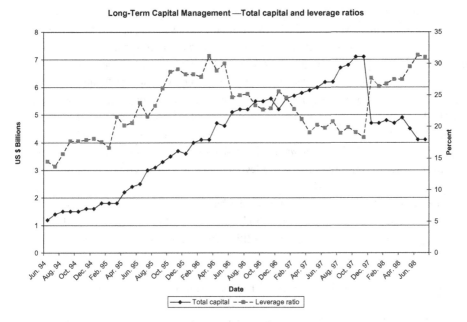

Figure 1   LTCM's performance.

physical configuration of LTCM's head offices in Greenwich (Connecticut) when he visited the firm:

> *"the floor it had constructed in Greenwich was a smaller version of a Wall Street trading floor, with subtle differences. The old wall between the trading floor and the research department had been pulled down. For most of Wall Street the trading floor is a separate room, distinct from research. The people who pick up the phone and place the bets (the traders) are the highly paid risk takers, while the people who analyze and explain the more complicated securities (the researchers) are glorified clerks. Back in 1993, when Meriwether established LTCM, he also created a new status system. The title "trader" would no longer exist. At LTCM, anyone who had anything to do with thinking about how to make money in financial markets would be called a "strategist."*[159] *"*

THE ALCHEMY OF FINANCE

LTCM would search for market imperfections or pricing abnormalities which it could exploit through hedged trades. At its simplest, the trading strategy was built on "buying

---

[159] Lewis, M. How the Eggheads Cracked, *The New York Times* (January 24, 1999).

long" assets perceived to be slightly undervalued and "selling short" very similar assets considered as slightly overvalued. LTCM would then wait for the spread to narrow as convergence in prices was believed to be ineluctable: as a *"long-term"* investor *Long-Term* Capital Management would simply wait out for convergence to materialize. Such market-neutral quasi-arbitrage trades were believed to be very low risk and would be structured in such a way as to minimize the use of capital through skillful leverage of LTCM equity capital base. As the famous financial economist and Nobel laureate Merton Miller put it *"they are sucking nickels from all over the world. But because they are so leveraged, that amounts to a lot of money."* In short, LTCM's alchemy of finance was built on three pillars: (1) leverage enabled by (2) repo-financing, and (3) controlled by Value-at-Risk.

Leverage. LTCM spectacular returns were built on parsimonious use of its equity capital base and powered by extremely high leverage. At the outset of 1998, LTCM had an equity base of a little less than $5 billion for an asset portfolio of $125 billion or a leverage ratio of

$$\text{Assets/Equity} = \$125\,\text{billion}/\$5\,\text{billion} = 25.$$

To better understand the power of leverage simply consider LTCM without or with debt financing:

- Under an all equity-financed (no debt) scenario assume that LTCM invests in securities yielding 4% which would earn $5 billion × 0.04 = $200 million; its return on asset (ROA) = Earnings/Assets = $200 million/$5 billion = 4% is equal to its return on equity (ROE) = Earnings/Equity = $200 million/$5 billion = 4%.
- Under a highly leveraged scenario LTCM now borrows $120 billion at 3% and invest total assets of $125 billion at 4% for a net income of

$$\$125\,\text{billion} \times 0.04 - \$120\,\text{billion} \times 0.03 = \$1.4\,\text{billion}.$$

LTCM's ROA is still 4% but its ROE has now jumped from 4% to $1.4 billion/$5 billion = 28%.
- Such a high leverage ratio made LTCM highly vulnerable to small decline in its asset portfolio value. For example should asset values decline by 4% from $125 billion to $120 billion the $5 billion loss would wipe out LTCM's entire capital equity base. Leverage is truly a double-edge sword.

Financing. To build this mountain of debt on a very narrow equity base LTCM's technique of choice was the repurchase agreement (repo for short) — a form of collateralized loan — whereby LTCM would pledge a newly purchased fixed income security such as treasury bonds to raise a short-term loan for the full amount of the pledged asset minus a 1% or 2% margin of safety — also known as a "haircut". Such loans were generally negotiated at very low rates (typically below LIBOR) of say 3.00% with which LTCM would buy additional fixed income securities yielding the higher rate of say 4%. Repos are typically short-term loans (with maturities of 7, 30, or 90 days) and would need to be continuously rolled over at expiration. What LTCM could do once it could do again and again as often as 25 times: assuming a starting equity capital in the amount of $1 billion LTCM would buy $1 billion of treasury bonds, simply pledge the newly acquired bonds to borrow $1 billion minus a 1% "haircut" which in turn would be invested at the higher rate of 4%. Critical to this leverage scheme was LTCM ability to borrow consistently at a lower rate than it would invest at and its ability to keep the "haircut" at 1% (or less) of the pledged security; an initial equity investment of $1 billion could be leveraged 25 times into an asset portfolio of

$$25 \times \$1 \text{ billion} (1 - 0.01)^{25} = \$19,446 \text{ billion}.$$

However funding through repos is risky because the value of the collateral is itself exposed to market risk — that is the market value of the pledged security is exposed to interest rate fluctuations — specifically, increasing interest rates which could trigger a margin call from the lender. Because of LTCM's secretive policy lenders — mostly commercial banks and brokerage firms — were not aware of the Fund's true leverage or — if they did — they felt protected by the collateralized nature of the loan.

Risk Management. LTCM prided itself on a scientific risk management system to protect its highly leveraged portfolio from adverse market movements: after all it had the who's who of "rocket finance" as partners. The instrument of choice was Value-at-Risk which is a summary statistic measuring in a single number the total risk of a portfolio of financial assets. History has it that the CEO of JP Morgan had asked his staff to provide him with one single number at 4:15 pm everyday of the risk faced by the bank for the next day. He was served with Value at Risk.

"We are x percent certain that we will not lose more than L dollars in the next N days."

In other words, value-at-risk (V@R) estimates the maximum loss L in dollar terms over a target horizon (N days) with a given probability x; it answers in pseudo-scientific terms the difficult question

"How much are we likely to lose?"

To arrive at such a compellingly simple statistic a major effort at estimating correlation amongst the different asset classes is critical. LTCM relied on recent history to model its V@R avoiding "Black Swans" such as the crash of 1987. In the words of the famed hedge fund manager David Einhorn

"V@R is a very limited tool which is relatively useless as a risk management tool and potentially catastrophic when its use creates a false sense of security among senior managers and watchdog. This is like an airbag which works all the time, except when you have a car accident."

RELATIVE VALUE OR CONVERGENCE TRADES

Convergence or relative value deals were LTCM signature trades and generally focused on fixed income securities. LTCM searched far and wide the US domestic bond market and beyond for market imperfections and abnormal pricing opportunities. It did reach out also to European and Japanese treasuries and mortgage-backed securities; nevertheless it avoided high-yield bonds and emerging market sovereigns when default risk was a primary concern.

Arbitraging US Government Bonds. A good example of this strategy is the quasi-arbitrage of "on-the-run" for "off-the run" long-term US treasuries which LTCM perfected to science as early as 1994. "On-the-run" 30 year treasuries are newly issued bonds auctioned off by the US government every six month to finance the budget deficit: they are very liquid — that is easy to trade — and were perceived by LTCM to be slightly overpriced (investors are willing to pay a small premium for treasuries deemed the most liquid — so called "liquidity premium"). By contrast "off-the run" 29.5 year treasuries — that is 30 year treasuries which have been issued more than 6 months ago — seemed to be hoarded by institutional investors or Asian central banks such as The Bank of China and are illiquid because they trade infrequently and are therefore somewhat difficult to find: LTCM believed that they were slightly undervalued. For example in 1994, LTCM observed that the spread was abnormally large between 30-year treasuries issued in February 1993 (off-the-run) offering a yield of 7.36% (see Box B) whereas 30-year treasuries issued 6 month later in August 1993 (so-called

---

Box B. Interest Rates and Bond Prices. Bonds are securities which pay a set annual or semiannual interest or coupon and repay principal at maturity. Bond prices are determined as the present value of future periodic interest payments and principal repayment discounted at the market interest rate for similar bonds in terms of credit risk and maturity. The discount rate that equates the present value of future interest payments and principal repayment to the current value of the bond is the yield-to-maturity. As the level of interest rates (discount rate) rise in the economy the value of bonds will adjust downward and conversely lower interest rate will drive bond prices higher as long as the credit quality of the bond remains unchanged: bond prices and interest rates move in opposite directions.

on-the-run) were yielding only 7.24% (see Box C).[160] The spread of 12 basis points corresponded to a difference in bond prices of approximately $15. LTCM purchased a billion dollars worth of the cheaper bond yielding 7.36% and simultaneously sold short the same amount of the more expensive bond yielding 7.24%. The two bonds are identical except for a slight difference in maturity which partly accounted for the very small difference in yields. For the trade to be profitable the spread had to narrow — that is the short sale and/or the long purchase had to be profitable. LTCM would not necessarily wait for 29.5 years to realize the profit and would expect the spread to start converging in short order. Most likely there would be a slight drop in the price of the on-the-run bond when it would shift to the off-the-run category six months after its issuance. LTCM would be closely hedged since it would be both "long" (owns) and "short" (owes) 30-year treasuries: should long-term interest rates move up or down during the six-month holding period both prices and yields on 30-year treasuries would move in unison. In the above example the bond price spread was only $15 per $1,000. Assuming that the spread would narrow to $10 the profit per trade would amount to $5 per $1,000. To make it worth its time LTCM would have to carry out the trade on a very, very large scale: for the purchase of $1 billion worth of bonds the trade would deliver a profit of $1 billion $\times$ 0.005 = $5 million. Here comes in the power of leverage: LTCM would first purchase bonds which it would in turn lend to a bank.

Box C. What is a Short Sale? *To sell a bond short LTCM would first borrow the bond and sell it immediately. Upon maturity of the loan — say 90 days later — LTCM would have to return the bond to its rightful owner who lent it to LTCM in the first place. LTCM would have to buy on the 90th day or sooner the bond at whatever prevailing price in order to return it to its owner and therefore close the short sale. For example assume that LTCM borrowed 30 year treasuries with face value of $1,000 and sold them immediately at the prevailing price of say $998. Ninety days later — or sooner — to close its short sale LTCM would purchase the same bond which now trades at say $995 thereby generating a net profit of $998 − $995 + $998(0.04/4) = $13 where the last term accounts for the interest earned on the cash proceeds from the short sale. The cash proceed from the short sale would be deposited with the owner/lender of the bond who effectively gets a collateralized loan from the short seller. Typically, a small amount of 1% or 2% would be added to the cash deposit should the value of the bonds sold short to increase. Should 30 year treasuries increase in value to say $1010 LTCM would close its short sale at a loss of $998 − $1010 + $998(0.04/4) = −$2. The coupon interest payments collected by the short seller during the short sale are returned to the owner/lender.*

---

[160] This numerical illustration is drawn from the excellent book by Lowenstein, Roger, *When Genius Failed: The Rise and Fall of Long Term Capital Management* (Random House, 2000).

Said bank would pledge the bonds as collateral to LTCM which it would, in turn, deposit with the owner of the bonds it borrowed for the purpose of the short sale. In the actual example introduced above LTCM committed to a $1 billion transaction to earn $1 billion × 0.005 = $5 million.

Such trades were predicated on an assumption of *convergence* in bonds price for the quasi-arbitrage transaction to be successful. Should the spread widen rather than narrow an unrealized loss would be incurred when the position would be marked-to-market but LTCM was in this for the long term (actually in the name of the hedge fund): it would wait out for a reversal of the widening spread until the trade could be closed at a profit which could take several months. In sum the not so simple quasi-arbitrage trade can be summed up as follows:

(1) **Selling short.** LTCM borrows $1 billion of 30 year treasuries "on-the-run." LTCM sells treasuries immediately at the current price of say $998 for a total cash proceeds of $998 million which are immediately deposited with the owner of the treasuries plus a 1% haircut. Short seller receives interest at 4% per annum on proceeds pledged to bond owner but pays coupon interest on sold treasuries to bond owner.
(2) **Closing short position.** Six months later LTCM closes its short sale by buying treasuries at then prevailing spot price of say $993. Bonds are returned to their rightful owner. LTCM earns the difference of $998 million − $993 million + $0.04/2 × $998 million − $3.62 million = $6.37 million with coupon at 7.24% paid to the bond owner and interest earned at 4% per annum on sale proceeds kept by the short seller.
(3) **Buying long.** LTCM buys $1 billion of 30-year "off-the-run" treasuries at current price of $992 for $992 million. LTCM enters into a repurchase agreement at 4% with a bank and receives 100% of market value of bonds plus a 1% haircut.
(4) **Closing long position.** LTCM sells it long bond position at then prevailing price of $995 for a profit of $995 million − $992 million = $3 million. Interest coupon at the annual rate of 7.34% will generate an additional $995 million × 0.0734/2 = $3.75 million but pays interest at 4% on repo in the amount of $995 million × (0.04/2) = $1.95 million. In sum LTCM would earn:

$$\$3\,\text{million} + \$3.75\,\text{million} − \$1.95\,\text{million} = \$4.80\,\text{million}.$$

(5) **LTCM maintained a hedged position at all times since long bond position = short bond position.** It earned a total $11.17 million without taking any risk nor committing any capital to the trade. Interest rate risk was not in contention because both sides of the trade would have responded identically (or almost identically) to a rise or fall in interest rates.

Arbitraging Interest Rate Swap Spreads. A variation on the same convergence theme was the arbitrage of swap spreads which would also generate small profits at very low risk: however thanks to the power of leverage LTCM could turn them

> **Box D. What are Interest Rate Swaps?** *LTCM could borrow fixed rate five year debt at 5% and wanted to take advantage of the lower commercial paper market floating interest rate of approximately 3.25%. By entering into an interest rate swap LTCM would now pay the floating rate on commercial paper to its counter-party while receiving the fixed 5% interest payment. Each payment would be based on a notional amount of say one $1 billion. For all practical purposes — once the swap is in place — it is as if LTCM had borrowed short term floating rate commercial paper with its fixed rate debt obligation assumed by the swap counter-party.*
>
> *The terms of an interest swap are set so that the present value of the "fixed interest cost leg" is equal to the present value of the "floating leg" so that neither party would gain or lose from entering into the swap. The value of the "fixed interest rate leg" is easy to compute since interest payments are contractually defined at the outset (see Box B on bond valuation) but valuing the "floating rate leg" faces the problem of not knowing what future short-term interest rates are going to be. By extracting forward rates from the zero-coupon yield curve it is possible to generate market-based forecasts of what those future short-term interest rate are going to be. With that information one can value the "floating rate" leg of the swap the way it is done for the fixed rate leg of the same swap. Interest rate swaps are used mostly to reduce the cost of financing as well as the firm's exposure to interest rate movements.*

into sizeable earnings. The swap rate is the fixed long term interest rate that banks, insurance companies and other institutional investors demand to be paid in exchange for agreeing to pay the 6 month floating LIBOR rate. The swap spread itself is the difference between the fixed interest rate received/paid and the yield on a treasury of matching maturity. An important benchmark in developed capital markets swap rates typically trade at a small spread above government treasuries of matching maturities. In the United States, for example swap spreads had hovered in a narrow range of 17–35 basis points throughout the nineties with brief spikes at 84 basis points during the recession of 1990 and at 48 basis points in April 1998.

LTCM would construct a convergence trade whenever the spread would hit the bottom or reach the top of the range expecting the spread to revert closer to its mean value. The trade was built on the simple notion that an interest rate swap replicates at slightly different rates a long position in treasuries financed by a floating rate loan: being long treasuries means owning bonds paying a fixed rate coupon (the fixed rate leg of the swap) while being short (borrowing) at a floating loan corresponds to the floating rate leg of the interest rate swap. Let us consider the mechanics of the trade[161]:

---

[161] Perold provides a detailed and lucid discussion of the trade in *Long Term Capital Management LP (A)*, *9-200-007* (Harvard Business School, 1999), pp. 4–6.

Scenario 1 (low swap spread): When the spread between the fixed interest payment on the swap and the yield on a similar maturity treasury was abnormally low by historical standards LTCM would purchase treasuries financed through a repurchase agreement and enter in a symmetrical interest rate swap paying fixed and receiving floating six month LIBOR. The net cash flow of the transaction would amount to[162]:

$$(\textbf{Treasuries yield} - \textit{fixed swap interest rate}) + (\textbf{LIBOR} - \textit{repo rate})$$

$$= -\textit{swap spread} + [\textbf{LIBOR} - (\textbf{LIBOR} - \textbf{20 basis points})]$$

$$= \textbf{20 basis points} - \textit{swap spread}$$

given that typically the rate on repo financing was LIBOR − 20 basis points and would compensate for the loss due to the differential between receiving lower treasury yield and paying higher fixed swap rate. The risk would be that over time (depending on how long LTCM would have to hold on the trade) the positive differential between LIBOR and repo rate would narrow and become insufficient to compensate for the negative differential on fixed interest rates. LTCM would expect the swap spread to widen back to past equilibrium value and would combine a positive carry (typically only a few basis points) with a capital gain on liquidating the swap.

Scenario 2 (high swap spread): when the swap spread would reach the ceiling of its historical range LTCM would enter into an interest rate swap receiving fixed and paying LIBOR while borrowing/shorting treasuries to earn a reverse repurchase agreement rate at LIBOR − 40 basis points. The convergence trade constructed under this scenario was symmetrical to the one described under a low swap spread scenario. The net cash flow would amount to

$$(\textbf{Fixed swap interest rate} - \textit{treasury yield}) + (\textbf{Reverse repo rate} - \textit{LIBOR})$$

$$= \textit{Swap spread} - 40 \textit{ basis points}.$$

Both trades would generate profits as low as 3–5 basis points (in some cases barely break-even) but provide a valuable option on swap spread volatility and would be magnified many times over through leverage. Because exposures to fixed and floating interest rates were perfectly hedged as long as the spread between LIBOR and repo rate remained invariant LTCM considered this convergence trade to be ideally congruent with its trading philosophy (see Box E for other convergence trades in European bond markets).

---

[162] Bold types signify interest income. Non-bold types refer to interest payments.

> **Box E. The Extended Family of "Converging Spreads."** *Similar pricing inefficiencies could be found in many foreign bond markets which by and large are not as liquid as the US bond market and generally more prone to pricing abnormalities. Perhaps fewer computer-enhanced arbitrageurs competed with LTCM in chasing such inefficient yield spreads outside the US market. Relying on its prowess honed in the US bond market LTCM was thus able to exploit similar convergence trades between foreign treasuries and interest rate swaps in the United Kingdom, Germany, Italy and Japan. It also ventured in the mortgage-backed securities market of several European countries — most notably Denmark.*
>
> **Italian swap spreads.** *LTCM noticed an unusually bearish pricing of Italian treasuries whose yield was higher (rather than lower) than the fixed rate at which Italian corporations could enter into interest rate swaps. This unusual swap spread reversal was attributed to the market sentiment that Italian government bonds were somewhat riskier than AAA-rated Italian corporate bonds. LTCM estimated that the spread should narrow and reverse itself as Europe was readying itself for the launch of the single currency (Euro) in 1999. LTCM bought Italian treasuries (receiving higher yield) financed through a repurchase agreement and entered in an interest swap paying fixed rate (lower than treasury yield) and receiving Lira LIBOR (higher than repo rate).*[163] *LTCM was thus able to lock in a positive spread without taking a position on the direction of interest rates while betting that a narrowing of the swap spread would also deliver a capital gain when the positions would be closed.*
>
> **Danish mortgage bonds.** *In the same spirit of yield convergence LTCM constructed a riskier trade on the assumption that 140 basis point spread between 30-year Danish mortgage bonds and 10 year Danish government bonds would narrow. In early 1998 LTCM became the largest investor in Danish mortgage bonds accumulating an $8 billion position while shorting a matching amount of 10-year government bonds. In the summer of 1998 the Russian crisis roiled capital markets the world around pushing spreads to all time highs: instead of narrowing the Danish Mortgage/Government bond spread skyrocketed from 140 to 200 basis points.*

THE CENTRAL BANK OF VOLATILITY

As prices discrepancies in the bond markets were dwindling because of LTCM success at arbitraging them on a mammoth scale LTCM turned increasingly to riskier trades which were bundling directional bets with convergence plays. In early 1998 LTCM started to write large amount of long-term options on major stock indices such as the

---

[163] Initially, LTCM purchased default insurance on both treasury and corporate bonds; as the trade mushroomed in magnitude and LTCM grew more comfortable with the transaction it allowed the default insurance to lapse.

> **Box F. Volatility and the Value of Options.** *Volatility is difficult to measure. It is usually proxied by the standard deviation of past stock index price fluctuations. This approximation, in turn, assumes that the prices of stock market indices are well enough behaved to follow a lognormal probability distribution. "Historic" (ex-post) volatility is not necessarily a reliable predictor of future (ex-ante) volatility whereas "implied" volatility (derived from the options market price) captures the market consensus. Practically, as volatility rises, option premia should increase and vice versa. Implied volatility at any given point in time can be extracted from current option prices by solving option pricing models for volatility since all the other parameters are known. However one should keep in mind that option prices are themselves set by traders who feed into the option valuation models their own subjective measure of volatility — itself based on some measure of past volatility.*

US Standard & Poor 500, the French CAC40 or the German DAX. Writing options on stock market indices is the same thing as shorting or what professionals refer to as "selling volatility" (see Box F). In the aftermath of the Asian financial crisis stock markets were very jittery with doomsday scenarios periodically predicting the crash of all crashes. In this climate of heightened volatility banks were facing a growing demand by retail investors who sought protection against downside stock prices while still being able to partake in their upside potential. To that effect banks structured products which would generally combine a zero coupon bond — thereby guaranteeing the value of the principal invested in stocks — with a five-year call option on the stock market index. Alternatively a long position in the stock index would be combined with a five-year put option on the same index.

The Rationale for "Selling Volatility." LTCM was keen on selling long-term options because it was convinced that the implied volatility of these options far exceeded their historical volatility. European stock indices such as the French CAC 40 and the German DAX had averaged long term historical volatility of approximately 15%. In late 1997 and early 1998 in the aftermath of the Asian financial crisis, options on the CAC 40 and the DAX were trading at levels which implied volatility of 22% — in other words these options were expensive (commanded a high premium). LTCM was more than ready to oblige the hefty demand from investors to "buy volatility" protection by selling options on stock market indices which it believed were overpriced. It did so on such a large scale — estimated by some observers as amounting to a quarter of the overall market — that it was soon dubbed by one of its competitors *"the central bank of volatility."*[164] LTCM was convinced that volatility would trend back to more normal and lower level at which time it would buy back the options it

---

[164] Lowenstein, op.cit., p. 126.

had sold at a lower price (option premium are closely related to the volatility of the underlying asset — stock market indices in this case). LTCM was now in effect in the business of forecasting volatility and it was doing so on the basis of historical data — in other words it was simply betting that *the past would prove to be a reliable predictor of the future*! Interestingly and somewhat ironically LTCM partners — who through their PhD studies had been brought up with the gospel of market efficiency — were rejecting the forward looking market forecast of volatility embedded in option prices in favor of historical volatility trends.

This single category of trades proved to be a disaster for LTCM when volatility refuses to behave according to the laws of linear extrapolation to which LTCM adhered. In fact LTCM was now embarking on a trading strategy that deviated markedly from its earlier more cautious convergence trades which were always based on paired/matched transactions and therefore largely immunized against market moves in one direction or another.

In fact LTCM had no interest in holding its short option positions to maturity and was looking to periodic drop in volatility to lock in profits. By betting on volatility understand that the stock market indices had been fluctuating wildly over a short period of time. LTCM wagered that their prices were soon going to become far steadier or less volatile. Since option premia are closely linked to the volatility of the underlying stock index, at high volatility option premia were expensive; dampened volatility would bring premia down. Whatever option combination LTCM had sold/written at a high price it was counting on being able to close its positions by buying them back at a much lower price thereby netting a sizeable profit. Indeed options — when appropriately combined — can provide lucrative results on specific volatility scenarios.

The Mechanics of Selling Volatility. Let us now turn to a more technical discussion of how these volatility trades were actually put to work in practice. Most appropriate to plays on volatility are options strategies known as *straddle and strangles*. LTCM wrote a large portfolio of put and call options[165] combined in the mold of these two option strategies. The key word is "wrote" (rather than bought) put and call options. In so doing LTCM collected hefty option premia hoping that these options would never be exercised if held to maturity or could be bought back at a lower price before maturity. If LTCM guessed wrong and the options were to be exercised LTCM would face very large losses.

Straddle. Buying a straddle is the simultaneous purchase of one put and one call option at the same exercise price and with the same maturity. This strategy is especially attractive when one anticipates high stock index volatility but is hard-pressed to forecast the direction of the stock market. LTCM was actually selling (rather than buying) straddles on the premise that the CAC 40 index volatility was going to subside

---

[165] For a primer on option see chapter on Société Générale, pp. 179–196.

and would stabilize at a lower rate. Consider the following market situation faced by LTCM on January 14, 1998 and how it constructed the writing/sale of a straddle.

Written:	1/14/98		
Assume:	March 98 option	on CAC 40	
Call strike:	FF 1,900	Put strike:	FF 1,900
Call premium:	FF 50	Put premium:	FF 50.

Let us now sketch with precision the building blocks of a straddle strategy — that is the writing of a call and put options on the CAC 40 index at the same strike price of 1,900.

Writing of a Call. For a cash premium of FF 50 collected on January 14, 1998 LTCM would commit to delivering one CAC 40 index futures at the strike price of 1,900. If the stock index were to remain below the strike price of 1,900 the option will not be exercised and LTCM keeps the option premium. Should the stock index rise above the strike price LTCM will have to deliver the stock index futures at 1,900. These stock index futures would have to be purchased at a higher price. The more expensive the CAC 40 index gets the higher the losses incurred by LTCM. Line (1), in Figure 2, sketches the payoff profile from the writing of a call option. LTCM makes a profit equal to the premium FF 50 at any level up to the strike price of 1,900 since the call option would not be exercised. Beyond 1,900 the profit/loss line is downward sloping. However, between 1,900 and 1,950 (strike price + premium) the premium is at least partially covering losses due to the movement of the stock index. At 1,950, the loss due to stock index movement is exactly equal to the premium. This is the break-even point. Beyond 1,950 LTCM incurs ever-increasing losses.

Writing of a Put. For a cash premium of FF 50 LTCM would commit to buying the CAC 40 at the strike price of 1,900. Line (2) in Figure 2 sketches the payoff profile from writing a put. Until the strike price of 1,900, the buyer will exercise his option to sell the CAC 40 at 1,900. LTCM will incur a cash flow loss in this range due to the fact that it must buy the CAC 40 at 1,900 and can only resell them at the lower price. Losses will be incurred up until the break-even price of 1,850 (strike price — premium) where the loss due to the stock index movements equals the profit from the premium. Beyond the strike price of 1,900 the option will not be exercised and LTCM retains the full premium of FF 50 per stock index transacted.

Plotting the Straddle. Writing the straddle is the bundling of a put and a call shown in Figure 2 as the graphical sum[166] (line 3) of a call (line 1) and put (line 2).

---

[166] Referring to Figure 2, the graphical sum of lines 1 and 2 for each level of the CAC 40 index (horizontal axis) shows the algebraic sum of gains/losses measured on lines 1 and 2 (vertical axis).

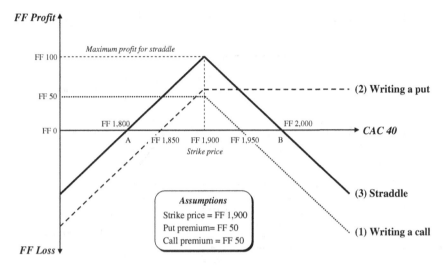

Figure 2   Payoff from writing a straddle.

Please note the pyramid top (in bold) of a straddle where LTCM nets a profit. Of interest are the break-even exchange rates A and B within which LTCM makes money because of very low volatility and outside of which it incurs deepening losses because of increased volatilities. To figure out the prices at which the straddle will cross the *x*-axis (the break-even points), we simply add/subtract the *sum* of the call and put premia to/from the strike price.

Break-even A: $S(90)^A = $ strike price $-$ (call premium $+$ put premium)
$$S(90)^A = 1,900 - (50 + 50) = 1,800$$

Break-even B: $S(90)^B = $ strike price $+$ (call premium $+$ put premium)
$$S(90)^B = 1,900 + (50 + 50) = 2,000.$$

Therefore, when the stock index is below 1,800 or above 2,000, LTCM will lose money and the loss is literally unlimited should the stock index fall way below 1,800 or appreciate well above 2,000. Conversely, within the same range, when volatility is low, LTCM stands to gain. Its maximum profit comes when the stock index is exactly equal to the strike price of 1,900. At that point neither options will be exercised. Therefore, it suffers no loss due to stock index movement and it retains the full amount of both premia, equal to FF 100 per CAC 40 index futures transacted.

Writing a Strangle. It is another speculative strategy based on volatility which also combines the writing of calls and puts. The main difference with a straddle is that the strangle combines out-of-the-money puts and calls at different strike prices. Correspondingly, the options are cheaper and the premia collected lower than in the

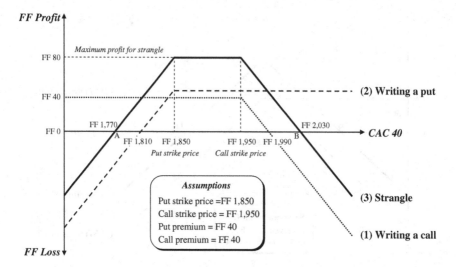

Figure 3   Payoff from writing a strangle.

case of straddle built on at-the-money put and call options. A strangle is less speculative than a straddle because, as we can see in Figure 3, there is a wider range over which the seller/writer of a strangle makes a profit. The downside is that, because of lower risk, the premia earned are lower.

Written: 1/14/98. Assume March 98 options on eAC40
   Call strike: 1,950   *Put strike*: 1,850
   Call premium: FF 40   *Put premium*: FF 40

We first plot the payoff profile of writing a call. See line (1) in Figure 3. The break-even is 1,990 (strike price of 1,950 + premium of FF 40). In the same way, we can plot the writing of the put where the break-even point is 1,810 (strike price of 1,850 − premium of FF 40) as shown by line (2) in Figure 3. Writing the strangle is the bundling of the call option (line 1) and the put option (line 2) and is shown by line 3 as the graphical sum of lines 1 and 2. Of interest are the strangle break-even points when the payoff line crosses the horizontal axis (premium income equals option losses):

Break-even A: $S(90)^A$ = put strike price − (call premium + put premium)
$$S(90)^A = 1,850 - (40 + 40) = 1,770$$

Break-even B: $S(90)^B$ = call strike price + (call premium + put premium)
$$S(90)^B = 1,950 + (40 + 40) = 2,030.$$

Between the break-even points of 1,770 and 2,030 the strangle is profitable with maximum gains earned between the strike prices of the put and call option when neither option is exercised and LTCM would collect the full sum of the put and call premia in the amount of FF 40 + FF 40 = FF 80.

Betting on Volatility: "The Long and Short of It." Long-term options are not actively traded but are nonetheless subject to day-to-day posting of margins or collateral to protect the option buyer from non-performance (default) on the part of the option seller. LTCM had collected upfront very hefty cash premium from writing long-dated options which were posted as collateral. Should volatility subside and long-dated options become "in-the-money" LTCM would be allowed to reduce its cash collateral. Conversely should volatility increase markedly LTCM would have to increase its cash collateral to compensate for options becoming "out-of-the-money." Compounding LTCM's exposure was the fact that its bet on diminishing volatility was a long term bet — but what about short term fluctuations in the level of volatility? LTCM had put itself at the mercy of investors who would not necessarily behave rationally which ultimately proved to be one of the principal causes for the fund's demise.

STRAYING AWAY FROM THE MASTER PLAN

As "convergence" plays in the bond and option markets were proving increasingly difficult to arbitrage profitably LTCM turned to riskier trades, which were stretching the philosophy of convergence into uncharted territory. Most notably were trades on pair of stocks issued by the same firm and listed on different exchanges as well as risk arbitrage on mergers and acquisitions.

Paired Stocks. LTCM targeted the Royal Dutch/ Shell group which had been separately controlled by two holding companies and which were listed on the Amsterdam exchange (Royal Dutch Petroleum N.V.) and the London exchange (Shell Transport & Trading plc.). Even though both stocks were equivalent claims on the Royal Dutch/Shell group's operating cash flows in terms of share of profits and dividends, since 1992 Royal Dutch had traded at premium ranging from 7% to 12% to its British cousin Shell. How could one explain why investors would prefer to invest in one stock over the other? It seemed that factors such as investors' country of domicile, their tax status, their ability to benefit from foreign tax treaties and to waive withholding taxes on dividends largely accounted for their choice to favor one stock versus the other thereby driving the price difference between the two.[167]

---

[167] Perold (1999) op. cit., p. 9 illustrates this point: "For example US pension funds received a full withholding tax refund from Royal Dutch but not from Shell (i.e., they would receive 100% of declared dividends by holding Royal Dutch, and only 58% by holding Shell); on the other hand UK taxable corporates would prefer holding Shell — after-tax they would receive 80% of dividends on Shell but only 69% on Royal Dutch."

LTCM bought $2 billion of Shell stock and sold short the matching amount of the more expensive Royal Dutch on the expectation that both stock prices should converge. The convergence trade was based on a pending change in the UK tax legislation which was supposed to make holding of Shell preferable to holding Royal Dutch for several classes of investors. There were even rumors that the two securities could be merged once for all. Thus LTCM was still toying with a "stretched out" version of the convergence principle but one had to be skeptical about the intellectual foundation of the trade. Unfortunately instead of converging the premium of Royal Dutch Petroleum versus Shell Transport & Trading shares sky-rocketed to 22% as the summer 1998 crisis roiled financial markets: LTCM lost $286 million in such matched trades — more than half being accounted by the Royal Dutch/Shell bet.

Risk Arbitrage. LTCM sought to exploit the uncertainty surrounding the closure of merger or acquisition deals. When a merger/acquisition between two firms is first announced the price of the target firm being acquired jumps to a level close but inferior to the announced official price at which the deal should close. The price discrepancy simply reflects the uncertainty about the deal winning regulatory approval in a timely fashion. As the deal gets closer to completion the price discrepancy narrows until it dissipates entirely when the deal closes which may take several months and sometimes more than a year. LTCM would purchase the temporarily undervalued stock of the acquired firm and short the acquirer. The risk was that the deal would break: indeed LTCM lost $150 million when Tellabs failed to complete its acquisition of Ciena. LTCM which was betting that the deal would close had owned Ciena's stock which plummeted from $56 to $31.25 on August 21, 1998.

Generally, LTCM favored lower risk deals avoiding hostile takeovers or situations characterized by high regulatory hurdles. Risk arbitrage is far removed from arbitraging yield spreads in the bond market and requires unique expertise about the companies involved, their industry dynamics, antitrust and other idiosyncratic regulatory issues which clearly LTCM never had. Investment banks which are active in the risk arbitrage business would typically build small team of specialists but LTCM never did.

THE FALL OF LTCM

In late 1997, LTCM returned $2.7 billion of capital to its investors. This rather unusual but by no means unique decision by a hedge fund was motivated by the recognition that price inefficiencies and arbitrage opportunities in capital markets were becoming fewer and further between: in a sense LTCM had done good work mining them away and thereby contributing to greater market efficiency. Indeed in 1997, LTCM returned only 17% thereby grossly underperforming the S&P index which delivered a return of 35%. Besides, hedge funds which had been a minor player in the world of global investment were, in the mid-1990s, gaining in relative importance and if they had not quite become *"the market"* yet they certainly loomed a lot larger on the Wall Street horizon. LTCM was falling victim to its own success and was being honest with its investors; as Meriwether put it:

> *"we will be hard-pressed to continue delivering the outsized returns that we have been blessed with and are therefore downsizing to give ourselves a better chance to outperform the market."*

The year 1997 was also the year when the Asian financial crisis first struck the Asian tigers. Several of East Asian and South-East Asian economies which had allowed their exchange rates pegged to the US dollar to become grossly overvalued saw the value of their currencies plunge under relentless speculative attacks. In short succession the Thai baht, the Indonesian Rupiah, the Philippines Peso, and the Korean Won lost half or more of their value during the summer of 1997. Explosive growth in Asia which had been largely powered by massive foreign capital inflows coupled with leveraged speculation came to a screeching halt when the same foreign capital fled. A deep recession gripped Asia. As a result of this large-scale capital outflow in search for safe haven investments in highly liquid US and European treasuries spreads between zero-risk treasuries and riskier mortgages, investment grade corporate and junk bonds widened drastically. LTCM — which had been a perpetual gambler on spread convergence — was caught on the wrong side of the equation. Some of its classic trades such as bets on convergence between "on the run" and "off the run" 30 year treasuries diverged instead of converging thereby triggering collateral call from its lenders as their periodic marking-to-market showed losses rather than gains.

Capital flow reversals also heightened volatility on stock markets which collided with LCTM long established belief in volatility subsiding and reverting to lower historical levels. As discussed earlier LTCM was known as *"the central bank of volatility"* and was a major seller of volatility in the form of writing/shorting stock index options bundled as straddles and strangles. When the turmoil of Asian stock exchanges spread to Russia in the summer of 1998 and reverberated through major financial centers LTCM's extensive short positions in long dated options on stock indices such as S&P 500 and CAC 40 became deep "out-the-money" prompting massive margin calls.

Compounding LTCM's burgeoning difficulties and unrelated to world financial market gyrations was the announced merger in the spring of 2008 between Travelers and Citicorp. As part of the deal, Travelers inherited Salomon Brothers — the alma mater to many of LTCM's key players (see Table 1) and a bond arbitrage house which mimicked many of LTCM's convergence trades. Travelers' CEO Sandi Weill and his lieutenant Jamie Dimon had misgivings about Salomon's business model which they considered as a disguised form of pseudo-scientific gambling and soon decided to pare down its positions. As a result many of LTCM's outstanding convergence trades involving fixed income securities and interest rate swaps were severely disrupted by Salomon Brothers hurried exit of the market. The losses started to mushroom on July 17: *"for the rest of that month, LTCM dropped about* 10% *because Salomon Brothers was selling all the things that LTCM owned."*[168] Because Salomon was on the same side of many of LTCM's trades its sales of illiquid positions exacerbated spreads rather than pushing them towards convergence; as a result LTCM experienced in July 1998 one of its worst month which brought the fund down for 1998 by 14%. Ironically Meriwether had outdone its creator Salomon but the latter's demise would — in the end — fatally wound LTCM.

One month later, on August 17, 1998 Russia devalued the rubble and declared a moratorium on its government debt. The default roiled world financial markets as Russian banks and financed companies claimed *"force majeure"* to default on derivatives contracts which left their western counterparties fully exposed to major losses. LTCM had a sizeable position in rubble-denominated Russian government bonds (also known as GKOs); its exposure was hedged by a matching amount of rubble forward sales on the assumption that a Russian bond default (loss of principal) would be compensated by exchange gains on the forward contracts (rubble depreciates): for example for an investment of 1,000 rubbles in GKO, LTCM would sell forward 2,000 rubbles with the expectation that a default on GKO (value collapses from 1,000 to 500) would be compensated by an exchange gain should the rubble lose 50% of its value (sell rubble forward at R50 = \$1 and buy them back at R100 = \$1 for a profit of $R2,000 \times (1/50 - 1/100) \times 100 = R2,000$. In dollar terms the initial investment was preserved as the exchange gain on the forward compensated for the 50% drop in the value of the bond and the 50% devaluation of the rubble. Unfortunately when Russia defaulted on its GKOs it severely damaged the Russian banks which defaulted on their forward contracts. The Russian bear had stripped off LTCM's hedge and left it naked!

As it is often the case in financial crises the default triggered a capital flight to "quality" and "liquidity," which merely compounded the losses that LTCM had started to experience with the Salomon Brothers exit. As panicked investors abandoned riskier securities to seek refuge in the safest securities they drove up spreads: for example one of LTCM's signature convergence trades (discussed earlier) between "on-the-run" and "off-the run" treasuries saw the spread spike from 6 basis points to 19 basis points in the days following Russia's default. On August 21, 1998 LTCM lost \$550 million — its single day largest loss. Heightened volatility in stock markets also caused investors to seek downside protection by purchasing long-dated options for which LTCM had established itself as the dominant seller. Option prices naturally experienced a steep rise which caused LTCM major losses (margin calls) on its portfolio of long-dated stock index options: here again LTCM was on the wrong side of the fence and on September

---

[168] Lewis, M. How the eggheads cracked, *The New York Times* (January 24, 1999).

Table 2 LTCM losses according to the nature of its trades.

Russia and other emerging markets:	$430 million
Directional trades in developed countries (such as shorting Japanese bonds):	$371 million
Equity pairs (such as Volkswagen and Shell):	$286 million
Yield-curve arbitrage:	$215 million
Standard & Poor's 500 stocks:	$203 million
High-yield (junk bond) arbitrage:	$100 million
Merger arbitrage:	Roughly even
Swaps:	$1.6 billion
Equity volatility:	$1.3 billion

Source: Lowenstein, R. *When the Geniuses Failed: The Rise and Fall of Long Term Capital Management* (Random House, 2000), p. 234.

21 it experienced its second largest single day loss of $500 million. LTCM's equity was now down to $1 billion (it had been at $4.5 billion in April) for a total asset portfolio of more than $100 billion and off-balance sheet positions in derivatives of $1.2 trillion. Leverage had reached a flabbergasting 100 to 1 ratio. Overall the losses came primarily — $3 out of 4.4 billion — from the two trades on which LTCM claimed to have built a comparative advantage — convergence trades in the bond markets through interest rate swaps and volatility bets on stock indices through selling options (see Table 2 for a breakdown of trading losses). Ultimately of the $4.4 billion that LTCM lost $1.9 billion belonged to the partners personally, $700 million to Union Bank of Switzerland and $1.8 billion to other investors — half of them European banks. Interestingly since the original investment had long been paid back to most of the banks the losses really came out of profits which had been left in the fund. Bankruptcy was around the corner.

THE RESCUE OF LTCM

On September 2, Meriwether wrote to his investors:

> *"As you are all too aware, events surrounding the collapse in Russia caused large and dramatically increasing volatility in global markets throughout August... Unfortunately, Long Term Capital Management's portfolio has also experienced a sharp decline in net asset value... it is down 44 percent for the month of August and 52 percent for the year-to-date. Losses of this magnitude are a shock to us as they surely are to you, especially in light of the historical volatility of the fund."*[169] *"*

---

[169] Cited in Lowenstein, p. 161.

The letter was blunt and to the point but — as usual — very short on specifics and certainly did not report on the fund leverage which had now reached the level of 55 to 1. The letter was faxed to all LTCM investors the same day. One of the investors immediately leaked it to Bloomberg, a financial news service, which published it. In fact, LTCM was one of the best known secrets on Wall Street in spite of Meriwether's elaborate effort to cloak the fund in secrecy:

> *"LTCM traded in huge size and trumpeted their acumen with panache. Now they were like a hunted elephant trying to hide in knee-high grass. Most dealers and large hedge funds knew LTCM was short of cash and would need to sell, and they knew what it would sell."*[170] "

After Salomon Brothers and Russia this was to be the last straw which broke the camel's back. The Good Samaritan is not necessarily a much emulated role model in financial markets. Swirling rumors about LTCM losses led to further losses which in turn unleashed more rumors and more losses. Was Wall Street ganging up against a falling star?

Just as The Federal Reserve Bank of New York was calling on major Wall Street firms to mount a rescue, Warren Buffet along with Goldman Sachs and A.I.G. proposed on September 21 a $4 billion takeover of LTCM which — for all practical purposes -would have expropriated LTCM partners.[171] On that same day, LTCM had its second worst day losing $500 million — half of which were due to the fund's short position on five year stock index options: equity capital was now down to $1 billion and with assets still at the $100 billion mark leverage had reached 100 to 1. John Meriwether was tipped by traders at JP Morgan and UBS that the squeeze that LTCM was experiencing on its option book was due to aggressive bids by A.I.G. By adding to LTCM's woes A.I.G. was doing the bidding for the Buffet consortium hoping to pressure Meriwether to sell the fund cheaply. The offer was turned down by Meriwether who argued that given the very short notice (Warren Buffet insisted on an answer within one hour of making the offer) he could not commit without having consulted with his partners.

On September 23, 1998, The Federal Reserve Bank of New York convened a meeting of 14 major commercial and investment banks which all had major outstanding loans to LTCM and coaxed them into contributing $3.5 billion to LTCM's capital. Limited partners would lose most of their stake in the fund and would be left with only

---

[170] Bookstaber, R. *A Demon of Our Own Design* (John Wiley, 2007), p. 104.

[171] Berkshire Hathaway (Warren Buffet's investment vehicle), Goldman Sachs and AIG offered to buy LTCM for $250 million and to immediately inject $3.75 billion in the fund (with $3 billion coming from Berkshire Hathaway). The partners would be fired and Goldman Sachs would manage the fund's portfolio. For Meriwether who had been forced out of Salomon Brothers seven years earlier by the same Warren Buffet, this would have been the ultimate capitulation.

10% of the recapitalized entity. The rescue of the fund was not quite a "bail-out" but rather a form of "negotiated bankruptcy" and no taxpayers money had been contributed to its recapitalization.

> *"The rescuers had effectively taken control of the fund's assets — still they hired LTCM's former employees to manage the portfolio under their direct supervision and with sufficient incentives to undertake the task efficiently. Although the Federal Reserve Bank of New York facilitated the take-over, it did not bail out LTCM. Many debtor entities found it in their self-interest not to post the collateral that was owed to LTCM and other creditors claimed to be ahead of others to secure earlier payoffs. Without the Federal Reserve Bank of New York acting quickly to mitigate these hold-up activities, LTCM would have had to file for bankruptcy ... If there were a bail out it failed: LTCM has been effectively liquidated."[172]*

Yet, the heavy hand of the Federal Government seemed to vindicate the "too big to fail" adage whereby any large financial institutions whose failure could trigger havoc with the stability of the global financial system would somehow be rescued.

One may wonder why major Wall Street firms could be convinced to bail out LTCM at a time when most of them were suffering from punishing losses and beaten down stock prices.[173] In view of the fund's stratospheric leverage and its calamitous demise what was the true motivation of Wall Street to come to LTCM's rescue? In large part this can be explained by the complex exposure of most major banks to LTCM: loans were bad enough but the true exposure came in the trillions of dollar in over-the-counter derivatives contracts woven into an intricate web that engulfed all the key players on Wall Street. Default of LTCM would trigger a domino effect throughout the financial system whose scope could not be gauged because of the opaque nature of over-the-counter (OTC) contracts: there was no centralized clearing house and no systematic margining system providing an accounting data base for everyone to see and which could be easily monitored. With OTC derivative contracts each party is on its own when it comes to assessing counterparty risk before the contract is signed and then during its life. But bailing out LTCM was not only about self-preservation it was also old fashioned greed. Most of the houses which were part of the consortium were well aware of many of LTCM's trades as they often had mimicked them: they knew what the upside potential was once financial markets would revert to normalcy and they "wanted in" on terms that only a few months ago were unheard of.

---

[172] Lowenstein, R. op. cit.
[173] Goldman Sachs was particularly concerned that a seismic LTCM collapse would damage the prospect for a successful initial public offering of its stock. Similarly Sandy Weil feared any disruption of the pending merger of Travelers with Citibank.

THE MORAL OF THE STORY

Lessons for Investors: in the Name of Disclosure. Investing in hedge funds is not for the faint-hearted. Pension funds, university endowments, billionaires and other likely investors are all savvy investors who will dedicate a limited part of their investment portfolio to such enticing opportunities: they do so knowingly and at their own perils. The search is for risk adjusted returns in excess of what market indices would yield — sometimes referred to as the "alpha" return — in excess of the "beta" market return. Should such pursuit of the alpha be at the cost of sacrificing investors' prerogatives of access to meaningful information? Hedge funds protect their proprietary trading strategies by disclosing minimal information. Meriwether's letters to his investors were a model of vagueness. Investors had no idea of the level of leverage built into LTCM's model and did not really ask pressing questions as long as LTCM delivered stellar returns.

Lessons for Hedge Funds Risk Managers: History Does not Necessarily Repeat Itself. Many of LTCM convergence trades were predicated on stable historical trends: bond spreads and stock index volatilities which may have temporarily wandered out of established ranges would inexorably revert back to normalcy. In the words of Victor Haghani — LTCM London-based star trader and strategist — *"what we did is rely on experience. And all science is based on experience. And if you are not willing to draw any conclusions from experience, you might as well sit on your hands and do nothing."* Except for the once in a hundred year flood linear extrapolation is a reasonable approach to modeling the future. Unfortunately financial history is populated — albeit sparsely — by "Black Swans" or unlikely but catastrophic events which devastate the global economy.

LTCM put great faith in the value-at-risk (V@R) metric as the all encompassing gauge of the fund risk exposure. In August 1998, LTCM estimated its one-day V@R to be $35 million with a 99% probability: on September 21, 1998 the fund lost $550 million. V@R is a very useful gauge of risk exposure as long as close attention is paid to the time frame over which its key parameters are estimated. LTCM seemed to have relied on relatively recent history as the relevant time period to build its models and failed to make allowance for "Black Swans."

Lessons for Hedge Funds Strategists (I): Heed the Call for Diversification. Under the pretense that it was actively involved in many of the major capital markets LTCM misleadingly believed that it was truly diversified and yet most of its trades were different variation on one central theme: convergence of spreads. In time of crisis flight to quality spikes spreads across the fixed income universe at once. It also heightens the correlation among the same spreads because risky and illiquid securities are all abandoned at the same time and therefore become riskier and more illiquid — that is their spreads against no-risk government securities all surge in unison.

Lessons for Hedge Funds Strategists (II): Fear the "leverage-illiquidity axis of evil." Leverage by itself is perilous enough but when it is paired with investing in illiquid assets it becomes deadly. LTCM sought matched trades which combined underpriced and generally illiquid fixed-income securities with very similar but slightly overpriced liquid securities such as "off-the-run/on-the-run" 30-year treasuries expecting that over time their market value would revert to fair value and the gap would narrow or disappear. This strategy was clearly predicated on "patient" capital and LTCM certainly had long-term commitment from its investors. But most of LTCM's capital was borrowed capital and lenders are not necessarily patient when their clients are highly leveraged. Indeed in times of crisis when capital seeks safe haven in quality and liquid assets illiquid assets become even more illiquid. If they have to be liquidated on a short notice to meet margin calls because lenders become impatient they become even cheaper. In fact, in times of crisis what matters is market value (very sensitive to liquidity) — not fair value and the more illiquid the security the wider the gap between the two. LTCM was truly exposed to "liquidity risk" as the long side of its portfolio was generally made up of illiquid securities. LTCM fell victim to this vicious cycle. What LTCM overlooked was its exposure to "liquidity risk" and it should have classified and balanced its portfolio according to this simple criterion.

Lessons for Lenders to Hedge Funds: Do Not Abdicate Due Diligence. Wall Street had a blind spot when it came to lending to LTCM. Major commercial banks were overly eager to do business with LTCM and let themselves being talked into granting mammoth loans without being able to have access to vital financial information. In a bizarre twist of "crony capitalism" several of the lenders' senior management also made personal investments in LTCM which must have clouded their judgment in assessing their institution's true credit exposure. Indeed knowing about LTCM true leverage and the extent of its off balance sheet web of over-the-counter derivatives may have led many of the unsuspecting lenders to reconsider the terms of engagement. Meriwether drove a hard bargain and was able to leverage the LTCM mystique to safeguard his fund's total lack of transparency and extract much reduced haircuts from its lenders. It is ironic to see the same financial institutions demanding detailed information from retail customers before granting consumer loans in the thousands of dollars and yet extending billions of dollar in unsecured loans to highly leveraged LTCM without asking any questions.

Lesson for Regulators: Tame the OTC Derivatives Monster. Unlike Amaranth Advisors — the hedge fund which lost $6 billion in gas futures in 2006 without much of a ripple on financial markets — LTCM's loss of $4.6 billion eight years earlier nearly bankrupted the entire global financial system. Both were hedge funds with an unbridled appetite for daring speculative trades: the key difference was LTCM's use of over-the-counter (OTC) derivatives as opposed to Amaranth's quasi-exclusive dealing with exchange traded derivatives such as natural gas futures and options.

OTC derivatives are tailor-made financial contracts between two independent parties which are not cleared through any central processing entity nor are they subjected to any disciplined margining system. In fact it is difficult to know at any given time what is the precise amount of outstanding OTC contracts. By contrast, exchange traded products are standardized contracts with capitalized exchanges such as the NYMEX or the Chicago Board of Trade. Margin posting and twice daily marking-to-market (with margin calls when necessary) ensures that counter-party risk is never an issue.

Regulators should have learned the lessons from the near-collapse of LTCM in 1998. Untamed webs of over-the-counter derivatives contracts without any proper posting of collateral or margins allowed LTCM to amass more than a notional trillion dollars of derivatives contracts with a puny capital base of $4.5 billion. LTCM's counterparties had no clear understanding of LTCM's true leverage nor of its exposure to various financial risk nor had they insisted on proper protection in the form of adequate collateral. The financial tsunami of 2008 and the bail-out of AIG is largely a replay on a much larger scale of the LTCM 1998 debacle. Here again hundreds of notional trillions of dollar in derivatives — most notably credit-default swaps — were OTC contracts. Regulators should steer the "OTC derivatives monster" towards central clearing and automated processing. The resulting transparency provides regulators with much needed information about traders and their trades which in turn facilitates prevention of price manipulation and fraud. Standardization of contracts will by necessity become part of the reform to bring about transparency and to reduce counterparty risk thereby mitigating systemic risk.

EPILOGUE

Once rescued with a capital infusion of $3.7 billion in September 2008 LTCM continued to lose money — as much as $300 million — but by the close of 1998 it was starting to rebound as the partners had predicted. By mid 1999 LTCM was up by 14.1% net of fees on its post-rescue capital base and on July 6, 1999 it returned $300 million to its original investors whose residual stake — post rescue — had been reduced to only 9% of the fund. $1 billion were also returned to the 14 consortium banks which had taken over the fund. Later that fall all monies were returned to the banks and LTCM was disbanded.

All **creditors** were paid in full. **Investors** who were refunded $2.7 billion in late 1997 and who had felt discriminated against by LTCM partners when they were forcibly asked to take their money back were largely insulated from the 1998 collapse and earned an average of 20% annual return. Six month later Alan Greenspan further relaxed the use of derivatives on the ground that financial markets were best at self-regulation.

Shortly after leaving LTCM, **John Meriwether** resurfaced with the launch of a new hedge fund named after his initials — JWM Partners LLC — which intended to replicate many of LTCM trades with less leverage. At its height, before the onslaught of the 2008 financial crisis, JWM Partners controlled $2.6 billion having enjoyed eight very successful years.

Myron Scholes is intimately involved in the management of Platinum Grove Asset — a California-based hedge fund overseeing $5 billion.

Robert Merton returned to Harvard Business School while maintaining an active consulting practice with leading Wall Street houses most notably JP Morgan Chase.

Bibliography

Dunbar, N. *Inventing Money: The Story of Long Term Capital Management and the Legends Behind It* (John Wiley & Sons, 2000).

Edwards, F. R. Hedge funds and the collapse of Long-Term Capital Management, *Journal of Economic Perspectives*, 189–210 (Spring 1999).

Lowenstein, R. *When the Genius Failed: The Rise and Fall of Long Term Capital Management* (Random House, 2000).

Perold, A. Long term capital management LP:(A) 9-200-007 *Harvard Business School* (1999).

Stein, M. Unbounded irrationality: Risk and organizational narcissism at Long-Term Capital Management, *Human Relations*, **56**(5), 523–540.

Stulz, R. M. Hedge funds: Past, present and future. *Journal of Economic Perspectives*, 175–194 (Spring 2007).

Questions for discussion

1. Explain the differences between relative value, convergence and directional trades.
2. Referring to swap spread trades identify the nature of risk(s) taken on by LTCM. Explain why this trade accounted for such a large amount of losses incurred by LTCM in the summer of 1998.
3. Would you characterize LTCM volatility trades as convergence or directional trades?
4. Why was LTCM dubbed "the central bank of volatility"?
5. Why was LTCM progressively digressing from its convergence trades?
6. Are hedge funds a source of systemic risk? Should hedge funds be regulated like other financial institutions?
7. What are the lessons that regulators should have learnt from the LTCM debacle?

16 AIG

The models suggested that the risk (about credit default swaps) was so remote that the fees were almost free money ... Just put it on your books and enjoy the money.[172]

Tom Savage, President of AIG Financial Products

In the mother of all derivative debacles which nearly brought down the insurance colossus AIG,[173] the villain is a relatively recent financial product known as the credit default swap (CDS). How could a derivative akin to a form of insurance policy against bond default unleash the default AIG itself? First, we need to explain how CDS became a key linchpin of the securitization revolution to understand AIG's collapse.

SECURITIZATION AND CREDIT DEFAULT SWAPS

Between the subprime crisis of 2007 and the demise of the insurance colossus, AIG stands the securitization revolution which made consumer finance more accessible to American households. Securitization, at its simplest, transforms old fashioned and illiquid automobile loans, home mortgages, and credit card receivables into liquid,

---

[172] Brady D. and R. O'Harrow. A crack in the system, *The Washington Post* (December 30, 2008).
[173] It required an unprecedented bail out by the US federal government — now exceeding $150 billion and counting.

Box A. What is Securitization?[174] *First pioneered in the United States by Ginny Mae and Freddie Mac in the mid-70s, the technology of securitization has truly transformed consumer finance. By repackaging illiquid consumer loans such as residential mortgages, automobile, and credit card receivables — which are traditionally held by commercial banks, thrifts, finance companies, and other financial institutions — into liquid tradable securities, securitization is a form of elaborate "disintermediation," which results into a lower cost of consumer finance. As illustrated in Figure 1, a typical securitization transaction is structured around six building blocks:*

1. **Origination** *— carried out by the financial institution which traditionally financed the transaction. It consists of managing the credit-granting process ("booking" the loan) to consumers applying for a loan to facilitate the purchase of a home, automobile, or the use of a credit card.*
2. **Structuring** *— creating a legal entity generally known as a special purpose vehicle (SPV) for the sole purpose of the transaction using the loans as the asset collateral for issuing bonds. The SPV would typically purchase without recourse the receivables/loans from the originators, who are usually invited to be one of the credit enhancers — admittedly the ultimate incentive in performing as reliable loan originators.*
3. **Credit enhancement** *— improving the credit risk profile of the original loans by procuring insurance coverage against default from insurance carriers such as AIG. Because default rates on large portfolios of small consumer loans can be accurately gauged through actuarial techniques, it is relatively easy to price the insurance premium for enhancing credit. This assumes that consumer loans are granted under normal and consistent prudential rules and that the information disclosed is accurate, which was not the case during the subprime crisis. This is where CDS play a critical role in making securitization a cost-effective technique.*
4, 5. **Underwriting and placing** *—the newly-created securities with appropriate investors.*
6. **Servicing** *— finally, the loans by collecting interest and principal repayments from borrowers to insure the proper cash-flow disbursement to noteholders.*

---

tradable fixed income securities which institutional investors such as pension funds can readily purchase (see Box A).

Most importantly, the technology of securitization hinges on credit enhancement of the newly issued securities also known as mortgage-backed securities (because they are collateralized by the cash-flows of the original borrower's mortgage). Credit

---

[174] Jacque, L. L. Financial Innovations and the Dynamics of Emerging Capital Markets. *Financial Innovations and the Welfare of Nations*, edited by Jacque L. L. and P. M. Vaaler (Kulwer Academic publishers, 2001), pp. 1–21.

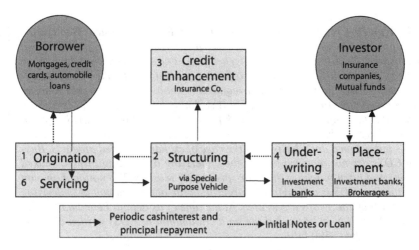

Figure 1   Building blocks of securitization.

enhancement is about providing some form of partial or full insurance against the risk of default and concretized either through more traditional bond insurance and more recently through credit default swaps. As a result, the credit-enhanced securities are better-rated and can therefore be issued at a lesser yield. Of course, credit enhancement only makes sense as long as its cost (often as low as 35–50 basis points) is less than the resulting reduction in interest rate paid out by the issuer of the mortgage-backed securities.

AIG, with its AAA credit rating, was a much sought after provider of such protection and indeed readily obliged by building over the last decade a portfolio of credit default swaps, which had reached $500 billions in notional value by 2008. AIG would lend its strong credit rating to lesser-rated securities, which as a result would now enjoy the AAA rating of the insurance carrier. AIG would receive a fee for providing the protection from default to investors. So far so good. As for any insurance coverage provided by an insurance carrier such as AIG the two key questions to answer are: what premium to charge and how much of that premium should be reserved to pay for future losses. Before answering these two questions, let us review further CDS as financial derivatives.

WHAT ARE CREDIT DEFAULT SWAPS (CDS)?

Credit default swaps were introduced in the mid-90s as a new and more flexible form of bond insurance. Credit default swaps are over-the-counter contracts whereby the buyer (insured) agrees to pay the seller (insurer) periodic fees (insurance premium)

> **Box B. How Do Credit Default Swap Differ From Bond Insurance?** *Bond insur-
> ance is provided by regulated insurance carriers to entities which own the bond
> being insured. Its purpose is clearly of a hedging nature unlike CDSs which allow
> anyone to place a bet on the risk of a firm's bond default. Banks or any unreg-
> ulated entities writing CDSs are not required to set aside loss reserves (but are
> nonetheless subject to regulatory capital) and may hedge themselves by selling
> CDSs to third parties. Counterparty risk for anyone purchasing a CDS is a real
> issue mitigated by the posting of margin which should be updated on a periodic
> basis — but not on a daily basis as in the case of exchange-traded products. Buy-
> ers of CDSs are not required to own the underlying bond being insured (naked
> position) and often purchase them for speculative reasons. The notional amount
> of outstanding CDS is considerably larger than the actual amount of underlying
> bonds on which the swaps are written. At the time of its default Lehman Brothers
> owned $125 billion in bonds but the notional amount of CDSs written on those
> bonds approached $500 billion.*

in exchange for receiving protection against default (event) of a loan or bond (loss).
The event triggering the payment of the loss is usually the debtor's default but can
also be a credit rating downgrade or restructuring of the debtor. Unlike bond insurance
policy whereby the buyer purchases protection on a loan/bond he owns (see Box B),
the buyer of a credit default swap may not have any material relationship with the
debtor (so-called "naked" CDS). Purchase of a credit swap is therefore motivated not
only by hedging, but also by arbitrage and speculative reasons.

As an illustration consider the pension fund TIAA-CREF holding on January 1,
2008 $100 million of five year bonds issued by Lehman Brothers with a coupon yield
of 7.50% and purchasing a CDS from AIG for a semesterly fee/premium of $350,000
to protect itself against the default of Lehman Brothers. TIAA-CREF is committed to
making 10 payments through the life of the five year bond as long as Lehman Brothers
is solvent. Should Lehman Brothers default — as it did in September 2008 — AIG
will pay the full $100 million to TIAA-CREF.

Were credit default swaps written by AIG fairly priced? Was AIG properly reserv-
ing for potential losses? Unlike traditional insurance products such as life or property
and casualty where the insurance carrier amply reserves for each risk it underwrites
AIG never reserved in any meaningful way for the credit default swaps that it was writing. In part its CDS valuation models consistently showed a miniscule risk of default
and in part because CDS are not traditional insurance products subjected to the same
stringent capitalization requirements and regulations which are imposed on the rest of
the insurance industry.

Interestingly CDS originated out of a separate unit known as AIG Financial Products which was created in 1987 by three ex-Drexel Lambert bankers. For the first 10

years of its existence, it prospered on selling products such as plain vanilla interest rate swaps until JP Morgan approached AIG Financial Products in 1998 with a proposal to credit enhance (write insurance against default) collateralized debt obligations (CDOs).

AIG Financial Products' revenue (insurance premia) peaked in 2005 at $3.26 billion with operating income accounting for 17.5% of the firm's total operating income. Unlike its many siblings in the extended AIG family, AIG Financial Products did not believe in proper reserving and capitalization of the insurance products it was selling. As the President of AIG Financial Products so eloquently remarked: *"The models suggested that the risk (about credit default swaps) was so remote that the fees were almost free money... Just put it on your books and enjoy the money."*[175] Because of its faulty business model, it misled itself, its parent and investors in reporting a profit margin of 83% in 2005 and unsurprisingly it lavished on its employees outlandish salaries and bonuses:

> *Mr. Cassano and his colleagues minted tidy fortunes during these cotton years. Since 2001, compensation at the small unit ranged from $423 million to $616 million each year, according to corporate filing. That meant that on average each person in the unit made more than $1million a year. In fact compensation expenses took a large percentage of the unit's revenue. In lean years it was 33 percent; in fatter ones 46 percent. Overall AIG Financial Products paid its employees $3.56 billion during the last seven years.*[176]

THE MORAL OF THE STORY

In the end, AIG ignored the basic core principles of finance and insurance. *"There is no free lunch"* in life and the fact that AIG was naïve enough to believe that it could underwrite billions of bond insurance coverage without having to ever pay on losses is truly mystifying when it comes from one of the colossus in the insurance world.

Second, even though there may be some debate as to whether CDS are more akin to financial than insurance products, it remains that CDS are closely related to traditional insurance products and that valuation of any insurance business is actuarial in nature. By extracting from long-dated loss tables the probability of facing default the insurer is able to charge a fair premium and will accumulate appropriate reserves so that when losses do hit they can be paid off. More fundamentally, there is a reason

---

[175] Brady D. and R. O'Harrow. A crack in the system, *The Washington Post* (December 30, 2008).

[176] Morgenson, G. Behind biggest insurer's crisis, a blind eye to a web of risk, *The New York Times* (September 28, 2008).

why — for generations — insurance companies have thrived on selling life insurance contracts or coverage policies on property and casualty risks but have avoided business risk. It has to do with the fundamental nature of risk and the insurance carrier's ability to measure it: mortality table for life insurance products have a great virtue — they are reasonably stationary from an actuarial point of view and each loss (when someone dies) is statistically independent from another loss (someone else death is unrelated unless there is an epidemic). Similarly floods, fires, and tornados are acts of nature and are statistically uncorrelated. Business risk — that is the risk of defaulting — is different as the population of firms (and their insured loans) are subject to the vagaries of business cycles in unison (so-called domino effect): in other words, probabilities of default on business loans are highly correlated and much more difficult to gauge with accuracy.

And even if one can gauge in probabilistic terms the likelihood of default on loans, it is generally easier to do it with small consumer retail loans than with larger business loans. Actuarial tables on default of mortgages and automobile loans have by and large shown great stability over the last 75 years as long as the prudential rules of loan granting are respected. However, reliability of these tables hinges on the assumptions that each mortgage or automobile loan is granted under the same prudential rules. Clearly, the subprime crisis signaled a major departure from past practices and had a lot to do with the rules of mortgage lending being ignored: no down payment required from the home buyer (instead of the usual 20–30% initial down payment) and after tax income failing to be at least three times the carrying cost of home ownership (mortgage interest + principal repayment, real estate taxes, and insurance cost). Once actuarial projections of future default are corrupted by changing the underlying premises, setting fairly valued insurance premia on credit default swaps become also flawed. As AIG believed that risk of default on mortgage-backed securities it was credit enhancing was miniscule, it was under-pricing its insurance protection, over insuring, and under-reserving. Unsurprisingly, disaster struck AIG when default rates on subprime mortgage-backed securities started to accelerate in 2008.

FROM THEORY TO MALPRACTICE: LESSONS LEARNED

All of life is the management of risk, not its elimination.

Walter B. Wriston, former Chairman of Citicorp

The collective wisdom of the financial services industry should make the conclusions of this book redundant. The lessons of each derivative debacle were all self-evident and yet *"Plus cela change plus c'est la même chose"*: the name of the derivatives and techniques involved have changed and multiplied over the years while the debacles grew significantly larger but the same prudential principles which guide the wise management of financial activities in both financial and non-financial firms continue to be ignored or violated: from the rogue trader's $8 million loss at the Citibank's branch in Brussels in the mid-1960s to SoGen's $7.2 billion blowout and AIG's $150 billion bailout in 2008 it is *déjà vu all over again* .... This chapter consolidates the many lessons learned from the perspectives of non-financial firms, financial institutions, regulatory agencies and investors.

SOME FIRST PRINCIPLES

Failings of the risk management function are at the core of the unsavory tales of derivative debacles told in this book. At its basics risk management is about identifying risks faced by the firm (market, credit, liquidity, and operational risks — see Box A), gauging its degree of exposure to each of them (from 0% to 100%), formulating and implementing risk management policies (optimal hedge ratio for each type of

---

Box A. Operational Risk. *One of the recurring lessons of the derivative deba-*
cles recounted in this book is the daunting nature of operational risk — that is
the risk of catastrophic loss (often due to unauthorized trading) associated with
internal processes, faulty models or computer systems, derelict employees or
external events. Unlike market or counterparty risk for which insurance products
or derivative markets offer comprehensive protection operational risk cannot be
easily hedged. Indeed there is a scarcity of insurance products providing cov-
erage against operational risk: one exception is Swiss Re — one of the largest
re-insurance company in the world — which offers "financial institution opera-
tional risk insurance" to protect against unauthorized trading (rogue traders) and
other types of operational risk.[177] *In the same vein and recognizing its importance*
Basel II is mandating a new operational risk charge as part of regulatory capital
imposed on financial institutions.

---

exposure) which are consistent with the firm's appetite for risk. This presupposes that
the Board of Directors has set clear strategic objectives and risk tolerance parameters
within which risk management policies can be formulated and implemented. Defining
the firm's risk appetite is one of the cornerstones of a risk management strategy: It
rests squarely with the firm's senior management which will decide on its level of
risk–aversion and therefore how conservative its risk management strategy will be. It
will also shape major risk taking decisions: for example setting a certain level of credit
rating for the firm as a risk management objective will constrain the risk–return trade-
offs within which investment decisions will have to be made. Last but not least senior
management must also insure that such policies be woven into the fabric of the firm's
daily operations. A word of caution though: as we argue for tighter risk management
rules the firm has to make difficult trade-offs:

> *A company's risk management function could, at least in theory, be designed to*
> *know everything at all times. But if it were organized that way, the risk management*
> *function, besides being hugely costly, would likely stifle innovation and reduce the*
> *competitiveness of the firm. In fast moving markets, employees need flexibility.*[178]

POLICY RECOMMENDATIONS FOR NON-FINANCIAL FIRMS

Derivatives are a key risk management tool used widely by non-financial firms. The
acid-test for any use of such instruments — and for that matter any risk management

---

[177] Jorion, P. *Value at risk: the New Benchmark for Managing Financial Risk* (McGraw Hill,
3rd edn: 2007), p. 507.
[178] Stulz, R. M. Risk management failures: What are they and when do they happen, *Journal of*
Applied Corporate Finance (Fall, 2008), p. 66.

Table 1   Vulnerability to derivative debacles for non-financial firms.

	Over-the-counter derivatives	Exchange-traded derivatives
Treasury as a nonprofit center	Medium	Low
Treasury as a profit center	High	Medium

policy — is whether they are truly value-creating for the firm. The evidence provided in this book clearly indicates otherwise. Derivatives debacles which involved non-financial firms were rooted in ill-devised financial engineering (Metallgesellschaft), non-authorized speculative trading (Allied-Lyons), misunderstood products (Proctor & Gamble) and concealed losing speculative trades (Showa Shell).

Upon closer scrutiny of the above cases a simple taxonomy of corporate vulnerability to the malpractice of derivatives can be presented in a matrix which — on one dimension — will distinguish whether firms set up their treasury as a profit center and — on the second dimension — whether treasury operations rely mostly on over-the-counter (OTC) derivatives as opposed to exchange traded products (see Table 1).

As the book amply illustrated failure to set clear and unambiguous objectives for the treasury office compounds the firm's vulnerability to derivatives' malpractice (see lesson #1 below). Most non-financial firms are better off keeping their treasury operations as a nonprofit center unless they developed unique expertise in a speculative market — e.g., energy companies in gas or oil derivatives. When treasury is set as a profit center it is important to clearly delineate the proprietary trading activities from traditional treasury operations and to set very tight monitoring guidelines for the newly embedded "hedge fund."

Reliance on OTC products also compounds the firm's exposure to debacles because enforcing positions and more importantly trading loss limits requires an in-house marking-to-market algorithm (see lesson #2 below). The absence of any cash margin requirements for OTC products (margins are the hallmark of exchange traded products) makes it easier to conceal large positions from the firm's comptroller.

Lesson 1: Failure to Set a Clear Mission for Treasury as a Profit Center. A company's treasury department is charged with two principal tasks: (1) procuring financing at the lowest possible cost of capital with financing running the gamut from short-term suppliers' funding in the form of account payables from suppliers to medium and long term bank loans or various forms of capital market debt and (2) hedging risk by limiting the firm's exposure to exchange rate, commodity price and interest rate risk in a manner consistent with its risk appetite. Neither funding nor hedging are profit making activities *per se* since the goal of financing is to minimize costs while hedging is all about minimizing risks. And yet many corporations have in the last 25 years redefined the mission of their treasury operations to turn them into profit centers.

For example, with the overhauling of its treasury function as early as 1987 Allied-Lyons' treasury seemed to have morphed into a de facto profit center without ever articulating clearly the risk-return profile within which it could operate. Indeed Allied-Lyons had reported increasingly significant profits from foreign exchange trading and success clearly emboldened its treasury to pursue high stakes currency gambits. Profits came from the firm taking on sizeable speculative positions to which the governance of the firm seemed to acquiesce. Unfortunately, there was no charter prepared by the treasury, supported by the finance director and debated before being blessed by the Board of Directors. Speculation within the treasury was no secret and the alarm bells did ring on a number of occasions without any formal attempt by senior management to rein in the treasury's activities. Similarly Procter & Gamble was committed to lowering its cost of capital through creative financial engineering courtesy of Bankers Trust: unfortunately it exposed itself foolishly to risk that it failed to fully comprehend.

Lesson 2: Failure to Enforce Position and Trading Loss Limits. When it comes to the effective use of derivatives the trading room all too often happens to be the Achilles' heel of the firm. Most trading rooms within large industrial or financial institutions have reporting guidelines in place with tight net position and trading loss limits. Allied-Lyons claimed to have had position limits of £500 million which were easily circumscribed by Bartlett and his acolytes. Similarly Showa Shell had a $300 million trading limit. In both cases position limits were not monitored nor enforced. Position limits are actually not enough and should be superseded by more revealing *trading loss limits* which can be enforced by a "*marking-to-market*" of each outstanding derivative product. Because forward contracts and over-the-counter swaps and options are not traded continuously — unlike futures and other exchange-traded derivatives — "*marking them to market*" would require careful valuation at the close of every business day. In fact a "shadow" margining system attached to OTC products would greatly enhance the transparency of the trading room. This can be readily done through the Interest Rate Parity theorem (in the case of foreign exchange), Cost-of-Carry formula (in the case of commodities), Black and Scholes model (in the case of options) and appropriate valuation models for interest rate, currency or credit default swaps.

Close monitoring of the trading room will further require that each trade, when executed, be recorded via a trade ticket with the "back-office" accompanied by its rationale. Presumably an industrial corporation such as Allied-Lyons or Showa Shell should primarily trade currencies paired with real transactions — that is transactions having to do with imports/exports of goods or services. This is known as the legitimate activity of managing transaction or translation exposures. More speculative proprietary trading — if tolerated as part of profit center mandate — should be closely supervised with stress-testing of pessimistic scenarios accompanied by Value-at-Risk analysis and measurement. Unfortunately, at Allied-Lyons overly lax controls allowed currency traders to build an overall speculative position in excess of £1.5 billion which bore no relationship to the scope of its international operations. Similarly traders at Showa Shell built a mammoth dollar position in excess of $6 billion without senior management ever finding out.

Lesson 3: Failure to Report. When it comes to derivatives what to report, when to report and to whom to report are often questions ill addressed by large organizations. A breakdown of aggregate derivative positions by tenor/maturity is necessary to avoid creative yet noxious speculative schemes as illustrated in the Citibank case. Reporting should be on a daily basis and reach not only Treasury's senior management, but also the very governance of the firm albeit on a less frequent basis. At Nippon Oil, Japan's largest oil refiner and a direct competitor of Showa Shell, the Treasury's deputy manager of foreign exchange was required to report to the company's Board of Directors at their monthly meeting on their foreign exchange positions and associated hedging policy. The very sizeable positions built up by the treasury of Allied-Lyons and Showa Shell should have been periodically scrutinized by senior management (possibly at the board level) outside the treasury department.

Lesson 4: Failure to Audit. Given the complexity and multitude of transactions flowing through a trading room, systematic audits are a vital complement to reporting. All too often the auditing process of derivatives used is inadequate because it is understaffed by accountants ill-versed in the subtleties of derivatives' valuation and trading. Auditing should be internal and external to the firm and based on principles of independence between the auditor and "auditee." Trade tickets are the informational foundation on which auditors will be able to uncover illicit transactions when they reconcile trades recorded by the "front" and "back" offices. But any transaction involves a counter-party: establishing channels of communications with such independent parties — typically the trading rooms at banks or clearing houses at organized exchanges — is a critical adjunct to this process. In fact, in several instances of major derivative malpractices — including the case of Showa Shell — the plot was uncovered through counter-parties which had commented on abnormal trades.

Lesson 5: Failure to Integrate the Risk Management Function. In manufacturing firms the use of derivatives is driven by risk exposure resulting from "real" (as opposed to financial) activities. Because hedging commodity, currency and interest rate risk may involve different units in the firm it is important to coordinate their use of derivatives so as to keep the overall exposure portfolio within the risk tolerance boundaries set by the Board of Directors. For example, the procurement department at Showa Shell in charge of oil purchase was not communicating with the treasury department nor was it in contact with the currency traders who were, presumably, hedging the yen cost of the company's oil bill. Close coordination between these different departments is clearly crucial to the effective design and implementation of a hedging policy. For a domestic Japanese company whose risk exposure was limited to the value of the dollar and the price of oil it seems surprising — to say the least — that hedging exchange rate risk would be conducted independently from oil price risk management. Oil procurement managers and treasury executives should make their decisions conjointly rather than independently or sequentially.

Lesson 6: Failure of Risk Management Systems. By nature derivatives and audacious financial transactions built around them are risky propositions whose ultimate outcome is derived from the price of an underlying currency, commodity, security or index. There are many techniques available for gauging what the value of the derivative will end up being — some rely on statistical techniques such as Value-at-Risk and others or more linear simulation of worst case scenario. All too often a basic approach is to extrapolate from past trends future relationships. History however does not necessarily repeat itself. The daring and innovative hedging program designed by Metallgesellschaft (MG) depended on extrapolating into the future past trends characterized by an oil futures market consistently in backwardation. Humans have a tendency to project into the future what they have experienced in the past — at their own peril!

To correct for this inherent bias stress-testing and multiple scenario analysis are simple yet powerful methodologies for probing doomsday scenarios or "outlier" events. Stress-testing emphasizes one noncontrollable variable which would typically be the price of a given currency or commodity or the level of interest rates. Multiple scenario analysis allows to schematize states of the world built on two or more key noncontrollable variables.

As an illustration it is ironic that the pseudo-hedge designed by MG's North American subsidiary and amounting to a notional value in excess of $3 billion (twice the equity value of its parent) would not trigger a careful review of what would happen under the most adverse scenario. More specifically, MG's supervisory board should have raised two related questions: "how much could MG lose? and 'how much was MG likely to lose?" Neither question were necessarily easy to answer. The first question would have typically been addressed with the help of stress-testing and multiple scenario analysis while the second would have been gauged by the more sophisticated Value-at-Risk metric.

Similarly, Proctor & Gamble was willing to enter into a leveraged interest swap seemingly unaware of its exorbitant cost should interest rates start to rise instead of staying level or declining. Simple stress-testing of the swap exposure to increasing interest rates would have sufficed to avoid a $150 million loss not too mention the reputational damage that Proctor & Gamble suffered in the aftermath.

POLICY RECOMMENDATIONS FOR FINANCIAL INSTITUTIONS

Financial institutions are both "dealers" and "end-users" of derivatives. As they generate an increasing percentage of their net profit from proprietary trading — as opposed

Table 2 Vulnerability to derivative malpractice for financial institutions.

	Exchange-traded derivatives	Over-the-counter derivatives
Agency trading	Low	Medium
Proprietary trading	Medium	High

to more traditional agency business — they exposed themselves to rogue traders and operational risk. Most of the recommendations formulated for non-financial firms are relevant for financial institutions. Additional scrutiny of their trading operations warrants careful management of their exposure to operational risk. To focus where maximum scrutiny should be exercised a taxonomy of vulnerability to derivatives debacles can be set by distinguishing between agency and proprietary trading and the balance between exchange-traded products and OTC derivatives: clearly maximum vulnerability would be expected with financial institutions trading primarily OTC derivatives for proprietary purposes (see Table 2).

Lesson #1: Failure to Enforce Position and Trading Loss Limits. Of paramount importance is establishing trading loss limits by forcing a daily *"marking-to-market"* of each outstanding contract. This would be typically done by the middle office in cooperation with the back office. This is easily done for exchange-traded products since market values are readily available in real time. Because OTC contracts are tailor-made contracts and are not continuously traded (unlike exchange-traded products) *"marking them to market"* would require their "in-house" valuation at the close of every business day.

By establishing a trading loss limit of say x dollars for a given trader (perhaps $500,000), the back office would be in a position to halt early on any speculative scheme: further trading activities would be actually frozen until proper accounting of the position was made available. As we learnt in the case of Citibank this is a far more effective way of keeping a lid on the bank's overall exposure than the "square position" requirement which can hide all kinds of contrived transactions which — in turn — may or may not have large cash-flow loss implications. Furthermore numerical trading limits would be strengthened if every trader would spell out clearly the nature of the underlying transaction: who are the end-users of the derivative products? Here it is critical to keep the front office clearly separate and independent from the back office (accounting/control) function.

Almost as important is the requirement for a breakdown of aggregate positions by tenor/maturity: even though a matched aggregate position should keep the bank reasonably safe it may hide speculative schemes which are contrary to the mission of the bank's trading desk.

For firms actively engaged in proprietary trading a separate entity akin to embedding a hedge fund should be established under a different charter and different rules of engagement as agency (low risk/low return) and proprietary trading (high risk/high return) are at opposite ends of the risk-return continuum. Commingling agency and proprietary trading activities as Barings allowed blurs the boundary line between the two activities and confuses the control system. Many investment banks have such separate departments and many of them are very profitable.

Lesson #2. Failure to Control. At its simplest the mechanics of daily reporting and control between the "front" and "back" office of the bank's trading operations works as follows: the derivative trader executes his trades, keeps a daily log and writes e-trade tickets which are entered by the back office into the bank's accounting system. This latter department will, in turn, verify independently each trade against a broker or counterparty to validate and ensure accuracy of the transaction. Independent confirmation is really the backbone of the control process. The "middle" office or risk department will then compute the daily trading gains/losses associated with the book of outstanding contracts and compare it with daily trading limits.

In order to implement such a control system commercial banks put great emphasis on enforcing a foolproof rule book and charge the back office with implementing it. However the best administrative guidelines will never fully discourage inventive traders from circumventing them. Both Allfirst's and SoGen's control processes failed both the letter and spirit of their intent.

The Letter. In several cases recounted in this book the back office ignored one of its basic responsibilities: to get proper and independent confirmation directly from the counterparty rather than the trader himself. Since the bank is trying to get independent confirmation of what its front office is dealing it stands to reason that it should not rely on the trader itself to get confirmation. The back office should apply a healthy dose of mistrust to the front office questioning the letter as well as the spirit of each transaction.

The spirit of the trader's activities has also been ignored more than once: it is not enough to seemingly follow the rules, the trader should be asked to provide a simple narrative allowing for each transaction to be put in an understandable strategic context. In the case of Allied Irish Banks no one questioned the rationale of Rusnak's booking pairs of bogus options with the same strike price with different maturities. Nor was the writing of actual deep-in-the-money yen put options ever challenged by the middle nor the back office. Raising $300 million in option premium should have caught someone attention — it did not.

Lesson #3: Failure to Follow the Cash Flow Trail. Trading futures and writing options leaves an indelible cash flow trace. When the futures contract is first bought or an option written the Exchange will ask for a margin; in the case of Barings' trading with the Singapore Monetary Exchange (SIMEX) margins were set at 15% of the nominal value of the contract. Second, when the contract is "marked-to-market" at the close of each trading day any loss resulting from a drop in the cash value of the contract will be debited from the contract holder's margin account. A margin call will ensue whereby the contract holder will be asked to replenish the margin account to bring it back to the 15% of the notional value of the contract. Lastly, when the contract is liquidated or simply expires at a loss a cash outflow will immediately ensue. Barings' senior management and auditors clearly lost the cash-flow trail early on. Reconciling the margin account against the SIMEX and the Osaka Stock Exchange (OSE) records should have been carried out by external auditors to the firm. Massive loan requests by Leeson for financing his margin account were met without much questioning what the funds were specifically used for. When such a request exceeded the book value of Barings it would stand to reason that whoever authorized the transfer — and given the amount it had to be someone very senior within the firm — would want to investigate thoroughly the rationale for the request. Blind trust and naïve gullibility from Barings' various echelons of management were just incredible!

Financial accounting documents can be easily misleading. Realized and unrealized amounts (in a cash-flow sense) are commingled and the practice of marking-to-market outstanding derivative contracts only exacerbates the confusion. All too often attention is wrongly given to the income statement rather than to the cash-flow statement or how else could AIB's Rusnak and SoGen's Kerviel fool for so long the accounting and the auditing staff of their respective bank.

Tailor-made over-the-counter trades — unlike standardized exchange traded products — are not subjected to margin calls: this only makes OTC trading activities that much more difficult to control since there is no cash-flow trail to follow. Attaching a "shadow" margin account to the currency trading desk and treating every single over-the-counter currency trade as if it were exchange traded would have forced Citibank, AIB and SoGen to follow the cash-flow trail rather than the accounting trail. Eventually AIB started in 2001 to charge its proprietary trader Rusnak for his usage of its balance sheet which was a commendable attempt to rein in its currency trader reckless activities: a margin account would de facto have achieved the same goal while forcing the transparency and discipline of a cash-flow account.

Lesson #4: Failure to Break the "Routine Chain." When all else fails, rotating employees and enforcing consecutive vacation rules will unveil elaborate and fraudulent concealment schemes. US laws require that traders take 10 consecutive days of vacation off from trading activities every year. The intent of the law is clearly that someone else would take over temporarily the activities of the trader on leave and thereby facilitate the uncovering of fraud.

Apparently AIB's Allfirst did not enforce the law and Rusnak never strayed away from his trading desk. In fact, Allfirst equipped Rusnak with Travel Bloomberg software so that he could trade from home or on vacation allowing him to exercise uninterrupted control over the currency trading desk. Similarly, SoGen allowed Kerviel to skip for all practical purposes vacations time since he never strayed away from his trading desks for more than four days.

Lesson #5: Failure to Enforce Division of Labor and Separation of Power Between Front and Back Offices. One of the golden rules of the securities and brokerage business is to segregate front and back office duties. Both desks should be staffed independently with frequent rotation at the back office to avoid collusion between the front and back office. The clerical responsibilities of the back office are focused on confirming, settling and recording the securities trades made by the front office. Most critical to these administrative responsibilities is the reconciliation of the details of each trade provided by the bank's counterparties and by the front office in terms of type of trade, price and amount of each transaction. Upon satisfactory verification the back office will authorize payment and release of relevant securities. Such tight checks are meant to prevent unauthorized trading or criminal activities such as embezzlement. Leeson (Barings) was allowed to run both front and back offices in spite of several warnings from successive auditors. Kerviel at Société Générale had spent five years in the back and middle office of Sogen and even though he had become a full-time trader he had retained easy access to internal control systems which should be the privy of the back offices including passwords access to critical data bases. More generally allowing back office and front office responsibilities to be performed either conjointly (as in the case of Leeson) or sequentially (as in the case of Kerviel) seems to be a lethal combination. Do not promote back or middle office managers to front office positions!

Lesson #6. Failure to Understand Your Business. Warren Buffet is famously known — among other things — for investing only in businesses he understands. All too often senior management at leading financial institutions is ill versed in the nuts and bolts of derivative products and financial engineering — relying on junior staff to deal with such technicalities. There is ample evidence that senior management on both the banking and securities broking side of Barings betrayed ignorance of the fundamental workings of derivatives market:

> *A colleague once had a good position, where he had bought a very deep discount warrant on Hong Kong listed Guandgong Investments and had sold the underlying stock to create what was effectively a fully hedged long put position. But Peter Norris, chief executive of Baring Securities, called him from London and said that, as he thought Guandgong Investments was heading for a fall, the position should be closed out. My colleague was unable to explain that we would have made money if the stock price had fallen.*[179]

Board members and senior management would be well-served to school themselves into the guts of their business by attending training seminars, which in 2–3 days

---

[179] Barings "wear death experience" (March 1995), p. 40.

can convey the essence of derivatives products, their valuation and how they can be controlled and configured in an elaborate financial architecture.

Lesson #7: Failure to Perform Analysis of Variance. As part of the financial planning and control process every unit within a given financial institution would prepare a pro-forma income statement based on clear assumptions about the economic and business contexts within which the unit profit would be earned. Barings was certainly no exception: when Leeson's unit reported 500% of his projected profit in 1994 — supposedly from arbitraging Nikkei 225 index futures between the SIMEX and the OSE — his supervisors should have asked questions about the unique reasons behind the abnormal results. Peter Barings declared that he was "pleasantly surprised"! Specifically, analysis of variance is all about understanding differences between projected and actual performance/profit and tracing abnormal results to specific factors. Barings' senior management was happy to take in the profits without asking too many embarrassing questions. SoGen fell in the same trap of allowing its trader Kerviel to report a $43 million profit when his objective was a more modest $3–5 million without asking any hard questions.

Lesson #8: Failure to Monitor Open Interests. Exchanges should monitor carefully who are the key holders of open interests in their different products. Financial institutions' senior management should also monitor open interest positions that their various trading operations may be responsible for thereby creating an external channel for auditing purposes. Sudden and dramatic change in positions in any given products by one prominent client should automatically trigger an investigation into the matter. Before Barings' collapse Leeson was responsible for an amazing 49% of open interest in Nikkei 225 March 95 futures on the SIMEX. Derivative Exchanges should keep channels of communications open with the trading entity itself — as well as with more senior overseers to be able to ascertain the veracity of the information obtained: traders should be held guilty of rogue behavior before proven innocent!

Lesson #9: Failure to Segregate Agency from Proprietary Trading. When the same trader executes orders on behalf of a bank's client (agency trading) and for the bank itself (proprietary trading) an obvious conflict of interest arises and the client is typically shortchanged. Proprietary trading should be ring-fenced from agency trading with each activity relying on its own separate trading desk and back office. Auditing and control mechanisms will be inherently different: agency trading is performed as a service to the bank's customer: the bank should not in principle be exposed to any risk if credit risk and account management are properly carried out. Proprietary trading on the other hand commits the bank's capital and careful control of traders' activities is vital: each trader should be subjected to tight position limits and daily reporting is an absolute necessity. Leeson was commingling both activities with neither audit nor control being carefully exercised on either one. Margin positions were combined and senior management had no clue which part belonged to the agency or the proprietary business. Position limits on Nikkei 225 futures and JGB futures were continuously flouted with no supervisory control mechanisms able to stop Leeson.

Lesson 10: The "Long and Short" of Derivatives Trading. The hectic pace of feverish activities in a trading room leaves little time for elaborating grand strategy and thoughtful consideration of the "big picture." Traders suffer from tunnel vision and immediate term scheming about their next trade. For traders the going long or short does not extend to their trading horizon when their long term horizon is the end of the day and "now" is therefore anything less than long term! For example how much consideration did Amaranth traders give to the fact that many of the Fund's positions in the natural gas future markets accounted for more than 50% of open interests on the NYMEX. The larger the position accumulated by a trader the more treacherous the exit. Amaranth traders ignored liquidity risk: their risk managers should have enforced tight position limits as a percentage of open interest — normally a ceiling at 12.5% to insure smooth exit when necessary. They did not and paid the ultimate price — bankruptcy!

POLICY RECOMMENDATIONS FOR INVESTORS

Derivatives are embedded in most investment products in one form or another. It is a fact of life which investors have to live with and that should be welcomed rather than feared. At the two extremes of the investment spectrum — high risk/high return hedge funds and low risk/low return municipal bonds and anywhere in between — misuse of derivatives have distorted the otherwise orderly investment landscape. Traditional investment guidelines should be supplemented by the following:

Lesson 1: Investing in Hedge Funds. Such investments are not for the faint-hearted. Pension funds, university endowments, billionaires or simply wealthy investors and other likely investors in hedge funds are all savvy investors who will dedicate a limited part of their investment portfolio to such enticing opportunities: they do so knowingly and at their own peril. The search is for risk adjusted returns in excess of what market indices would yield — sometimes referred to as the "alpha" return — in excess of the "beta" market return. Hedge funds are of course savvy users of derivatives and the debacles of two hugely successful funds — Long Term Capital Management and Amaranth Advisors LLC — were largely driven by their malpractice of derivatives.

For investors simple questions should be centered around the fund's basic investment philosophy, its trading team and record as well the efficacy of its risk management system. Paramount is probably a gauge of how leveraged the fund is as a basic proxy of its riskiness. Value-at-Risk (V@R) will also be helpful if the fund is willing to disclose the underlying premises upon which estimation of key correlation coefficients are based. If the time series from which the key metrics are extracted are too short and/or ignore past crisis situations V@R will lull the fund's managers and its investors into a false sense of security. Long-Term Capital Management had measures of its V@R derived from the very recent past which proved useless when the Asian financial crisis hit global financial markets. Unfortunately hedge funds prefer to cloak their activities in secrecy and tend to be very parsimonious in the amount and relevance of information they disclose to their investors. Long-Term Capital Management was notorious in this respect.

In the case of commodity-focused hedge funds which have become popular of late, diversification and the gauging of their relative derivatives positions to markets' outstanding open interests is paramount. Outsized open interest positions for specific traded contracts should be clearly monitored as they may be indication of excessive concentration in shallow markets. Last but not least, marking-to-market of commodity futures or options positions may appear to be a relatively straightforward exercise under normal market conditions: in reality, under "abnormal" conditions (contract holder controls an "abnormally" high percentage of outstanding open interests), exiting excessively large positions — as Amaranth attempted on several occasions — may happen at prices that are quite different from pretrade levels. This process clearly distorts a realistic valuation process and misleads investors as to the real performance and riskiness of their investments.

Lesson 2: Investing in Municipal Bonds. Retail or institutional investors who are inclined to invest in safe municipal bonds may want to engage in self-directed due diligence with regards to the credit risk of the bond issuer. The borrower's abnormal performance in the form of consistently superior yield should have been a red flag to any investor in Orange County's bonds: indeed wide press coverage hailing Orange County's treasurer as an investment genius made the information widely available. The theory of finance has long established the robust relationship between risk and return. As Citron was delivering high returns to his grateful constituents, higher level of exposure to risk had to be taken. Clearly credit rating agencies failed to ask this basic question and were willing to uphold a strong AA rating for Orange County's bond issues. Prudent investors would want to adhere to portfolio diversification and credit enhancement through bond insurance as guiding investment principles in municipal bonds. Reliance on credit ratings agencies may fail to unveil fundamental flaws such as leverage and over-reliance on derivatives-cum-fixed income securities. Access to publically available reports issued by Orange County should have been enough to raise questions which — if remained unanswered — should have discouraged investors.

POLICY RECOMMENDATIONS FOR REGULATORS

Lesson 1: Systemic Risk and Over-the-Counter (OTC) vs. Exchange-Traded Derivatives. OTC derivatives are tailor-made financial contracts between two independent parties which are not cleared through any central processing entity nor are they subjected to any disciplined margining system. In fact it is difficult to know at any given time what is the precise amount of outstanding OTC contracts. By contrast, exchange traded products are standardized contracts with capitalized exchanges such as the NYMEX or the Chicago Board of Trade. Margin posting and twice daily marking-to-market (with margin calls when necessary) ensures that counter-party risk is never an issue.

The reader will recall the vivid debacles of two high-flying hedge funds discussed in this book: unlike Amaranth Advisors LLC — the hedge fund which lost $6 billion in gas futures in 2006 without much of a ripple on financial markets — Long-Term Capital Management's loss of $4.6 billion eight years earlier nearly bankrupted the entire global financial system. Both were hedge funds with an unbridled appetite for daring speculative trades: the key difference was LTCM's use of OTC derivatives as opposed to Amaranth's quasi-exclusive dealing with exchange traded derivatives such as natural gas futures and options.

Regulators should have learned the lessons from the near-collapse of LTCM in 1998. Untamed webs of OTC derivatives contracts without any proper posting of collateral or margins allowed LTCM to amass more than a notional trillion dollars of derivatives contracts with a puny capital base of $4.5 billion. LTCM's counterparties had no clear understanding of LTCM's true leverage nor of its exposure to various financial risks nor had they insisted on proper protection in the form of adequate collateral. The financial tsunami of 2008 is largely a replay on a much larger scale of the LTCM 1998 debacle. Here again hundreds of notional trillions of dollar in derivatives — most notably credit-default swaps — were OTC contracts held primarily by AIG. It was not only that AIG was too big to fail it was that it was too intrinsically enmeshed in the global financial system to be allowed to collapse: the US government in the end mounted the mother of all bail-outs to rescue AIG — $150 billion and counting! Regulators should steer the "OTC derivatives monster" towards central clearing houses and automated processing. The resulting transparency provides regulators with much needed information about traders and their trades which in turn facilitates prevention of price manipulation and fraud. Standardization of contracts will by necessity become part of the reform to bring about transparency and to reduce counterparty risk thereby mitigating systemic risk.

Lesson 2: Surveillance of Derivatives Markets. Derivative markets perform an important economic function by enabling an efficient transfer of risk bearing from market participants least equipped to bear risk to market participants best equipped to bear risk. Speculators have an important role to play as offsetting parties to non-financial firms in search of a price hedge. However outsized positions in derivative markets controlled by one entity will distort price and volatility patterns which in turn will distort the risk allocation process and may end up causing harm to end-consumers. This is especially true for commodity derivative markets. For example in the natural gas derivative market Amaranth was not slightly above the ceiling but several times over the limit with positions on specific contract dates in excess of 100,000 contracts. The NYMEX lapsed in its watchdog capacity when it failed to enforce the simple rule of maximum position of 12,000 contracts for any-one market participant. When NYMEX finally pressured Amaranth to comply with position limits Amaranth simply moved its position to ICE which has no position nor any reporting requirement. Clearly disclosure requirements and position limits should be extended to ICE — what is referred to as closing the "Enron loophole." As one of several institutional end-users of natural gas the Municipal Gas Authority of Georgia testified to the US Senate subcommittee that it incurred unnecessary hedging costs of $18 million over actual spot market prices for the winter season 2006–2007 which ultimately had to be passed on to consumers. This abnormal hedging premium can be directly attributed to excessive speculation and market manipulation by Amaranth and others.

Lesson 3: Governance and Regulation of Municipal Finance. At both, the state and federal level regulation should be enacted dictating explicit investment charters and governance mechanisms for managing municipal investment pools. Ironically, federal regulation covering various types of mutual funds has existed for many years protecting unsuspecting retail investors. Municipal investment pools should be obvious targets for similar regulation with clear guidelines protecting agencies participating in such pools and investors financing them.

At the very least a charter defining clearly the investment objectives of the pool and what would constitute acceptable assets for investment purposes spelled out in terms of tenors, credit and market risk terms should be carefully formulated. Should leverage be tolerated and at what level? As discussed in the Orange County chapter leverage can be found at two levels: (1) directly, in terms of borrowing in order to increase the total size of an asset portfolio: if one believes in the mutual fund model Orange County would have been forbidden to use leverage to morph itself into a hedge fund and (2) indirectly, as leverage can be directly imbedded in derivative investment products such as leveraged inverse floaters or leveraged interest rate swaps. Should such toxic securities be prohibited or — at very least — severely limited? If a moderate level of leverage is allowed, clear, monitorable and enforceable limits/threshold should be spelled out.

A charter would also spell out the nature, timing and frequency of reporting and disclosure requirements. Beyond reporting monthly or quarterly balance sheets, income statements and cash-flow statements key information on the risk profile of the pool in terms of Value at Risk and other risk metrics is critical. Orange County should also have been required to stress-test its marked-to-market value under different interest rate scenarios.

Oversight of municipal investment pool activities is also paramount. Electing or appointing a Board of Directors including a majority of independent investment-savvy professionals without any conflict of interest with service/product providers should be mandatory. The Treasurer should be elected from a list of prescreened contenders with meaningful professional qualifications in the field of asset management: said individual and his/her team should be required to periodically enlist in executive seminars and should abide to a term limit. Last but not least independent auditors should be required to prepare detailed analysis of variance for each quarter between investment pool's planned goals and actual performance by reaching out to financial institutions which are service/product providers.

Last but not least, to strengthen further the protection of municipal finance, specific guidelines enacted as federal regulation should be forced on financial institutions selling sophisticated and complicated securities to treasurers of public entities such as Orange County. "Buyer beware" is legitimate when the buyer is a hedge fund or the CFO of the Microsoft or ExxonMobil of this world but municipal finance officers should be handled with "kids' gloves."

***

As we close this book, repeated occurrences of derivative malpractices resulting in mammoth losses continue to make front page news in the financial press. We hope that there is a silver lining to our bullet of sad tales about derivative debacles and that in the best of Darwinian tradition we can learn the necessary lessons to strengthen the governance of the international financial system.

INDEX

H

Haircut, 234, 251, 254, 271
Hamanaka, Yasuo, 97–99
Hatch, Clifford, 106–108, 121
Hawawini, Gabriel, 3
Hedge
    money market, 20
    ratio, 89, 92, 166, 204, 218, 232, 250, 281
Hedge fund, 3, 8–10, 35, 39, 43, 49, 50, 52, 60, 70, 72, 101, 126, 221, 232, 236, 240, 242, 244–248, 251, 254, 264, 268, 270, 271, 273, 283, 287, 292–296
    categories of, 87, 227
    defined, 25, 31, 213
    see also Long-Term Capital Management
Hedging
    cost of hedging, 80
    with forwards, 2, 9, 10, 13, 21, 27, 44, 77, 79, 90, 99, 126, 127, 133, 134, 186, 188
    with futures, 2–11, 16, 17, 19, 23, 25, 26, 29, 32, 33, 39, 43, 47, 49–61, 63–71, 74–77, 79–85, 87–96, 98–101, 109, 110, 112, 117, 122, 124, 127, 141, 143, 146–160, 162–164, 166–169, 171–179, 182–186, 188–194, 201, 206, 219, 236, 238, 247, 252, 255, 258–261, 270–273, 277, 280, 284, 286, 288, 291–294
    with options, 1, 3–5, 7, 9, 10, 20, 21, 24, 34, 36, 51–54, 57, 58, 105, 107–115, 117–124, 126, 129, 130, 132, 134–139, 141, 145–147, 155–169, 171, 174, 178, 182–185, 189, 193, 196, 206–211, 214, 217, 218, 231, 247, 248, 256–268, 272, 284, 288, 293, 294
    with swaps, 1, 3, 4, 7, 9–11, 34, 99, 199–201, 209, 213, 217–220, 255, 257, 266, 267, 272, 275, 277–280, 284, 294, 295
Hero, 51, 52, 71, 223, 292
Hunt Brothers, 99

Hunter, Brian, 51, 52, 69, 71, 72
Hurricane Katrina, 8, 52

I

ICE or Intercontinental Commodity Exchange, 57, 60, 62, 67, 71, 295
IMF, *see* International Monetary Fund
Import-export bank, 26, 123, 284
Index-amortizing notes, 228, 229, 233
Index futures
    defined, 25, 31, 57, 77, 82, 98, 124, 146, 149, 201–203, 205, 213, 226, 229, 255
    home-made, 148–150
Index options, 156, 265, 266, 268
Infamous spread formula, 22, 174, 200, 211, 222
ING Bank, 100, 177
Insurance, 5, 31, 56, 74, 98, 241, 255, 257, 275–280, 282, 293
Intel, 264
Intercontinental Commodity Exchange (ICE), 56, 57, 60, 62, 67, 71, 295
Interest Rate Parity Theory, 23, 24, 26, 31, 35, 36, 39, 44, 96, 123, 129
Interest rates, 1–3, 20, 23, 24, 26, 27, 32, 35–39, 43, 44
    bond prices and, 202, 203, 226
Interest rate swaps, 3
see also Procter & Gamble vs. Bankers Trust interest rate swap
International Monetary Fund, 7
Intrinsic value of options, 58, 115, 160
Inverse floating-rate notes, 228–231

J

Jacque, Laurent L., 3, 44, 89, 276
Jaffar bin Hussein, 41
Japanese government bond, 143, 154, 155, 169, 173
Jorion, Philippe P., 4, 223, 224, 225, 227, 238–240, 282
J. P. Morgan, 49, 51, 67, 69, 101, 146, 238, 243, 251, 268, 273, 279
Junk bond arbitrage, 267
    losses due to, 118, 134, 163, 167, 227, 260